THE

ERRANT ART OF *MOBY-DICK*

LIT CRIT

NEW AMERICANISTS

A SERIES EDITED BY DONALD E. PEASE

THE

ERRANT ART OF *MOBY-DICK*

THE CANON, THE COLD WAR, AND THE STRUGGLE FOR AMERICAN STUDIES

WILLIAM V. SPANOS

DUKE UNIVERSITY PRESS DURHAM AND LONDON

1995

© 1995 Duke University Press

All rights reserved

Printed in the United States on acid-free paper ∞

Designed by Cherie H. Westmoreland

Typeset in Weiss with Eras display by Keystone Typesetting, Inc.

Permissions and Library of Congress Cataloging-in-Publication Data

appear on the last printed page of this book.

To the memory of "William Slothrup," the exorbitant whom

"they did finally 86 out of Massachusetts Bay Colony,"

his pigs, and "all the Preterites" in "our crippled Zone"—those

to whom he would give back their histories.

There is time, if you need the comfort, to touch the person
next to you, or to reach between your own cold legs . . . or, if song
must find you, here's one They never taught anyone to sing, a hymn by
William Slothrup, centuries forgotten and out of print, sung to a simple
and pleasant air of the period. Follow the bouncing ball:

> There is a hand to turn the time,
> Though thy Glass today be run,
> Till the Light that hath brought the Towers low
> Find the last poor Pret'rite one . . .
> Till the Riders sleep by ev'ry road,
> All through our crippl'd Zone,
> With a face on ev'ry mountainside,
> And a Soul in ev'ry stone . . .

Now everybody—

> Thomas Pynchon, *Gravity's Rainbow*

I would like to write the history of this prison, with all the political
investments of the body that it gathers together in its closed architecture.
Why? Simply because I am interested in the past? No, if one means by
that writing a history of the past in terms of the present. Yes, if one
means writing the history of the present.

> Michel Foucault, *Discipline and Punish*

Moby-Dick is a giant stutter in the Manner of *Magnalia Christi Americana*.

> Susan Howe, *The Birth-Mark*

CONTENTS

ACKNOWLEDGMENTS

This book on Herman Melville's *Moby-Dick* is the third in a tetralogy of related studies. The first two—*The End of Education: Toward Posthumanism* and *Heidegger and Criticism: Retrieving the Cultural Politics of Destruction*—were published in 1993, and the fourth, an interrogation of the history of the American Cultural Memory's representation of the Vietnam War since the dedication of the Vietnam Veterans' Memorial in Washington, D.C., is still in draft form. Despite the chronology of publication, however, I have worked on all four projects more or less simultaneously for over a decade. In fact, *The Errant Art of "Moby-Dick"* was begun during a sabbatical spent on Kalymnos (the Greek island in the Dodecanese, made famous by Ovid's invocation "Kalymne, rich in honey," in his undecidable story about the prodigal son of a master maker) in the spring semester of 1981. It was originally intended to serve as a third, alternative last chapter of application (the first was a destructive reading of Tolstoy's *The Death of Ivan Illyich* and the second, a destructive reading of T. S. Eliot's "The Waste Land") for a book intended to work out the implications of Heidegger's destruction (*Destruktion*) for a hermeneutics of literature entitled *Icon and Time*. This book was begun—indeed, completed—considerably earlier (in 1974) than my study of Melville's novel, but it was never published in its original form. For the sudden apotheosis and rapid institutionalization of Jacques Derrida's deconstruction by America literary critics—and a university press responding to academic fashion—had, according to the experts of that time, rendered Heidegger's "ontological difference"—the temporal thematic informing his ontic/ontological understanding of being—"anachronistic." Since Derrida had definitively located Heidegger, so the argument seemed to go, reading him was superfluous. In its appropriation of Heidegger's "de-struction" for "dis-closive" or "e-mergent" or "e-mancipatory" purposes, however, *Icon and Time* was the matrix from which both *Heidegger and Criticism* and (as the allusion to Heidegger's judgment of the latest, anthropological phase of the ontotheological tradition in the title suggests) *The End of Education* emerged.

I refer to this abbreviated history not simply to orient the reader to the continuity of my intellectual work and to the transdisciplinary imperatives of my appropriation of Heidegger's destruction—to the multicultural range of reference enabled by thinking being as an indissoluble relay of sites or force fields—which might otherwise be missed in an all-too-likely disciplinary reading of *The Errant Art of "Moby-Dick"* (its overdetermination of the ontological site). I want also unashamedly to suggest the scope, depth, and continuity of my debt to Martin Heidegger's thought, in the face of the mounting campaign by the custodians of the American Cultural Memory to prosecute "the case of Heidegger"—a campaign, not incidentally, that few American deconstructionists have challenged. I mean their unerringly hostile will to discredit his philosophical thought—and the emancipatory discourses it has in large part enabled—licensed by Victor Farias's anecdotal history (1987) of Heidegger's complicitous relation to Nazism.

I want to convey how difficult it is to acknowledge the more immediate, but no less substantial, intellectual debts I owe to those friends, colleagues, and students whose specific contributions to my intellectual "identity"—and the ontological and sociopolitical horizon that has given this book its "shape"—have become unidentifiable traces in the corrosive process of a long and variously lived time. I have often been compelled, by a profound sense of gratitude to the people whom I have-been-with in my life, to retrieve the living force of these traces, but to do so would require an intellectual autobiography that I feel would be incommensurate with such a purpose. So I pass over these traces in a silence that I hope says something, if only regret.

I can, however, be certain about some of the people who have made an irreversible difference in my sense of the task of criticism at a historical conjuncture that is now, in the wake of the "revolutions" in Eastern and Central Europe and the former Soviet Union, being ominously represented as the advent of the "new world order" and the "end of history." They are, above all, that critically significant group of critics of the *boundary 2* editorial collective with whom I have had the privilege of being closely associated for many richly productive years: Jonathan Arac, Paul

Bové, Joseph Buttigieg, Margaret Ferguson, Nancy Fraser, Daniel O'Hara, Michael Hays, Ronald Judy, Donald Pease, and Cornel West. Of this remarkably intelligent, original, profoundly and variously engaged group— a group that, in my mind, has produced some of the most significant critical writing in America since the demise of the New Criticism—I want for this particular occasion to single out Donald Pease, not only for his encouragement of my appropriation of Heidegger's thought to American literary studies in the face of the residual but active American exceptionalism in contemporary Americanist literary and cultural studies, but also for his exemplary New Americanist criticism. His is a discourse that I have found profoundly enabling, despite my reservations about his reading of *Moby-Dick*, which I articulate in my text. After Pease's disclosure that the "field-Imaginary" established by the founders of American literary studies was in complicity with the ideology of the Cold War, there is no turning back to the Old Americanists' "American Renaissance." What his work signals, in fact, is an American discourse dedicated to the deterrence of American democracy, or, to put it positively, to the fulfillment of the multicultural democratic imperatives of a truly multicultural society.

I can also be certain about the persons who have most made a difference in my representation of my self and world in the process of writing this book, even if I can't name that difference. They are my son, Adam, and my dear friend and former student, Jeanette McVicker. To Adam, I am profoundly grateful not simply for *being there*, an always awesomely transforming presence, but for being there in care when he's not. To Jan I am deeply grateful for her acutely intelligent criticism of my thinking, but, equally important, for her nearness, even in the unhappy context of a variety of literal and symbolic distances. These (they are somehow one) have been insistently regenerative when the all-too-easy institutional accommodation of emergency has precipitated a pale cast of doubt over my expectations concerning my work—which is to say, when, against my better judgment, I have succumbed to the temptation of taking myself too seriously.

In a different register, I want to thank my colleague Bernard Rosenthal, and Joseph Kronick and Bainard Cowan for acute and suggestive readings of the very first version of *The Errant Art of "Moby-Dick."* Not least, I wish to thank Christopher Fynsk of the Comparative Literature Department at Binghamton University and my former student Sandra Jameson, both of whom have been close and supportive friends in difficult times as well as dialogic partners on matters ranging from Heidegger's thought through pedagogy to politics. I also deeply appreciate the intelligent copyediting of Maura High.

Finally, I wish to record my debt to the fiction of Thomas Pynchon, especially to the American motif of the *preterite,* that differential constituency of American society that "America," since the Puritans, has insistently disinherited in the process of naming itself. It is, perhaps, the impact of this resonant motif that, in the end, instigated my effort to think Melville's fiction.

THE

ERRANT ART OF *MOBY-DICK*

MOBY-DICK AND THE AMERICAN CANON

Israel Potter well merits the present tribute—a private of Bunker Hill, who for his faithful services was years ago promoted to a still deeper privacy under the ground, with a posthumous pension, in default of any during life, annually paid him by the spring in ever-new mosses and sward. . . . From a tattered copy, rescued by the merest chance from the rag-pickers, the present account has been drawn, which, with the exception of some expansions, and additions of historic and personal details, and one or two shiftings of scenes, may, perhaps, be not unfitly regarded something in the light of a dilapidated old tombstone retouched.

Herman Melville, "To *His Majesty,* the Bunker-hill Monument," *Israel Potter, His Fifty Years of Exile*

According to traditional practice, the spoils are carried along in the procession. They are called cultural treasures, and a historical materialist views them with cautious detachment. For without exception the cultural treasures he surveys have an origin which he cannot contemplate without horror. They owe their existence not only to the efforts of the great minds and talents who have created them, but also to the anonymous toil of their contemporaries. There is no document of civilization which is not at the same time a document of barbarism. And just as such a document is not free of barbarism, barbarism taints also the manner in which it was transmitted from one owner to another. A historical materialist therefore dissociates himself from it as far as possible. He regards it as his task to brush history against the grain.

Walter Benjamin, "Theses on the Philosophy of History"

Traditional American literary critics have insisted that "theory" is a European import inappropriate to the historically specific conditions of American cultural production. It is the enabling claim of this study of Herman Melville's *Moby-Dick* that, on the contrary, what has been called "postmodern" or "poststructuralist" or, as I prefer, "posthumanist" theory—far from being an imposition of a discourse foreign to the particularities of the American context—has its enabling origins, however indirectly, in the modern American occasion. If the inaugural theorists were European, it was, I submit, a fundamentally American event whose epochal implications resonated and continue to resonate beyond the borders of the United States to encompass the West at large that precipitated their subversive discourses and rendered their interrogation of truth/power relations in the modern West in some essential sense revelatory for American literary intellectuals, whose cultural tradition, in separating theory and practice in favor of the latter, had deprived them of a theoretically viable critical discourse.

This epochal American event was the Vietnam War, a war that bore spontaneous historical witness to the spectacle of a brutal—indeed, monomaniacal—American intervention in a Third-World space, which was justified by invoking the "free world" (Western-style democracies), and, more tellingly, was conducted in terms of the very self-representation of America, synecdochically represented by President John F. Kennedy's "New Frontier," inscribed in the American literary canon. I am referring to that empowering cultural imaginary whose origins lie in the American Puritan theological/theocratic "errand in the wilderness" ("to build a city on the hill"); was secularized by post-Revolutionary writers like James Fenimore Cooper and Robert Montgomery Bird, who transformed the westering frontier experience of individuals like Daniel Boone, Davy Crockett, and Kit Carson into cultural myths of "manifest destiny"; was legitimated philosophically (however unintentionally) by "American Renaissance" thinkers like Ralph Waldo Emerson, Henry David Thoreau, and Theodore Parker, who represented the difference between the American errand in the wilderness and the European experience in terms of the difference between the creative principle of new-world "self-reliance" and the decadent principle of old-world authority; and was finally institutionalized by the American culture industry (both the information media and the institutions of learning): that is, the naturalized cultural imaginary, in the name of which America has perennially justified its essentially imperial, racist, and patriarchal historical project.[1]

What I am suggesting, in thus insisting on the relevance of posthumanist theory for the contemporary American cultural occasion is a matter of crucial import for the post–Cold War occasion. It emerged in the aftermath of the Vietnam War as a critical discourse intended to theorize the contradictions spontaneously disclosed by the self-destruction of the self-representation of the American cultural/sociopolitical mission (and by the ensuing refusal of spontaneous consent by various social constituencies to its hegemonic imperatives). As such, it has theoretically precluded the possibility any longer of referring to the American canon as if these *aporias* in the discourse of canon formation did not exist. More specifically, to practice literary criticism now in terms of the discourse of canon formation that has determined the content and form of American literary studies and their institutional organization (according, that is, to the rules of discursive formation that privileges disinterested inquiry and the transparency of language, in the face of the interrogation of its very "problematic"),[2] is to betray a resistance to "theory" grounded in recuperative ideological presuppositions of dubious lineage. For, however various the manifestations of contemporary theory, what they have essentially in common is their persuasive disclosure—also supported by the inordinate efforts of public officials, the custodians of the American Cultural Memory, and the media to police them—that the American literary history elaborated by the "disinterested" discourse of canon formation is a social construct—a mode of cultural production—which has served to legitimate and reproduce the power of the dominant sociopolitical order both in the United States and abroad.

And yet traditional (humanist) critics continue to resist theory in the name of the constellation of principles that has informed and determined the American canon: the disinterestedness of inquiry, the sovereign individual, pluralism, the genetic model of history, and so on. Indeed, the radical, adversarial critical initiative momentarily achieved by theory in the early 1980s appears to have all but dissipated in the 1990s. This is suggested by the increasing momentum of the campaign to delegitimize theory, inaugurated by traditional humanist critics such as William Bennett, Walter Jackson Bate, Allan Bloom, E. D. Hirsch, and Wayne Booth, and by institutions such as Harvard University (in its adoption of the "core curriculum") in the aftermath of the Vietnam War. I mean the campaign that has culminated in the identification of theory at large with "political correctness" by such politically conservative intellectuals as Roger Kimball and Dinesh D'Souza, and, in the area of American literary studies, by politically liberal intellectuals such as Frederick Crews.[3] It is also suggested by the noticeable retreat from the radical imperatives of theory by certain practitioners of the New Historicism, a retreat taking the symptomatic form of forgetting that in theory history is always the history of the present.[4] What, then, is it about the traditional discourse of canon formation that has enabled it to resist the compelling ideological disclosures of theory? Or, to put this question differently, what is it about theory that has rendered it more or less ineffectual in the face of the resistance of the traditional discourse of canon formation? Despite the obviousness of these questions, they have been strangely but symptomatically ignored by contemporary theory. It is one of the purposes of this book on Herman Melville's *Moby-Dick*, not to proffer answers to these questions as such—they are too complex for easy and definitive settlement—but simply to address them with the hope of reactivating their urgency in the face of the curious and, in my mind, disabling tendency on the part of contemporary theorists, who ought to know better, to overlook their historically specific occasion.

Why Melville's *Moby-Dick*? Because, perhaps, nothing in the history of American cultural production and consumption can teach us more about the ideological operations of canon formation in general and the formation of the American canon in particular than the apparently erratic history of the reception of the texts of a writer whose *raison d'être*, as *Israel Potter* most clearly suggests, was to interrogate the relationship between cultural monuments and sociopolitical power. I am not simply invoking the by now well-known period of rejection or benign neglect of *Moby-Dick*, extending throughout Melville's lifetime until the 1920s and the period extending from its apotheosis as an American "masterpiece" following World War I to its accommodation to a different historical context during World War II and, above all, the Cold War. I am also referring to the most recent extension of this third phase, which, as a glance at the recent study guide published by the Modern Language Association and the volume of "new essays" published in the Cambridge University Press series entitled "The American Novel" will make clear,[5] continues to represent *Moby-Dick* as an "American" Classic, a monumental "work" of the

American literary tradition, despite the disclosures during and after the Vietnam decade that have put the American literary canon into question.

Appropriating the deconstructive criticism of Jacques Derrida, Paul de Man, and their American followers, it could be said that this history of the reception of *Moby-Dick*, far from being the consequence of disinterested inquiry, has been adjudicated by a logocentrism that has measured Melville's text in terms of its correspondence to the metaphysical *logos*. This would be a valid judgment; but in situating it at the site of textuality, it would also be an extremely rarified one, that is, devoid of historically specific reference. It is preferable, therefore, despite the risk of misunderstanding, to invoke Heidegger's diagnosis of the "ontotheological" tradition, at least as a point of departure, in interpreting this history. But let me be clear about what I mean by this much misunderstood term. Unlike Derrida's and de Man's "logocentrism," Heidegger's "ontotheology" distinguishes between three broad historical phases of the discourse of Western metaphysics: the *onto*-logical (Greco-Roman, with the decisive emphasis on the latter), the *theo*-logical (medieval/Protestant), and the *anthropo*- or *ratio*-logical (post-Enlightenment or humanist). It thus foregrounds more clearly than the utterly generalized "logocentrism" of deconstruction an epochal transformation of the relationship between the discourses of truth and sociopolitical power: that which bore witness to the displacement of the *theologos* by the *anthropologos*, which is to say, of a *visible* (and hence *resistible*) by an *invisible* and thus virtually *irresistible* center of authority, one which, in fact, enhanced its positive capability of commanding assent, of compelling/pacifying "deviant" elements—whether temporality, words, or differential sociopolitical forces—into its "imperial" orbit.

To be more specific, Heidegger's interrogation of the ontotheological tradition disclosed the all-but-anthropologized ("humanized") modern age (what he calls appropriately the "age of the world picture" [*Die Zeit des Weltbild*]) to have its enabling origin, not simply in Roman antiquity—the transformation of an always already originative Greek thinking (*a-letheia*) into a secondary and derivative (technologized)—and calculative—that is, meta-physical, thinking (*veritas*: truth as the correspondence of mind and thing)—as it is formulaically put by both his sympathetic and antagonistic critics. Heidegger's interrogation of this tradition also and simultaneously disclosed the genealogy of Occidental modernity to lie in a historical transformation of the Roman discourse of truth (and the political practice it authorized) in the posttheological Enlightenment. It was a transformation, in other words, in which an earlier, direct (unmediated) use of power in discourse and practice authorized by the visible center and its commanding gaze was replaced by indirection or deception: a "going around" or "going behind," no less authorized by the centered commanding gaze. Heidegger's resonant formulation of this epochal transformation of truth/power relations in the modern West in his lectures on the *Parmenides* (no doubt to settle his accounts with German National Socialism)[6] warrants extended quotation:

> The essential domain which prevails for the deployment of the Roman *"falsum"* [the opposite of *veritas*] is that of the *"imperium"* and of the "imperial." . . . *"Imperium"* means "command." . . .
>
> To commanding as the essential foundation of sovereignty belongs "being above" [*Obensein*]. That is only possible through constant surmounting [*Überhöhung*] in relation to others, who are thus the inferiors [*Unteren*]. In the surmounting, in turn, resides "the constant ability to oversee" [*Übersehen-können:* supervise and dominate]. We say "to oversee something," which means to "master it" [*beherrschen*]. To this commanding view, which carries with it surmounting, belongs the "always-being-on-the-lookout." That is the form of all the action that oversees [dominates from the gaze], but that holds to itself, in Latin the *actio* of the *actus*. The commanding overseeing is the dominating "vision" which is expressed in the often cited phrase of Caesar: *veni, vedi, vici*—I came, I *oversaw* [*übersah*], I conquered. Victory is already nothing but the consequence of the Caesarian gaze that dominates [*Übersehens*] and the look [*Sehens*] which has the character of *actio*. The essence of the *imperium* reposes in the *actus* of constant action [*Aktion*]. The imperial *actio* of the constant surmounting over others implies that the others . . . are fallen [*gefällt werden*]—in Roman: *fallere* (participle: *falsum*). The "bringing-to-fall" [*das Zu-Fall-bringen*] belongs necessarily to the domain of the imperial. The "bringing-to-fall" can be accomplished in a "direct" assault [*Ansturm*] and an overthrowing [*Niederwerfen;* "throwing down"]. But the other can also be brought to fall by being outflanked [*Um-gehung*] and tripped up from behind. The "bringing-to-fall" is now the way of deceptive circumvention [*Hinter-gehen*]. . . . Considered from the outside, going behind the back is a complicated, circumstantial, and thus mediate "bringing-to-fall" as opposed to an immediate overthrowing. In this way, what is brought to fall does not thereby become annihilated, but in a certain manner redressed within the boundaries [*in den Grenzen*] which are staked out by the dominators. This "staking out" is called in Latin: *pango*, from which the word *pax*, peace. This, thought imperially, is [in the present age] the firmly established

condition of what has been brought-to-fall. In truth, the bringing-to-fall in the sense of deception [*Hintergehens*] and outflanking [*Umgehens*] is not the mediate and derived imperial *actio* but the imperial *actio* proper. It is not in war, but in the *fallere* of deceptive outflanking [*hintergehenden Umgehens*] and its appropriation to the service of domination that the proper and "great" trait of the imperial reveals itself.[7]

Admittedly, Heidegger's genealogy of truth/power relations in modernity addresses the modern European occasion and is Occidental in scope. To apply it to the historically specific American context as it pertains to the history of the reception of Melville's *Moby-Dick*, therefore, is to open oneself to the charge of misapplication (the practice that Edward Said has appropriately called "traveling theory").[8] Nevertheless, Heidegger's thematization of the distinction between the theological (medieval/Protestant) and the anthropological (humanist or post-Enlightenment) moments of the discursive and political practices to which the metaphysical *logos* has been put—the distinction between the direct and indirect use of force in the practice of domination—is suggestive as a point of departure in the face of an American "critical" tradition (including its most recent New Historicist phase) that has insistently failed to examine the *ontological* sources of its own problematic. To think the history of the reception of Melville's text in terms of Heidegger's distinction is to locate it within the period in American cultural history that bore witness to the sublation of the *theologos* of American Puritanism into the *anthropologos* of the American "Republic." I mean the moment that precipitated supplementation of a visible center elsewhere that justified the New England theocracy and its pacification of "heresy" by violence, including the "diabolic" way of life of the native Americans (in this respect, see Melville's interrogation of "the metaphysics of Indian-hating" in *The Confidence-Man*), by an invisible center elsewhere that, structured largely on the Roman model, positively enabled a national consensus, specifically, a cultural self-representation that legitimated the imperial practice of Manifest Destiny.[9]

Without discounting or effacing the force of the ontological disclosures concerning truth and power enabled by Heidegger, let me put these three broad moments in the history of the reception of *Moby-Dick* in the sociopolitical terms made familiar by the general appropriation by contemporary literary/cultural critics of the Left of the discourses of Antonio Gramsci, Louis Althusser, Raymond Williams, and, especially, Michel Foucault. It might be said that these moments synecdochically reenact, at the site of literary production and consumption, the history of the transformation of truth/power relations at large since the Enlightenment or the rise of bourgeois/capitalist culture. I am referring to what happens when the overt and visible use of force (repression, exclusion, marginalization, censorship, indoctrination) against an indissoluble *relay* of deviances (ranging from the subject through discourse to sociopolitics) is displaced by an indirect and invisible coercion of this relay of differences in the benign name of amelioration, but which in fact harnesses the wasteful and potentially disruptive energies of this relay in behalf of "discipline" and the material interests of the privileged norm.[10] I mean, in short, the epochal transformation of *domination* into *hegemony*[11] or, in Foucault's brilliant appropriation of Gramsci's insight in his genealogy of the discourse and practice of Man (the modernity that privileges the "sovereign subject"), of truth/power understood and practiced as arbitrary repression into truth/power understood and practiced as productivity:

It is often said that the model of a society that has individuals as its constituent elements is borrowed from the abstract juridical forms of contract and exchange. . . . Indeed, the political theory of the seventeenth and eighteenth centuries often seems to follow this schema. But it should not be forgotten that there existed at the same time period a technique for constituting individuals as correlative elements of power and knowledge. The individual is no doubt the fictitious atom of an 'ideological' representation of society; but he is also a reality fabricated by this specific technology of power that I have called 'discipline'. We must cease once and for all to describe the effects of power in negative terms: it 'excludes', it 'represses', it 'censors', it 'abstracts', it 'masks', it 'conceals'. In fact, power produces; it produces reality; it produces domains of objects and rituals of truth. The individual and the knowledge that may be gained of him belong to this production.[12]

To put this epochal historical transition in knowledge/power relations in the terms Foucault crystallized in *The History of Sexuality*—terms remarkably similar to, if far more historically specific than, Heidegger's ontological version—the change inaugurated by the humanist reformers of the Enlightenment entailed the establishment of the ruse of "the repressive hypothesis." Whereas the truth (of the *theologos*) under the aegis of the pre-Enlightenment—the occasion of the *ancien régime*, which derived its absolute authority to repress and punish from the principle of the divine right of kings—sanctioned the overt use of power in the repression of difference (representing it as heresy and/or as threat to the body of the sovereign), the truth (of the *anthropologos*) in the post-Enlightenment came to be represented as a logical economy external to and the adversary of— the agency of "liberation" from—power:

One can raise three serious doubts concerning what I shall term the "repressive hypothesis". First doubt: Is sexual repression [read cultural, social, and political, as well] truly an established historical fact? Is what comes into view—and conse- quently permits one to advance an initial hypothesis—really the accentuation or even the establishment of a regime of sexual repression beginning in the seven- teenth century? . . . Second doubt: Do the workings of power, and in particular those mechanisms that are brought into play in societies such as ours, really belong primarily to the category of repression? Are prohibition, censorship, and denial truly the forms through which power is exercised in a general way, if not in every society, most certainly in ours? . . . A third and final doubt: Did the critical discourse that addresses itself to repression come to act as a roadblock to a power mechanism that had operated unchallenged up to that point, or is it not in fact part of the same historical network as the thing it denounces (and doubtless misrepresents) by calling it "repression"? Was there really a historical rupture between the age of repression and the critical analysis of repression?[13]

During both historical occasions, the age of monarchy and the age of liberal humanism, it is the metaphysical principle that Identity (or, put figuratively, the Center) is the condition for the possibility of difference, which determines discourse and practice. But in the earlier age Identity (centeredness or closure) was achieved by *exclusion*—by the use of force— and was thus materially and politically wasteful, whereas in the later age, Identity (consensus, as it were) came to be achieved by *inclusion*—the accommodation of difference to Identity, the periphery to the Center:

At bottom, despite the differences in epochs and objectives, the representation of power has remained under the spell of monarchy [and the *theologos*]. In political thought and analysis, we still have not cut off the head of the king. Hence the importance that the theory of power gives to the problem of right and violence, law and illegality, freedom and will, and especially the state and sovereignty (even if the latter is questioned insofar as it is personified in a collective being and no longer as sovereign individual). To conceive of power on the basis of these problems is to conceive of it in terms of a historical form that is characteristic of our [present] societies: the juridical monarchy.[14]

To be sure, Foucault emphasizes the sociopolitical effects of the logical economy of knowledge/power relations in his analysis of the transformation of the theological-monarchical social order into the anthropological-humanist social order. Let us not be misled, however, by Foucault's emphasis. For it is clear that the repressive hypothesis enabled by the disciplinary/specular technology developed in the Enlightenment—specifically, that subsumed under the logic of the centered circle, the figure of Truth/Beauty/Perfection that sustains both the theological and anthropological *epistemes*—is, as he says of Jeremy Bentham's Panopticon, infinitely polyvalent in its applicability:

The Panopticon . . . must be understood as a generalizable model of functioning; a way of defining power relations in terms of the everyday life of men. . . . The fact that it should have given rise, even in our time, to so many variations, projected or realized, is evidence of the imaginary intensity that it has possessed for almost two hundred years. But the Panopticon must not be understood as a dream building: it is the diagram of a mechanism of power reduced to its ideal form; its functioning, abstracted from any obstacle, resistance or friction, must be represented as a pure architectural and optical system: it is in fact a figure of political technology that may and must be detached from any specific use.[15]

In other words, the repressive hypothesis (and its disciplinary panoptics) of what Foucault calls oxymoronically "the regime of truth" serves not only to discipline deviation in the social sphere, "to reform prisoners, . . . to treat patients, to instruct schoolchildren, to confine the insane, to supervise workers, to put beggars and idlers to work."[16] It also, however unevenly, serves to discipline deviation in the sphere of language: to accommodate, domesticate, and pacify the production and consumption (interpretation) of words: not least, of literary texts and, more important for our present purposes, the production and interpretation of the text of literary history.[17]

The difference between the theological-monarchical and the post-Enlightenment or humanist comportment toward literary texts and literary history is that the former disciplines by condemnation and exclusion, whereas the latter disciplines by accommodation and inclusion: as in the public sphere, it is a matter of economy and efficiency. Within the theological occasion the texts that received the imprimatur of the established authority and were endowed canonical status were those the form and content of which "represented" the *theologos* and its providential history, and the texts that deviated from the *theologos* and its providential history were pronounced heretical. However, no less than the spectacle of the *auto da fé*, or the public execution that Foucault describes in *Discipline and Punish*, the process of evaluating and determining the fate of literary texts came to be seen as politically uneconomical, in the sense that its visible inquisitional character instigated more than it inhibited the production of deviant texts. In the context of the anthropological occasion, therefore, the process of reception, under the aegis of the repressive hypothesis, became progressively far more complex, but no less repressive. If, early on, the adjudication of deviant texts took the form of exclusionary censorship, it became clear, under the pressure of the dissidence ostensibly enabled by the substitution of the *anthropologos* for the *theologos*, that the practice of arbitrary exclusion was inoperable. To put it positively, the adjudication of the aesthetic, cultural, and social status of texts gradually but inexorably came to manifest itself, not as a practice of demonization and exclusion on the grounds of their departure from the anthropological norm as such, but as a practice of *accommodation*.[18] Like, for example, Rabelais's *Gargantua and Pantagruel* or Cervantes's *Don Quixote* or Sterne's *Tristram Shandy* or Flaubert's *Madame Bovary* or Joyce's *Ulysses* (to name only the most prominent), they were interpreted in such a way as to *over-look* or *super-vise* the differential elements that, left intact, would subvert the canon and the humanist *logos* determining it. By the hermeneutics of *over-sight* I mean the interpretive practice that is inscribed by the already fulfilled form/content privileged by the anthropological *episteme* and that thus precludes the possibility of perceiving disruptive *aporias* in the text or must represent them as "flaws" or "excrescences" or, as Derrida has tellingly observed in a critique of "structuralist" interpretive practice, as "sins" of "lack" or "excess,"[19] which, however much they might mar the final design, cannot subvert its monumental authority. By the hermeneutics of *super-vision*, I mean the imposition of meaning from the normative/panoptic perspective on the subversive aporetic elements—the differential force—to make them conform to the larger (imperial) design. And what I have said about the genealogy of the post-Enlightenment comportment in the face of the individual text applies as well to the text of literary history.[20]

In sum, what theory has disclosed in its interrogation of the ontotheological literary tradition is that the history of canon formation since the epoch of the *theologos* bears witness to a transformation of the operations of power relations at the site of textuality analogous to and complicitous with the transformation of power relations at the site of sociopolitics. It is no longer the censorship—the active rejection or marginalization of deviant texts—that determines the structure of the canon. Like the disciplinary operations obscured by the ruse of the repressive hypothesis or, alternatively, of hegemony, it is, rather, the domestication or pacification of their duplicitous, disruptive force in the name of deliverance but in behalf of national consensus. Theory has taught us, in other words, that the institutional production and consumption of literary texts constitutes one of the most important and powerful means of legitimating and reproducing the dominant cultural and sociopolitical formation. It is in this multiple sense that one can now speak of interpretation and canon formation (and the institutional machinery—literature departments, presses, journals, professional literary associations, accrediting agencies, and so on—which transmit their forms and contents) in the post-Enlightenment age as a form of (neo-)colonialism and the intended accomplishment of a *Pax Anthropologica.*

A GENEALOGICAL HISTORY OF THE RECEPTION OF *MOBY-DICK*, 1850–1945

The general significance of the posthumanist disclosure of the logocentric will to power informing canon formation for the history of the reception of Melville's *Moby-Dick* should now be obvious. In the historical context of a still powerful Puritan tradition, however secularized as the "spirit of capitalism,"[21] the Melville of *Moby-Dick* (1851), indeed, of *Pierre; or, The Ambiguities* (1852), "Bartleby the Scrivener" (1853), "Benito Cereno" (1855), *The Confidence-Man* (1857), and the other texts that followed, was arbitrarily dismissed by his early critics as exorbitant, if not exactly pronounced to be heretical: too radical in his departure from the Puritan/capitalist *logos*. The official custodians of the American Cultural Memory (often repeating the judgment of Victorian English critics), that is, found Melville's text, especially those baroque stylistic and rhetorical elements associated with his representation of Captain Ahab, utterly alien, despite intimations of the writer's remarkable talent, even genius, to the Puritan/capitalist problematic determining their critical discourse; specifically, the "realist"/autobiographical form inherited from the Puritan confessional discursive tradition and exploited by Richard Henry Dana Jr. in *Two Years before the Mast* (1840) and by Melville himself in *Typee* (1846),

Omoo (1847), *Redburn* (1849), and *White Jacket* (1850). Blinded by the oversight of an empirical problematic that rationalized a providential history, they read Melville's deliberately "errant" text—the structural oscillation between the personal discourse of common sense or experiential verisimilitude and the more predominant "eccentric" flights of imagination (which they reduced to "Fancy")—as the manifestation of something between lunacy (possession) and blasphemy: the confirmation of a tendency already latent, not least in *Mardi* (1849), but "under control" in his earlier seafaring romances:[22]

> In all those portions of this volume which relate directly to the whale, his appearance in the ocean which he inhabits; his habits, powers and peculiarities; his pursuit and capture; the interest of the reader will be kept alive, and his attention fully rewarded. We should judge, from what is before us, that Mr. Melville has as much personal knowledge of the whale as any living man, and is better able, than any man living, to display this knowledge in print. In all the scenes where the whale is the performer or the sufferer, the delineation and action are highly vivid and exciting. In all other respects, the book is sad stuff, dull and dreary, or ridiculous. Mr. Melville's Quakers are the wretchedest dolts and drivellers, and his Mad Captain, who pursues his personal revenges against the fish who has taken off his leg, at the expense of ship, crew, and owners, is a monstrous bore, whom Mr. Melville has no way helped, by enveloping him in a sort of mystery. His ravings, and the ravings of some of the tributary characters, and the ravings of Mr. Melville himself, meant for eloquent declamation, are such as would justify a writ *de lunatico* against all parties.[23]

Despite variations, this overall judgment against the excessiveness of *Moby-Dick*, which barely conceals its privileging of the ideological relay between the economic and materially useful knowledge of empirical observation and the Protestant ethic over a disturbingly forceful discourse represented as wasteful—a discourse that, from outside the empirical problematic, could be characterized as an originative *poiesis*—is not simply that of the critics repelled by the exorbitant force of Melville's writing. This reactive judgment is also that of those critics who, like Evert Duyckinck, acknowledged *Moby-Dick* as the work of an American writer of genius, but were ideologically incapable of reconciling what their problematic compelled them to see as a radical and disabling division in Melville's psyche. It was not simply, as Duyckinck puts it, "the double character under which [*Moby-Dick*]" and "one or two other of Mr. Melville's books present themselves" (as both "romantic fiction" and "state-ments of absolute fact") that makes it difficult to judge their value in a disinterested and impartial way. It was also that these early critics' insis-tence on representing this split as a speculative extravagance that contra-dicted and disabled the fiction of factuality masked a consensually vali-dated refusal of assent to a polyglossic fictional discourse that thematizes and travesties the complicity between empirical verisimilitude and the theological/ethical tenets of the American Protestant tradition, including its secularized version in Emerson. One catches a glimpse of this discur-sive regularity—this ideologically compelled blindness to the projective as well as destructive possibilities of Melville's polyglossia in Duyckinck's commentary on the third of the "three" distinct and incommensurable "books in Moby Dick" that together render the novel "an intellectual chowder of romance, philosophy, natural history, fine writing, good feel-ing, bad sayings": that part of Melville's book in which Ishmael unleashes his "quaint" and "extravagant" speculative "wit" "against everything on land, as his hand is against everything at sea." Though Duyckinck would dissociate Melville from Ishmael's demystifying sentiments by vaguely offering that this multiply subversive narrative "be taken as in some sense dramatic," his rhetoric here and in the essay at large makes it quite clear that his collective judgment is ultimately addressed against Melville's art:

This piratical running down of creeds and opinions, the conceited indifferentism of Emerson, or the run-a-muck style of Carlyle is, we will not say dangerous in such cases, *for there are various forces at work to meet more powerful onslaught*, but it is out of place and uncomfortable. We do not like to see what, under any view, must be to the world the most sacred associations of life violated and defaced.[24]

In short, it might be said that the ascetic/realist problematic of the first phase in the history of the reception of Melville's *Moby-Dick* was in some degree or other informed by what Nietzsche called *ressentiment*: the reactive response of an "ascetic" consensus to what exceeds its problematic that guarantees its productive identity and authority by an inversion of "the value-positing eye" that represents this threatening excess as the Other that this eye is not; by, as it were, demonizing its creative—originative—force:

The slave revolt in morality begins when *ressentiment* itself becomes creative and gives birth to values: the *ressentiment* of natures that are denied the true reaction, that of deeds, and compensate themselves with an imaginary revenge. While every noble morality develops from a triumphant affirmation of itself, slave morality from the outset says No to what is "outside," what is "different," what is "not itself": and *this* No is its creative deed. This inversion of the value-positing eye—this *need* to direct one's view outward instead of back to oneself—is of the essence of *ressentiment*: in order to exist, slave morality always first needs a hostile external world; it needs, physiologically speaking, external stimuli in order to act at all—its action is fundamentally reaction.[25]

The effects on Melville's literary reputation and on American literary history of this arbitrary marginalization of *Moby-Dick* in the name of the more or less visible Puritan/capitalist *logos* around which the American literary canon was being formed is now, thanks to the "Melville revival," a matter of historical record, even if, as I will suggest, this revised record betrays a significant failure to perceive, or a refusal to acknowledge, the ideological agenda informing its celebrated renarrativization: Melville's differential or ec-centric fiction was in his lifetime sufficiently subversive in its reading of the self-representation of American culture against the grain to warrant the invocation of the executive power of the American Jeremiad by the custodians of the American Cultural Memory against its violations of the Protestant/capitalist *logos* and the colonialist practice of Manifest Destiny it authorized. This project of the fiction of the *Moby-Dick* period to decenter and demystify the American cultural identity was not only forgotten by the oppositional memory of the Melville revival. The American cultural identity Melville intended his texts to subvert was recuperated, albeit in a more subtle form.

This second phase of the history of the American reception of Melville's fiction was inaugurated in the 1890s, following Melville's death in 1891, but was not brought to fulfillment until the 1920s.[26] It was characterized by a significant transformation—based on (the representation of) Melville's life—of the rules of discursive formation that were brought to bear on the representation and evaluation of his work, the genealogy of which is only now being analyzed by the so-called New Americanists. Building on the theme of American society's neglect of Melville or Melville's self-imposed withdrawal from a materialist society incapable of appreciating the life of the spirit central to the problematic of the critics of the 1890s (Arthur Stedman, H. S. Salt, and so on), the biographical critics of the 1920s—Raymond Weaver, Lewis Mumford, John Freeman, Van Wyck

Brooks—read Melville's texts according to this representation of Melville's biography, especially the latter version.

The revivalist critics represented Melville's time (and their own) from an elitist—essentially humanist—perspective that attributed the vulgar materialism of the age to the abstractive, reductionist, and normalizing (that is, antiartistic) essence of Puritanism.[27] They thus also represented Melville's "withdrawal" from the American literary scene as a consequence of his alienating cultural context. According to the discursive rules of this narrative, then, it was the postautobiographical (or postrealist) novels that emerged as the focus of renewed interest. In other words, that characteristic breach of the decorum of empirical rationality (the "realism" deriving from the rationalization of the inscrutable Calvinist deity's providential design) became the qualities henceforth to be privileged, insofar as these were manifestations of the *spirit* or *soul* that American society denied in its vulgar pursuit of the material life. The Modernist revival, that is, chose to celebrate precisely that differential speculative extravagance of style, form, and content which, in the eyes of Melville's early critics, interrupted the promise latent in the documentary veracity of his first romances and disqualified him from a place in the emergent American canon. This shift in evaluative emphasis from "low" to "high" culture resulted in the apotheosis of *Moby-Dick* not simply as Melville's "masterpiece" but as an American "masterpiece." It enabled a representation of the novel that viewed it as the apex—the mature fruit—of the genetically propelled narrative of his (and America's) *genius*. I mean a narrative, like that projected by all structuralist or preformationist interpretative perspectives, in which everything that precedes (the realistic sea romances) and everything that follows (*Pierre, The Confidence-Man, Israel Potter*, for example) are necessarily represented in terms of the structural economy of promise and decline, modes of partiality or incompleteness (and inferiority), in comparison to the plenary, organic unity of *Moby-Dick*.[28]

The Melville revival inaugurated by such biographers and critics as Raymond Weaver, John Freeman, Van Wyck Brooks, and Lewis Mumford was not, in other words, simply a revival of interest in Melville; it was also an ideological victory over the problematic of a previous generation of critics. It went far, if not the whole way (a project fulfilled by the next generation of Americanists), to reverse the judgment of the earlier critics, without, however, disturbing the *logos* informing the earlier representation of America's cultural identity and its canon. These critics of the revival apotheosized *Moby-Dick* as an American masterpiece because it intuited and expressed an essentially *human* "spiritual" Real that, in its integral and universal comprehensiveness, transcended the ideological partiality—the Hebraism, as it were—of American sociopolitical existence, an existence precipitated by the inevitable reduction of the Protestant prohibition of art to the vulgar materialism of post–Civil War capitalism.[29] This reversal, based on an "opposition" between the reductive and alienating (repressive) Puritan/capitalist ethos and the "emancipatory" spirit of individual genius (the self-reliant and all-incorporating subject of an earlier American time) is, *mutatis mutandis*, a discursive regularity of the revival criticism of the 1920s. It is also, not incidentally, a reversal based on an opposition that derived as much from Matthew Arnold's "English" classical humanism (his "best self") as from Emerson's "American" transcendentalism.

What the discursive regularity of this Modernist discourse—its anthropological problematic—precluded it from saying, in its representation of the recuperation of Melville's late texts from the virtual oblivion to which they were relegated by the Puritan/capitalist tradition, is that it took place in the context of a momentous historical disruption of American sociopolitical life: specifically, the acceleration of the demographic shift from country to city, the massive influx of a southern European immigrant population, the rapid expansion of industry, the "universalization" of primary educational opportunity, the emergence of working-class, racial, ethnic, and feminist consciousness, and so on. In other words, these critics of the revival obscured by overlooking or "supervising" the fact that the rehabilitation of Melville, especially of *Moby-Dick*, was a synecdochical manifestation of a momentous transformation of American cultural discourse—a transformation given massive immediate impetus by the representation of World War I as a "crusade" of the civilized ("Western") nations against barbarism, first the "Huns" and, after the defeat of Germany, the "Bolsheviks"[30]—that bore witness, not to the radical rejection of the Puritan problematic, but to its total secularization. To put it another way, the rehabilitation of *Moby-Dick* was a symptomatic manifestation of the achievement of the hegemony of the American *anthropologos*: the Emersonian principle of "self-reliance" or, more precisely, "central man," which, in the name of "American" freedom, was ultimately intended to domesticate the threat of resistance by a multiplicity of "alien" subject positions against the dominant sociopolitical order. In this, as I have suggested, they repeated—quite consciously—in the American historical space the compensatory English strategy represented by Matthew Arnold's recuperative project, especially in *Culture and Anarchy*. In this English jeremiad, we will recall, in which the "sweetness and light" of a universal art grounded in "disinterested" inquiry ("seeing life steadily and seeing it whole") replaced the partiality of a triumphant Puritan "Hebraism" (that individualism symptomatic of "our ineptitude for seeing more than one side of a thing"),[31] thus sublimating social conflict, specifically the struggle for the enfranchisement of the working class, into the national (middle-class) identity embodied in the English literary canon. As Terry Eagleton describes this *Aufhebung*:

Literature was in several ways a suitable candidate for this ideological enterprise [hitherto the responsibility of the religious tradition]. As a liberal, "humanizing" pursuit, [literature] could provide a potent antidote to political bigotry and ideological extremism. Since literature, as we know, deals in universal human values rather than in such historical trivia as civil wars, the oppression of women or the dispossession of the English peasantry, it could serve to place in cosmic perspective the petty demands of working people for decent living conditions or greater control over their own lives, and might even with luck come to render them oblivious of such issues in their high-minded contemplation of eternal truths. English, as a Victorian handbook for English teachers put it, helps to "promote sympathy and fellow feeling among all classes"; another Victorian writer speaks of literature as opening a "serene and luminous region of truth where all may meet and expatiate in common," above "the smoke and stir, the din and turmoil of man's lower life of care and business and debate". Literature would rehearse the masses in the habits of pluralistic thought and feeling, persuading them to acknowledge that more than one viewpoint than theirs existed—namely, that of their masters. It would communicate to them the moral riches of bourgeois civilization, impress upon them a reverence for middle-class achievements, and, since reading is an essentially solitary, contemplative activity, curb in them any disruptive tendency to collective political action.[32]

Like Arnold's discourse of "culture" and the discourse of other liberal Victorian founders of English studies, which demonized the *"populace"*— the emergent working-class consciousness—by identifying it with the threat of "anarchy," the Americanist discourse of the early exponents of autonomous "genius" and what they represented as Melville's anti-Puritan, that is, humanist, texts barely obscured their ideological commitment to an aristocracy of the universal human spirit at the expense of the flagrantly grim inequalities of American economic and sociopolitical life in the 1920s.

To put this transformation of the rules of discursive formation determining the status of Melville's *Moby-Dick* in the destructive/ontological terms of a posthumanist "Heideggerian" discourse, these "adversaries" of the nineteenth-century critical consensus, grounded in the still effective American Jeremiad and its providentially sanctioned "errand in the wilderness," made the hitherto visible *logos*—the "center elsewhere," "beyond the reach of freeplay" (of criticism), in Derrida's apt phrase—invisible.[33] They did not, in effect, reject the Puritan/capitalist *logos* (and its commanding gaze); rather, they put this imperial principle out of sight by secularizing and internalizing it in the deceptive form of the self-reliant and self-present art of individual genius. "The bringing-to-fall" of the "other," as Heidegger wrote in the passage quoted at length in the previous section, "is now the way of deceptive circumvention," in which "the proper and 'great' trait of the imperial reveals itself."

To put this transformation in the affiliated genealogical/sociopolitical terms of the posthumanist Foucauldian discourse, these "avant-garde" American critics and biographers appropriated the liberal humanist ruse of the "repressive hypothesis," which, according to Foucault, rendered the newly enfranchised individual subject in modernity the bearer of his or her own coercion. Analogous to the discourse of the Enlightenment, which represented the ("objective") truth as external and adversary to the will to power, yet which left the king's divinely ordained head intact, the discourse of the American avant-garde represented itself as a discourse of deliverance that, in fact, obscured its reinscription of the repressive Puritan paradigm that it was ostensibly resisting. Specifically, their rehabilitation of Melville as the authentic adversary of Puritan capitalism and Melville's post-"realist" texts as the creative (self-reliant) acts of resistance—and, in the case of *Moby-Dick*, of spiritual transcendence—of an alienated (and finally silenced) genius in an intolerant conformist society mirroring their own, did not delegitimize the *logos* informing this reductive materialist society. Rather, it put out of sight their reinscription of a differently repressive (*anthropo*)*logos*. Just as the reformers of the Enlightenment did not, in fact, cut off the "divine" head of the king, so the modern avant-garde American critics did not cut off the head of the Puritan *Theos*. Like the Enlightenment reformers, they gave it another—benign—name, one deceptively consonant with the discourse of the American Revolution. What Foucault says about the European humanist subject constructed in the wake of the French Revolution applies as well to the comportment of this early-twentieth-century American subject towards American literary texts, not least *Moby-Dick*, and the text of American literary history:

By humanism I mean the totality of discourse through which Western man is told: "Even though you don't exercise power, you can still be a ruler. Better yet, the more you deny yourself the exercise of power, the more you submit to those in power, then the more this increases your sovereignty." Humanism invented a whole series of subjected sovereignties: the soul (ruling the body, but subjected to God), consciousness (sovereign in a context of judgment, but subjected to the necessities of truth), the individual (a titular control of personal rights subjected to the laws of nature and society), basic freedom (sovereign within, but accepting the demands of an outside world and "aligned with destiny"). In short, humanism is everything in Western civilization that restricts *the desire for power*: it prohibits the desire for power and excludes the possibility of power being seized. The theory of the subject (in the double sense of the word) is at the heart of humanism and this is why our culture has tenaciously rejected anything that could weaken its hold upon us.[34]

At the site of ontological origins, the revival critics' appeal to a discourse of emancipation obscured their renarrativization of Melville's relative neglect in the resonant terms of the perennial American ideology of the "saving remnant": like their own cultural discourse, the Melville of *Moby-Dick* was a bearer of the seminal Word that engendered the Republic in the diaspora precipitated by the Puritan/capitalist tradition.[35] At the site of cultural production, their appeal to the "autonomous" work of genius obscured the affiliation of literature with historically specific events. At the site of sociopolitics, their appeal to the sovereign individual obscured its essentially antidemocratic—elitist—ideology. In short, their discourse would make Melville's *Moby-Dick*—what these critics took to be its celebration of the sovereign individual in its self-present and plenary form and content—a cultural/spiritual paradigm, a measure or criterion of the civilized American consciousness in the face of the threat of barbarism posed by the "enfranchisement" of the hitherto quiescent immigrant masses and, not incidentally, the emergent "Red Scare." For in representing Melville's *Moby-Dick* (and their own "renewed" Americanist discourse) as paradigmatic re-presentation of a universal truth in struggle against the repressiveness of the "puritanical," if not Puritan, ideological tradition, these critics did not merely authorize an American critical tradition that viewed Melville's text as an autonomous and free-floating essence, an autotelic and totalized "world elsewhere," that symbolically compensated for the contradictions of American cultural and sociopolitical life. In so doing, they also went far to authorize an institutional American literary tradition that was—and continues to be—complicitous with an "aristocratic," that is, hierarchized, democracy, which is to say, one with a discursive tradition that transforms every differential historical *event* threatening its hegemony—whether subject position (women, blacks, ethnic minorities, working-class, gay), cultural product (jazz, rock and roll, rap, cinema, video), or Third-World initiative (the Vietnamese or Palestinian struggle against American [neo-]colonialism, for example) into a radically limited "Other" to be as-similated into and by its imperialist problematic.

What, in other words, should be remarked about the discursive regularity of the biographical criticism of the 1920s Melville revival (one might, paradoxically, call this Americanist discourse Arnoldian), is its proleptic prejudice against historicity. By identifying Melville's art with his spiritual condition in a crassly puritanical and materialist—and hostile—America and by representing *Moby-Dick*—its reconciliation and fulfillment of the partial and uneven tensions activated by this vulgarized America—as a spiritual triumph over his alienated condition in the public sphere, this criticism, in fact, inaugurated an ideological interpretive discursive practice characterized by its suspicion of temporality, specific history, and sociopolitics that was to achieve fulfillment and hegemony, by way of its amalgamation of cultural concerns with New Critical poetics, during and immediately after World War II, when the study of American literature was accorded institutional status. I mean the "dialectical" cultural interpretive/critical practice that, in opposition to the Parringtonian tradition—the reading of American literary history as a progressive history of social criticism—privileged that American literary art which internalized and reconciled the conflicts generated by the social divisions in American society within the all-accommodating consciousness of the self-present, pluralistic, humanist Self.

This is the "field-Imaginary" (as Donald Pease, following Lacan and Althusser, has called this dialectics in his brilliant interrogation of its political unconscious)[36] that was institutionalized by the founders of American literary studies in the context of the onset of the Cold War. I am referring, more specifically, to the Modernist cultural discourse that, according to Pease, was inaugurated by F. O. Matthiessen's *American Renaissance* as a response to European fascism, but which was crystallized and given its essential shape by Lionel Trilling's appropriation of the (Arnoldian) "liberal imagination" to define American democracy against Soviet communism. Pease's thematization of the ideological agenda informing Trilling's "liberal imagination" deserves quotation at length for the light it throws on an entire founding generation of Americanist literary criticism:

Trilling's splitting off of the literary imagination from any public world constitutes the ideological work, what might be called the field-defining *action* [of his substitution of the discourse of *The Liberal Imagination* for F. O. Matthiessen's *American Renaissance*]. . . . The experience of this separation, by which literary possibilities can be realized as determinate actions or as particular referents [which Trilling calls, after Keats, negative capability], in turn results in the internalization of that dialectical contradiction (the yes and no) Trilling earlier defined as the agency of American cultural history. When exercising liberal imagination, an otherwise politically engaged liberal subject can experience the disconnection between what commits him and the place where commitment can be realized. Thus, Trilling's liberal imagination produces two disconnected realms—the cultural and the public. And in diverting their attention from the "limited" world of politics (preoccupied by the larger and permanent dialectical contradictions that sets, for Trilling, the United States' freedom against the Soviets' totalitarianism) to the densely nuanced, complexly differentiated realm of high modernist culture, American readers/writers experience a surrogate fulfillment of their deepest drives and an ersatz wholeness for their authentic selves. By promising wholeness for selves partitized within the public world and an infinity of private locations for the fulfillment of drives left unrealized in the public realm, the cultural sphere's attraction increases, according to Trilling, in direct proportion to the needs for such compensatory gratifications produced within the public realm.[37]

In short, in valorizing the intensely imaginative inventiveness of *Moby-Dick* or, rather, the synthesis of its imaginative and realistic elements—the characteristics that Melville's earlier critics seized on to dismiss the novel as incommensurable with the rules of discursive formation inscribed in their Puritan/capitalist problematic—the "avant-garde" of the 1920s *accommodated* what I will show to be the novel's multi-situated decentering force to the invisible *anthropologos* informing their notion of creative genius. They thus prepared for its accommodation to the American canon (its institutionalization) as it was constructed in the next generation by the "liberal imagination": by Modernist cultural critics such as Trilling, F. O. Matthiessen (*The American Renaissance*, 1941); Henry Nash Smith (*The Virgin Land*, 1950); R. W. B. Lewis (*The American Adam*, 1955); Richard Chase (*The American Novel and Its Tradition*, 1957); Harry Levin (*The Power of Blackness: Hawthorne, Poe, Melville*, 1958); Leslie Fiedler (*Love and Death in the American Novel*, 1960); Marcus Bewley (*The Eccentric Design*, 1963); Leo Marx (*The Machine in the Garden*, 1965); Richard Poirier (*A World Elsewhere*, 1966); and Quentin Anderson (*The Imperial Self*, 1971). And, of course, to the "new" national self-image: that which extended and refined the elitist spirit of genius privileged by the 1920s against massification (and the masses) to include an international or geopolitical dimension. In order to compensate for the inevitable leveling cultural and sociopolitical processes endemic to industrial expansion and the materialist ethos latent in the abstract Puritan discipline *and* to accommodate the cultural and political "enfranchise-ment" of the hitherto disenfranchised, largely immigrant masses, the Americanist discourse of the Melville revival rendered the transcendent spirit of genius (Arnold's "best self") the measure of all (not only American) things. As the enormous impact of Arnold's cultural criticism on Lionel Trilling clearly suggests,[38] the American cultural critics of the 1940s did not break with this curiously English problematic; they gave it greater cultural and sociopolitical specificity and widened its (geopolitical) scope. To accommodate the contradictions in the historically specific discursive practices of American ("liberal") democracy exposed by the United States' assumption of superpower status after World War II, they lent their "liberal" discourse, as a number of the New Americanists, most notably Donald Pease, have persuasively demonstrated, to the ideological struggle for world hegemony in the Cold War against the Soviet Union.[39]

THE NEW AMERICANIST "FIELD-IMAGINARY" AND THE VIETNAM WAR

This third phase of the history of the reception of Melville's *Moby-Dick*, however, has not yet been played out. Despite the valuable interventions of recent Americanists like Sacvan Bercovitch, Michael Paul Rogin, Sharon Cameron, Wai-chee Dimock, and especially Pease, the ideological subtext(s) informing mainstream Americanist critical discourse on Mel-ville's novel since the 1920s has not, I submit, been adequately thematized. Why I think this has been the case will become clear in the process of the "reading" of *Moby-Dick* that follows. Suffice it here to say provisionally that their criticism, like that of the nineteenth- and twentieth-century forebears they ostensibly are subverting, have in varying disabling degrees remained too parochially within the framework of the Americanist cultural discourse they would interrogate, not realizing, among other things, that the provenance of this last is, in large part, English. This is not to say that they all have resisted or ignored European theory. On the contrary it is, according to many of them, their appropriation of this discourse that distinguishes their criticism from their predecessors'. But if they have invoked contemporary continental thought, they have, as in the case of Bercovitch's appeal to Antonio Gramsci, accommodated it to the discourse of America rather than utilizing its estranging perspective to interrogate it.[40] They have thus inhibited, if not precluded, the perspectives of the outside of this inside, namely, the *relay* of "others" disaffiliated by the totalizing American Imaginary, which it is the imperative of posthumanist theory to thematize. As Paul Bové has observed in an important critique of Sacvan Bercovitch's revisionist New Americanist project, for example,

While honoring the values of distance and the experience of exile that theorize it as a critical necessity, one must also wonder if the study of culture does not require an even more complex and difficult position: being in and of one's locale while understanding its needs and hence one's own projects in terms of a global or transnational set of interlocking perspectives. The best critical emblem for our time might be what Gayatri Spivak has taught us to call the "post-colonial subject," that is, the gendered intellectual engaged in agonistic analysis of global issues central to regional and national concerns and always motivated by an understanding of the complex position that any citizen of a postmodern cultural multiplicity must occupy.

I want to suggest . . . that "American Studies" taken as a field in its "theoretical fullness" . . . has not yet reached the point of "exile" in relation to itself and its nationalist projects. This is an intolerable situation to be in because, like it or not, the citizens who carry out even "New Americanist" discourses do so precisely as persons whose own positionality—despite the appearance of their practice—is not solely determined or defined by their inscription within the professions that train them. . . . This has, of course, always been true as any look at the monuments of the subdiscipline would show. But it is intensely true now precisely because the historical multi-positionality of the critic is a determining "fact" that has already been partly theorized within criticism in the work not only of Spivak but of Foucault, Gramsci, and others.[41]

As a consequence of this vestigial—untheorized—nationalism, Melville's *Moby-Dick*, however large the space of its incarceration granted by the "New Americanists," remains a captive of the literary/cultural/political tradition that it was, I submit, Melville's purpose in some fundamentally counterhegemonic way to call radically into question. That this is the case, one need only to cite the recent synecdochal "revisionary" institutional critical anthologies referred to earlier, which, in characteristically pluralist fashion, include token—and, in the case of the MLA publication, extraordinarily weak—essays written from a broadly "poststructuralist" perspective, but finally only to replicate the monumentalized representation (and its ideology) of *Moby-Dick* elaborated and institutionalized by the recuperative critics of the "Melville Revival" and after.[42]

The "New Americanist" task of demonumentalizing *Moby-Dick*—of liberating it from its colonization by a mainstream Americanist criticism that would legitimize an alleged "revolutionary" cultural identity that guaranteed America's world hegemony—can no longer, as I have been arguing, be conducted according to the dictates of disciplinarity, as either a purely aesthetic/literary or textual or cultural or economic or historical or political project restricted within the parameters of the discourse of "America." It must, rather, take the form of a *transdisciplinary* critical practice undertaken from a global perspective or, in Bové's terms, from the "point of 'exile' in relation to itself and its nationalist projects." I mean an alienated comportment toward national inquiry that has penetrated the disabling humanist disciplinarity—the Enlightenment's seductive strategy *vis à vis* knowledge production of domination by division—into the recognition of the *indissoluble*, however unevenly developed or asymmetrical, *relationship* between all the "disciplinary" sites on the continuum of being, from ontological representation as such through the construction of the subject and knowledge production to economics and sociopolitics. As I have suggested elsewhere, this disclosure of the affiliative relay that traverses the "disciplinary" sites on the continuum of being constitutes the fundamental lesson of contemporary theory, although it has yet to be adequately thought. Since this still-to-be-thought disclosure is crucial to the argument of this book, I hope to be forgiven for quoting myself at some length:

ver decisive their demystification of the binary logic of logocentric think-
e various practitioners of postmodern theory have failed to break out of the
shed disciplinary parameters. They tend in practice, despite their interroga-
f boundaries, to limit critical inquiry to more or less specific sites, with only
minimal (though quite suggestive) gestures of crossover into others. It is this
general failure to fulfill the radical *transdisciplinary* imperatives of the decentering
of the anthropologos that accounts for the easy accommodation of a number of
these discourses to the established curriculum; not least, deconstruction and the
new historicism. To put it another way, the tendency . . . of the various postmodernist theoretical discourses to work inside the university's disciplinary structure
has, as the now highly visible example of the conflict between deconstructionist
and Left social and neo-Marxist critics suggests, rendered these practitioners more
like adversaries of each other's discourse—adversaries, furthermore, in the non-
conflictual, rarefied arena of institutional economy, where what is at stake is
celebrity, professional advancement, and rate of consumption—than adversaries
of the discourse and practice of the dominant culture at large. As such they
inadvertently tend to fulfill the productive and hegemonic ends of the disciplinary
logic of division and mastery, the logic, that is, which constituted the sovereign
subject and the sovereign disciplines. The theoretical recognition of the polyglossic necessity of a nonfoundational mode of inquiry to always already reex-
amine its own discourse is what distinguishes posthumanist thinking in general
from the monoglossic "pluralist" discursive practices of "disinterested" humanist
inquiry. In some sense the debates internal to "theory" are symptomatic evidence
of this openness to self-criticism. But the failure to theorize the positive possibilities of this absolute imperative of a mode of inquiry professing the decentered
center as point of departure is disabling. The particular discourse must, of course,
be understood in its own historically specific terms. . . . But in focusing *too*
exclusively on a chosen disciplinary site, the practitioner of a particular postmodern discourse is too often blinded by his or her particular insight to the relay of
differences—the constituencies or bloc of repressed—that affiliates their discourses in a common adversarial enterprise against the dominant culture.[43]

But this transdisciplinary imperative of the postmodern occasion is also
the inadequately thought lesson of the Vietnam War. For, as I shall suggest
in the last chapter, the massive American intervention in Southeast Asia in
the 1960s, undertaken as an extension, if not the culmination, of the Cold
War, did not simply betray the will to power and the latent violence

informing a particular American government's foreign policy. It disclosed the will to power informing an indissoluble relay of specific "emancipatory" discourses and sociopolitical practices justified by its "American" problematic. In other words, the Vietnam War bore witness to the self-destruction, not only of the political discourse of the administrations of John F. Kennedy, Lyndon B. Johnson, and Richard M. Nixon, but also of the relay of benign discourses and practices harnessed by the United States to accomplish its "errand in the wilderness" of Vietnam in the name of "America," which is to say, the "free world." It disclosed the complicity of American ontological, cultural, economic, and sociopolitical discourses with a military tactics and practice that unleashed high-technology violence in the face of a maddening elusive "enemy," a violence that destroyed Vietnam as a culture without winning the war. As such, this multisituated self-destruction of America's self-representation constituted an uncanny fulfillment of Melville's disclosure of the complicity—however uneven—of the relay of "American" discourses privileged by his age (Puritan exegesis, Emersonian transcendentalism, natural science, the fiction of romantic realism, the discourse of the republic) and the relay of "American" social, political, and economic practices (the *Pequod* as state and manufactory) with Captain Ahab's apocalyptic destructive *monomania*—his "unerring" fulfillment of the (onto)logical economy of self-reliance or self-presence in his disastrous pursuit of the elusive white whale.

Equally pertinent to this decolonizing project is the massive and multisituated campaign inaugurated sometime between the dedication of the Vietnam Veterans' War Memorial in November 1982 and the tenth anniversary of the fall of Saigon by the anxiety-ridden American Cultural Memory to obliterate (by once and for all accommodating) the contradictions—those circulating around the violent interest inscribed in the disinterested discourse of truth—disclosed by the disintegration of the collective American psyche in the pursuit of its anthropologically ordained westward "mission" in Southeast Asia. I mean the amnesiac project that came first to be referred to euphemistically and tentatively as "healing the wound" and then, in the wake of the events of 1989–91 in Eastern and Central Europe and the Soviet Union, and especially in the aftermath of the Gulf War, more aggressively, overtly, and revealingly, as "kicking the Vietnam Syndrome." For one of the primary agencies of this cultural project to recuperate a lost national consensus has been from the begin-

ning the "reform" movement in higher education, which would rehabilitate the "core curriculum"—and within this, the American canon—
"shattered" on its account by the "collective loss of nerve and faith on the
part of both faculty and academic administrators during the late 1960s and
early 1970s,"[44] but which could as easily be attributed to the refusal of
spontaneous consent to the hegemony of the institutional discourse of
deliverance by the various but interrelated cultural and sociopolitical
constituencies—blacks, women, ethnic minorities, students (youth), and
so on—that protested the war in Vietnam. I am referring, of course, to the
recuperative initiative undertaken by Harvard University in 1978,[45] "theorized" by such humanist (universal) intellectuals as Walter Jackson Bate,
Allan Bloom, Roger Kimball, Dinesh D'Souza, and E. D. Hirsch Jr., and, in
the field of American literary studies, Frederick Crews, and politicized by
such ideological bureaucrats of the United States government as William J. Bennett (secretary of education in the Reagan administration) and
Lynne Cheney (director of the National Endowment for the Humanities
in the Bush administration).

What I am suggesting in thus putting the Vietnam War back into play,
in other words, is that "*Moby-Dick*"—by which I mean the representation
of the text as the *center* and *apogee* of the American literary canon by the
third (Cold War) phase of Melville criticism—must be addressed in terms
of the stakes *vis à vis* national and international sociopolitical power
involved in this massive postwar amnesiac recollection of the American
canon. Despite the significant contribution of deconstruction to the project of decentering the "center elsewhere" that has hitherto governed the
"structurality" of the structural representation of American literary studies
and Melville's text in particular, it is not adequate, I submit, to limit inquiry
into this history and this writing to the context of a historically indifferent
textuality as, say, Edgar Dryden or Henry Sussman or Barbara Johnson
have proposed.[46] Nor, though preferable, is it adequate to restrict such
inquiry to an all inclusive and necessarily rarefied cultural paradigm (the
American Jeremiad) as Sacvan Bercovitch does from his New Historicist
perspective. As I have been suggesting, criticism must also take into
account the historically specific sociopolitical context in which "Moby-
Dick" is imbedded. In other words, it must be genealogical, always, in
Foucault's terms, a "history of the present." The struggle to decolonize
Moby-Dick must understand the massive post-Vietnam effort to recuperate

the American canon as simultaneously an effort of the American Cultural Memory to recuperate the American cultural/political identity which, in self-destructing in the decade of the 1960s, precipitated a "crisis of command" in the public sphere—a refusal of "'spontaneous' consent" to the discourse of hegemony by a large part of American society.[47] Criticism, that is to say, must recognize this contemporary recuperative initiative as a strategy to reestablish what the various posthumanist discourses in their analyses of specific power relations have collectively shown—some implicitly, others explicitly—to be the primary (though not sole) agency of power in modernity: cultural production, that is, the active *invisible* "center elsewhere . . . beyond the reach of freeplay," which guarantees the effective operation of power in the public sphere precisely by producing the illusion of freeplay in the private sphere.

To put it in terms of this Gramscian modality of the posthumanist critical perspective, what is at stake in the struggle over Melville's text is the discourse of *hegemony,* provided one understands this situated discourse—especially the metaphorics of depth in the following definition by Raymond Williams—as *ontological* as well as cultural and/or political:

The concept of hegemony often, in practice, resembles these definitions [of ideology], but it is distinct in its refusal to equate consciousness with the articulate formal system which can be and ordinarily is abstracted as 'ideology'. It of course does not exclude the articulate and formal meanings, values and beliefs which a dominant class develops and propagates. But it does not equate these with consciousness, or rather it does not reduce consciousness to them. Instead it sees the relations of domination and subordination, in their forms as practical consciousness, as in effect a saturation of the whole process of living—not only of political and economic activity, nor only of manifest social activity, but of the whole substance of lived identities and relationships, to such a depth that the pressures and limits of what can ultimately be seen as a specific economic, political, and cultural system seem to most of us the pressures and limits of simple experience and common sense. Hegemony is then not only the articulate upper level of 'ideology', nor are its forms of control only those ordinarily seen as 'manipulation' or 'indoctrination'. It is a whole body of practices and expectations, over the whole of living: our senses and assignments of energy, our shaping perceptions of ourselves and our world. It is a lived system of meanings and values—constitutive and constituting—which as they are experienced as practices appear as reciprocally confirming. It thus constitutes a sense of reality for most people in the society, a sense of absolute because experienced reality beyond which it is very difficult for most members of the society to move, in most areas of their lives. It is, that is to say, in the strongest sense a 'culture', but a culture which has also to be seen as the lived dominance and subordination of particular classes.[48]

Indeed, this "totalizing" critical perspective, I submit, has been made an imperative by the global events of 1989–91 in Eastern Europe and the former Soviet Union and the Gulf War. For these events have defused, if not entirely delegitimized, any purely disciplinary economic or social or political critique of capitalist democracy and, more important, have enabled a totalization of the recuperative amnesiac initiative that is epochal in its scope and significance. I mean that post–Cold War development that now represents these events not simply as the triumph of (the ontological principles of) "liberal democracy" over "totalitarian communism" and the establishment of a "New World Order" presided over by "America," but also, in a gesture that boldly airbrushes the Vietnam War, as the "end of history": the completion of a "Hegelian"—an ontologically grounded historical—dialectic:

The fact that there will be setbacks and disappointments in the process of democratization, or that not every market economy will prosper, should not distract us from the larger pattern that is emerging in world history. The apparent number of choices that countries face in determining how they will organize themselves politically and economically has been diminishing over time. Of the different types of regimes that have emerged in the course of human history, from monarchies and aristocracies, to religious theocracies, to the fascist and communist dictatorships of this century, the only form of government that has survived intact to the end of the twentieth century has been liberal democracy.

What is emerging victorious, in other words, is not so much liberal practice, as the liberal *idea*. That is to say, for a very large part of the world, there is now no ideology with pretensions to universality that is in a position to challenge liberal democracy, and no universal principle of legitimacy, other than the sovereignty of the people. Monarchism in its various forms had been largely defeated by the beginning of this century. Fascism and communism, liberal democracy's main competitors up till now, have both discredited themselves. . . . Even non-democrats will have to speak the language of democracy in order to justify their deviations from the single universal standard.[49]

The narrative of the New Americanist countermemory locates the origins of the discourse that has dominated American literary studies—and the interpretation of *Moby-Dick*—in the 1940s, when, that is, liberal democracy was threatened, first by Nazi totalitarianism and, immediately after the war, by Stalinist communism. According to this genealogical account, most notably represented by Donald Pease and Jonathan Arac,[50] this enabling discourse, inaugurated by F. O. Matthiessen in *American Renaissance* (1941) but accommodated to the Cold War context by Lionel Trilling, Richard Chase, Charles Feidelson, and others, ventriloquized the texts of the so-called American Renaissance in the terms of the discursive regularities of their Modernist age, thus distorting both the Renaissance writers' and their own historical context. Specifically, these founding cultural critics, whatever their particular political persuasions, represented the texts of Emerson, Thoreau, Hawthorne, Whitman, Melville, and (sometimes) Poe as a collective achievement of an autochthonic and autonomous American literature that transcended the politics of its occasion: the multifaceted divisions of the antebellum period that had disintegrated the national consensus grounded on the cohesive discourse of the American Revolution. For these Modernists the writers of the American Renaissance had achieved a literary/cultural consensus that was beyond ideology. What this "end of ideology" discourse concealed, in thus sublimating the divisive political questions that engaged these writers into the "world elsewhere" of (American) art was its ideological purposes: the reestablishment, by way of invoking the canonical status of this literature, of a national consensus in the face of emergent (hitherto spoken for) social constituencies (the working class, racial and ethnic minorities, women) adequate to the national task, first, of defeating German and Italian fascism and, then, of countering the "threat" of international communism both at home and abroad:

But in the twentieth-century commentary on American Renaissance literature, these divisive political questions [that were its fundamental concern], as well as the pre–Civil War cultural context, tend to drop out of sight. They are supplanted by more rarefied struggles. . . .

Critics whose politics were as different as F. O. Matthiessen's and Charles Feidelson's could not claim the Civil War as the basis for their elimination of the pre–Civil War context. But these critics did share a predisposition with Americans who wrote immediately after the Civil War [Mark Twain, for example, who "along with the rest of the nation needed to believe himself forever free from divisive contexts"]. They too needed to believe in an end to ideology in America. Writing in the years immediately preceding World War II, Matthiessen needed to put aside internal disputes over ideology, the better to defeat the totalitarian powers Germany and Japan. And in the Cold War that followed World War II, Feidelson had reason to dissolve all signs of literary dissent into an organicist process. His book *Symbolism and American Literature* uses the literary term "symbolism" to separate America's literature from any merely local or national identity so that it can the better enter the modern world.

Here "symbolism" becomes indistinguishable from the process of change and the activity of modernization. Like symbolism these two processes include every determinate form—whether it be a character, a theme, or their setting—in an open-ended process, capable of dissolving their objective structure into its movements. Feidelson sets up an opposition between this organicist, utterly free process and forms of closure intent on containing the freedom of this process within structures; the parallel with the Cold War is obvious. A Cold War consensus on the question of liberty opposes the freedom of an open-ended process to the totalitarianism of closed systems.[51]

This sublimation of historically specific conflict into a "nonideological"— "free"—canonical art, which surreptitiously served the ideological purposes of the Cold War, was not restricted to American literary studies. It was, as I have shown elsewhere, exactly replicated in macrocosmic form in *General Education in a Free Society* (better known as "The Harvard Redbook"), the master text (strongly influenced by the Modernist pedagogical project of I. A. Richards) that became the model for the "reform" of higher education in the United States—above all, for the programming of the core curriculum and the teaching of the "Great Books"—after World War II.[52]

In the specific case of the recuperation and canonization of Melville's *Moby-Dick*, according to Donald Pease, the founding of American literary studies by American Modernists entailed not simply the transformation of "a nineteenth-century social text" into "a modern classic." Behind this effort—and analogous to the Modernist ideology that transformed pre–Civil War American writing into an "American Renaissance"—also lies the transformation of a novel that "resisted or more precisely disarticulated the ruling mythos in the nineteenth century" (the mythos of the American

Revolution embodied in the American Jeremiad), which, in Melville's pre-Jacksonian occasion, lacked "anything other than a sheerly rhetorical relationship with the scene of the Revolution,"[53] into the paradigm of the American Revolution now accommodated to the Cold War context.

This transformation, according to Pease's brilliant reading, was inaugurated by F. O. Matthiessen, specifically in his engaged analysis of the quarterdeck scene. Here, Matthiessen discovers the complicity of the Emersonian doctrine of *self-reliance*—which constituted the fundamental characteristic around which he wished to build a national consensus adequate to the task of defeating Nazi totalitarianism—with the totalitarian will and persuasive singular rhetoric of Captain Ahab, a rhetoric that, for Matthiessen, evoked the image of Adolph Hitler.[54] Through the power of Matthiessen's persuasion, commentators on *Moby-Dick* henceforth transferred the focus of critical interest from Ahab to Ishmael:

Ahab, in transforming Starbuck's dissent into a demonstration of the force of his own character, silenced all other opposition. As if to supply the opposition to Ahab the crew could not, a lineage of commentators, from F. O. Matthiessen to the present, have found an alternative figure of dissent. They find freedom displayed not in Starbuck's argument but in Ishmael's narrative. And they set Ishmael's subversive narrative energies against the totalitarian will at work in Ahab's policy. . . . [The] canonical reading appropriated *Moby-Dick* to a modern scene of cultural persuasion analogous to the one at work in Melville's age. This modern scene of persuasion is the global scenario popularly designated as the Cold War.[55]

Following Lionel Trilling, postwar Melville criticism, according to Pease, obscured Matthiessen's ideological intention by representing *Moby-Dick* (as well as the literature of the American Renaissance) as the embodiment of the "liberal imagination," that is, as representative of a cultural project committed, against the "progressive" ideological project of V. L. Parrington (and of the pre– and post–*American Renaissance* Matthiessen) to the "end of ideology" (the disengagement of American literature from its historical/political occasion).[56] But it was Matthiessen's inaugural dissociation of Ishmael from Ahab and his identification of Melville's "Americanism" with the former that enabled the harnessing of *Moby-Dick* as such to the global Cold War scenario, the scenario that privileged Ishmaelite America as the symbolic agent of the "free world" in its self-ordained effort to resist Ahabian communist aggression and by thus incorporating specific or local dissent into its total and completed structure, annulled the possibility of effective emancipatory praxis. Whatever the variations in the interpretation of the novel, in other words, Melville criticism since World War II has been informed by the rules of discursive formation established by Matthiessen's elevation of *Moby-Dick* to canonical status, more specifically, by his inaugural representation of the novel as the essence of American Renaissance writing and (implicitly) Ishmael's effort to free himself from the mesmerizing bondage of Ahab's totalitarian rhetoric of persuasion as the *canonical* (idealized) essence of the American nation.

Pease's (and the New Americanists') genealogy of modern Americanist discourse on *Moby-Dick*, specifically its transferral of the canonical principle of self-reliance from Ahab to Ishmael, is stunningly persuasive, not simply in its disclosure of the Cold War ideology hidden within its rhetoric of autonomy at "the scene of persuasion," but also in its analysis of the enormously effective repressive operations of "emancipatory" discursive practices enabled by this totalizing Cold War scenario:

Unlike other paradigms in the American sphere of political discussion (but like Ahab in his "dialogue" with Starbuck), the Cold War scenario does not mediate or adjudicate discussion. It is persuasive, that is to say, without either having resulted from discussion among individuals with differing opinions or having persuaded a liberal nation to any action other than the acceptance of the scenario. Instead of arguing its persuasion, the Cold War simply exemplifies it.

The best way to ascertain the compelling force of its persuasiveness is to attempt locating any geographical territory or political question that could not be accommodated by the Cold War frame. In portraying the globe as a super opposition between the two superpowers (the free world supervised by the United States and the totalitarian countries under Soviet domination), the Cold War can recast all conflicts, in any place in the world, and at any time, in terms of this pervasive opposition. So inclusive is this frame and so pervasive is its control of the interpretation of world events that there appear to be no alternatives to it. Since this scenario coopts the universe of argumentation with a global opposition, there is no moving outside the frame. . . .

What we understand through this paradigm are not historical facts or specific historical events but a way of organizing their relationship. In positing the conclusion rather than arriving at it through argument, the Cold War scenario produces as implicit the resolution that never has to become explicit. And in translating explicit political argument into the implicit resolution of that argument, the Cold War scenario silences dissent as effectively as did Ahab in the quarterdeck scene.[57]

Since the publication of Pease's book, the Cold War has "come to its end." But the essential validity of what he says about the effectiveness of the Cold War discourse is demonstrated not simply by the degree to which the "end" of the Cold War has been represented as the triumph of the principles of democracy, which is to say, of the canonical texts that have been the agency of disseminating those principles, and has been harnessed against a "politically correct" academic Left.[58] It is also evident, even more tellingly, in the ease with which this "end" of the Cold War has been incorporated into a larger speculative scenario, that of the Hegelian dialectic of history: an incorporation that has obliterated the last vestiges of the memory of the Vietnam War, not least, by way of his concurrent apotheosis, of the presidency of Richard Nixon, the simulacral Ahabian, whose paranoid conduct of the war entailed the irreversible demolition of the democratic process.

Specifically, Pease's New Americanist genealogy of the dominant critical tradition that has displaced Ahab in favor of Ishmael as the horizonal center of Melville's narrative discloses this displacement as a reconfiguration of the narrative intended to recuperate the threatened ideological ground on which this tradition was founded. He shows that it is a strategy committed not only to thematizing the contradictions inhering in the privileged Emersonian principle of self-reliance (the totalitarianism latent in the logic of self-presence, which Matthiessen inadvertently discovered in his encounter with Melville's Captain Ahab), but to separating this singular logic into two distinct, opposing, and incommensurable logics: that of "individual freedom" (Ishmael) and that of "absolute freedom" (Ahab). Pease, that is, demonstrates that this strategy is finally intended to *accommodate* this disabling contradiction to the inclusive binary framework of the Cold War scenario.

In thus disclosing the ideological origins of the mainstream postwar reading of *Moby-Dick*, Pease's genealogy has rendered this privileged interpretation permanently suspect. Indeed, it could be said that Pease's genealogy has synecdochically theorized what the events of the Vietnam decade exposed spontaneously: that the American canon constructed in the name of the American Renaissance principle of self-reliance was complicitous in the formation of the national consensus on which the state apparatuses, from the Eisenhower administration in the 1950s through the Kennedy and Johnson administrations in the 1960s to the Nixon administration in the 1970s, relied, not simply to intervene in the "wilderness" of Vietnam but to execute its mission in the relentless and brutally genocidal way it did. It is a theorization that delegitimizes the rationale posited by Frederick Crews and all the other Old Americanists who would recuperate the American canon established by the "liberal imagination"—and the national consensus "shattered" by the "irresponsibility" of those who protested the Vietnam War. It is also a theorization that renders hollow the triumphant rhetoric of persuasion of the humanists—conservative and liberal alike—who are now representing the end of the Cold War not simply as the vindication of America's intervention in Vietnam, but also as the triumph of American democratic ideals and the advent of the *pax* of the New World Order.

THE LIMITS OF THE NEW AMERICANIST DISCOURSE

All this, however, is not to say that I am entirely in agreement with Pease's New Americanist (genealogical) revision of post-Matthiessen commentary on *Moby-Dick.* While I find his disclosure of the Cold War ideology informing the canonical criticism that displaces the focus of critical attention from Captain Ahab to Ishmael, that, in other words, represents Ishmael as the principle of "individual freedom," to be entirely convincing, I have significant reservations about his critically unelaborated and thus putative suggestion that Melville intended Ishmael's *story* to be complicitous with Ahab's mesmerizing rhetoric in a "scene of persuasion":

[If] Ahab was a figure who ambivalently recalled the scene of persuasion in the American jeremiad, Ishmael recalls nothing if not the pure persuasion at work in Emerson's rhetoric. Like Emerson, Ishmael uncouples the actions that occur from the motives giving rise to them, thereby turning virtually all events in the narrative into an opportunity to display the powers of eloquence capable of taking possession of them. Indeed, nothing and no one resists Ishmael's power to convert the world that he sees into the forms of the rhetoric that he wants. . . . Is a will capable of moving from one intellectual model to another—to seize each, to invest each with the subjunctive power of his personality, then, in a display of restlessness no eloquence can arrest, to turn away from each model as if it existed only for this ever-unsatisfied movement of attention—is such a will any less totalitarian, however indeterminate its local exertions, than a will to convert all the world into a single struggle?[59]

The reasons compelling my skepticism about Pease's triple identification (Emerson = Ishmael = Ahab) will be elaborated at length in the concluding sections of my reading of *Moby-Dick* in chapter 3. Here it will suffice to say provisionally that, however more suggestively than that of most other New Americanists, Pease's New Historicist problematic overlooks the *ontological* site in its otherwise productive disclosure of the "political unconscious" of the Old Americanists' reading of American Renaissance writing and *Moby-Dick* in particular. Because of a vestigial adherence to disciplinarity, he fails to see, even as his discourse (unlike that of other New Americanists such as Bercovitch and Walter Benn Michaels) circles around it, that the Cold War "scenario" is not simply a cultural and/or political discursive practice, but also and simultaneously (as its epochal accommodation in the post–Cold War period to the "end of history" thesis makes clear) an ontological one. In other words, he fails to see that the discourse of the "liberal imagination" is informed by metaphysics: an ontological representation of being that, in perceiving *meta-ta-physika*—from after or above an always already e-mergent *physis*—spatializes time or, rather, the differences that time disseminates. As a consequence of this failure to think the "liberal imagination" beyond the Cold War scenario to its "grounding" in the ontological spatialization of temporality, Pease also fails to perceive that the ideological project of Melville's deliberately antinarrative art in *Moby-Dick* (like the destructive discourse of the posthumanist occasion) is not restricted to the decolonization of politically colonized human constituencies as such, but also includes, indeed, prioritizes, the decolonization of time: the liberation of the ontological other—the differences that temporality disseminates—from the imperial metaphysical/spatial imagination.

In other words, the very strength of Pease's argument is also, paradoxically, its weakness. Despite his brilliant disclosure of the Cold War "scenario"[60] informing the canonical commentary centering on Ishmael, Pease I would suggest, imposes this same scenario of cultural persuasion on his own (implicit) interpretation—his purpose is to "produce a historical context sufficiently alienated from the Cold War to make *Moby-Dick* susceptible to another reading."[61] I am referring particularly to his analysis of the relationship between Ishmael and Ahab. To bring this scenario to its prefigured conclusion, he is compelled—against a better knowledge—to overlook Melville's ontological destruction of the spatial form authorized by the speculative philosophy of the American Renaissance (Emersonian transcendentalism). He is compelled, that is, to coerce what, after Heidegger, I will call the "errancy" of Ishmael's radically temporal narrative into the inclusive, comprehensive, and fixed binary terms of this "imperial" metaphysical scenario. (This reduction of Ishmael's errant narrative by way of obeying the imperatives of a totalizing scenario is, not incidentally, duplicated by another prominent New Americanist, Wai-chee Dimock.)[62] In so doing, Pease precludes by overlooking—and ultimately supervising—the possibility of a *different*(ial) reading of Ishmael's "story." I mean a reading that does not implicate its teller in a free-floating scene of persuasion that, emptied of *events* by the adherence to a totalizing center elsewhere, is appropriatable by both the American Jeremiad and the Cold War discourse. I mean, to put it positively, a reading that discovers Ishmael's centerless and errant "narrative" to be in the "end" a multiply situated de-structive *praxis*: not simply a *praxis* that resists containment and/or constitutes a counterhegemonic critique of *both* the sociopolitical effects *and* the ontological "ground" of the American Jeremiad and its Cold War allotrope, but also one that pro-jects the lineaments of a social democracy "grounded" in decenteredness or rather, the decentered "occasion."[63]

This is the "reading" of *Moby-Dick* that I will proffer, not against this New Americanist reading, but in Heidegger's resonant term, as an *Auseinandersetzung*—an agonistic dialogue[64]—with it, in the central chapter of this book. But before beginning, it will be necessary for the sake of justifying my rehearsal of much of the same ground traversed by Pease and other New Americanists to retrieve the Modernist interpretive orientation toward *Moby-Dick*, the perspective that immediately precedes but continues to be concurrent with what is the overdetermined object of the New Americanists' critique but which significantly they have overlooked in their narrative of the history of the reception of Melville's novel. I am referring to that essentially humanist perspective of the Melville revival, still influential, if displaced from the center as a nostalgia, which assumes *Moby-Dick* to be an American tragedy: a work, that is, which appropriates the modern European ("Aristotelian") representation of tragedy—the overdetermined German (and English) representation that Nietzsche called "Apollonian" in the process of his sustained critique of modern

European high art as an enervatingly repressive anthropocentrism—for the mid-nineteenth century American context. It is a form, not incidentally, the balanced opposing tensions of which can, in a time of national crisis (such as that precipitated by the advent of the Cold War), be easily shifted to accommodate the need of consensus: away, that is, from the cathartic lament over the catastrophic fate of the tragic hero to the condemnation of his repressive and overpowering hubris. In the case of *Moby-Dick*, from the revivalist celebration of the triumph-in-defeat of Ahab to the Cold War apotheosis of Ishmael for his liberatory resistance to Ahab's sultanism. Though Pease overlooks its prominence, it is, in fact, this tragic form that, no less than Lewis Mumford's, for example, determines F. O. Matthiessen's reading of *Moby-Dick*:

This cleavage [between perception and feeling] is at the root of Ahab's dilemma. He can see nothing but his own burning thoughts since he no longer shares in any normal fellow-feelings. His resolve to take it upon himself to seek out and annihilate the source of malignity, is god-like, for it represents human effort in its highest reach. But as he himself declares, it is likewise "demoniac," the sanity of a controlled madness. The control depends upon "that certain sultanism of his brain," which cunningly builds its power over the others into "an irresistible dictatorship." At the moment of the initial announcement of his vengeance, he rises to a staggering *hubris*, as he shouts, "Who's over me?" Starbuck, powerless before such madness, can only think: "Horrible old man!" . . . Yet Starbuck is forced not simply to resent but to pity him, since he reads in the lurid eyes the captain's desperation. And in sleep, when alone the grip of the conscious mind has been relaxed, Ahab's tortured soul shrieks out in nightmares, in a frantic effort to escape from the drive of his obsession. At such moments Melville finds an image for his state in calling him a Prometheus whose intense thinking has created the vulture that feeds upon his heart forever. It is significant that Melville wrote on the back cover of the last volume of his Shakespeare, "Eschylus' *Tragedies*," as though intending to read them. Prometheus, whose desire to help humanity was also misdirected and led him into crime, makes a not unfitting counterpart for Ahab, for the stark grandeur of Melville's creation is comparable even to that of Aeschylus.[65]

The retrieval of this revivalist criticism, which represents *Moby-Dick* as high tragedy, from the oblivion to which it has been relegated by the New Americanists is not, as I hope to show in what follows, an insignificant arbitrary gesture. Tragedy thus understood in Apollonian terms is a cathartic cultural form the dialectical/teleological economy of which enacts a

"Hegelian" *Aufhebung*: a sublimation of the conflicts of actual and immedi-ate individual and collective human experience in the name of an anthro-pological End, variously called Center, Logos, Transcendental Signified, Principle of Presence, and so on. In this, the (Apollonian) form of tragedy is not simply affiliated with the dialectical form that, according to the Old Americanist representation, was intrinsic to the American romance; it also focuses more clearly the ideological function of the dialectic than the American romance. Further, it should not be forgotten, as too often New Americanists do, that the overdetermined object of Melville's parodic (I will call it destructive) text—as well as of *Pierre, The Confidence-Man,* and *Israel Potter*—was precisely, if not exclusively, the anthropological meta-physics of presence of those optimistic Yankee "Pantheists" who dreamed their sweet self-fulfilling unworldly dreams unheedful of the "Descartian vortices" over which they "hovered." As I will show, its adversarial object was also—and simultaneously—what Melville took to be this confidence game's privileged (because most deceptive) cultural agency: high tragedy.

In other words, such a retrieval of the "tragic" interpretation of *Moby-Dick* will, I submit, disclose a crucial dimension of the ideological subtext of postwar canonical readings of Melville's novel to which the New Historicist problematic of the New Americanists is in some disabling degree blinded by its otherwise illuminating sociopolitical oversight. I mean the discreetly repressive ideology of anthropologocentrism which, however indirectly, is indissolubly continuous with the sociopolitical ideology disclosed by the critical genealogy of the New Americanists. In so doing, it will also activate a reading of *Moby-Dick* that renders its eccentric fictional/documentary confrontation of its historically specific American occasion an uncanny precursor of what I take to be two broadly related contemporary cultural projects of emancipation, which, however tentatively and whatever the internal antagonisms, finally represent being, cultural production, and sociopolitics not as discrete and/or incommen-surable sites of struggle, but as overdetermined nodes of an inclusive relay that are, however unevenly developed at any historically specific con-juncture, indissolubly affiliated. I am referring (1) to the radically parodic (intertextual) project of postmodern "literature," best exemplified perhaps by Bertolt Brecht's anti-Aristotelian epic theater, but also, whatever the variation in situational emphasis, by the writing of contemporary Ameri-cans like Thomas Pynchon, William Gaddis, Robert Coover, Donald Barthelme, Stanley Elkin, E. L. Doctorow, Kathy Acker, Don DeLillo and, at least in his powerful documentary fiction about the Vietnam War, *Dispatches*, Michael Herr; and (2) to the destructive or deconstructive or genealogical project of posthumanist "philosophy" (best exemplified, I feel, by the Foucault of "Nietzsche, Genealogy, History" and *Discipline and Punish*, but also, however unevenly, by Heidegger, Derrida, Lacan, Gramsci, Althusser, and Spivak among many others) and by the "cultural criticism" this essentially transdisciplinary mode of inquiry has precipitated, not least, I suggest, that of the New Americanists.

In his boundary-breaking introduction to the special *boundary 2* issue "New Americanists: Revisionist Interventions into the Canon," Donald Pease extends his retrieval of the "visionary compacts" of antebellum American writing—the renegotiation of the American social compact that would reunite the cultural and political spheres split into disconnected and incommensurable practices by the elevation of the historically anachronistic discourse of the American Revolution in a "scene of persuasion"—into the contemporary American occasion. In opposition to the ineffectual political discourse of "dissensus" that characterizes Sacvan Bercovitch's and his Cambridge history of American literature project, Pease posits the formation of a "counterhegemony" that closes the gap between art and politics as the essential task of the New Americanists in the face of the dissociation of the cultural and public spheres accomplished by the discourse of the "liberal imagination" in the Cold War era. This is, indeed, the crucial imperative disclosed by the crisis of legitimation precipitated by the self-destruction of the Cold War scenario during the Vietnam decade, and, in invoking history as countermemory, the New Americanists like Pease have disclosed the way to the formation of a collectivity of new visionary compacts. Still, given the relative ease with which the "liberal imagination" and the dominant culture it represents have recuperated the lost national consensus in the wake of the representation of the demise of the Soviet Union as the "end of history" or the advent of a "New World Order" grounded in the triumphant ontological principles of liberal democracy, one is permitted to ask this question: Is the "field-Imaginary" that Pease attributes to the New Americanists finally any more adequate, in its appeal to the vision of the visionary, to the task of deterring democracy than the economic or sociopolitical discourses of the old Left? Is a New Historicism that discounts, overlooks, marginalizes, or leaves unthematized the ontological site in privileging the more visible and worldly sites of culture and sociopolitics in its critique finally capable of delegitimizing the authority of the repressive hegemony in place and of forming the more truly democratic counterhegemony it "envisions"? These are not intended as rhetorical questions. They are posed, rather, in the spirit of the *Auseinandersetzung* and are, as such, intended to provide a *raison d'être* for undertaking a "reading" of *Moby-Dick* that would alienate the scene of interpretation (in Brecht's sense of the word) by taking as its point of departure the retrieval and demystification of the continuing post-revival critical discourse that represents Melville's novel as the canonical American tragedy, the most *metaphysical* of all forms privileged by the Occident. I leave it to the reader to decide whether or not this "reading" contributes to or diminishes the emergent Americanist field-Imaginary.

2

METAPHYSICS AND SPATIAL FORM:

MELVILLE'S CRITIQUE OF SPECULATIVE

PHILOSOPHY AND FICTION

Desecrated as the body is, a vengeful ghost survives and hovers over it to scare. Espied by some timid man-of-war or blundering discovery-vessel from afar, when the distance obscuring the swarming fowls, nevertheless still shows the white mass floating in the sun, and the spray heaving high against it; straightway the whale's unharming corpse, with trembling fingers is set down in the log—*shoals, rocks, and breakers hereabouts: beware!* And for years afterwards, perhaps, ships shun the place; leaping over it as silly sheep leap over a vacuum, because their leader originally leaped there when a stick was held. There's your law of precedents; there's your utility of traditions; there's the story of your obstinate survival of old beliefs never bottomed on the earth, and now not even hovering in the air! There's orthodoxy!

Thus, while in life the great whale's body may have been a real terror to his foes, in death his ghost becomes a powerless panic to a world.

Herman Melville, "The Funeral," *Moby-Dick*

Having become a dense and consistent historical reality, language forms the locus of tradition, of the unspoken habits of thought in a people's mind; it accumulates an ineluctable memory which does not even know itself as memory. Expressing their thoughts in words of which they are not the masters, enclosing them in verbal forms whose historical dimensions they are unaware of, men believe that their speech is their servant and do not realize that they are submitting to its demands. The grammatical arrangements of a language are the *a priori* of what can be expressed in it. The truth of discourse is caught in the trap of philology.

Michel Foucault, *The Order of Things*

O, reader, list! I've chartless voyaged.

Herman Melville, *Mardi*

The Modernist critics of the Melville revival in the 1920s represented *Moby-Dick* as the mature culmination of his art, prior to which everything he wrote was tentative and preparatory, the exercises of a developing genius, and after which everything he wrote was fatally flawed by his retreat from a callously materialist culture into his private spiritual world. It is not simply that these American "preformationist" or "panorographic" critics[1] interpreted Melville's radical departure in *Moby-Dick* from the realistic autobiographical fiction of "verisimilitude" (*Omoo, Typee, White Jacket, Redburn*), on the one hand, and the extravagant fiction of "fancy" (*Mardi*), on the other, as a process that fulfilled the prefigured reconciliatory imperatives of Melville's Coleridgean imagination, that "esemplastic power" which "reveal[s] itself in the balance or reconciliation of opposites or discordant qualities: of sameness, with difference; of the general, with the concrete; the idea with the image."[2] More important, they represented *Moby-Dick* as the fulfillment of what they understood to be the Coleridgean imagination's privileged form: tragedy. In other words, these critics ventriloquized their Modernist poetics into what I am calling Melville's errant art, specifically that humanist (Arnoldian) concept of the universality, if not quite the autonomy, of art, the practice of which, as T. S. Eliot (echoing Arnold) put it about the same time, would be "a way of controlling, of ordering, of giving a shape and a significance to the immense panorama of futility and anarchy" precipitated by the disintegration of the Occidental identity during and after World War I.[3] This representation of Melville's novel as tragedy was not entirely obliterated in the post–World War II period as the New Americanists imply in shifting the focus of critical attention from tragedy to romance and from Ahab to Ishmael. As I have shown, it was determinative, however problematized, in the interpretation articulated by F. O. Matthiessen, who, according to Donald Pease, established the critical frame of reference of the third (Cold War) generation of Americanists. And this interpretation of the form of *Moby-Dick* has continued, despite its displacement from the center, to affect modern commentaries up to the very advent of the New Americanists.

The New Historicist perspective of contemporary Americanist critics, as I have conceded, has gone far to demystify the canonical status of *Moby-Dick* in tracing its genealogy back to the sociopolitical ideology informing the cultural discourse of the Cold War. But in disregarding the tradition of Modernist American commentary that identified *Moby-Dick* with the

Coleridgean (English/German) imagination and its privileged genre, tragedy, this criticism, I want to suggest, also bypasses the very locus Melville's novel overdetermines. I mean the *ontological* site, which, if it does not function exactly as the base to the superstructural, sociopolitical sites, certainly is the primary focus of his engagement with antebellum American culture. More specifically, the New Americanist discourse overlooks Melville's exposure, by way of Ishmael's errant narrative, of the specular philosophy of presence—the metaphysics that perceives temporality from after or beyond or above "its" differential occasioning—that informs both the art of tragedy and the whole indissoluble relay of apparently different and competing discourses and sociopolitical practices which constitutes American being-in-the-world not simply in the period designated as the "American Renaissance," but throughout American history since that inaugural moment. To put Melville's project positively, this criticism overlooks that ontological decenteredness of *Moby-Dick* which, in resisting the hegemonic discourse of the "American Renaissance" (the transcendentalist-inspired discourse of "self-reliance"), also resists appropriation by both the *essentialist* hegemonic discourse of Modernist humanism (the elitist, class-determined discourse of "high culture") and of the Cold War. And, I would add, by the emergent post–Cold War discourse (the discourse of the truth of late capitalist democracy, which is assuming credit for the "revolutions" in the communist world). In thus overlooking Melville's decentering ontological project, the New Americanist criticism also forecloses the possibility of perceiving that *Moby-Dick* provides a context for the articulation of a counterhegemony that is not *essentially* hegemonic.

What I wish to claim provisionally and in general, in thus putting the representation of *Moby-Dick* as tragedy back into play as point of departure, is that a criticism adequate to the task of interrogating its canonical status must resist the inscribed temptation to separate and hierarchize the sociopolitical and the ontological sites, to render the former a base to the superstructural (and epiphenomenal) latter. Indeed, in overdetermining the site of ontology on the continuum of the text's being, Melville's novel, in fact, interdicts such a move. As Raymond Williams suggests in his revision of classical Marxism (and, I think, as contemporary theory at large, despite its internal antagonisms, demands), criticism must, rather, acknowledge these sites as an indissoluble, however unevenly developed, material relay:

In the transition from Marx to Marxism . . . the words used in the original arguments were projected, first, as if they were precise concepts, the second, as if they were descriptive terms for observable 'areas' of social life. The main sense of the words in the original arguments had been *relational*, but the popularity of the terms tended to indicate either (a) relatively enclosed categories or (b) relatively enclosed areas of activity. These were then correlated either temporally (first material production, then consciousness, then politics and culture) or in effect, forcing the metaphor, spatially (visible and distinguishable 'levels' or 'layers'— politics and culture, then forms of consciousness, and so on down to the base). The serious practical problems of method, which the original words had indicated, were then usually in effect bypassed by methods derived from a confidence, rooted in the popularity of the terms, in the relative enclosure of categories or areas expressed as 'the base', 'the superstructure'.

It is then ironic to remember that the force of Marx's original criticism had been mainly directed against the *separation* of 'areas' of thought and activity (as in the separation of consciousness from material production) and against the related evacuation of specific content—real human activities—by the imposition of abstract categories. . . .

What was fundamentally lacking, in this theoretical formulation [the orthodox base/superstructure model] of this important period, is any adequate recognition of the *indissoluble connections* between material production, political and cultural institutions, and activity, and consciousness.[4]

To put this imperative in terms of the theoretical orientation I intend to follow, a criticism adequate to the task of reclaiming *Moby-Dick* as an oppositional text must be simultaneously destructive and genealogical. More specifically, I want to claim that Ishmael's art is an errant art that is finally intended to disclose the totalizing—and totalitarian—ideological agenda of the "unerring" art privileged by his American contemporaries. His "story" is a narrative that destroys the tragic form imbedded intertextually in it: the form that both his contemporaries and the humanist critics of the Melville revival, regardless of their judgment of the novel, took to be the essence and apogee of literary art in order to sublate the conflicts of their own historically specific American occasions, above all, though by no means exclusively, the conflict between an oppressed class and the dominant middle-class order. In the case of Melville's contemporaries, this was the potential conflict represented by the preterition, oppression, and exploitation of a derelict seaman class by the dominant Puritan/capitalist

order; in the case of the critics of the 1920s, it was tl
represented by the marginalization, oppression, and
emergent immigrant, urban working class by the dor
capitalist order. As such an antitragic narrative, the "stc
ontological totalization—and, however unevenly, the e(
ciopolitical totalitarianism—the "sultanism" (Nietzsche's
term for this relay of coercions, not incidentally, is "Eg)
latent in both Captain Ahab's metaphysics of the free or sove
ual (the will to knowledge enabled by the Puritan principle o.   . ́cɪ1ance
mediated through the anthropological metaphysical discourse of Emersonianism). To put Melville's project positively, I want to claim provisionally
that Ishmael's errant narrative constitutes neither a "negative capability"
that "both negates a reader/writer's need to realize literary ideas in the
public realm and enables her experience of the *separation* between what is
and what is not literary,"[6] nor a positive capability that reinscribes the self-
present subject and its will to power over difference, but an emancipatory
theoretical *and* sociopolitical praxis. Though it overdetermines the critique of the ontological site (Captain Ahab's anthropological metaphysics), this critique of the American representation of being as such
nevertheless relays itself into the sites of American knowledge production
(the discourse on "cetology"), economic production (the *Pequod* as factory)
and sociopolitics (the *Pequod* as the state).

TRAGIC VISION AND METAPHYSICS

Friedrich Nietzsche's *The Birth of Tragedy* constitutes a genealogy of the
modern Occidental understanding of tragic form as a self-contained and
consoling microcosm reflecting the universal condition of human being. It
discloses the Occident's representation of this privileged form to have its
origin in the figural imposition of the Apollonian principle of closure (and
individuation) on Dionysiac force in order to domesticate and pacify its
disruptive threat. Nietzsche claimed that tragedy thus represented in and
by modernity was, in fact, a historical construction motivated by the
resentment of the dominant (bourgeois/humanistic) culture and intended
to annul by sublating its formless Other. Despite the persuasiveness of
Nietzsche's genealogy, the American criticism that monumentalized
Moby-Dick as the great American tragedy in the process of rehabilitating

...erary reputation derived its understanding of tragedy in large ...m Matthew Arnold's British Apollonianism: his humanist and spec-...r representation of Greek tragedy, itself derived from the German classicists (from Winckelmann to Schiller) in the terms of that "adequate" and "comprehensive" Sophoclean vision capable of "seeing life steadily and seeing it whole":

I propose, in this my first occasion of speaking here [at Oxford] to attempt . . . a general survey of ancient classical literature and history as may afford us the conviction—in presence of the doubts so often expressed of the profitableness, in the present day, of our study of this literature . . . that, even admitting to their fullest extent the legitimate demands of our age, the literature of ancient Greece is, even for modern times, a mighty agent of intellectual deliverance. . . .

But first let us ask ourselves why the demand for an intellectual deliverance arises in such an age as the present, and in what deliverance itself consists? The demand arises, because our present age has around it a copious and complex past; it arises because the present age exhibits to the individual man who contemplates it the spectacle of a vast multitude of facts awaiting and inciting his comprehension of this present and past. It begins when our mind begins to enter into possession of the general ideas which are the law of this vast multitude of facts. It is perfect when we have acquired [as the Greeks did] that harmonious *acquiescence of mind which we feel in contemplating a grand spectacle that is intelligible to us; when we have lost that impatient irritation of mind which we feel in presence of an immense, moving, confused spectacle* which, while it perpetually excites our curiosity, perpetually baffles our comprehension.

This, then, is what distinguishes certain epochs in the history of the human race [especially the age of Pericles]. . . : on the one hand, the presence of a significant spectacle to contemplate; on the other hand, the desire to find the true point of view from which to contemplate this spectacle. He who has found that point of view, he who *adequately comprehends* this spectacle, *has risen to the comprehension of his age.*[7]

Like Arnold, the Americanist critics of the Melville revival assumed the tragic form to be inherent in nature itself, that is, the natural precipitation of a "disinterested" panoptic view that was capable of perceiving the comprehensive law informing the bewilderingly—and imprisoning— "immense, moving, confused spectacle" of immediate contemporaneity: the conflicts in a public sphere volatilized by the emergence of class consciousness. And like Arnold, they assumed that this distanced, steady, and comprehensive vision was a powerful agent of deliverance.

Since those New Americanist genealogists who now bypass the tragic reading of *Moby-Dick* leave this ontological assumption more or less intact in addressing the novel as social text, it will be necessary, despite the risk of repeating what by this late date should be obvious, to undertake an interrogation of "tragic vision" as this vision was understood by the Modernists who appropriated it to read *Moby-Dick*. To be more specific, it will be necessary, in order to solicit this derivative and sedimented discourse of tragedy, to "de-stroy" "*Moby-Dick*"—the representation of Melville's novel as tragedy: to "wrest" Melville's *Moby-Dick* from its naturalized "everyday" (ontic) representation by "violence." For, as Heidegger observes, "Dasein's *kind of being demands* that any ontological Interpretation which sets itself the goal of exhibiting the phenomena in their primordiality, *should capture the Being of this entity, in spite of this entity's own tendency to cover things up.* Existential analysis, therefore, constantly has the character of doing violence [*Gewaltsamkeit*], whether to the claim of the everyday interpretation, or to its complacency and its tranquilized obviousness." By thus "following the *opposite course* from that taken by the falling ontico-ontological tendency" of interpretation,[8] by "brushing [monumentalized] history against the grain," as it were,[9] we alienate the self-evident, familiar, and tranquilizing claims of the everyday tragic interpretation of *Moby-Dick* and retrieve the aura of uncanniness Melville intended it to instigate. Like Arsine in Samuel Beckett's great posthumanist novel *Watt*, we become in the wake of such a destructive solicitation of Melville's text acutely and anxiously aware that "something [has] slipped, some little tiny thing. Gliss-iss-iss-STOP!" and everything, while remaining exactly the same, has been irreversibly changed:

The sun on the wall, since I was looking at the sun on the wall at the time, underwent an instantaneous and I venture to say a radical change of appearance. It was the same sun and the same wall, or so little older that the difference may safely be disregarded, but so changed that I felt I had been transported, without my having remarked it, to some quite different yard, and to some quite different season, in an unfamiliar country. . . . What was changed, and how? What was changed, if my information is correct, was the sentiment that a change, other than a change of degree, had taken place. What was changed was existence off the ladder. Do not come down the ladder, Ifor, I have taken it away. This I am happy to inform you is the reversed metamorphosis. The Laurel into Daphne. The old thing where it always was, back again.[10]

From the decentered perspective of a destructive hermeneutics—off the Platonic ladder, as it were, where Apollo's projections are recognized as the derivative and coercive ideological phantasms they are—to perceive *Moby-Dick* in the light of the monumental rhetoric of tragedy is also to see it in the light of the metaphysical eye's esemplastic will to spatialize—and repress—its elusively differential and disconcerting force. For "tragedy," whether understood in terms of the imperial economy of Aristotle's rhetoric or the Modernists' dialectical version of Aristotle's rhetoric (which is simply a supplementary displacement of the Aristotelian definition) is the literary genre *par excellence* that succeeds in figuring or iconizing temporality and its disseminations. This is precisely the equation Stephen Dedalus makes in James Joyce's *A Portrait of the Artist as a Young Man*, when, in his effort to articulate a "proper" iconic poetics of *stasis*, he privileges the drama—the "aesthetic image" of which is "life purified in and reprojected from the imagination" of the invisible god/ artist—over the lyric and epic as the highest form of literary art. As his culminating analysis of the psychological effects of iconic art suggests, it is the tragic drama he has particularly in mind:

The tragic emotion, in fact, is a face looking two ways, towards terror and towards pity, both of which are phases of it. You see, I use the word *arrest*. I mean that the tragic emotion is static. Or rather the dramatic emotion is. The feelings excited by improper art are kinetic, desire or loathing. Desire urges us to possess, to go to something; loathing urges us to abandon, to go from something. These are kinetic emotions. The arts which excite them, pornographical or didactic, are therefore improper arts. The aesthetic emotion (I use the general term) is therefore static. The mind is arrested and raised above desire and loathing.[11]

This identification of tragedy and spatial form sublates and interiorizes the conflicting tensions of being-in-the-world (desire and loathing) into a comprehensive static figure or icon that brings peace. Significantly, it also lies at the hidden center of the "autotelic" poetics of the New Criticism, which Stephen's specular discourse authorized and/or legitimized. In his influential *Principles of Literary Criticism* (published in 1924, during the period of the Melville revival), for example, I. A. Richards, like Stephen, not only privileges tragedy as the essential form of the (Coleridgean) imagination, but also as that form which, precisely because of its "inclusive" and "balanced" economy, is, better than any other, capable of recuperating the psychic discordances precipitated by being-in the fragmented modern world:

What clearer instance of the "balance or reconciliation of opposite and discordant qualities" can be found than Tragedy? Pity, the impulse to approach, and Terror, the impulse to retreat, are brought in Tragedy to a reconciliation which they find nowhere else, and with them who knows what other allied groups of equally discordant impulses. Their union in an ordered single response is the *catharsis* by which Tragedy is recognized, whether Aristotle meant anything of this kind or not. This is the explanation of that sense of release, of repose in the midst of stress, of balance and composure, given by Tragedy.[12]

and again:

The metaphor of balance or poise will bear consideration. . . . Tragedy is perhaps the most general, all-accepting, all-ordering experience known. It can take any-thing into its organization, modifying it so that it finds a place. It is invulnerable; there is nothing which does not present to the tragic attitude *when fully developed* a fitting aspect and only a fitting aspect. . . .

This balanced poise, stable through its power of inclusion, not through the force of its exclusions, is not peculiar to Tragedy. It is a general characteristic of all the most valuable experiences of the arts.[13]

The familiar and tranquilized rhetoric of these discursive regularities of Modernist theory seems innocuous enough. But if we read the "dead," that is, naturalized, metaphorics of these white passages against the grain, we discover the violent imperial ontological and epistemological assumptions informing and generating Richards's benignly "disinterested" or "objective" discourse. We discover that the origin of tragic form thus represented is, in Derrida's phrase, "a center elsewhere," specifically the *anthropologos*, invul-nerable to the freeplay of worldly criticism. In so doing we also discover that its end, since Aristotle (but especially from Aristotle's Renaissance commentators, who represented Greek tragedy from a Roman perspec-tive, through the German Romantics and Coleridge to I. A. Richards and the New Critics) is the reduction or accommodation of difference to Identity—the many to the One—for the sake of comprehending the dislocating conflicts of temporal being; its end thereby is the effecting of what Arnold called "deliverance": the distanced "rest"—the "acquiescence of mind" as Richards's mentor puts it—that comprehension, even of the catastrophic, promises in bringing the absent or secret "cause" to presence. We discover, in other words, that the *telos* of this representation of tragedy is the *Pax Metaphysica*. What Derrida says, following Heidegger, about the restricted economy of logocentrism in general applies as well, indeed, especially, to the anthropological tragic vision of Modernism:

[I]t has always been thought that the center, which is by definition unique, constituted the very thing within a structure which while governing the structure, escapes structurality. This is why classical thought concerning structure could say that the center is, paradoxically, *within* the structure and *outside it*. The center is at the center of the totality, and yet, since the center does not belong to the totality (is not part of the totality), the totality *has its center elsewhere*. The center is not the center. The concept of centered structure—although it represents coherence itself, the condition of the *epistémé* as philosophy or science [or tragedy]—is contradictorily coherent. And as always, coherence in contradiction expresses the force of a desire. The concept of centered structure is in fact the concept of a play based on a fundamental ground, a play constituted on the basis of a fundamental immobility and a reassuring certitude, which itself is beyond the reach of play. And on the basis of this certitude anxiety can be mastered.[14]

As the insistent analogy—explicit in Stephen Dedalus's account, implicit in Richards's—between author and God the Creator suggests, the "tragic *vision*" (I emphasize the noun to estrange it) assumes in advance a *model* of being in which temporality and the differences it disseminates are only apparent or, to put it positively, in which a hidden and enabling—imperial—center, simultaneously outside and inside, informs the ever-expanding but predictably directive circle of being. Nothing in this model is in excess of the end. No detail or event escapes the distanced and concealed but ever-present shaping gaze of its (patriarchal/imperial) maker, not even the fall of a sparrow. Every thing and event, however irrelevant (or "playful") in appearance, plays its proper structural part—is accounted for and accountable—in the containing circle of this metaphysical cosmic drama.

Thus, like the transcendent God of Catholic—but especially Protestant—Christianity, the tragic author, whether he believes in a theological or anthropological cosmos, begins his textual creation from the *end*, that is, beyond the reach of freeplay. Confronted by the disturbing and deviant ambiguities or contradictions of the human occasion and the psychological imbalances—the desires and loathings or, as Richards puts them in his pseudoscientific rhetoric, "the appetancies and aversions"[15]—they precipitate, the tragic author coerces the threatening Other—the differences—into an inclusive, unified imperial space, which, in giving everything it "takes in" its "fitting" place, thus becomes "invulnerable" to irony, which is to say, to the threat of criticism.[16] In terms of a privileged Modernist metaphor, the tragic author creates a "microcosm," a reduced internalized but comprehensive spatial figure of the larger temporal universe, the immediate experience of which precludes an inclusive and ordered view: its presentation. In this microcosm, which the author, hidden or otherwise, can see and grasp simultaneously, the apparent differences of the otherwise unpresentable and unmanageable macrocosm do, indeed, achieve a condensed and mediated equilibrium, and the psychological tensions, the desires and loathings of being-in-the-world that they activate (what Heidegger calls the "dread" [Angst] which has "no thing" as its object),[17] a cathartic stasis or peace. But they are won by the repression and defusing of temporality and its threatening "errant" motion (kinesis). We are reminded by this "all-accepting, all-ordering" vision, of course, of Lévi-Strauss's structuralist analysis of the "small-scale model or miniature," which constitutes "the universal type of the work of art": "reduction in scale," he observes "reverses [the process of understanding, which moves from (temporal) parts to whole]. Being smaller the [real] object as a whole seems less formidable. Being quantitatively diminished it seems to us qualitatively simplified. More exactly, this qualitative transposition extends and diversifies our power over a homologue of the thing; and by means of it the latter can be grasped, assessed and apprehended at a glance."[18]

Analogous to the act of creation, the interpretive process implied by Stephen Dedalus's and I. A. Richards's tragic vision assumes an all-seeing Reader elsewhere, one who is therefore also immune to the freeplay of criticism. His single-minded and unequivocal purpose is to locate the "center," the "secret cause" (in Stephen's phrase), the "still point" in the troping text: to name and domesticate what Derrida, after Nietzsche, calls its (Dionysiac) "force."[19] With this end in view, the Reader's inclusive gaze enables a further miniaturization, one that coerces or accommodates the apparent deviations in the text into the inclusive and balanced circle of tragic form, or, if the text resists this move, justifies the conclusion that the artist has not "mastered" his recalcitrant material, has not satisfied the formal imperatives of tragic/dramatic vision. This ontological rhetoric of imperial vision that circulates around the idea of tragedy, it needs to be emphasized, is not my imposition; it is the rhetorical currency—authorized by metaphysics—of traditional and especially Modernist (including structuralist) literary discourse. It is a rhetoric, as I will show more fully later, affiliated with the sociopolitical rhetoric of panopticism (the discursive practices of the disciplinary society) brilliantly analyzed by Michel Foucault in *Madness and Civilization, The Birth of the Clinic*, and, above all, *Discipline and Punish*.

In thus undertaking a critique of the "inclusive" (spatial/circular) form of the autotelic Modernist poem, I do not want to be read as giving privileged status to the linear form of the "exclusive" narrative that is the object of the Modernist critique. Such a reversal of this binary opposition would be tantamount to identifying the Ishmael I discover in *Moby-Dick* with the Ishmael implied by the "progressive" Parringtonian tradition, the tradition that the "liberal imagination" of Cold War Americanist criticism would delegitimize in favor of a Modernist Ishmael. What needs to be emphasized is that these two "oppositional" perspectives are, in fact, different faces of the same problematic: affiliative oppositional perspectives within—variants of—an identical class. They are differential perspectives, that is, informed by the metaphysical principle of self-presence and, as such, project specular narratives: narratives characterized by their spatialization of time. The linearity of the poetry of "exclusion" is no less centered and circular than the simultaneity of the poetry of "inclusion": both have their end in their beginning and their beginning in their end. As a result, their fields of visibility preclude the dynamics of temporal differentiation. The Ishmael I would put into play in the struggle over *Moby-Dick* is precisely this invisible because differential Ishmael. He is a decentered, a marginal, Ishmael, and the "story" he articulates from the margin is his errant narrative.

TRAGIC VISION AND *MOBY-DICK*

Tell my why you should grieve so terribly
over the Argives and the fall of Troy.
That was all gods' work, weaving ruin there
so it should make a song for men to come!

    Alkinoös, King of the Phaiakians, to Demokos [Odysseus] in Bk. 8, *The Odyssey*

The criticism of *Moby-Dick* (not to say of *Pierre* and *The Confidence-Man*) from the revival to the present that would endow the novel with canonical status or underscore its paradigmatic canonicity has assumed that Melville, like all the great masters of Occidental literature, was attempting to write a book in which all the (temporal) parts, "peripheral" or "central," "accidental" or "calculated," "irrelevant" or "relevant," "digressive" or "directional," "dark" or "light," were integrated into a larger, illuminated and illuminating organic whole, one, that is, which accounted for all its details no matter how apparently ec-centric to its centered design. Whether, as at first, *Moby-Dick* has been represented as an American (prose) tragedy or, as later, an American romance, its interpretation and its place in American literary history has been determined by the rules of this metaphysical discursive formation, this Modernist spatial problematic. It is, I suggest, the failure of the New Americanists adequately to thematize the affiliation between tragedy and the romance as represented by the second and third phases of Melville criticism and thus the deep enabling ontological structure in their analysis of the Cold War interpretation of *Moby-Dick* that accounts for the obfuscation of the disruptive or rather de-structive "essence" of Melville's artistic "achievement." This is why it seems to me useful to begin the task of retrieving *Moby-Dick* as an anticanonical text by interrogating the 1920s interpretation of *Moby-Dick* as an American tragedy written in the modern Aristotelian (Apollonian) mode. Because tragedy—like monarchy, its political allotrope (in the discourse of humanism)—has been surpassed by history in the sense of rendering its ruthlessly autotelic (closed) form incommensurable to its postmetaphysical occasion, the conservative or elitist ideological agenda informing the metaphysical structure attributed to *Moby-Dick* is more accessible in the tragic form attributed to it by the revival critics than in the allegedly "open-ended" romance form attributed to it by the "liberal imagination" of the founders of American literary studies.

   The great majority of critics during and immediately after the revival (including F. O. Matthiessen) conceptualized tragedy more in visionary terms than as a dramatic genre and thus in applying the name to *Moby-Dick* overlooked or excused its "erratic" form. Despite its structural digressiveness, they found that in the end the novel fulfilled the thematic imperatives of "tragic vision." Despite its affective imbalances, they found it achieved an inclusive "equilibrium" between heroic "Man" and indifferent or malevolent nature, the inevitable glory and horror of moral action in the face of "Man's" difficult predicament, victory and defeat, pity and terror, light and dark—the essentially permanent (fated) ontological contradictions of the human condition—that, according to Matthew Arnold, constituted "intellectual deliverance." I mean that distanced/internalized consolatory repose (the ontological *and* sociopolitical "quiescence of mind") both within the self-identical protagonist ("the representative man") and the self-identical "spectator" ("the ordinary man") which comes with the "tragic knowledge" gained by the comprehensive anthropological/humanistic vision of tragedy. This, for example, is the inflated Arnoldian conclusion of Henry Alonzo Myers, one of a number of post–World War II Melville critics who transformed the rather crude biographical interpretive discourse of the revival into something like literary criticism:

The end of Ahab is not unrelieved defeat, but victory in defeat; and the main point of *Moby-Dick* is that any great human action will show that the heavens and the deeps, eternal symbols of man's triumphs and disasters, are merely the limits of his experience related to each other through that experience and dependent upon each other and upon him for their meaning. . . . Even to the degree in which he differs from the ordinary man, Ahab is well-chosen as the representative man. He is neither saint nor sinner and his madness is beyond common experience only in its intensity. His grand passion to do and to know makes evident human destiny on a scale larger than life. . . . Ahab, furthermore, is the captain, the leader of his company; his fate is their fate; all that happens to him is significant to others. But in the last analysis we can generalize from the story of one man only if some common law governs the fortunes of all. *Moby-Dick,* like all tragedies, stresses the inevitability with which fate flows from character and by which the lot of the individual is governed by fixed conditions and not chance. These conditions, if we judge by Ahab, are in human nature, chief among them the principle whereby man is equal to himself. . . . Not until his discovery, does Ahab realize [this] truth. Then in feeling that his greatness lies in the grief, he discovers that the only compensations for this fact are to be found in himself, in the nature that is capable of an exaltation exactly equal to his grief. . . . Ahab's victory equals his defeat, his joy equals his sorrow.[20]

With a slightly different (but telling) emphasis that, by way of the New Critical discourse, substitutes "precarious balance" for Myers's "equivalence" in his humanist problematic, Richard Sewall reaches the same universal—and, in its similar indifference to the others on the *Pequod,* politically callous—conclusion in 1959:

Should [Ahab] or should he not have done what he did? Should or should he not have followed his "fatal pride," as Melville calls it, to the end? If the book is to be read as saying that he *should*, then it is a "wicked" book, justifying monomania, sultanism, blasphemy, and the all-but-total destruction they wrought. But the book neither justifies nor condemns Ahab. Tragedy is witness to the moral ambiguity of every action, and Melville is true to the witness of *Job*, *Dr. Faustus*, and *Lear* in conceiving of Ahab's action in just this light. Melville keeps the precarious balance in many ways—not only through Ishmael's comments and experience and Ahab's brooding awareness of the ethics of his actions, which comes to the surface in some calmer soliloquies and in his gentler replies to Starbuck, but in the perspective that Starbuck and the visiting captains in the gams give to Ahab's purpose; in the constant reminder, through imagery and (later) direct comment, of the beauty, the goodness, the truth that make (with the vision of evil) the dual vision of tragedy. . . . The book leaves us, again true to its tradition, somewhere between pity and terror, faith and doubt, heaven and hell; it leaves us in what Ishmael-Melville calls . . . "manhood's pondering repose of If." *But we have seen the conditions of pity and terror, good and evil, heaven and hell, more clearly.*[21]

In substituting "precarious balance" for "equivalence," Sewall, it is true, attempts to differentiate his reading of Melville's "tragic vision" from that represented in Myers's essay: "The metaphor of [exact] equivalence," he says in a footnote appended to his text, "suggests too neat and precise an equation." But this crucial distinction (further amplified in the footnote by revising "precarious balance" to "precarious and imperfect balance"), which threatens to deconstruct his reconstruction of Melville's novel, is finally neutralized. In a move clearly determined by Matthiessen's and the later Cold War critics' American Renaissance reading, Sewall denies Ahab the "Whole" "tragic knowledge" and the Arnoldian/Richardsian repose that comes with "look[ing] on life steadily,"[22] attributing it instead to Ishmael and the reader/spectator (which is to say, to himself): "If the world [*Moby-Dick*] presents is the starkest kind of answer to the Emersonian dream, it is not a world for despair or rejection—as long as there is even one who escapes to tell its *full story.*"[23] Thus on the ontological level, Sewall achieves a Hegelian *Aufhebung*—an internalized reconciliation in the re-collective and totalizing artistic imagination (*Er-innerung*) of the resistant existential contradictions of Melville's text. No less than the cruder version of Myers's traditional humanist representation, Sewall's "hovering" Hegelian dialectical perspective (as Kierkegaard puts it against Hegel's metaphysics) accommodates Melville's eccentric text to the humanist *anthropologos* and its totalizing circle. To put this sublating and spatializing operation in terms of its ideological effects, this attribution of "tragic vision" to *Moby-Dick* ends in the domestication of its heretical or insurrectionary ontological force. In identifying Melville's "witness" with that luminous global witness attributed by the modern humanist tradition at large to the authors of *Job, Dr. Faustus,* and *Lear*—in universalizing its American context—this criticism also colonizes and pacifies its historically specific insurrectionary sociopolitical force. In other words, to *arrive* at this state of "deliverance"—what Matthew Arnold referred to as this "harmonious acquiescence of mind which we feel in contemplating a grand spectacle that is intelligible to us"—these critics have had in their "reading" to overlook or suppress the minute and, as we shall see in the case of Father Mapple's sermon, not-so-minute particulars precipitated in and by the temporal process of Melville's text. They have, that is, transformed their being-in-the world into a panoptic gaze.

To counter this representation of *Moby-Dick* as an American cultural monument, let me begin by invoking the all-but-forgotten, but powerfully persuasive witness of the New Critic, R. P. Blackmur, who was acutely aware of the interpretive violence perpetrated by the post-revivalists on *Moby-Dick* in imposing the tragic vision on the errancy of Melville's text. Unlike Mumford, Myers, and Sewall (and even Matthiessen), Blackmur insisted on a close or intrinsic, which is to say, a "temporal" reading of the novel, precisely to counter such impositions of larger, spatial categories to justify a preconceived ideological agenda. And this insistence on the details ended in his denial of canonical status to *Moby-Dick* on the grounds that Melville was careless with "the tools of his craft."[24] Like the Tolstoy read by Henry James and Percy Lubbock,[25] Melville, according to Blackmur, failed to achieve the objective distance that would allow him to "see" and economically "render" the whole complex experience he would imitate: that would, in other words, empower his eye to control his resistant centrifugal materials and to bring them into the circle of a resolved dramatic, that is, *visible* and *plenary* unity. Melville was too *immersed* in the differential temporal experience he was narrating to be able to see it wholly and thus to gain knowledge—and power—over it. For Blackmur,

[t]he dramatic form of a novel is what *holds it together, makes it move, gives it a center and establishes a direction;* and it includes the agency of perception, the consciousness set up in the book upon which, or through which, the story is registered . . . we may think of different ways in which things go together in a given work, and strangely,

the labor of abstraction and violation will seem to deepen our intimacy with the substance of the work and, more valuable, to *heighten our sense of how that substance is controlled. The sense of control is perhaps the highest form of apprehension; it is understanding without immersion.*

The question we have here to ask then is how did Melville go about controlling his two novels, *Moby Dick* and *Pierre?* The general, strictly true . . . answer would be: *haphazardly*—that is, through an attitude which varied from arrogance of extreme carelessness to the humility of complete attention. It is not that he attended only to what seriously interested him, *for he was as careless of what he thought important as of what he thought trivial,* but that apparently *he had no sure rule* as to what required *management* and what would take care of itself. *His rule was vagary,* where consequential necessities did not determine otherwise. And even there, Melville's *eye* was not good.[26]

Blackmur, I submit, is quite justified in thematizing the erraticness of Melville's fictive art against those post-revival cultural critics who overlooked its obvious disruptive irregularities in favor of focusing its monumental—visionary or prophetic—American essence. And it is high time to acknowledge this errancy, given the increasingly hardening "postmodern" tendency to eschew the New Critical imperative of close reading in favor of reading literary texts as symptomatic mirrors of deterministic cultural *epistemes* or, what is worse, in terms of the degree to which they confirm or depart from a particular identity politics. But Blackmur's critical problematic is finally no different from that of the Americanists to whom he is responding: as New Critic, he reads Melville's novels meta-physically, without pausing to ask the question that fictive errancy asks of the directionality of canonical fiction. What his otherwise valuable New Critical insight necessarily precludes, in other words, is the possibility of reading Melville's "rule of vagary" as an emancipatory "measure," of perceiving the positivity of Melville's "errant" art in the context of a tradition of fiction that privileged the transcendent eye and the principle of metaphysical closure. It is not simply that Blackmur's specular problematic (that "highest form of apprehension" which is "understanding without immersion") as well as that of the critical tradition he is opposing will entail the violent repression of Melville's insistently voiced interrogation—indeed, indictment—of vision and visionary writing as a metaphysical confidence game, a game grounded in the ontological principle of presence, a game, that is, which is always won by precisely this kind of repression or marginalization of the disruptive "Other." More important, it will also foreclose the possibility of thinking the relay of specifically situated terms repressed or marginalized by the visionary gaze in other modes than the binary logic that demonizes and incarcerates them in its inclusive, circular iron cage.

I want to suggest provisionally, then, that Melville overdetermines the "tragic" in *Moby-Dick* in order to expose the discourse of "tragic vision" as a ruse constructed by metaphysical confidence men (and thus, as a more subtle form of the blindness he finds in the "optimism" of the legacy of Emerson and Thoreau to the unequal, historically specific, lived experience of men and women). Far from writing or failing to write a novel that enacts the encompassing epiphanic closure of tragedy, Melville wrote a novel that exists to destroy not simply the idea of tragedy but the *metaphysical vision* that has given privileged status to tragic form, indeed, to *all* structurally teleological literary forms—including what came to be called the American romance—grounded in the certainty of an ultimate presence and a determinate meaning. However constrained by the philosophical, scientific, and literary discourses of his time and place, Melville had an intuition, not simply of the *disabling* internalization and resolution of existential contradictions incumbent on the reduction of being-in-the-world to miniaturized representation. He also had an intuition of the imperial will to power over being—and, as I will show, of the cultural, economic, and sociopolitical implications of this will to power—informing the miniaturizing tragic vision and the archival critical discourse it has produced. It is this intuition, I will suggest, that disaffiliates him from the exhausted and exhausting metaphysical tradition at large and its literary monuments and affiliates him in a proleptic way with the postmodern, or, more specifically, posthumanist distrust of tragedy as metaphysical confidence game. "Tragedy," Roland Barthes writes, echoing Bertolt Brecht, "is merely a means of 'recovering' human misery, of subsuming and thereby justifying it in the form of a necessity, a wisdom, or a purification: to refuse the recuperation and to investigate the techniques of not treacherously succumbing to it (nothing is more insidious than tragedy) is today a necessary enterprise."[27]

I want to suggest, in other words, that *Moby-Dick* is a destructive social text—I am tempted to call it, after Nietzsche and Foucault, a work of "genealogy" in its parodic modality, or, after Mikhail Bakhtin, a "carnivalesque" novel—that finally exists to de-structure the "competent reader's" archivally inscribed—and thus always confident—impulse to read and "master" texts spatially: not simply to expose its gaze's "imperial" project of decipherment, but to release the temporality—and the sociopolitical forces—it has colonized. To approach Melville's fiction with such a future anterior perspective—a geometric measure, as it were—is precisely to practice the restricted (imperial) economy of the ontology and epistemology he is calling radically into question in *Moby-Dick* (and the fiction that follows): specifically, the monomania that impels Captain Ahab on his murderous pursuit of the ineffable white whale. For the archival Americanist's assumption of and obsessive quest for tragic unity—the "talismanic secret," as it were—in Melville's radically elusive text is precisely analogous to Ahab's will to knowledge: a paranoid effort to coerce the multiplicity—the differential force—of being into Oneness. In interrogating this hermeneutic monomania, which imperially reduces difference to the indifferent and enervating Same, *Moby-Dick* discloses a different—a differential—measure, a de-centered and falling and errant measure, a cadence, as it were, that, in deference to its unnameability, will be named by resisting the impulse to name it in the sequel.

MELVILLE'S ERRANT MEASURE: THE TESTIMONY OF THE FICTION FOLLOWING *MOBY-DICK*

The most significant symptomatic instance of the obstinate effort to repress the contradictions in Melville's novel that would disclose vision and visionary writing as a metaphysical confidence game of metaphysical confidence men is the failure by virtually all the commentators—Old and New Americanists alike—to address the narrative evidence of Ishmael's representation and response to Father Mapple's sermon on the biblical Jonah text: more specifically, its function in the narrative at large. But because the subversive/emancipatory effect of this crucial but obliterated intertextual occasion works by way of a complex indirection, I will invoke other such suppressed occasions in Melville's post-*Moby-Dick* fiction, the retrieval of which will help to clarify not only the subversive function of Father Mapple's sermon in the novel at large, but also what is at stake in Melville's errant art, what Melville's ontological interrogation of vision is intended to compel the American cultural identity to (re-)think.

In the novels following *Moby-Dick* and their more or less indifferent reception, especially *Pierre*, *The Confidence-Man*, and *Israel Potter*, Melville explicitly indicates his acute awareness of the ideological coerciveness inherent in Anglo-American philosophies of presence (metaphysics), not least Puritan theology and its post-Revolutionary anthropological allotrope, transcendentalism (and the cultural discourses they legitimized). In this fiction, in other words, he affirms "immersion without [final] understanding" (he reiteratively calls it "diving") against "control" as "the highest form of apprehension." In opposition to the centered speculative perspective whose "truth" turns out to be an ideologically motivated lie, Melville posits the decentered finite and thus interested horizonal perspective of being-in-the-world: *interesse*, the being in the midst, which, as Heidegger, following Kierkegaard, has shown, is the condition of possibility for care (*Sorge*), the sense that difference makes a difference. As Melville puts this ontological reversal in *Pierre* in commenting on the state of his protagonist's mind during his exilic journey from Saddle Meadows to the city:

Hereupon then in the soul of the enthusiastic youth two armies come to the shock; and unless he prove recreant, or unless he prove gullible, or unless he can find the talismanic secret to reconcile this world with his own soul, then there is no peace for him, no slightest truce for him in this life. Now without doubt this Talismanic Secret has never yet been found; and in the nature of human things it seems as though it never can be. Certain philosophers have time and again pretended to have found it; but if they do not in the end discover their own delusion, other people soon discover it for themselves, and so those philosophers and their vain philosophy are let glide away into practical oblivion. Plato, and Spinoza, and Goethe, and many more belong to this guild of self-imposters, with a preposterous rabble of Muggletonian Scots and Yankees, whose vile brogue still the more bestreaks the stripedness of their Greek or German Neoplatonical originals. That profound Silence, that only Voice of our God, which I before spoke of; from that divine thing without name, those imposter philosophers pretend somehow to have got an answer; which is as absurd, as though they should say they had got water out of stone; for how can a man get a Voice out of Silence?[28]

But Melville's project to de-structure the world picture enabled by metaphysics is not restricted to the discourse of American theology/philosophy. It extends across a relay of American discursive practices: not simply the Calvinist Christianity and Emersonian transcendentalism (the secularized Puritanism authorized by German idealism and mediated by

Thomas Carlyle) to which he alludes in the above passage, but also, however unevenly, the affiliated discourses of positive science, Linnaean natural history, Lockean political economy, Smithsonian capitalism, and, not least, American cultural, especially literary, production. For these ultimately optimistic or consolatory logocentric and teleological systems of thought, according to Melville's late texts, constitute secondary or derivative (spatial/specular) strategies of knowledge production that overlook-and-suppress the originary—e-mergent—"things themselves" in their pursuit of the "talismanic secret." That is, they reduce the differential, elusive, and ambiguous mystery of being to one kind of reassuring Book of the Word or another, to a prophetic fiction the beginning-middle-end or promise/fulfillment narrative structure of which, at best, renders being presentable and graspable and, at worst, an object of manipulation and plunder: "practically assailable," as it were. Under their encompassing eyes, the disseminations of being are, to appropriate Heidegger's critique of modern technology, subjected to "enframement" (Ge-stell), reified, and reduced to "standing reserve" (Bestand)[29] or, to appropriate Foucault's genealogy of modern Enlightenment, to "useful and docile bodies."[30]

Indeed, Melville's effort to de-structure the relay of systems shaped into a world picture by the affiliated versions of nineteenth-century (American) metaphysics (and to expose the will to power over the be-ing of being informing them) becomes one of the most insistent purposes of his late fiction. This intention is determinative in *The Confidence-Man*, for example, a novel that recalls Voltaire's *Candide* and anticipates Samuel Beckett's *Watt*, both of which parody Leibniz's doctrine of "preestablished harmony": the metaphysical representation of being that annuls the painful contradictions of immediacy by accommodating them to a larger mediated teleological Identity and its panoptic eye. As Alexander Pope represents this "best of all possible worlds" in "The Essay on Man," a poem that Melville surely has in mind in satirizing the "New World" (exceptionalist) optimism:

Cease then, nor ORDER Imperfection name:
Our proper bliss depends on what we blame.
Know thy own point: This kind, this due degree
Of blindness, weakness, Heaven bestows on thee.
Submit.—In this, or any other sphere,
Secure to be as blest as thou canst bear:

Safe in the hand of one disposing Power,
Or in the natal, or the mortal hour.
All Nature is but Art, unknown to thee;
All Chance, Direction, which thou canst not see;
All Discord, Harmony not understood;
All partial Evil, universal Good:
And, spite of Pride, in erring Reason's spite,
One truth is clear, WHATEVER IS, IS RIGHT.[31]

In *The Confidence-Man* Melville not only parodies the specifically American version of this specular Old-World doctrine (the naturalized supernaturalism of New England transcendentalism) by demonstrating that the benignly disinterested logic of Mark Winsome's (Emerson's) optimistic metaphysics ends in practice in Egbert's (Thoreau's) cold-blooded indifference to the suffering of actual men and women ("The Story of China Aster").[32] His parody also implicates all the allotropes of this kind of reassuring specular metaphysics by exposing the absurd lengths its imperial logic will "unerringly" go to contain and master—to colonize—the radically differential entities that threaten to dissolve it. (I draw attention to this word not simply to anticipate the "unerring" directedness of Captain Ahab's pursuit of the white whale, enabled by his metaphysical representation of being: "Swerve me? The path to my fixed purpose is laid with iron rails, whereon my soul is grooved to run. Over unsounded gorges, through the rifled hearts of mountains, under torrents' beds, unerringly I rush! Naught's an obstacle, naught's an angle to the iron way!"[33] I want, for the sake of orientation, also to recall Wai-chee Dimock's New Americanist attribution of Ahab's inexorable locomotive practice to Melville's imperial effort to "blame the victim.")[34]

The absurdity and violence of this logic's imperial economy is made explicit in the following passage from *The Confidence-Man*, where Melville undermines the rules of discursive formation that privilege consistency of character—the self-present subject—in the American fiction of his day by pointing to the radical inconsistencies, the differences, that nature itself disseminates. This carnivalesque passage should also make it clear that Melville's intention in the "cetology" chapters in *Moby-Dick*, on which I will elaborate in the next chapter, is not, as Wai-chee Dimock's all-too-literalist reading claims, to work out an "imperial folio" on natural science that reflects the structure of *Moby-Dick*, but to parody and demystify the specular and totalizing Linnaean system of zoological classification that was then being appropriated to master and exploit the American earth:

If reason be judge, no writer has produced such inconsistent characters as nature herself has. It must call for no small sagacity in a reader unerringly to discriminate in a novel between inconsistencies of conception and those of life. As elsewhere, experience is the only guide here; but as no one man's experience can be coexistent with *what is*, it may be unwise in every case to rest upon it. When the duck-billed beaver of Australia was first brought stuffed to England, the naturalists, appealing to their classifications, maintained that there was, in reality, no such creature; the bill in the specimen must needs be, in some way, artificially stuck on.[35]

Again, in the crucial last chapter of *The Confidence-Man*, which harks back specifically to the figural exegetical practice of Father Mapple's sermon in *Moby-Dick*, Melville parodically evokes the origins of biblical hermeneutics to suggest its historical affiliation with the optimist philosophy of New England transcendentalism. His genealogy, that is, not only exposes the coercive impulse to totalize informing the typological or prefigural exegetical strategies of the Church Fathers (surely with the American Puritan exegetes in mind), who are compelled in advance to rewrite the Old Testament (and its historical occasion) in order to make it conform to the Word—the providential design—of the New (and its historical occasion). It also exposes the will to power informing the affiliated secularized—naturalized supernatural—strategy of interpretation practiced in the schools: the "unerring" archival hermeneutics—the "high seriousness," as it were—that must necessarily exclude from the canon as "apocryphal" the texts whose content and form deviate from and, in their "differential play," threaten to undermine the patriarchal authority of the original privileged Book.

In this unfinalizing final episode of *The Confidence-Man*, the "optimistic" "cosmopolitan" most clearly reveals his function in the novel. He is, like the enchanter in Cervantes's *Don Quixote*, the metaphysical principle of last resort in the face of the finally unnameable and uncontainable differential force of being: the "end"—the fulfillment and self-destruction—of the undeviating and undeviatable representational logic of metaphysics.[36] He is, in other words, Melville's derisive "principle" of ontological absence *masquerading* as free-floating citizen of the world—as one who "lives" in no historically specific place or time. Like the Satan of the Ur–Book of Job,

whose original destructive force, according to modern Christian existentialist scholarship, was accommodated to the Word of God by the inter-
polations of a later Herbraic tradition, Melville's cosmopolitan "[has]
moved much about the world, and still keep[s] at it" (p. 250), testing men's
and women's faith in God and exposing the inscribed logocentric assumptions informing it.[37] Specifically, he "anxiously" confronts and bewilders an
old "gentleman" reading the Bible with what appears to be scandalous—
and dread-provoking—contradictions within the Word of the text:
"'With much communication he will tempt thee; he will smile upon thee;
and speak thee fair, and say What wantest thou? If thou be for his profit he
will use thee; he will make thee bare, and will not be sorry for it. Observe
and take good heed. When thou hearest these things, awake in thy sleep'"
(p. 242). And the following dialogue, constantly disrupted by an anti-
choric figure from one of the berths in the cabin of this Ship of Fools,
ensues:

"Ah!" cried the old man, brightening up, "now I know. Look," turning the leaves
forward and back, till all the Old Testament lay flat on one side, and all the New
Testament flat on the other, while in his fingers he supported vertically the portion
between, "look, sir, all this to the right is certain truth, and all this to the left is
certain truth, but all I hold in my hand here is apocrypha."

"Apocrypha?"

"Yes; and there's the word in black and white," pointing to it. "And what says the
word? It says as much as 'not warranted'; for what do college men say of anything
of that sort? They say it is apocryphal. The word itself, I've heard from the pulpit,
implies something of uncertain credit. So if your disturbance be raised from aught
in this apocrypha," again taking up the pages, "in that case, think no more of it, for
it's apocrypha."

"What's that about Apocalypse?" here, a third time, came from the berth.

"He's seeing visions now, ain't he?" said the cosmopolitan, once more looking in
the direction of the interruptions. "But, sir," resuming, "I cannot tell you how
thankful I am for your reminding me about the apocrypha here. For the moment,
its being such escaped me. Fact is, when all is bound up together, it's sometimes
confusing. The uncanonical part should be bound distinct. *And, now that I think of it,
how well did those learned doctors who rejected for us this whole book of Sirach. I never read
anything so calculated to destroy man's confidence in man.* This Son of Sirach even says—I
saw it but just now: 'Take heed of thy friends;' not, observe, thy seeming friends,
thy hypocritical friends, thy false friends, but thy *friends*, thy real friends—that is

to say, not the truest friend in the world is to be implicitly trusted. Can Rochefoucault equal that? I should not wonder if his view of human nature, like Machiavelli's, was taken from the Son of Sirach. And to call it wisdom—the Wisdom of the Son of Sirach! Wisdom, indeed! *What an ugly thing wisdom must be! Give me the folly that dimples the cheek, say I, rather than the wisdom that curdles the blood. But no, no; it ain't wisdom; it's apocrypha, as you say, sir. For how can that be trustworthy that teaches distrust?*" (p. 243; my emphasis)

Melville, of course, situates his destructive interrogation of the biblical canon at the site of friendship, which, by way of pursuing the rarefied logic of Mark Winsome's transcendentalist metaphysics to its end in the practice of Egbert, is disclosed to be a ruthlessly calculative capitalism. But this interrogation resonates across the (uneven) continuum of represented being. The parodic—or, rather, the "carnivalesque"—rhetoric of this tellingly neglected (i.e., invisible) passage does not simply disclose the folly of the "Wisdom" of confidence in man's moral relation to man, but also, and more important, of the "sage" ontology and epistemology and, even, of the secular cultural tradition and sociopolitical institutions that are indissolubly affiliated with this optimistic morality. For informing the morality of confidence in Man is an original and originating confidence in the presiding *logos*—the seminal, patriarchal Word—of metaphysics (in Heidegger's sense) and in an unerring epistemology, a truth discourse grounded in the *logos*, the gravely linear interpretive imperative of which is to "read" (re-present) actual existence *sub specie aeternitatis*. This means to rely for the "certain truth," not on the primary things themselves, on the evidences of human being's temporal occasion, but on a secondary or mediating and regulative common text simultaneous in and above time— what Derrida calls a Transcendental Signified or, alternatively, a center elsewhere. To read the being of being from a providential perspective is necessarily—unerringly—to overlook and forget (to repress) the uncanny or dread-provoking decentered measure of the "excluded middle" (*interesse*): the differences precipitated by time, the contradictions, the *aporias*, the discontinuities, the accidents, the differential play, that "curdle the blood," that would "destroy man's confidence in man" ("So if your disturbances be raised from aught in the apocrypha . . . in that case, *think no more of it*, for it's apocrypha" [my emphasis]).

Further, and for my purposes even more important, confidence in a patriarchally prescribed Archive[38] modeled on this speculative epistemology justifies the coercive project of the "learned doctors" to legitimize and reproduce the dynastic tradition, to canonize the texts that conform to and confirm the authority of the abiding center and to reject as "uncanonical part," "apocryphal," "not warranted," "of uncertain credit," those that do not. Surely, given his acute awareness of the fate of his novels, Melville is referring here not only to the seminal, recollective, exegetical strategies of the American Puritan biblical exegetes, from Winthrop through Cotton Mather to Jonathan Edwards, but simultaneously—and more immediately—to that of the secular "learned doctors" past and future—presiding over the American literary scene, the academic critics (the "college men") who, in the name of the Emersonian testament (one central target of this "satanic" or, rather, "diabolic" anti-Book) read *Moby-Dick* and *Pierre* as eccentric deviations and excluded them from the canon of American literary history. Surely, too, Melville is proleptically anticipating the fate of the heretical "novel" from which the above passage is taken.

What, in fact, is especially remarkable about this synecdochical passage on the hermeneutic practice of mid-nineteenth-century American biblical exegetes *and* secular college "doctors" is its stunning similarity to the genealogical project of posthumanist theory *vis à vis* what Foucault calls "the author function" in his effort to think the disappearance of the author as subject. I mean its disclosure not simply of the totalizing logocentrism informing authorship and canon formation in general, but also of the historical affiliation between the typological or prefigurative hermeneutics of Christianity and the privileged "disinterested" exegetical practice of modern humanist criticism, between the visibly coercive interpretive operations of the *theologos* and the invisible coercive operations of the *anthropologos*. We may bear witness to Melville's proleptic intuition of this ideological complicity by juxtaposing the above passage from *The Confidence-Man* with the following resonant passage from Foucault's "What is an Author?" provided we read the latter's focus on the ideological determination of textual authorship and canon formation as particular superstructural corollaries of the prefigurative determination of God's authorship, enabled by the providential (meta)narrative of history. I quote at length to suggest the remarkable similarity between Melville's and Foucault's postmodern genealogy of modern hermeneutics:

> In [modern] literary criticism . . . the traditional methods for defining an author—or, rather, for determining the configuration of the author from existing

texts—derive in large part from those used in the Christian tradition to authenticate (or to reject) the particular texts in its possession. Modern criticism, in its desire to "recover" the author from a work, employs devices strongly reminiscent of Christian exegesis when it wished to prove the value of a text by ascertaining the holiness of its author. In *De Viris Illustribus* Saint Jerome maintains that homonymy is not proof of the common authorship of several works, since many individuals could have the same name or someone could have perversely appropriated another's name. The name, as an individual mark, is not sufficient as it relates to a textual tradition. How, then, can several texts be attributed to an individual author? What norms, related to the function of the author, will disclose the involvement of several authors? According to Jerome, there are four criteria: the texts that must be eliminated from the list of works attributed to a single author are those inferior to the others (thus the author is defined as a standard level of quality); those whose ideas conflict with the doctrine expressed in the others (here the author is defined as a certain field of conceptual or theoretical coherence); those written in a different style and containing words and phrases not ordinarily found in the other works (the author is seen as a stylistic uniformity); and those referring to events or historical figures subsequent to the death of the author (the author is thus a definite historical figure in which a series of events converge). Although modern criticism does not appear to have these same suspicions concerning authentication, its strategies of defining the author present striking similarities. The author explains the presence of certain events within a text, as well as their transformations, distortions, and their various modifications (and this through an author's biography or by reference to his particular point of view, in analysis of his social preferences and his position within a class or by delineating his fundamental objectives). The author also constitutes a principle of unity in writing where any unevenness of production is ascribed to changes caused by evolution, maturation, or outside influence. In addition, the author serves to neutralize the contradictions that are found in a series of texts. Governing this function is the belief that there must be—at a particular level of an author's thought, of his conscious or unconscious desire—a point where contradictions are resolved, where the incompatible elements can be shown to relate to one another or to cohere around a fundamental originating contradiction. Finally, the author is a particular source of expression who, in more or less finished forms, is manifested equally well, and with similar validity, in a text, in letters, fragments, drafts, and so forth.[39]

Nor is Melville's reiterated interrogation of American hermeneutic practices limited to his disclosure of the will to power informing their thematics. Indeed, as the passages I have quoted from *The Confidence-Man* suggest, especially that identifying the conventional demand for consistency of character (the proper self) with the conventional appeal to consistency in nature, his repeated disclosures of the recuperative violence done to temporal phenomena in the name of the metaphysical *logos* are intended in some significant degree to foreground the indissoluble relay between ontological interpretation and literary form. *Pierre,* for example, significantly subtitled *or the Ambiguities,* is, if not itself a *Künstlerroman* in the tradition of Schlegel's *Lucinde,* an interrogation of that form as much as it is of tragedy. In this novel, which continues to remain problematic even for Melville's sympathetic critics, the "innocent" protagonist, whose identity as sovereign subject has been determined by the hegemonic discourse of "patrician" America (embodied in his mother and her world), is confronted by the unyielding disruptive mystery of being in his pursuit of the "talismanic secret." With the sudden intrusion of Isabel into this tranquilized and tranquilizing Edenic world, Pierre is driven into radical questioning of the principle of presence (the Father/*Logos*) and its re-presentational structural imperatives—symbolized by the demystification of the painted representations of Pierre's father—all along the continuum of being of the American symbolic order: the proper self, the domestic order, the language of rationality, the genetic/dynastic or, in Nietzsche's term, monumental, historical model (his patriarchal Revolutionary heritage), the romance narrative itself (the imperative of the American scene of cultural production)—and, not least, the male-determined order of gender relations.[40] Indeed, he is driven out of his illusory "homeland" into consciousness of the unnameable and abyssal ambiguities that underlie the socially constituted "rock" of his American Identity. In his "extraordinary e[-]mergency" (p. 89), that is, he becomes another "infant Ishmael," "now doubly orphan," exiled from his paradisal homeland in "the desolate places" (p. 90). In terms of the subsuming destructive/archeological metaphorics of Melville's text—a metaphorics predating Henry Adams's, and, not incidentally, Nietzsche's, Heidegger's, and Foucault's, in its exposure of the relay between self-presence, knowledge production, and (male) power—this American Adam is exiled into the realm of the uncanny (*die Unheimlichkeit*), at the "axis" of which is not the "talismanic secret," an ultimate presence that renders every recalcitrantly differential thing and event reassuringly intelligible, but a sign of a sign of a sign . . . that bespeaks *différance,* an always deferred presence, which is to say, an abysmal absence:

Ten million things were as yet uncovered to Pierre. The old mummy lies buried in cloth on cloth; it takes time to unwrap this Egyptian king. Yet now, forsooth, because Pierre began to see through the first superficiality of the world, he fondly weens he has come to the unlayered substance. But, far as any geologist has yet gone down into the world, it is found to consist of nothing but surface stratified on surface. To its axis, the world being nothing but superinduced superficies. By vast pains we mine into the pyramid; by horrible gropings we come to the central room; with joy we espy the sarcophagus; but we lift the lid—and no body is there!—appallingly vacant as vast is the soul of man! (p. 285)

In the process of Melville's corrosive narrative, this essentially de-structive ontological theme implicates fictional structure with the "Egyptianism" of a historiographic narrative grounded in metaphysics. By way of his commentary on Pierre's disintegrating sovereign subjectivity, he mocks the enlightened, subservient, pacified, and reassuring—reified—form that the re-presentation of such a dark, uncanny world all too easily assumes under the disciplinary gaze of the tradition of the American Enlightenment. Conversely, he points to the quite different kind of novel he is himself struggling to write in the face of the linear narrative syntax privileged and demanded by literary America. In an often commonly overlooked passage following the irruption of Isabel into Pierre's New-Adamic world and the estranging metamorphosis of his father's portraits, Melville destroys not only the narrative of verisimilitude, that is, dis-closes precisely the circular (spatial) structure of realistic representation, but also the naturalized metaphorics of light and dark, of (prophetic) "vision," it privileges (in this instance, its historically specific allotrope, the classificatory table) and the imperial will to power over being that is its underlying motive. This passage needs to be quoted at length, not only because it demonstrates Melville's contempt for logocentric ontologies in general. In mocking the domesticated and commodified family romance privileged by the antebellum American market, it also points suggestively back to the de-structive form of *Moby-Dick* and, not incidentally, forward to the troping fiction of the contemporary occasion, as the remarkably resonant parallel with Jean-Paul Sartre's enabling distinction between "*l'aventure*" and "*la vie*" in his seminal postmodern novel, *Nausea*, suggests:[41]

In [Isabel's] life there was an unraveled plot; and he felt that unraveled it would eternally remain to him. No slightest hope or dream had he, that what was dark and mournful in her would ever be cleared up into some coming atmosphere of light and mirth. Like all youths, Pierre had conned his novel-lessons; had read more novels than most persons of his years; *but their false, inverted attempts at systemizing eternally unsystemizable elements; their audacious, intermeddling impotency, in trying to unravel, and spread out, and classify,* the more thin than gossamer threads which make up the complex web of life; *these things over Pierre had no power now.* Straight through their helpless miserableness he pierced; the one sensational truth in him, transfixed like beetles the *speculative* lies in them. He saw that human life doth truly come from that, which all men are agreed to call by the name of *God.* [For Melville, "God," as the cryptic qualification—"that which"—indirectly suggests, is the *deus absconditus,* i.e., the "principle" of absence.] By infallible presentiment he saw, that not always doth life's beginning gloom conclude in gladness; that wedding-bells peal not ever in the last scene of life's fifth act; that while the countless tribes of common novels laboriously spin vails of mystery, only to clear them up at last; and while the countless tribe of common dramas do but repeat the same; yet profounder emanations of the human mind, intended to illustrate all that can be humanly known of human life; these never unravel their own intricacies, and have *no proper endings; but in imperfect unanticipated, and disappointing sequels (as mutilated stumps), hurry to abrupt intermerging with the eternal tides of time and fate.* (p. 141; my emphasis)

Admittedly, Melville does not entirely fulfill the antistructuralist narrative imperatives of the decentered ontology which is at the absent heart of the thematics of *Pierre.* Despite his ironically critical affiliation with Pierre (his awareness, for example, of the contradictoriness of the "Ahabian" metaphorics he attributes to Pierre's sudden insight in the above passage), he maintains a vestigial control over the narrative that propels his protagonist inexorably to his and his "dependents'" doom (though it could be plausibly argued, as Edgar Dryden implies in his provocative reading of *Pierre,* that Melville accomplishes this subversive project more subtly by undertaking it at the scene of writing as such, rather than at the site of structure, that is, as a proleptic deconstructionist).[42] This is perhaps because of his impossible relationship to his contemporary critics and the American cultural conditions they represent. After the reception of *Moby-Dick,* which, however favorable, represented its eccentric formal experiments as a finally incommensurable and disabling clash between the discourse of documentary truth and an extravagant fancy that was symptomatic of a dangerously imbalanced creative mind, Melville, that is, became, understandably, more preoccupied with the negative than with the positive phase of his destructive fictive project. He chose to concentrate on revealing the inevitably disastrous consequences of an unerring American cultural logic which privileged the principle of self-presence and its patriarchal allotrope in its fully developed, i.e., commodified, form (the discourse and practice of positive "Truth")—the logic that alienated, indeed, crushed, not "creative genius," but the cultural imagination—than with what his preoccupation also disclosed: the "projective" potentialities of his de-struction of the ontology informing mid-nineteenth-century American cultural self-representation, specifically its "errant" measure.

Be that as it may, the evidence from Melville's post-*Moby-Dick* fiction that I have invoked to displace the reader's gaze from the content to the form of the novel or rather to their indissoluble relationship (that is, to foreground the marginalized errancy of *Moby-Dick*) is compelling. Each of the passages of critique quoted above overdetermines a particular site of the indissoluble continuum that constituted the privileged representation of the American cultural tradition: consistency of fictive characterization, the theological interpretation of texts (canon-formation), the self-present (patriarchal) subject, the classificatory or disciplinary table, the transparency of writing, and the beginning-middle-end structure of narrative form. But what the different objects of Melville's critique are shown to have in common—what informs, if not subsumes, their particular "truths"—is precisely *metaphysics*: the re-presentational mode of inquiry that posits Identity as the condition of possibility for difference. Which is to say, each "reads" the differential phenomena under scrutiny *meta-ta-physika* or spatially: from a speculative "center elsewhere" or from a "panoptic" perspective, the logical economy of which either reduces the "other" to the Same or excludes it as the "untruth." Each, that is, betrays its objectivity to be an "imperialist" project of the ocularcentric gaze.

Given Melville's more or less explicit identification of the metaphysical model with one form of imperialism or another in these post-*Moby-Dick* texts, therefore, we would do well to resist the inscribed impulse to spatialize the differential temporal dynamics of *Moby-Dick*: to read this novel, which precedes *Pierre* by a mere year and *The Confidence-Man* by six, from the end, as Melville's critics, both Old and New Americanists—whether Evert Duyckinck or Lewis Mumford or Richard Sewall or F. O. Matthiessen or Walter Benzanson or R. W. B. Lewis, on the one hand, or Donald Pease and Wai-chee Dimock, on the other—have read it. We would do well, that is, to abjure the inscribed temptation to *see* the digressive particulars—what Blackmur rightly referred to as the "rule of vagary," but which I would call, with the oxymoron in mind, the "measure of errancy"—according to the dictates of one *logos* or another, whether the benign Word informing the "tragic vision" of the humanist tradition in general or the sovereign subject of American democracy or, conversely, as Dimock has alleged, the repressive Jeffersonian Word informing the American "empire for liberty." To put it positively, Melville's insistent interrogation of the specular imperatives of metaphysics invites us to encounter *Moby-Dick* temporally, not as Word, but as words. As I hope to suggest, such a comportment toward the being of Melville's text will open up an interpretation of the novel—both the thematic and formal aspects of their being—that not only reconfigures the incommensurable critical terms of its reception in Melville's lifetime, but also the reconciliatory critical terms of its reception after the Melville revival to the present occasion, including those of the New Americanists.

3

THE ERRANT ART OF *MOBY-DICK*

Without errancy . . . there would be no history.

　Martin Heidegger, "The Anaximander Fragment"

THE QUESTION OF ISHMAEL'S NAME

"Call me Ishmael."[1] So, unexpectedly, Melville begins *Moby-Dick*. The narrator does not say, "My *name is* Ishmael." He says, "*Call* me Ishmael," thus orienting the reader/listener's attention to the possibility that the name is a mask, that Melville's inaugural use of this strange and resonant biblical/American Puritan name is a temporary "convenience" rather than a strategic reference to a proper self that, like Percy Lubbock's hidden Jamesian "showman" in *The Craft of Fiction*,[2] he is creating from outside and above the narrative: an invisible panoptic presence or a definite, if hidden, essence or seed that, like Emerson's "Thinking Man," will "reveal itself"—its *Identity*—in all its multifoliate plenitude at the end of the organic dramatic process, "in the fullness of time," as it were.[3] "Ishmael: This 'name' is as good as any to initiate the 'story' I want to tell you, but am certainly 'uncertain' as to how to proceed." By calling attention to the fictional status of the narrator, to his name *as sign*, Melville simultaneously reiterates and breaks down the distinction between the privileged author and the first-person narrator he "creates" to tell his story. He thus "announces" his intention to demystify the mystique of authorship—to call into question the shaping (or structuring) role of the transcendent author as self-present "subject" of the *logos*. In identifying with the narrator who, in discarding his patronym, has opened naming to question, Melville as author, unlike James's and Lubbock's "showman," also puts himself into the arena of historicity—and freeplay. The story he will tell by way of his fictional voice, "Ishmael," will begin "in the midst," not from the end—"beyond the reach of [free]play"—despite its reliance on recall.

To put this narrative consequence of the solicitation of naming in the posthumanist terms enabled by Kierkegaard's critique of Hegelian Recollection (Er-innerung), Ishmael's story will be (re)told, not from the end (in both senses of the word), from a certain outside perspective—"a center elsewhere" that enables a remembering that, in its future-anterior logical economy, is, in fact, a forgetting. It will be told, rather, from the *inside* (*interesse*), from the decentered horizontal perspective of engaged, explorative, and uncertain being-in-the-world: as an act of Repetition:

Repeating is handing down explicitly—that is to say, going back into the possibilities of the Dasein that has-been-there. The authentic repetition of a possibility of existence that has been . . . is grounded existentially in anticipatory resoluteness; for it is in resoluteness that one first chooses the choice which makes one free for the struggle of loyally following in the footsteps of that which can be repeated. But when one has, by repetition, handed down to oneself a possibility that has been, the Dasein that has-been-there is not disclosed in order to be actualized over again. The repeating of that which is possible does not bring again [*Wieder-bringen*] something that is 'past', nor does it bind the 'Present' back to that which has already been 'outstripped'. Arising, as it does, from a resolute projection of oneself, repetition does not let itself be persuaded of something by what is 'past', just in order that this, as something which was formerly actual, may recur. Rather, the repetition makes a *reciprocative rejoinder* [*erwidert*] to the possibility of that existence which has-been-there. But when such a rejoinder [*Erwiderung*] is made to this possibility in a resolution, it is made *in a moment of vision; and as such* it is at the same time a *disavowal* [*Widerruf*] of that which in the "today", is working itself out as the 'past'. Repetition does not abandon itself to that which is past, nor does it aim at progress. In the moment of vision authentic existence is indifferent to both these alternatives.[4]

In other words, Melville puts *Ishmael* as proper name, as identity, under erasure. The narrator, as the sequel more explicitly and audaciously reveals, becomes "Ishmael/Melville," which is to say, with Heidegger, an inquiring subject who is himself the object of inquiry, a "constitutor" who is himself the "constituted," as it were, the seer, who is himself the seen. Melville's purpose is not to establish an alternative privileged discourse, but to force an opening of the de-differentiating—imperial and finally enervating—closure of the traditional narrator and the metaphysical discourse that is its enabling origin. The exigencies of interpretation require reference to the narrator as "Ishmael," but, as Melville's first sentence insists, it is in this erased sense of the "proper self" that such reference has to be understood.[5]

"Call me Ishmael." Thus from the outset, this "simple sailor" (p. 5), this seaman (even on land he's "at sea"), puts into question the traditional relationship, Adamic in origin, appropriated anew by the American Puritans, between Naming and Identity. He is not going to allow his reader/ listener what he himself refuses: the habitual reliance on an absolute *arché* and *telos*, an authorial certainty and, through this, the viciously circular habit of suspending attention to the temporal process of the narrative in the name of a concealed, preordained and preconceived end. For, as seaman, he knows this kind of hovering above to be the care-less archival perspective of "landsmen" or "inlanders" (p. 4), who have conveniently forgotten or repressed the mysterious and dreadful sea, despite its awful magnetic attraction, its "loomings," in their obsessive imperial effort to colonize, measure, chart, and domesticate the American earth:[6] "Inlanders all, they come from lanes and alleys, streets and avenues—north, east, south, and west" (p. 4). On the simplest level, Ishmael will destroy this amnesiac archival perspective, transform by narrative violence the distanced recollective reader into an immediate listener or, in his own terms, the domestic and domesticating landsman into a "seaman." He will compel the landsman reader to recall, even against his inscribed logocentric will to forget, the suppressed relationship between the disturbing image of the sea and the "ungraspable phantom of life" (p. 14).

The "learned" or "competent" reader will know, of course, the story of Ishmael, son of Abraham and his wife Sarah's Egyptian slave, Hagar, in the Old Testament: "He will be a wild man, his hand will be against every man, and every man's hand against him; and he shall dwell in the presence of all his brethren."[7] But beyond the relationship between a seaman and an exile, there is little in this narrator's apparently sociable tone or what he says in these playful introductory remarks to suggest that he is referring to *this* particular Ishmael of the six very different Ishmaels in the Old Testament.[8] Nor, even if he is, is there anything in his text to imply that he, any more than Israel Potter, is aware of a deeper symbolic significance of his traditional Puritan name. Like the sea itself, it resonates as a vague intimation, a looming or, to appropriate Heidegger's existential analysis of Dasein's being-in-the-world, a "forestructure," whose "meaning" will only come near (not to presence), "loom larger," as it were, in and through repetition: the temporal process of his explorative narrative, after he has literally plunged into the hermeneutic circle—the destructive element— "primordially and wholly":

> What is decisive is not to get out of the circle but to come into it in the right way. This circle of understanding is not an orbit in which any random kind of knowledge may move; it is the expression of the existential *fore-structure* of Dasein itself. It is not to be reduced to the level of a vicious circle, or even of a circle which is merely tolerated. In the circle is hidden a positive possibility of the most primordial kind of knowing. To be sure, we genuinely take hold of this possibility only when, in our interpretation, we have understood that our first, last, and constant task is never to allow our fore-having, fore-sight, and fore-conception to be presented to us by fancies and popular conceptions, but rather to make the scientific theme secure by working out these fore-structures in terms of the things themselves.[9]

"Call me Ishmael." In the "beginning," the narrator, to appropriate T. S. Eliot's rhetoric in *Murder in the Cathedral*, "knows and does not know" who he "is" and what his experience on the *Pequod*, "some years ago—never mind how long precisely," (p. 3) was all about. In the "end," after his "repetition" or "retrieval" of—his existentially immersed and devious encounter with—the terrible events he and his shipmates on the *Pequod* had suffered (a death by drowning, a baptism, as it were), he will return to the beginning, to his name, and "know [it] for the first time." *But the truth he discovers will not be the Truth of the identical circle, the Truth as it has been understood in the ontotheological tradition up to Eliot* (or, at any rate, the exegetes of Eliot's poetry and drama).[10] It will not be the "still point," the final Truth of Presence, of Confirmation, of Identity, but the endless, always already unconcealing/concealing truth of *a-letheia*, of the broken circle, of absence, of difference or, to appropriate Derrida, of *différance*, in which the infinite deferral of presence makes time and its disseminations make a difference in the world. He and the American readers he has engaged in an agonistic dialogue will learn that being Ishmael is his—and "every(American)man's (and woman's)"—decentered and differential "calling."

To put the relationship between Ishmael's narrative and his identity in this equivocal way is, indeed, to displace the "center" of the novel from

Ahab to Ishmael. But it is not, therefore, to reinscribe and endorse the post-Matthiessen interpretation of *Moby-Dick*, which, as Donald Pease shows, represents Ishmael as the *principle* of individual freedom that finally triumphs over "Ahab's totalitarian will" in order to harness the narrative of *Moby-Dick* to the preconceived (teleological) American scenario of the Cold War, the interpretation epitomized by Walter Bezanson:

The story, this fiction, is not so much about Ahab or the White Whale as it is about Ishmael. . . . The point becomes clearer when one realizes that in *Moby-Dick*, there are two Ishmaels, not one. The first Ishmael is the *enfolding sensibility of the novel*, the hand that writes the tale, *the imagination* through which all matters of the book pass. He is the narrator. . . . The second Ishmael is not the narrator, *not the informing presence*, but the young man of whom, among others, narrator Ishmael tells us his story.[11]

On the contrary, to claim that Ishmael's narrative is a leap of a Dasein into the hermeneutic circle "primordially and wholly"—is itself, in other words, a de-structive process precipitated by the desire to understand the prior experience and "ending" in the disclosure, not of presence, but the absence of presence—is precisely to subvert an interpretation that reads Ishmael, the narrator, as the "enfolding sensibility of the novel," the "informing presence," who, like the masterful narrator of *The Divine Comedy* (clearly Bezanson's ultimate model), has already discovered the *meaning* of the "first," the "young" and immature, Ishmael's experience before the telling.

"Call me Ishmael." This first sentence is Melville's negative "annunciation." It introduces a twilight narrative, that, from the beginning exists not to confirm but to interrogate the privileged status of and thus disaffiliates its "author" from the structure of the novel he inherited as an American from the Puritan tradition (mediated, of course, by the American version of the Enlightenment). I mean the promise/fulfillment structure authorized by the specular/dynastic (recollective) memory of the ontotheological tradition, the memory, which, whatever its historically specific figuration, is understood as the agency that recuperates the dispersed Word (Idea) occasioned by the catastrophic "Fall" into time. By questioning the authority of authorship, Melville implies that the unerring linear logic—at least in intention—of a novel like Cooper's *The Deerslayer*, for example, or, in anticipation, of James's *The Ambassadors*, constitutes, in fact, a circular logic. It is a lying, speculative inversion of the errant dynamics of the temporal process of being-in-the-world that has its immediate source in American transcendentalism and its ultimate source in what I have called, after Kierkegaard's and Heidegger's critique of the "Hegelian system," the (amnesiac) recollective consciousness, the consciousness that re-collects, regularizes, and internalizes the "scatter," "the dispersions," the "accidents," of history or, rather, of historicity into a logically and emotionally totalized, ordered, redeemed and redeeming whole—in fact, into a circle moving around an unmoving center.[12] With this ironic invitation to the reader, in other words, Melville "announces" a narrative the ultimate purpose of which will be to de-stroy the kind of novel that, in beginning from the end, willfully and systematically spreads out and levels the termless and radically differential minute particulars of American existence into a palpable aesthetic object or, more specifically, into a figured carpet, which can, without risk, be apprehended with voyeuristic pleasure and/or comprehended and utilized for sociopolitical purposes from an "objective" panoptic distance.

Like Pierre Glendinning, Melville "had conned his novel-lessons; had read more novels than most persons of his years; but their false, inverted attempts at systematizing eternally unsystemizable elements; their audacious, intermeddling [read: arrogantly willful] impotency in trying to unravel and spread out and classify, the more than thin gossamer threads which make up the complex web of life; these things over [him] had no power now" (*Pierre*, p. 141). Unlike Pierre, however, who is brought to an artistic impasse by his discovery of the absent center, the Melville of *Moby-Dick*, as I will argue, finds this nothing to be liberating.

To put it positively, Melville's first sentence "announces" a "narrative" that, in Kierkegaard's and Heidegger's sense of the word, will, in fact, enact a "repetition" (*Wiederholung*). It will not constitute a "recollecting backwards" grounded in the regulative measure of one *logos* or another, but a "recollecting forwards" "grounded" in the absence of presence or, better, in the differential temporal measure of its occasion. If in the traditional novel Form (Identity) is ontologically prior to—is the condition for the possibility of—temporality, in *Moby-Dick*, as the resonant first sentence suggests, temporality (difference) will be ontologically prior to Form, words to the Word. Responding to precisely this inversion of traditional narrative priorities (which post-revivalist critics like Bezanson largely disregarded), R. P. Blackmur, we recall, accuses the Melville of *Moby-Dick* (and *Pierre*) of carelessness in his craft, of indifference to technique, and thus of failing to achieve that aesthetic distance which alone allows for "control . . . perhaps the highest form of apprehension." In the midst, in other words, Melville inevitably failed to arrive at that "understanding without immersion," which "distinguishes the great novelist from the journeyman."[13] Finally, Blackmur criticizes Melville for carelessly abandoning the "dramatic form" he initially chose, the form he announces in making Ishmael his narrator—and thus of having to resort to the "putative statement" of allegory in articulating the tragedy of Ahab:

> For example, in *Moby-Dick*, after setting up a single consciousness to get inside of, he shifted from that consciousness at will without sense of inconsistency, and therefore, which is the important thing, without making any effort to warrant the shifts and make them credible. . . . Melville was right, granting the theme of *Moby-Dick*, in choosing Ishmael the novice, to represent a story in which he had only a presumed and minor but omnipresent part. . . . The mere interposition of a participating consciousness between story [which is to say, "author"] and its readers, once it has been made logical by tying the consciousness to the story, is a prime device of composition: it limits, compacts, and therefore controls what can be told and how. The only error Melville made is that he failed to distinguish between what Ishmael saw and what the author saw on his own account.[14]

The "reading" of *Moby-Dick* that follows will suggest, on the contrary, that Melville was acutely conscious of his "craft" and that his collapsing of the distinction between "Ishmael" and "Melville" or, better, that his rendering the distinction a fluid one, was no accident of inattentiveness, but a deliberate destruction of precisely the form that "limits, compacts, and therefore controls what can be told and how." I am going to suggest, in short, that Melville's "careless" "method" is a *care*-ful, however (or, rather, because) uncertain, "strategy." It is precisely intended to make a novel that will not proceed according to the calculative and regularizing measure of an author who, out of reach of the freeplay of finitude, coerces the "middle"—the "incidental" (like "accident" and "case," also from *cadere*, to fall)—into the disciplinary space between Beginning and End, but according to the improvisational measure of its finite and decentered occasion. "To write poetry," Heidegger remarks in a passage about Hölderlin's poetic measure, but which could equally apply to the measure of Melville's *Moby-Dick*, is measure-taking, understood in the strict sense of the word by which man first receives the measure for the breadth of his being. Man exists as a mortal. He is called mortal because he can die. To be able to die means: to be capable of death as death. Only man dies—and indeed continually, so long as he stays on this earth, so long as he dwells. His dwelling, however, rests in the poetic. Hölderlin sees the nature of the "poetic" as the taking of the measure by which the measure-taking of human being is accomplished.

A strange measure for ordinary and in particular also for all merely scientific ideas, certainly not a palpable stick or rod [note the identification of calculation and doing violence] but in truth simpler to handle than they, provided our hands do not abruptly grasp but are guided by gestures befitting the measure here to be taken. This is done by a taking which at no time clutches at the standard but rather takes it in a concentrated perception, a gathering taking-in, that remains a listening.

But why should this measure, which is so strange to us men of today, be addressed to man and imparted by the measure-taking of poetry? Because only this measure gauges the very nature of man. For man dwells by spanning the "on the earth" and "beneath the sky." This "on" and "beneath" belong together. Their interplay is the span that man traverses at every moment insofar as he *is* an earthly being.[15]

Melville's rule was indeed vagary, as Blackmur observes, and his comportment in the face of his occasional materials, accordingly, one of immersion. Understood in its demystified sense, however, "immersion" means that Melville's vision was not panoptic, but horizonal.[16] Ishmael/Melville's narrative, in other words, will be "grounded" in the absence of presence, of a proper author, and thus will discover its own measureless measure on its *immersed* and errant way. Again, the passage on narration from *Pierre* comes to mind and bears repetition: "While the countless tribes of common novels laboriously spin vails of mystery, only to complacently clear them up at last . . . yet the profounder emanations of the human mind, intended to illustrate all that can be humanly known of human life; these never unravel their own intricacies, and have no proper endings; but in imperfect, unanticipated, and disappointing sequels (as mutilated stumps), hurry to abrupt intermergings with the eternal tides of time and fate" (p. 141).

In thus discovering this "errant" measure, Melville anticipates the Ezra Pound of *The Cantos*:

Periplum
not as land looks on a map
but as seabord by men sailing[17]

But Melville also, and more to the point of the "projective" American tradition Pound is "founding," anticipates the Charles Olson of *The Maximus Poems*, who, on the "basis" of "the old measure of care" pits the "local" against the will of his American contemporaries (specifically Vincent Ferrini) to universalize:

I'll put care where you are, on those streets I know as well as (or better:
I have the advantage
I was a letter carrier, read postcards, lamped checks, talked at the back doors

I'll meet you anywhere you say (the beer's best—the pipes are kept cleaner—
at the Anchor Inn (as the old captain called his bar,

with an old name.
You know it (at the head of the Atlantic Supply wharf, "Piney's wharf,"
it got called, from Ben's magazine fame, Collier's and all those

. . . . .

You see I can't get away from the old measure of care: how your magazine don't
     raise me,
not even Hugh Hill, whose triangles
are so nicely made but the course he's running
doesn't strike me as good enough
to come home a winner (as the Bluenose so often did
after the Columbia was lost
                         (did you know, by the way,
that it was off Sable
that she did go down?
that a trawler, a few years back,
caught her nose,
and she came up long enough,
before the beam broke,
for the letters to be read, gold
on black? COLUMBIA[18]

Confronted by the ineffable and increasingly disruptive force of being, Melville's other Ishmael, Pierre, renounces the innocently conventional poetry of that "sweet legendary time" (p. 283) prior to his fall into (American) experience and decides to write a novel as a way of facing its "nameless horror and terror" (p. 308). But, unlike Ishmael, Pierre betrays his profound insight into the decentered and endless duplicity of being by attempting to seize its ambiguities in a "comprehensive compacted work" (p. 283). More specifically, Pierre would reduce them to a binary opposition against the received view of things: Earth/Heaven; Man/God; Evil/Good, and so forth. His fiercely idealistic purpose as a Hegelian or Emersonian "Apostle" is to write a relentlessly inclusive and conclusive metaphysical book from the perspective of an omniscient eye (I), in which all experience, earthly and supernatural, is integrated and incorporated into a cosmic epiphany. It will be a "Titanic book," in which Man, like the Titan Enceladus, challenges the paternal authority of the established gods and the interpretation of being—the Book—that belief in the gods authorizes. Pierre intends his work to be an absolute inversion of the Christian (Puritan) myth of God as Origin, an Antibook or Antiscripture. But for that very reason, it will be, like the substitution of the *anthropologos* for the *theologos* in the ontotheological tradition, ultimately the same: teleological and, finally, narcissistic or, what is the same thing, monomaniacally anthropomorphic. About Pierre's Byronic or, rather, Quixotic "comprehensive" project to spatialize and name (and domesticate), the uncanny sublime, Melville says ironically—and in a metaphorics that, as in *Moby-Dick*, equates whiteness with a dread that has no thing as its object:

[A]s to the resolute traveler in Switzerland, the Alps do never in one wide and comprehensive sweep, instantaneously reveal their full awfulness of amplitude— their overawing extent of peak crowded on peak, and spur sloping on spur, and chain jammed behind chain, and all their wonderful battalionings of might; so hath heaven wisely ordained, that on first entering into the Switzerland of the soul, man shall not at once perceive its tremendous immensity; lest illy prepared for such an encounter, his spirit should sink and perish in the lowermost snows. Only by judicious degrees, appointed of God, does man come at last to gain his Mont Blanc and take an overtopping view of these Alps; and even then, the tithe is not shown; and far over the invisible Atlantic, the Rocky Mountains and the Andes are yet unbeheld. Appalling is the soul of man![19]

Ishmael, on the other hand, is uncertain about the kind of novel he will write, but, as I have suggested in my effort to think his first sentence, he is clear about one thing: it will be neither "well-made" (like those Melville criticizes in the passage quoted above) nor "Titanic," however much the content will dwell on Titanism. For, unlike the grave, inverted idealist, Pierre, who is sure of (even if, finally and necessarily, he is incapable of fulfilling) his authorial goal, Ishmael is not. All Ishmael knows at the beginning, as his tentative, loquacious, sometimes bantering, and erratic style itself suggests, is that gravity, in the pursuit of its period (whether in the name of the Titans' or Olympians', the Devil's or God's, Word—the Word of a transcendental presence that the postmodern novelist, Thomas Pynchon, will call "They"), inhibits the freeplay of mind: "I am quick to perceive a horror and could still be social with it—would they ["grave Fathers"] let me—since it is but well to be on friendly terms with all the inmates of this place one lodges in" (p. 161). Because of this, it also precludes the possibility of exploring and dis-covering.

In this respect, not incidentally, Ishmael recalls Tristram Shandy, who, in defense of the "digressive" or, rather, "transgressive" play of his eccentric narrative style—a style that, as I have suggested, could be called after Mikhail Bakhtin, carnivalesque—insistently mocks and subverts the relentlessly imperial circular linearity of the philosophy of the Enlightenment (not least John Locke's) and the authorial gravity it authorized:

> I need not tell your worships, that this [devaluation of wit by "your graver gentry"] was done with so much cunning and artifice,—that the great *Locke*, who was seldom outwitted by false sounds,—was nevertheless bubbled here. The cry, it seems, was so deep and solemn a one, and what with the help of great wigs, grave faces, and other implements of deceit, was rendered so general a one against the *poor wits* in this matter, that the philosopher himself was deceived by it,—it was his glory to free the world from the lumber of a thousand vulgar errors,—but this was not of the number. . . .
>
> This has been made the *Magna Charta* of stupidity ever since,—but your reverences plainly see, it has been obtained in such a manner, that the title to it is not worth a groat,—which by the by is one of the many and vile impositions which gravity and grave folks have to answer for hereafter.
>
> As for great wigs, upon which I may be thought to have spoken my mind too freely,—I beg leave to qualify whatever has been unguardedly said to their disparage or prejudice. . . . That I have no abhorrence whatever, nor do I detest and abjure either great wigs or long beards . . . peace be with them!— . . . mark only,— I write not for them.[20]

As I will show more fully, he also anticipates the Nietzsche who, as genealogist, according to Michel Foucault, subverts—"unrealizes"—the monumental history of the "graybeard" custodians of modern culture by parody, by "pushing their masquerades"—the constructions of their reverential comparative logic—to their grotesquely contradictory limits.[21] Ishmael's distrust of gravity (high seriousness) or, conversely, his irreverent levity, is not a casual impropriety; it is, rather, a deliberate means of preserving the freeplay of his mind against the imperial imperatives of logocentric structure. In the "projective" language of one of his most articulate postmodern American "heirs," his discourse will be a "forwarding," in which "one perception . . . [will] immediately and directly lead to a further perception."[22]

Where Pierre is a centered metaphysician, taking "himself, as subject, to be the standard for all beings,"[23] and his art a visionary instrument for tracking down the elusive and inscrutable One—the "talismanic secret"—Ishmael is a destructive phenomenologist.[24] He is attuned, in his interested uncertainty and need, to the occasional measure of being—the centerless cadence that takes the measure of man as self-identical subject (specifically, the self-reliant Emersonian Man). And his art is an "errant" art of *aletheia*, an opening or troping: a turning to and fro, an always already disclosing, which *at the same time* is an always already concealing. "Errancy," Heidegger writes in a way that provides a remarkable gloss on Ishmael's comportment toward being,

is the *essential* counter-essence to the primordial essence of truth. Errancy opens itself up as the open region for every opposite to essential truth. Errancy is the open site for and ground of *error*. Error is not just an isolated mistake but rather the realm (the domain) of the history of those entanglements in which all kinds of erring get interwoven.

In conformity with its openness and its relatedness to beings as a whole, every mode of comportment has its mode of erring. Error extends from the most ordinary wasting of time, making a mistake, and miscalculating, to going astray and venturing too far in one's essential attitudes and decisions. *However, what is ordinarily and even according to the teachings of philosophy recognized as error, incorrectness of judgments and falsity of knowledge, is only one mode of erring and, moreover, the most superficial one.* The errancy in which any given segment of historical humanity must proceed for its course to be errant is essentially connected with the openness of Dasein. By leading him astray, errancy dominates man through and through. But, as leading astray, errancy at the same time contributes to a possibility that man is capable of drawing up from his ek-sistence—the possibility that, by experiencing errancy itself and by not mistaking the mystery of Dasein, he *not* let himself be led astray.

Because man's in-sistent ek-sistence [his being simultaneously inside and outside, ontic and ontological] proceeds in errancy, and because errancy as leading astray always oppresses in some manner or other and is formidable on the basis of this oppression of the mystery, specifically as something forgotten, in the ek-sistence of his Dasein man is *especially* subjected to the rule of the mystery and the oppression of errancy. He is in the *needful condition of being constrained* by the one and the other. The full essence of truth, including its most proper non-essence, keeps Dasein in need by this perpetual turning to and fro. Dasein is a turning into need. From man's Dasein and from it alone arises the disclosure of necessity and, as a result, the possibility of being transposed into whatever is inevitable.[25]

Errancy, lest Heidegger's analysis be mistaken for error as such—the degraded *but correctable* binary opposite of truth as *adaequatio intellectus et rei*—is the condition for the possibility of necessity and not the other way around: errancy, in short, precludes closure. To put it positively, errancy "keeps Dasein in need by the perpetual turning to and fro." Necessity, "whatever is inevitable," is always a forestructure that the need of in-sistent ek-sistent Dasein will always de-stroy. As "the essential counter-essence of the primordial essence of truth" (*aletheia*), to put it otherwise, errancy is not a hierarchically subordinated opposite of truth subject to policing. It *belongs with* truth in strife, is a relationship always already characterized by what Heidegger, translating Heraclitus's *polemos*, calls *Auseinandersetzung*: the "questioning contending" in thinking, the agonic "rift" in art, that forestalls arrival and the indifferent peace of metaphysics, that, to put it positively, precipitates presen*cing (An-wesen)*: "What the Greeks meant by beauty was restraint. The gathering of the supreme antagonism is *polemos*, struggle . . . in the sense of setting apart [*Auseinandersetzung*]. For us moderns, on the contrary, the beautiful is what reposes and relaxes; it is intended for enjoyment and art is a matter of pastry cooks."[26]

ISHMAEL'S READING OF FATHER MAPPLE'S READING OF THE JONAH TEXT

The fact, therefore, that in the first chapter, Ishmael says he feels like a character in a dramatic fiction whose actions are predetermined from above by the policing fates does not constitute a contradiction of the preceding representation of Ishmael's (non)self:

But wherefore it was that after having repeatedly smelt the sea as a merchant sailor, I should now take it into my head to go on a whaling voyage; this the invisible police officer of the Fates, who has the constant surveillance of me, and secretly dogs me, and influences me in some unaccountable way—he can better answer than anyone else. And, doubtless, my going on this whaling voyage, formed part of the grand programme of Providence that was drawn up a long time ago. (P. 7)

Announcing itself at the beginning of Ishmael's narrative, this resonant metaphorics of fate and prophecy has misled many critics, both Old and New Americanists alike, into seeing the digressive and sprawling narrative in terms of a prophecy/fulfillment structure: as the necessary but redemptive tragic drama of Captain Ahab (the revival critics) or as the inevitable triumph of the self-reliant individual over Ahab's totalitarianism (the Cold War critics) or, as in the case of one highly regarded New Americanist, as the inexorable victimization of Ahab by the imperial author.[27] Despite the aporetic evidences of Melville's text—not least, as I will show, Ishmael's enabling "reading" of Father Mapple's sermon—virtually all commentators on Melville's elusive novel, like those artists or natural scientists who would capture "the living contours" of "the great leviathan" in paint or words (p. 264), have been tempted by the annunciatory aura of the beginning into assuming that the mysterious universe his narrator inhabits could reveal its integral wholeness by reading its differential but finally related shadowy signatures and thus into recklessly pursuing the original secret cause informing the organic form of the novel. But all these initial allusions to "those stage managers, the Fates" (p. 7) and the "grand programme of Providence" are, in fact, more ambiguous than they at first seem. If they are in part gestures of Ishmael's sense of cosmic entrapment, they are also, however tentatively, the sociable but no less destructive, subversion by mockery of the inscribed expectations of a nineteenth-century American readership still dominated by the teleological narrative form that had its origins in the Calvinist providential view of history: by, that is, its archival assumption that, to appropriate Sartre's genealogy of the modern novel, recounted beginnings are "annunciations" that "promise" an epiphanic end in the fullness of time. I mean the end-oriented narrative imposed by the Puritan exegetes on the biblical texts that enabled the discourse of the American Jeremiad—and the perpetual renewal of the imperial American errand in the wilderness. If Ishmael's playfully ironic tone does not suggest this alienation of the sedimented eschatological metaphorics—and the literature of promise and fulfillment—the conclusion of the chapter should:

Chief among these motives was the overwhelming idea of the great whale himself. Such a portentous and mysterious monster roused all my curiosity. Then the wild and distant seas where he rolled his island bulk; the undeliverable, nameless perils of the whale; these, with all the attending marvels of a thousand Patagonian sights and sounds, helped to sway me to my wish. With other men, perhaps, such things would not have been inducements; but for me, I am tormented with an everlasting itch for things remote. I love to sail forbidden seas, and land on barbarous coasts. Not ignoring what is good, I am quick to perceive a horror, and could still be social with it—would they let me—since it is best to be on friendly terms with all the inmates of the place one lodges in. (P. 7)

Here, Ishmael puts the policing Fates under erasure. Their commonplace meaning becomes duplicitous, not something outside, but that vague and disturbing attraction to the sea, its denizens, *terrae incognitae*: the homeland as not-at-home. And simultaneously the drama becomes antidrama and the "annunciations," "loomings." In thus undermining the sedimented meaning of the Fates, Ishmael/Melville suggests that it was not Being, an outside presence, that compelled him to go on a whaling voyage, but the always already prephenomenological understanding of the being—the differential and differentiating temporality—of being, the "average and vague understanding" that, according to Heidegger, Dasein opens up by existential immersion (or, as Melville prefers, "diving")[28] in the destructive element, the temporal circle without center. The Fates, that is, are not *symbols* (in the Coleridgean/Modernist sense)—the precipitate of an organic and continuous nature, but an inscribed forestructure that necessarily guides inquiry, but which leaping into the circle primordially and wholly always already destructures.

The next chapter of *Moby-Dick*, which is significantly entitled "The Carpet Bag," underscores this by suggesting that Ishmael is "leaving behind" the mental baggage of grounded landsmen. What he says here, immediately after invoking the eschatological metaphorics, is not what we would expect from one representing his experience in the light of the necessity of the providential design. His narrative does not proceed recollectively, by calculatively selecting and highlighting those *apparently* casual or superfluous objects or events that foreshadow and justify ("announce") the culminating event, their inclusive order and inexorably necessary ("promised") end, as, say, Fielding does Sophia Western's muff in *Tom Jones* (and Blackmur would wish).[29] We are given, rather, a devious narrative of Ishmael's more or less random passage through the streets of New Bedford in search of cheap lodgings (interspersed by inconclusive reflections on signs prompted by his insatiable interestedness) that "leads" him *accidentally* past several inns he might have stayed in had he the money, into and out of a black revival meeting, to the Spouter Inn, where, it just happens, Queequeg is staying. The errant movement of this chapter, in fact, epitomizes the movement of the entire narrative, from Ishmael's chance meeting with Queequeg, through his chance appointment as Captain Ahab's bowsman on the last day of the chase, to his chance expulsion from the rocking boat that is battling the white whale (p. 573), and his chance survival when the *Rachel* picks him up after the *Pequod* goes down.

It is true, of course, that Ishmael, like one of many of his postmodern American allotropes, Oedipa Maas, in Thomas Pynchon's *Crying of Lot 49*, betrays the characteristics of a "sensitive" in his penchant to "project a world," to read disparate places, objects, and events as "constellations."[30] And it is these characteristics that have teased critics, in spite of the aporetic resistance of the text, into assuming that the universe he inhabits could reveal an integrated wholeness through its apparently differential but finally related shadowy signatures and thus into recklessly pursuing the original secret cause informing the organic form of the novel. But Ishmael, however tempted early on by the impulse to symbolize the things themselves, finally and insistently resists the temptation to mystify them, to transform the minute particulars—the incidentals—of his occasion into a self-contained, total, and identical *mythos*. Thus, for example, after leaving the *Pequod*, where they have "signed" on with Captains Peleg and Bildad, Ishmael and Queequeg are accosted by a ragged stranger whose veiled reference to Captain Ahab's lost leg insinuates that their signing on is for them the ominous beginning of a voyage doomed from the start, "all fixed and arranged a'ready" (p. 93). Ishmael is made uneasy by these laconic "annunciations," especially when he learns at the end of the encounter that the stranger's name is Elijah, whose namesake, he knows from his Puritan heritage, is the Old Testament prophet who denounced King Ahab and prophesied his doom.[31] And thus "sensitized," he begins to infer connections in his mind between these otherwise incommensurable signs and what now seem to be earlier portents:

Elijah! thought I, and we walked away, both commenting, after each other's fashion, upon this ragged old sailor; and agreed that he was nothing but a humbug, trying to be a bugbear. But we had not gone perhaps above a hundred yards, when chancing to turn a corner, and looking back as I did so, who should be seen but Elijah following us, though at a distance. . . . This circumstance, couple with his ambiguous, half-hinting, half-revealing, shrouded sort of talk, now begat in me all kinds of vague wonderments and half-apprehensions, and all connected with the Pequod; and Captain Ahab; and the leg he had lost; and the Cape Horn fit; and the silver calabash; and what Captain Peleg had said of him, when I left the ship the day previous; and the prediction of the squaw Tistig; and the voyage we had bound ourselves to sail; and a hundred other shadowy things. (P. 93)

But Ishmael's counterimpulse to this retrospective penchant for reading phenomena as clues to a hidden and larger prefigurative design is to return "to the things themselves": "I was resolved to satisfy myself whether this ragged Elijah was really dogging us or not, and with that intent crossed the way with Queequeg, and on the other side of it retraced our steps. But Elijah passed on, without seeming to notice us. This relieved me; and once more, and finally as it now seemed to me, I pronounced him in my heart, a humbug" (p. 94). Clearly, Ishmael's anxiety about the stranger's portentous words is not diminished by this corporeal evidence. He is too definitive in pronouncing the "prophet" a humbug. Rather, he simply refuses to give the sign as "presentiment" a decisive symbolic status. The policing fates that "secretly dog" Ishmael and the "prophecy" of Elijah that Ishmael invokes are not finally intended by Melville as symbols (in the Coleridgean or Emersonian sense of the word): as "signs" that, read properly, will culminate in the revelation of a continuous and inclusive (prefigurative) historical design or, to put it alternatively, as annunciations of a promise that will be fulfilled and revealed in the fullness of time. They are, rather, as Ishmael's counterimpulse "to return to the things themselves"[32] suggests, simply "presentiments." They are the ambiguous and untrustworthy, however tempting, signifiers of a metanarrative which has its origins in the Calvinist providential view of history: the narrative of prefiguration imposed by the Puritan exegetes on the biblical texts, the narrative that enabled the cultural discourse of the American Jeremiad and the perpetual imperial American "errand in the wilderness."

Ishmael's predilection for symbolic reading, in other words, is not the symptom of a monistic hermeneutic quest for a Transcendental Signified—the "Talismanic Secret"—behind the pervasive duplicitous signs he encounters on the way. On the contrary, his invocation of the signs of fate implies, despite their necessity as point of departure, an essential distrust of the Symbolizing Imagination (insofar as it attempts to re-present and contain the un-imagable or in-effable). Conversely, it implies a willingness to let the dreadful ambiguities—the alterities—of being be. Seeming, like errancy, is not a degraded (and simply instrumental and disposable) copy of Being: "mere appearance" as, according to Heidegger, it came to be in the ontotheological tradition.[33] Seeming is always *seeming* or, rather, always already *belongs with* being. Ishmael comports himself in the face of the "presentiments" precipitated by the encounter with Elijah not as prefigurations as such, but, in the contestatory terms of Heidegger's Heraclitean *Auseinandersetzung* or, what is the same thing, of his version of the hermeneutic circle: as a risked "forestructure" that will guide his inquiry but that his immersion "wholly and primordially" in the temporal process will disclose as just that. It is not Fate—a (contradictorily) inside outside Presence—that compels Ishmael's quest for the meaning of his experience on board the *Pequod* (and of his narrative). It is, rather, the always pre-phenomenological understanding of being: its differential and differentiating temporality that the culturally dominant re-presentational discourse he has inherited from his ancestors has covered up and forgotten. It is the "average and vague understanding" of the being of being that, according to Heidegger, is opened up (disclosed) by existential immersion in the destructive element, the temporal circle without center.

At this initial stage of his erratic narrative, Ishmael's counterimpulse to risk, which is to say, to call into question, his (and his readers') archivally inscribed will to "detect" the secret cause behind seeming (appearance), to symbolize and regulate being in all its manifestations, is clearly symptomatic and provisional. It is in Ishmael's account of his digression into the Whaleman's Chapel before boarding the schooner that will take him and Queequeg to Nantucket and the "ill-fated" *Pequod*—a "digression"— which, as such, has been systematically overlooked by virtually all totalizing interpretations of *Moby-Dick*—that this counterimpulse will begin to be thought. It is, in other words, when this occasion of Melville's novel is retrieved from the benign oblivion to which the problematics of both Old and New Americanists have relegated it that Ishmael's symptomatic distrust of the traditional understanding of the sign as *figura* or symbol will be seen as an awakening recognition that it is an arbitrary construct and that its function is to reduce the ontological difference (the absent *real*, as it were) to "practically assailable" Thing (*Summum Ens*). It is, to put this disclosure alternatively, when the intertextual relation between Ishmael's "story" and Father Mapple's narrative sermon on Jonah and the Whale is thought, that Ishmael's provisional insight will take on the character of an ontic-ontological understanding of the sign, not as a signature of the truth of being, but as a forestructure to be interrogated by the things themselves. Indeed, Ishmael's emergent ontic-ontological understanding of the sign as forestructure and the absent real as the ontological difference—we can now call it a de-structive understanding—will gradually become explicit in the repetition of his interested encounter with the monomania of Captain Ahab.

Ishmael, as I have provisionally suggested, recounts his experience to the reader, somewhat like the Ancient Mariner in Coleridge's poem, from an interested perspective—horizonally and dialogically, as it were. The grave Father Mapple, on the other hand, tells his from the isolated vantage point of a symbolic pulpit above the congregation, after he has deliberately dragged up the "[rope] ladder step by step, till the whole was deposited within, leaving him impregnable in his little Quebec" (p. 39), and "ordered the scattered people to condense" (p. 41). It does not escape Ishmael that his elevated and distanced physical/spiritual perspective is embodied in a siege metaphor: "Can it be, then, that by that act of physical isolation he signifies his spiritual withdrawal for the time, from all outward worldly ties and connexions? Yes, for replenished with the meat and wine of the word, to the faithful man of God, this pulpit, I see, is a self-containing strong-hold—a lofty Ehrenbreitstein, with a perennial well of water within the walls" (p. 39).[34] From this elevated and self-contained vantage point, Father Mapple can panoramically survey and speak the Word to his congregation of seamen, or errant sinners, with immunity. (As Melville was quite aware, the laborers in the merchant marine and whaling industry constituted an outcast—because godless and socially undisciplined and volatile—subculture.)

Outside or above time and immured from its differential uncertainties, Father Mapple accordingly rehearses a far different kind of story from the one Ishmael attempts to tell. Whereas Ishmael narrates from inside and thus inevitably digresses in the explorative "to and fro" process, Father

Mapple, as "a pilot of the living God" (p. 42)—as the still center of a turning world—is unerring in his pursuit of his exegetical/didactic end. Inexorably determined by the prophecy/fulfillment structure of Puritan biblical exegesis, the story about Jonah and the Whale that he recounts thus begins from the allegorical end: "Beloved shipmates, clinch the last verse of the first chapter of Jonah—'And God had prepared a great fish to swallow up Jonah'" (p. 42). Following this annunciation, the temporal process, like that of the novels Melville contemptuously dismisses in *Pierre* for their "false inverted attempts at systematizing eternally unsystemizable elements," goes on in reverse. From this inverted temporal perspective nothing, not even the smallest detail in the narrative of Jonah, is allowed to escape into superfluity. Everything that *Father* Mapple relates points inexorably to the epiphanic and all-encompassing conclusion and to the integral place of "this smallest [of] strands in the mighty cable of the Scriptures" (p. 42).

The structure of this retrospective narrative is, in fact, an enactment of its (Calvinist) theo-logical content. Jonah, Father Mapple says to his contemporary audience of errant sinners, is chosen by the inscrutable God of the Old Testament to fulfill a command—"never mind now what that command was, or how conveyed" (p. 42). But finally it is "a hard command" (p. 42), so Jonah disobeys God and attempts to flee from Him. He boards a ship at Joppa bound for Tarshish, which Father Mapple interprets as the modern Jaffa and Cadiz to make it clear that this "God-fugitive" (p. 46) will go to the ends of the earth to escape the voice of His calling:

And where is Cadiz, shipmates? Cadiz is in Spain; as far by water, from Joppa, as Jonah could possibly have sailed in those ancient days, when the Atlantic was an almost unknown sea. Because Joppa, the modern Jaffa, shipmates, is on the most easterly coast of the Mediterranean, the Syrian; and Tarshish or Cadiz more than two thousand miles to the westward from that, just outside the Straits of Gibraltar. See ye then, shipmates, that Jonah sought to flee worldwide from God? Miserable man! Oh! most contemptible and worthy of all scorn . . . (P. 43)

But God, like the invisible police officer of the Fates, who "has the constant surveillance of me, and secretly dogs me," in Ishmael's story, is everywhere: no thing, no person, can escape his relentless and omnipresent gaze. Wherever this errant son of God goes to hide, His hovering and all-encompassing eye tracks him down. Even in the small cabin of the ship bound for Tarshish—"that contracted hole, sunk, too, beneath the ship's water-line"—Jonah feels "the heralding presentiment of that stifling hour when the whale shall hold him in the smallest of his bowel's wards" (p. 44). Geographical detail, captain, crew, ship, the lamp in Jonah's cabin, the sea, the very bones on the sea's floor, the whale: *all* are portentous signs that remind Jonah of the invisible presence of his pursuer, for he is being supervised by the *all*-seeing yet inscrutable (Puritan) God above. And *all* play their predestined role in the allegorized history that will reach its climax when, after his repentance "in the fish's belly" (p. 46), the whale "prepared" by God will come "breaching up towards the warm and pleasant sun, and all the delights of air and earth; and ['vomit'] out Jonah upon the dry land" to fulfill the hard command he had refused in the beginning: to become "an anointed pilot-prophet," another Jeremiah, "to speak hard things" and "to sound those unwelcome truths in the ears of a wicked Ninevah" (p. 47–48). Everything, as the very unerring momentum of Father Mapple's jeremiadic rhetoric suggests, conspires, in other words, to temporally enact and confirm the recuperative and disciplinary circular geometry that the center promises/demands from the annunciated beginning: "the sin, hard-heartedness, suddenly awakened fears, the swift punishments, repentance, prayers, and finally the deliverance and joy of Jonah" (p. 42).

Analogously, Father Mapple super-vises the materials of his text from the always-present end. Like the inscrutable God in his story of Jonah, he, too, as "anointed pilot-prophet," hovers high above the recalcitrantly obscure particulars of his biblical text, shaping them in the luminous light of the foreseen conclusion. His narrative thus never deviates from what it promises. No word in his contemporary seaman's plain style, no matter how apparently trivial or incidental in a different context, escapes his steady and steadying hermeneutic eye. Joppa, Tarshish, customs papers, passport, passage money, cargo, notice of a reward for the apprehension of a parricide, locked cabin, lamp: *all* are denied differential possibilities to become corresponding signatures of a totalized and unified metaphor and symbolic order: *all* are bent by his commanding gaze to form and bring to fulfillment—and light—the comprehensive circle of his single-minded and unerring purpose: "To preach the Truth in the face of Falsehood!" So, for example:

Thus far the busy Captain had not looked up to Jonah, though the man now stands before him; but no sooner does he hear the hollow voice, than he darts a scrutinizing glance. 'We sail with the next coming tide,' at last he slowly answered, still intently eyeing him. 'No sooner, sir?'—'Soon enough for any honest man that goes a passenger.' Ha! Jonah, that's another stab. But he swiftly calls away the Captain from the scent. 'I'll sail with ye,'—he says,—'the passage money, how much is that?—I'll pay you now.' For it is particularly written, shipmates, as if it were a thing not to be overlooked in this history, 'that he paid the fare thereof' ere the craft did sail. And taken with the context, this is full of meaning. (P. 44)

The ingeniously sustained figurative movement of this "well-wrought" narrative, in which the relentless metaphorics of the gaze renders cause and effect utterly tautological, makes it clear that Father Mapple's exegesis of the biblical Jonah text has its general archival origin—and here we recall Melville's parody in *The Confidence-Man* of the "learned doctors" who exclude the "whole Book of Sirach" from *the* Book as apocryphal—in the typological or figural method of the Patristic exegetical tradition: the hermeneutics of Paul, Justin Martyr, Iraneaus, Clement of Alexandria, Origen, Jerome, Theodore of Mopsuestea, Augustine, Tertullian, Vincent, Andrew of St. Victor, St. Thomas Aquinas, and so forth. I am referring, of course, to the pro*vid*ential Christian exegetical tradition whose purpose was to justify the permanent historical authority of the contemporary Church by reconciling—de-differentiating—the recalcitrantly past historical events represented in the Old Testament with the privileged Event (or Incarnate Word) represented in the New, by interpreting the former as prefigurations in temporal history of the latter. (It is, not incidentally, this prefigurative exegetical tradition that was eventually invoked to legitimize the idea of the Holy Roman Empire.) As Erich Auerbach puts this visually oriented hermeneutic method (in contrast to the allegorical, over which it triumphed):

Figural interpretation establishes a connection between two events or persons, the first of which signifies not only itself but also the second, while the second encompasses or fulfills the first. The two poles of the figure are separated in time, but both, being real events or figures, are within time, within the stream of historical life. Only the understanding of the two persons or events is a spiritual act, but this spiritual act deals with concrete events whether past, present, or future, and not with concepts or abstractions [as in the allegorical mode of the Philonian tradition]; these are quite secondary, since promise and fulfillment are real historical events, which have either happened in the incarnation of the Word, or will happen in the second coming. Of course purely spiritual elements enter in to the conceptions of ultimate fulfillment, since "my kingdom is not of this world";

yet it will be a real kingdom, not an immaterial abstraction; only the *figura*, not the *natura* of this world will pass away . . . and the flesh will rise again. Since in figural interpretation, one thing stands for another, since one thing represents and signifies the other, figural interpretation is "allegorical" in the widest sense. But it differs from most of the allegorical forms known to us by the historicity both of the sign and what it signifies.[35]

In his exegesis of the biblical Jonah story, Father Mapple, too, grounds his hermeneutics—and, not incidentally, his "low," that is, contemporary, style (*sermo humilis*)—on the Incarnation—the Word of God made flesh— and the providential history it legitimized and elaborated: the hierarchical system of spatial and temporal correspondences that, however "poetic," reduces all differential things in space and events in time to a *"lex naturae"*— a "world picture," as it were—under the inscriptive eye of the Creator/ Author/Exegete.

But the origins of Father Mapple's figural hermeneutics and the providential design it implies is, of course, far more historically specific than this. (I am invoking this fundamental continuity between the medieval and Puritan exegetical traditions to counter the exceptionalist thesis concerning the origins of American cultural identity.) It lies, as Melville is quite aware, in the American Puritans' revision of the Patristic exegetical tradition to accommodate its rejection of the decadent Old World order and its (imperial) errand in the wilderness of the "New World." As Sacvan Bercovitch puts it (curiously without reference either to the medieval Patristic Fathers or to Erich Auerbach—is it because he is reluctant to contaminate his "Americanist" discourse with continental theory?)[36] in his brilliant reading of Samuel Danforth's *Brief Recognition of New England's Errand into the Wilderness* (May 1670):

The parallels that Danforth urges upon his listeners, between John the Baptist and Danforth the preacher, between the Arabian and the New England desert, develop into a sweeping prophetic comparison—of the errand then, at the birth of Christianity, with the errand now, to bring history itself to an end. In this sense, *errand* means *progress*. It denotes the church's gradual conquest of Satan's wilderness world for Christ. Significantly, Danforth's exegesis devolves neither on "errand" nor on "wilderness," but as it were beyond these on the relative merit of John the Baptist. The question "What went ye out for to see?" [Matthew 11:7–9] is "determined and concluded," Danforth points out, when Christ describes John as "A prophet . . . and more than a prophet." The Baptist, that is, resembles *and supersedes* his predecessors ["Abraham, . . . or David . . . or Solomon"]; his role as exemplum is at once recapitulative and projective. . . .

All the prophets saw Christ. Who could excel Abraham or Moses?—this is history seen in the eye of eternity. All the faithful, Danforth is saying, are one in Christ; the errand here in New England is that of any other saint, or group of saints; the American wilderness no different essentially from that of Moses or John the Baptist. And yet the passage makes the difference abundantly clear. Sacred history unfolds in a series of stages or *dispensations,* each with it own (increasingly *greater*) *degree of revelation.* Hence the insistent temporality of the rhetoric: *prepare, foretold, herald, harbinger, forerunner,* and summarily, *types:* Finally, Danforth insists, there are crucial discriminations to be made. All of the Old Testament is an errand to the New; and all of history after the Incarnation, an errand to Christ's Second Coming. It leads from promise to fulfillment: from Moses to John the Baptist to Samuel Danforth; from the Old World to the New; from Israel to Canaan to New Israel in America; from Adam to Christ to the Second Adam of the Apocalypse. The wilderness that Danforth invokes is "typical" of New England's situation above all in that it reveals the dual nature of the errand as prophecy. In fulfilling the type, New England becomes itself a harbinger of things to come. . . .

For Danforth, in short, *errand* has the ambiguity of the *figura.* It unites allegory and chronicle in the framework of the work of redemption.[37]

Under the unerring gaze of the Puritan exegetical eye, according to Bercovitch, the "newness of New England becomes both literal and eschatological, and (in what was surely the most far-reaching of these rhetorical effects) [in its determination of future American discourse and practice *vis à vis* the frontier] the American *wilderness* takes on the double significance of secular and sacred place" (p. 15). As such, the Puritan prefigurative method of biblical exegesis established a metanarrative that became the foundation for the cultural discourse of the collective American self. I am, of course, referring to what Bercovitch has called the "American Jeremiad": the always available recuperative rhetorical practice inaugurated by the Puritans "to direct an imperial people of God towards the fulfillment of their destiny, to guide them individually towards salvation, and collectively towards the American city of God." This is the rhetorical practice that, in its secularized and hegemonic form, became the fundamental cultural means of recuperating a national consensus in the face of recurrent historical crises that threatened to disintegrate the national purpose: the American imperial mission.

To be more precise, then, Father Mapple's sermon in the Whaleman's Chapel in mid-nineteenth-century New Bedford has its origins in the Puritan Jeremiad. However restricted and overdetermined its locus, it constitutes a discourse of persuasion intended not simply to symbolically recuperate the Puritan Word and its hegemonic Symbolic Order, but, in so doing, the American national consensus that his motley congregation of errant seamen synecdochically represents. But, to anticipate, it is necessary to introduce a significant qualification of Bercovitch's otherwise valuable contribution to American studies in general and (implicitly, since he doesn't apply his analysis to it) to the reading of Father Mapple's sermon in particular. It is a qualification that renders historically specific what in Bercovitch's discourse is always and disablingly generalized: in the case of Melville's text, the sociopolitical consensus that Father Mapple's jeremiad is intended to achieve.

Father Mapple's jeremiad is not addressed to a general public that is falling away from the high national purposes commanded by the Word. It is addressed, rather, as I have suggested, to a mid-century congregation of errant American seamen, whom Melville in novels such as *Redburn* understands as an underclass of "offscourings" that the merchant marine, the American navy, the whaling industry—and the American government—exploits and alienates:

There are classes of men in the world, who bear the same relation to society at large, that the wheels do to a coach: and are just as indispensable. But however easy and delectable the springs upon which the insiders pleasantly vibrate; however sumptuous the hammer-cloth, and glossy the door-panels; yet, for all this, the wheels must still revolve in dusty, or muddy revolutions. No contrivance, no sagacity can lift *them* out of the mire; for upon something the coach must be bottomed; on something the insiders must roll.

Now, sailors form one of these wheels: they go and come round the globe; they are the true importers, and exporters of spices and silks; of fruits and wines and marbles; they carry missionaries, ambassadors, opera-singers, armies, merchants, tourists, scholars to their destination: they are a bridge of boats across the Atlantic; they are the *primum mobile* of all commerce; and, in short, were they to emigrate in a body to man the navies of the moon, almost every thing would stop here on earth except its revolution on its axis, and the orators in the American Congress.

And yet, what are sailors? What in your heart do you think of that fellow staggering along the dock? Do you not give him a wide berth, shun him, and account him but little above the brutes that perish. Will you throw open your parlors to him; invite him to dinner? or give him a season ticket to your pew in church?—No. You will do no such thing. . . . It is useless to gainsay it; they are deemed almost the refuse and offscourings of the earth; and the romantic view of them is principally had through romances.[38]

Father Mapple's jeremiad, in other words, is intended to recuperate the Puritan/capitalist sociopolitical order, the order, as C. L. R. James observed long ago in his unconscionably neglected book on *Moby-Dick*, that this subclass of "mariners, renegades, and outcasts" threatened. The purpose informing Father Mapple's American jeremiad, I am suggesting, is not the *conversion* of sinners as such. And if it is, as Bercovitch might say, to recuperate a national consensus, then this consensus, this specific context— not least the spatial economy that is indissolubly related to his discursive economy—compels us to understand the consensus in its historically specific form as well: as, in the terms of Michel Foucault's genealogy, the disciplinary normalization of an emergent, particular constituency of social "deviants": the multiracial and ethnic American working class.

This appropriation of a discourse that has its origins and its locus in Europe, specifically France, in behalf of a reading of a supremely "American" text will, I am sure, strike Americanists as an arbitrary and unwarranted imposition. To justify what some will surely call, after Edward Said, an example of "travelling theory,"[39] and to elaborate the above suggestion will require a repetition of the preceding matter.

Unlike Ishmael's narrative, which resonates with a distrust of the impulse to symbolize—his "hermeneutics of suspicion"—Father Mapple's Puritan exegetics is logocentric and teleological with a vengeance. He, too, it is suggested, has erred from the Way and has undergone some kind of immersion in the destructive element. But like the figure of Jonah, the wayward protagonist of his prefigurative narrative, of which he is a type, Father Mapple has emerged "converted" (turned toward the right Way) by and to the Word and is thus absolutely certain of its past, present, and future—that is, eternal—authority. From this exalted center—this metaphysical perspective, which is simultaneously within and above or beyond or after the differential realm of temporality—he is, as his privileged locus in the elevated pulpit suggests, out of reach of the freeplay of criticism. Thus in the name of the Calvinist God, for Whom he is an earthly pilot of errant seamen, he can or, rather, *must* interpret the words of his Old Testament text as a symbolic (Christian) Book, a Book—we might say, with an eye to its attribution by Wai-chee Dimock to Melville's novel—an "imperial Folio"—which, in the name of one original promise of the New Testament, comprehends and levels history—the text of the world—and makes *all* times one time, *all* things that time disseminates, one thing.

"But God is everywhere" (*Moby-Dick*, p. 50): In the Renaissance (Protestant) emblem books, one of the most commonplace figures depicts a naked man cowering futilely behind a fig tree from the all-seeing eye of God (at the upper left), which, inscribed by the word "UBI," gazes glaringly down on him from the distant heavens. The accompanying moral verse interpreting this allegorical emblem reads:

Behind a fig tree great, him selfe did ADAM hide:
And thought from God hee there might lurke, & should not be espied.
Oh foole, no corner seek, thoughe thou a sinner bee;
For none but God can thee forgive, who all thy ways doth see.[40]

Both in the content and form of his narrative about Jonah and the whale (its Puritan theology and the literary structure it authorizes) Father Mapple's text enacts in an appropriately contemporary local language addressed to his assumed audience of deviants the perennial emblem (spatial figuration) of the American Protestant tradition. It is not, I think, a fanciful imposition on his text and context to invoke the emergent mid-nineteenth-century—Protestant/capitalist—allotrope of this emblem. I am not simply referring to Max Weber's well-known metaphorical figuration of the "capitalist spirit" as "iron cage": that comprehensive image of the regime of discipline whose genealogy Weber persuasively traces back through the utilitarian sociopolitical discourses of American politicians such as Benjamin Franklin, to the ascetic theological discourses of everyday life of English and American Puritans such as Richard Baxter (*Saints' Everlasting Rest* and *Christian Directory*).[41] This is the image, more specifically, that has its origins in the Puritan work ethic—the obsessive "calling" to rationalize the American earth—determined by the transcendental, inscrutable, and circumscribing eye of the Calvinist God, whose gaze, which Weber describes as "beyond the reach of human understanding" (p. 103), accounts for and makes accountable everything and every event, however minute and apparently accidental, in the world and in history:

The Puritan wanted to work in a calling; we are forced to do so. For when asceticism was carried out of monastic cells into everyday life, and began to dominate worldly morality, it did its part in building the tremendous cosmos of the modern economic order. This order is now bound to the technical and economic conditions of machine production which today determine the lives of all the individuals who are born into this mechanism, not only those directly concerned with economic acquisition, with irresistible force. Perhaps it will so determine them until the last ton of fossilized coal is burnt. In Baxter's view the care for external goods should only lie on the shoulders of the "saint like a light cloak, which can be thrown aside at any moment." But fate decreed that the cloak should become an iron cage. (*Protestant Ethic*, p. 181)

I am also, and especially, referring to Jeremy Bentham's Panopticon, the very real "cruel, ingenious cage" of the post-Enlightenment, which Michel Foucault brilliantly analyzes in *Discipline and Punish* (*Surveiller et punir*), his genealogy of the modern disciplinary institutions—the prison, the hospital, the school, and the factory—of modern society.[42] It is no accident that this circular architectural model of surveillance, discipline, and normalization (for, that is, the re-formation of deviants from the bourgeois/capitalist order), according to Foucault's genealogy, had one of its most important enabling ontological origins in the obsession with detail:

There is a whole history to be written about such 'stone-cutting'—a history of the utilitarian rationalization of detail in moral accountability and political control. The classical age did not initiate it; rather it accelerated it, changed its scale, gave it precise instruments, and perhaps found some echoes for it in the calculation of the infinitely small or in the description of the most detailed characteristics of natural beings. In any case, 'detail' had long been a category of theology and asceticism: every detail is important since, in the sight of God, no immensity is greater than a detail, nor anything so small that it was not willed by one of his individual wishes. In this great tradition of the eminence of detail, all the minutiae of Christian education, of scholastic or military pedagogy, all forms of 'training' found their place easily enough. For the disciplined man, as for the true believer, no detail is unimportant but not so much for the meaning that it conceals within it as for the hold it provides for the power that wishes to seize it. (P. 139–40)

Nor is it an accident that Bentham's Panopticon had its most important practical precursor in the "Walnut Street Prison [in Philadelphia], opened in 1790, under the direct influence of the Quakers." This was the penal structure, according to Foucault, which more than any earlier models had historical significance because "it was associated in people's minds with the political innovations of the American system" and "was continuously re-examined and transformed right up to the great debates of the 1830s on penitentiary reforms" (p. 123), that is, more or less contemporary with Melville's *Moby-Dick*.[43]

I will elaborate this provisional suggestion of the complicity of Father Mapple's panoptic, Calvinist exegetical strategy with the emergent American capitalist sociopolitical order later in this chapter. It will suffice here for the purpose of distinguishing between Ishmael's and Father Mapple's discourses simply to point to the common *metaphysical* (and "architectural") ground (and the will to power over temporality and the differences it disseminates) that the latter shares with the discourse and practice of Bentham's Enlightenment panopticism. However more complex and indirect its panoptic functioning and disciplinary consequences, Bentham's anthropocentric Panopticon, as Foucault suggests, if only in passing, is historically continuous with and serves a remarkably similar purpose concerning power to that of Father Mapple's theocentric Puritan hermeneutics and the perennial emblem that figures its regulative economy of detail. Clearly the Panopticon's central tower, like Mapple's elevated and accessless pulpit and the transcendental eye of the emblem, affords a metaphysical/panoptic vantage point from which peripheral errancy (or what is always the same thing in this schema, detail) can be super-vised and contained with immunity.

But what *is* of crucial importance for my purposes at this conjuncture is not so much the historical specificity of the Panopticon (i.e., its representation by Bentham as a particular institution) as it is the *ontology* and its *figurative articulation*. For it is these, according to Foucault, that explain the "imaginary intensity that it has possessed for almost two hundred years." The Panopticon and its regulative economy "must be understood as a *generalizable model* of functioning," a "*diagram*" of a mechanism of power reduced to its *ideal* form," "a *pure* architectural and *optical system*," a "*figure* of political technology that may and must be detached from any specific use." And it is precisely this discursive imaginary that gives the guardians of the "sane and just society" a powerful, efficient, and invisible disciplinary instrument for converting and reforming all manner of deviants (those entities, as the Latin stem suggests, that err from the right [unerring] way):

It is polyvalent in its applications; it serves to reform prisoners, but also to treat patients, to instruct schoolchildren, to confine the insane, to supervise workers, to put beggars and idlers to work. It is a type of location of bodies in space, of distribution of individuals in relation to one another, of hierarchical organization, of disposition of centres and channels of power, of definition of the instruments and modes of intervention of power, which can be implemented in hospitals, workshops, schools, prisons. Whenever one is dealing with a multiplicity of individuals on whom a task or particular form of behaviour must be imposed, the panoptic schema may be used. (*Discipline and Punish*, p. 205)

To underscore the complicity I am suggesting between Father Mapple's sermon and the sociopolitical practices enabled by this polyvalent "diagram of a mechanism of power reduced to its ideal form"—and to suggest why discriminating between Ishmael's and Father Mapple's narratives is crucial in the contemporary struggle over Melville's text—one need only add the category of language to the relay of deviant constituencies that the polyvalent, panoptic Word is capable of turning around, that is, recentering, caging, and normalizing. I am referring to what in Foucault's genealogy (as well as Derrida's grammatology) is a fundamental and enabling disclosure: the troping—the errancy—of words.

Curiously, Ishmael does not comment directly on the hermeneutic strategy of Father Mapple's finished narrative. There is nothing explicit in his text to indicate that he has included this intertext at this conjuncture in order to mark an ideological distinction between his and the latter's discourses. Nevertheless, his introduction of Mapple's exegesis of the biblical Jonah text more or less immediately following his account of the encounter with Elijah is intended to distinguish between the coercive teleological panoptic mode of perception (and the spatializing/symbolic narrative it authorizes) and the differential ideological resonance of his own unmethodical mode of narration. This is clearly, however indirectly, suggested by the context of particulars in which Ishmael situates this intertext. I am referring, above all, to the symbolic painting that constitutes the visual backdrop for Father Mapple's sermon. Clearly reminiscent of the Hudson River School of landscape painting, specifically of Thomas Cole, whose pietistic version of the American sublime contributed to national self-exaltation,[44] this painting, so different in its privileging of light over darkness (and the pyramidal structure) from the obscurely amorphous and ambiguous one that profoundly engages, puzzles, and confounds him in the Spouter-Inn (p. 20), represents "a gallant ship beating against a terrible storm off a lee coast of black rocks and snowy beakers. But high above the flying scud and dark-rolling clouds, there floated a little isle of sunlight, from which beamed forth an angel's face; and this bright face shed a distinct spot of radiance upon the ship's tossed deck" (pp. 39–40). And if the optimistic sentimentalism of this painting, in which the agents are figured in a way precisely analogous to the hierarchical structure of the scene of Father Mapple's sermon (as well as the God/Adam emblem), does not cast an ironic shadow on the luminous authority of the exegesis that follows, surely Ishmael's parodic exegetical gloss on the angelic eye that sheds its radiant providential light in the midst of the tumultuous dark below does: "'Ah, noble ship,' the angel seemed to say, 'beat on, beat on, thou noble ship, and bear a hardy helm; for lo! the sun is breaking through; the clouds are rolling off—serenest azure is at hand'" (p. 40).

But it is Ishmael's abrupt transition from the sermon to his ecumenical participation in the religious rites of Queequeg in the next chapter that most tellingly suggests his uneasiness about, if not outright mockery of, the theology and formal economy of the sermon he has just heard. (Nor should we overlook Ishmael's apparently casual remark that the heathen, Queequeg, did not stay with the rest of the congregation to the end of Father Mapple's sermon.)[45]

Following his exegesis of the Jonah text, Father Mapple had concluded his sermon with the practical contemporary imperatives of the prefigurative history informing his reading of the Jonah text: the obligatory *applicatio* and *exhortatio* prescribed by the discursive rules of the Protestant hermeneutic tradition:

"This, shipmates, this ["to preach the Truth to the face of Falsehood"] is that other lesson; and woe to that pilot of the living God who slights it. Woe to him who seeks to pour oil upon the waters when God has brewed them into a gale! Woe to him who seeks to please rather then to appal! . . . Yea, woe to him who, as the great Pilot Paul has it, while preaching to others is himself a castaway!"

He drooped and fell away from himself for a moment; then lifting his face to them again, showed a deep joy in his eyes, as he cried out with heavenly enthusiasm,—"But oh! shipmates! on the starboard hand of every woe, there is a sure delight; and higher the top of that delight, than the bottom of the woe is deep. . . . Delight is to him—a far, far upward, and inward delight—who against the proud gods and commodores of this earth, ever stands forth his own inexorable self. Delight is to him whose strong arms yet support him, when the ship of this base treacherous world has gone down beneath him. Delight is to him, who gives no quarter in the truth, and kills, burns, and destroys all sin though he pluck it out from under the robes of Senators and Judges. Delight,—top-gallant delight is to him, who acknowledges no law or lord, but the Lord his God, and is only a patriot to heaven. Delight is to him, whom all the waves of the billows of the seas of the boisterous mob can never shake from this sure Keel of the Ages." (P. 48)

Disregarding the specifics of the narrative context surrounding its utterance in favor of the reference to "proud gods and commodores of this earth," founders of American studies such as Henry Nash Smith represented the joyous moral ferocity of this practical imperative of the providential Word as an indirect expression of the justified delight that Melville takes in scourging the "wicked Nineveh" that is American society: "Ishmael's admiration for 'deep, earnest thinking' and for the independence of the soul requires us to see a close parallel between him and the Jonah who was divinely appointed to a 'pilot prophet,' or 'speaker of true things.' And Melville evidently agrees with the *stirring exhortation* of Father Mapple."[46] Read in the context I have retrieved, however, a radically antithetical possibility asserts itself. And this is accentuated by what immediately follows the sermon. Far from indicating sympathy for Father Mapple's "stirring exhortation," Ishmael, having informed the reader of his return to Spouter-Inn, tells of his unfilial refusal to judge the "wild," idolatrous Queequeg from the point of view of the "infallible Presbyterian Church" in which he was "born and bred"—indeed, tells of his decision to participate in the cannibal's idolatry. Nor is it irrelevant that he does so in the carnivalesque terms that turn the inexorable, unerring logic of the Protestant *Logos* on its head:

I was a good Christian; born and bred in the bosom of the infallible Presbyterian Church. How then could I unite with this wild idolator in worshipping his piece of wood? But what is worship? thought I. Do you suppose now, Ishmael, that the magnanimous God of heaven and earth—pagans and all included—can possibly be jealous of an insignificant bit of black wood? Impossible! But what is worship?—to do the will of God—*that* is worship. And what is the will of God?—to do to my fellow man what I would have my fellow man to do to me—*that* is the will of God. Now, Queequeg is my fellow man. And what do I wish that this Queequeg would do to me? Why, unite with me in my particular Presbyterian form of worship. Consequently, I must then unite with him in his; ergo, I must turn idolator. So I kindled the shavings. (P. 52)

Surely Ishmael/Melville's thematization of the practical imperatives of Father Mapple's figural, exegetical practice is intended to recall the unrelenting, violent practices of the early American Puritans, which were justified by their providentially ordained "errand in the wilderness," specifically, of course, their genocidal disposition toward the native Americans—those diabolical "bloody Salvages," as Cotton Mather calls them in his epic Virgilian history of Christ's great works in America[47]—not to mention the theological or sociopolitical deviants they demonized and burned at the stake as witches. Is it, therefore, illegitimate to suggest as well that the *applicatio* and *exhortatio* that bring Father Mapple's exegesis of the biblical text to its blood-curdling climax is intended to establish the context for reading Captain Ahab's "fatal" monomania—his violent metaphysical reduction of the differential dynamics of being ("all that most maddens and torments; . . . the sum of all the general rage and hate felt by his whole race from Adam down" [p. 184]) to a named and "practically assailable" one (p. 184)—as the astonishing contradictory consequence, not of authorial imposition, but of the fulfillment of the unerring, divinely ordained logic of the Adamic American discourse?

This juxtaposition of Father Mapple's application and exhortation and Ishmael's ecumenical participation in pagan idolatrous rites, in other words, suggests that Ishmael/Melville is acutely aware of the materiality of discourse: that not only Father Mapple's utterly directed (economical) sermon, but his own errant (wasteful) narrative is, as Foucault would say, a *praxis*.[48]

Indeed, what is at this point implicit in the intertextual context I am focusing on surfaces much later in Ishmael's narrative, after the voyage has gotten well under way and the practical effects of Captain Ahab's monomania have become manifest. For here, in the chapter entitled "Jonah Historically Regarded," Ishmael returns to the Jonah text to mock the panoptic perspective of the "learned exegetes" and "revered clergy" (p. 365). "Arguing" against "one old Sage Harbor whaleman," who doubts the historicity of the biblical story on the grounds of "but little learning except what he had picked up from the sun and sea" (p. 365), he offers a defense of their prefigurative hermeneutics so obviously caricatured that it cannot be taken as other than a parody of their distanced—archival—

procedures and conclusions, a parody, not incidentally, analogous to Melville's travesty of the English natural scientists (quoted from *The Confidence-Man* in the previous chapter), who are compelled by the rigorous and austere logical economy of their system of classification to conclude that the offending bill of the Australian "duck-billed beaver" was "artificially stuck on." This "defense" reaches its parodic climax in an inevitable allusion to Father Mapple's exegesis of the geographics of the Jonah text. Against Sag-harbor's objection that the whale could not possibly have accomplished his divinely ordained mission to "vomit up" Jonah "somewhere within three day's journey of Nineveh, a city on the Tigris, very much more than three days' journey across from the nearest point of the Mediterranean coast" (p. 307), Ishmael, in the spirit of the interpretive logic of the "learned exegetes," proffers an alternative route that, by absurdly increasing rather than diminishing the hermeneutic difficulty, destroys his "argument":

> But was there no other way for the whale to land the prophet within that short distance to Nineveh? Yes. He might have carried him round by way of the Cape of Good Hope. But not to speak of the passage through the whole length of the Mediterranean, and another passage up the Persian Gulf and Red Sea, such a supposition would involve the complete circumnavigation of all Africa in three days, not to speak of the Tigris waters, near the site of Nineveh, being too shallow for any whale to swim in. (P. 365)

Finally, like Don Quixote, Ishmael is "driven" by the resistance of the things themselves to what, in the previous chapter I called the panoptic principle of last resort: the "enchanter."[49] Unable to accommodate this recalcitrant difference within his figural hermeneutics, he falls back, that is, on the "argument" of a Portuguese Catholic priest, who concludes that "this very idea of Jonah's going to Nineveh via the Cape of Good Hope" was "a signal magnification of the general miracle" (p. 366).

In thus pressing the logical economy of figural exegesis to its absurdly contradictory conclusion, Melville's parody—like Cervantes's, with which it has as significant, if unnoticed, affinities as with the American "tall tale"—reveals a remarkably resonant kinship with Nietzsche's genealogical criticism of the monumental historian's history. I mean, specifically, that modality of its uses that, according to Michel Foucault, adopted a decentered form of parody directed against the "reality" constituted by the totalizing metaphysical imaginary:

The new historian, the genealogist, will know what to make of this masquerade [which is assumed to be real]. He will not be too serious to enjoy it; on the contrary, he will push the masquerade to its limit and prepare the great carnival of time where masks are constantly reappearing. No longer the identification of our faint individuality with the solid identities of the past, but our "unrealization" through the excessive choice of identities. . . . Taking up these masks, revitalizing the buffoonery of history, we adopt an identity whose unreality surpasses that of God who started the charade. In this, we recognize the parodic double of what the second of the *Untimely Meditations* called "monumental history": a history given to reestablishing the high points of historical development and their maintenance in a perpetual presence, given to the recovery of works, actions, and creations through the monogram of their personal essence. But in 1874, Nietzsche accused this history, one totally devoted to veneration, of barring access to the actual intensities and creations of life. The parody of his last texts serves to emphasize that "monumental history" is itself a parody. Genealogy is history in the form of a concerted carnival.[50]

Like Foucault's Nietzsche, Melville not only parodically focalizes the mystified, de-differentiating, spatial perspective of the biblical exegetes—demonstrates its historical truth to be a masquerade—by pursuing the (supra)historical logic of figural interpretation to its limits. He also discloses the contradictory differentials—"the actual intensities and creations of life"—that their resentful imperial imaginary would, but finally cannot, colonize and thus vindicates the old seaman's—and Ishmael's—decentered/occasional measure. This genealogical movement of de-centering/dis-closure, to which virtually all Melville criticism has been blind, will, to put it provisionally, be repeated in Ishmael/Melville's representation of Captain Ahab's "fiery quest," this time, however, on a different but utterly related genealogical register: that which, according to Foucault, understands history as "sacrificial, directed against truth, and oppose[d to] knowledge": that which, in interrogating these last, discovers their origin in "instinct, passion, the inquisitor's devotion, cruel subtlety, and malice."[51]

Because, as I have suggested, most commentators, traditional and recent, have read the prodigally erratic movement of *Moby-Dick* with the filial "landsman's" panoptic and leveling, exegetical eye—have come to Melville's text encumbered by archival baggage, as it were—they have overlooked the crucial difference between Father Mapple's and Ishmael's narrative methods. Read temporally or horizontally, however—as Melville's mockery of "the false inverted attempts at systematizing eternally unsystemizable elements" of his contemporaries demands (not to say poststructuralist theory—whether that of Heidegger, Derrida, or Foucault) the intertextual sermon serves to thematize the deliberate carefulness of Ishmael's digressive "technique": its transgressive or destructive function. Ishmael's narrative comes to be understood as a "carpetbagging." Just as he goes to sea as a "simple sailor," unencumbered by the at-homing baggage of landsmen, so this American prodigal comes to his narrative without the constraining weight of the literary/hermeneutic tradition he inherits from his yea-saying American Fathers—and institutionalized by his yea-saying contemporaries, above all, Emerson and Thoreau. Or, rather, since he is indeed well read in the American tradition—its exhausted patriarchal signs—so, unlike his filial contemporaries, he will make unfilial light of its discursive and practical imperatives. Melville's critical genealogy, in other words, is intended to disclose that the patriarchal American Archive is inscribed by the commitment to a "secret cause" and thus justifies an indissoluble relay of imperial projects: not simply an ontological "center elsewhere" that legitimizes the colonization of the difference that temporality disseminates, but a sociopolitical "Capital" (metropolis) elsewhere that legitimizes the colonization of the different ("provincial" or "barbarous") worlds of historical others. To put it positively, it is intended to retrieve the centerless and inconclusive "actual intensities of life" to which the coercive, patriarchal American Archive has barred access.

This project of decolonization, I suggest, is the point Melville is struggling to articulate in his "well-known" "No! in thunder" letter to Hawthorne (written about the time *Moby-Dick* was published). This letter, which thinks the de-structive implications of Melville's own unfilial, irreverent, and unencumbered authorial stance in the face of being, though it is ostensibly referring to the author of *The House of the Seven Gables*, repeats the resonant carpetbag metaphor which opens *Moby-Dick*. In so doing, it invites us to understand "the last stages of metaphysics" that he refers to in terms of Heidegger's "end of philosophy." It invites us, in other words, to read the American cultural identity of the Jacksonian period (the imperialism, land speculation, Indian removal, and so forth) as the historical fulfillment *and* demise of the New Adamic tradition inaugurated by the prefigurative theology of Puritanism: as the (self)disclosure in these "last stages" of the absence of presence at the center of the American world picture, or, put positively, as the (self)disclosure of the ontological difference that its metaphysical problematic has always existed to de-differentiate and contain. Equally important, but more problematically, Melville's letter also solicits us, by way of its playful troping of "sovereign"/"power" (the Emersonian principle of self-reliance) to put the "Ego" he celebrates under erasure: to read this "self," not as the "imperial self" (as, say, Richard Chase or, for that matter, Wai-chee Dimock do, despite their differing evaluation of its moral and political implications), but as a social democratic "self" enabled by *negative capability*. I mean a free social self whose decenteredness distinguishes it from the unequal or "tributary" selves of both the hierarchical power structures of the Russian and British Empires *and* the reductive individualistic—disciplinary—self of American democracy. It warrants, that is, a reading that understands the "Ego" in terms neither of the sociopolitical passivity resulting from the dialectical internalization and resolution of the contradictions and conflicts of historicity, nor of the imperial practice of the sovereign subject, but, as the oxymoron itself suggests, of a negational praxis "grounded" in the non-self-identical self of finite (historical) human being ("we mortals"):

We think that into no recorded mind has the intense feeling of the visible truth ever entered more deeply than into this man's. *By visible truth, we mean the apprehension of the absolute condition of present things as they strike the eye of the man who fears them not*, though they do their worst to him,—the man who, like Russia or the British Empire, declares himself a sovereign nature (in himself) amid the powers of heaven, hell, and earth. He may perish; but so long as he exists he insists upon treating with all Powers upon an equal basis. If any of those Powers choose to withhold certain secrets, let them; that does not impair my sovereignty in myself; that does not make me tributary. And perhaps, after all, there is *no* secret. We incline to think that the Problem of the Universe is like the Freemason's mighty secret, *so terrible to all children*. It turns out, at last, to consist in a triangle, a mallet, and an apron,—nothing more! We incline to think that God cannot explain His own secrets, and that He would like a little information upon certain points Himself. We mortals astonish Him as much as He us. . . .

There is the grand truth about Nathaniel Hawthorne. He says NO! in thunder; but the devil himself cannot make him say *yes*. For all men who say *yes*, lie; and all men who say *no*,—why they are in the happy condition of judicious, unencumbered travellers in Europe; *they cross frontiers into Eternity with nothing but a carpet-bag,—that is to say, the Ego. Whereas those yes-gentry, they travel with heaps of baggage*, and, damn them! they will never get through the Custom House. What's the reason, Mr. Hawthorne, that in the *last stages* of metaphysics a fellow always fall to *swearing* so?[52]

"There are some enterprises," Ishmael/Melville says much later on (immediately before his return to the Jonah text), "in which a *careful disorderliness* is the true method" (p. 361; my emphasis). The great majority of Melville critics since the revival have overlooked or suppressed this resonant paradox in their panoptic effort to render *Moby-Dick* a monument of the American literary/cultural tradition or, more recently, to identify its monumentality with American cultural imperialism in general. This oversight and that which has relegated Father Mapple's sermon to critical oblivion are symptoms of the same spatializing problematic. They obscure their reciprocal relationship: that Father Mapple's narrative explains Ishmael's later affirmation of a "careful disorderliness" as "the true method," and vice versa. What the retrieval of Father Mapple's sermon suggests, in other words, is that Ishmael's narrative practice can be represented as neither the orderly and controlled process informed by the commanding gaze of the self-presence author (the representation of both those who have endowed *Moby-Dick* with canonical status and those who find its canonical status to be complicitous with imperialism), nor as the "immersion without understanding" that is the consequence of "the rule of vagary" (the representation of R. P. Blackmur and the New Critics). It is, rather, a deliberate nay-saying to the burdensome ontotheological tradition, not least, as Melville makes clear in *Pierre*, to that American version which was inaugurated by the Puritans' providential (New Adamic) theology and, for Melville, finds its naturalized "fulfillment" in the "delusory" metaphysics of "Yankee" transcendentalism and its "Greek and German Neoplatonical originals" and this metaphysics's repressive prophetic/dynastic structural imperative. And it is a nay-saying precisely because, as the letter to Hawthorne also makes clear, Melville understands this imposter tradition as coming to an exhausted end in disclosing its portentous self "at last," like the freemason's "mighty secret" (and power), to be a socially constituted mask: "a triangle, a mallet, and an apron—nothing more!"

In the rhetoric of this book, the retrieval of Father Mapple's sermon demonstrates that Ishmael/Melville's is a dis-affiliative enterprise and his "rule of vagary," a careful errancy—in Heidegger's sense of both words: an unmethodical method that simultaneously destroys the traditional narrative form (as structure) and the logocentric measure that authorizes it, and projects a "new" narrative "form" grounded in the ungrounded measure of its occasion and elaborated in the material language that its occasion demands. His purpose at this ontological site, again as his great refusal of the *logos* in the letter to Hawthorne suggests, is not like that of Father Mapple or the Muggletonian Scots and Yankees, whose "imposter philosophies"—their "masquerades"—secularized the prophetic economy of Mapple's Puritan providentialism by way of German idealism, to arrive at the "talismanic secret": the absolute—and imperial—Truth of *veritas*. It is, rather, like that of the postmodern American writers his fiction influenced, to disclose the always errant boundary-breaking truth of *a-letheia*.[53]

In his epilogue to *The American Jeremiad*, Sacvan Bercovitch concludes that Ishmael's narrative (*Moby-Dick*) is an American "anti-jeremiad" and, since "both the jeremiad and anti-jeremiad foreclosed alternatives,"[54] offer no way out of this cultural bind,

the novel offers no hope whatever. Melville's options, given his commitment to America, were either progress toward the millenium or regression toward doomsday. He simply could not envision a different set of ideals—an antinomian self-sufficiency, a non-American course of progress—beyond that which his culture imposed.[55]

This conclusion, I submit, is the inevitable consequence of an interpretive logic whose "vision" must render Father Mapple's sermon invisible. In retrieving the parodic function of Father Mapple's Jonah text—in revealing the repressive cultural and sociopolitical imperatives of the "benign" logic of his panoptic exegetical method, I have suggested (and will show more fully in what follows), on the contrary, that Melville's decentering of the imperial metaphysical ontology determining the discourse of the "American Renaissance" constitutes an overdetermined moment in an indissoluble, however unevenly developed, relay of decenterings that includes the scientific (the discursive practices of positivistic science parodied in the cetology chapters), the economic and the social sites (the *Pequod* as capitalist factory and *socius*), and the political site (the self-reliant subject whose fulfillment is Ahab's totalitarianism) of the antebellum American world picture.

If, further, Melville's parody of Father Mapple's prophetic mode of interpretation is understood as a critical genealogy of the indissoluble chain of values privileged by Jacksonian democracy, it will also be seen that his "errant" narrative, by contrast, constitutes an indissolubly multi-situated, negatively capable or de-structive project that *escapes*—indeed, exists to undermine—the totalizing, hegemonic American discourse. I mean, specifically, the discourse that operates within the comprehensive and abstracting parameters of a binary opposition between individual freedom and absolute freedom, American democracy and totalitarianism, liberty and empire: that is, within the closed (Thomas Pynchon would call it "paranoid") circle of the discourse of the American jeremiad—and anti-jeremiad. Such a recognition, in other words, will reveal that Melville's decentering of the American *logos* discloses the possibility of, if it does not fully develop, a counter*hegemonic* discourse and practice: precisely the alternative "set of ideals—an antinomian self-sufficiency, a non-American [American] course of progress"[56]—that Bercovitch's curiously "American-ist" scenario of the American jeremiad forecloses to *Moby-Dick* (and, in a different but equally disabling way, that Wai-chee Dimock's imperial and Donald Pease's Cold War scenarios foreclose to Ishmael).

THE CENTERED CIRCLE, THE IMPERIAL GAZE, AND ABASEMENT

If one understands Ishmael's comportment toward being as *interesse* (being-in-the-world) and his narrative as an interested and careful exploration of the ontological implications of his earlier experience on the *Pequod*, one would be naive to claim that his delayed introduction of Ahab to the narrative is simply an "artistic" preparation—a setting of the stage—for the unfolding of an American tragedy in the classical "Greek" or even Shakespearean manner. Nor would one be too quick to see Ishmael's role in the drama as that of a disengaged and peripheral choric observer of the tragic action or even, as Richard Sewall says, as a preliminary tactical convenience adopted by Melville to entice his "untragic American audience" into the tragic world of the novel:

And hence . . . the long preliminary phase of *Moby-Dick*, introducing Ishmael, the reassuring normal one who would go to sea now and again to drive off the spleen, or merely to satisfy "an everlasting itch for things remote", who would take "the universal thumps" with equanimity and cry three cheers for Nantucket—"and come a stove boat and stove body when they will, for stave my soul, Jove himself cannot. . . ." The rest of the story shows how shallow his optimism was, as Melville leads him (and the untragic American audience) by slow degrees, but remorselessly, towards tragic truth.[57]

Rather, this "long preliminary phase" of *Moby-Dick* dislocates the reader into perceiving Ishmael's *marginality* as "central" to the novel. He becomes a double participant (in the original events and in the narrative that interprets them), whose errant attempt to understand the catastrophe precipitated by Captain Ahab's "tremendous centralization" (p. 148) interrogates the tragic vision and the totalized symbolic *mythos* with which it invests the world. In other words, Ishmael puts at risk the autotelic tragic/mythic form—indeed, all teleological forms, including that linear, circular, anthropological one elaborated by the subject understood, as Bezanson and the Cold Warrior Americanists do understand it, as self-present and sovereign individual. And in the process of his submergence into the destructive element, or, in his own words, his "thought diving," Ishmael destroys it (and, as I will show, its cultural, social, and political allotropes). Ishmael's destructive narrative, his Repetition, that is, will retrieve the margin—and the marginalized—from the margin to which it has been relegated by the imperial center of teleological form.

It is true, of course, that Ishmael explicitly invokes the tragic vision precisely at the moment in his narrative ("Knights and Squires") when Ahab is about to make his appearance. But he does it against his uneasy intuition that there is something awry—not simply anachronistic—about its received form. It "is not the dignity of kings and robes, but that abounding dignity which has no robed investiture" (p. 174) that he will sing. Nor is it the tragic muse that he will apostrophize, but the "Spirit of Equality,"[58] which "hast spread one royal mantle of humanity over all my kind!" (p. 117). Since even the democratic impulse can, as we have seen all too frequently in the dismal history of modern American drama, be bent to the recuperative logocentric purposes of tragic form, Ishmael will exalt not so much Ahab, but the "meanest mariners, and renegades and castaways" (p. 117)—that demeaned, multicultural class of common seamen, as C. L. R. James has argued, which the emergent capitalist democracy of Melville's time impoverished and marginalized, rendered "*Isolatoes*," as the novel's next chapter puts it.

From the beginning of his mnemonic retrieval of Ahab's sudden appearance on the quarterdeck of the *Pequod*—an appearance that seemed to him then like the fulfillment of the ominous, inverted annunciation hinted at by "ragged Elijah's diabolical incoherences" (p. 122)—Ishmael recalls his profound and reverential awe before Ahab's silent, central, and commanding presence, not simply by the "nameless regal overbearing dignity of some mighty woe" that he read in the Cain-like mark on the captain's face, but also by "an infinity of firmest fortitude, a determinate unsurrenderable willfulness, in the fixed, and fearless, forward dedication of that glance" (p. 124). Even now—and despite his antisymbolic rhetoric, his invocation of the spirit of equality, his consciousness, like the Jonah of Father Mapple's sermon, of being *under* the gaze of a "master-eye" (p. 124), Ishmael is still haunted by Ahab's awesome, commanding image and his immediate impulse is to read symbolic significance into it, to envisage Ahab as the "regal" hero—the chosen, however base-born center—of a preordained tragic action.

Ishmael is aware of the possibility that Ahab's delayed entrance, his austere remoteness from the crew, and his exaction of absolute obedience, if not homage, from the men are more than simply the observances "of the paramount forms and usages of the sea" (p. 147). Based on a knowledge similar to that of the narrator of *White Jacket* that such established forms and usages bestow enormous power on the captains of literal and figurative ships, Ishmael realizes they may also reflect a calculative strategy for concealing and advancing "other and more private ends" (p. 142):

That certain sultanism of [Ahab's] brain, which had otherwise in a good degree remained unmanifested; through those forms that same sultanism became incarnate in an irresistible dictatorship. For be a man's intellectual superiority what it will, it can never assume the practical, available supremacy over other men, without the aid of some sort of external arts and entrenchments, always, in themselves, more or less paltry and base. (Pp. 148–49)

Despite Ishmael's characterization of Ahab's leadership in the rhetoric of hierarchical power, however, he is too magnetically drawn to the *image* of the captain's tragic presence to be quite able to perceive that this rhetoric contradicts his inscribed democratic and pluralistic leanings. However obsolescent, the monolithic metaphysical discourse of tragedy he has inherited from the tradition still effectively inhibits his ability to thematize the destructive import of his rhetoric. Instead, he tends to rationalize and accommodate its duplicities, to coerce the contradiction he now but half-perceives into a paradoxical justification of his continued attraction to Ahab's mystified grandeur. Indeed, Ishmael tends to read Ahab's strategy of concealment as the mark of his chosen, central, unmoving, and untouchable superiority over the circumscribing mass of "ordinary" men. Though he insists that it is not with "Emperors and Kings" but "with a poor old whale-hunter" he has to do, he nevertheless "invests"[59] Ahab with symbolic garb, the very "majestical trappings and housing" that, as he observes, his American subject matter denies him: "But Ahab, my Captain, still moves before me in all his Nantucket grimness and shagginess: and in this episode touching Emperors and Kings, I must not conceal that I have only to do with a poor old whale-hunter like him; and, therefore, all outward majestical trappings and housings are denied me. Oh, Ahab! what shall be grand in thee, it must needs be plucked at from the skies and dived for in the deep, and featured in the unbodied air!" (p. 148). But his intuition into the devastating power inhering in the (modern) representation of the classical tragic hero—one is tempted to call this intuition Nietzschean[60]—insistently deforms Ishmael's Apollonian rhetoric. And this distinction culminates in an ominously resonant trope suggesting, if it does not make explicit, that Ishmael has in some sense made the equation between the central "master-eye" of the tragic hero and its totalization and reduction of the Other it surveys to the dedifferentiated and docile Same:

Such large virtue lurks in these small things [the "forms and usages" sanctioned by a hierarchical social structure] when extreme political superstitions invest them, that in some royal instances even to idiot imbecility they have imparted potency. But when, as in the case of Nicholas the Czar, *the ringed crown of geographical empire circles an imperial brain; then, the plebeian herds crouch abased before the tremendous centralization.* Nor, will the tragic dramatist who would depict mortal indomitableness in its fullest sweep and direst swing, ever forget a hint, incidentally so important in his art, as the one now alluded to. (P. 148; my emphasis)

The specific reference of the "hint" to which Ishmael alludes is not entirely clear, simply because it is not yet focalized in his horizonal narrative consciousness. But the passage, which recalls his earlier reference to "the certain sultanism of [Ahab's] brain," does, in its identification of the metaphorics of centeredness (and light) with inordinate imperial power, at least suggest his ambiguous and uneasy attitude toward the tragic (Apollonian) vision and its encompassing and "abasing" circular specular geometry.

Following Ishmael's meditation on the relationship between the tragic hero and power ("The Specksnyder"), this generalized trope assumes a chillingly concrete form. As if the narration of the event is triggered by the preceding meditation, he recalls the calculated moment on the quarterdeck, when, nailing a gold doubloon to the mast, Ahab announces his hidden purpose, thus changing the intended course of the whaling voyage and, potentially, the course of Ishmael's narrative: "Whosoever of ye raises me a white-headed whale with a wrinkled brow and a crooked jaw; whosoever of ye raises me that white-headed whale, with three holes punctured in his starboard fluke—look ye, whosoever of ye raises me that same white whale, he shall have this gold ounce, my boys" (p. 162). True to the mystified image Ahab has deliberately projected, the language he uses to articulate his singular, determined, and vengeful purpose to destroy the white whale is an incantatory symbolic and totalizing rhetoric that both provokes his crew's anxiety in the face of uncertainty and appeals to its latent superstitiousness: its receptivity to the investiture of being with anthropomorphic significance. In opposition, Starbuck tries to call things by their right name: "Vengeance on a dumb brute! . . . that simply smote thee from blindest instinct! Madness! To be enraged with a dumb thing, Captain Ahab, seems blasphemous" (pp. 163–64). But his effort to persuade Ahab against the quest to which he has committed the *Pequod* and to break the spell his totalizing rhetoric has cast over the crew is futile. As Ahab's response to Starbuck's initial objection makes clear ("I came here to hunt whales, not my commander's vengeance. How many barrels will thy vengeance yield thee even if thou gettest it, Ahab? it will not fetch thee much in our Nantucket market."), it betrays a sociopolitical, ideological motive, which, in the superficiality of its principle of resistance against a dominating authority, is even more problematic than Ahab's: "'Nantucket market! Hoot! But come closer, Starbuck; thou requirest a little lower layer. If money's to be the measurer, man, and the accountants have computed their great counting-house the globe, by girdling it with guineas, one to every three parts of an inch; then, let me tell thee, that my vengeance will fetch a great premium *here!*' (He smites his heart.)" (p. 163). In reminding Captain Ahab that his business was to hunt whales for the Nantucket market and referring to his pursuit of the white whale as blasphemous, Starbuck, that is, exposes the Real to which he would recall him and the crew to be inscribed by a totalizing ideology and the principle of his resistance to be that form of freedom sanctioned by a developing Puritan Christianity that transformed the divine imperative to rationalize the earth into a justification to plunder being "for the Nantucket market."[61]

This ideological gesture annuls the force of Starbuck's invocation of the ship's occasion, and the enchanting power of Ahab's mystifying rhetoric of persuasion continues to work out its hypnotic, lulling, and abasing magic. Responding to his ritual call for "the measure" and the harpoon (cup and lance), the ship's company of wildly different *Isolatoes* forms a circle around Ahab, and his mates pass the "heavy charged flagon" around. Ahab, Ishmael recalls—in a way that cannot but evoke his earlier relinquishment of "all outward majestical trappings and housings"—insists on his absolute centrality: "Attend now, my braves. I have mustered ye all round this capstan; and ye mates, flank me with your lances; and ye harpooneers, stand there with your irons; and ye, stout mariners, *ring me in*, that I may in some sort revive a noble custom of my fisherman fathers before me" (p. 146; my emphasis). The ceremonialized figure of the circle becomes charged with greater power when he orders his officers to "cross your lances" so he can "touch the axis" (p. 163). And in a final ritual gesture to galvanize the crew's obedience to his imperial iron will, Ahab commands the harpooneers to detach the harpoon blades and fill them with drink, thus transforming harpooneers into "braves" who are "cup-bearers," the harpoons into "murderous chalices," and the entire communal ceremony, presided over by Ahab (who now refers to himself as "Pope" and harpooneers as "cardinals"), into a kind of black mass that reduces all the otherwise differential crew "parties to this indissoluble league" (p. 146) against the white whale: "'Drink, ye harpooneers! drink and swear, ye men that man the deathful whaleboat's bow—Death to Moby Dick! . . .' and to cries and maledictions against the white whale, the spirits were simultaneously quaffed down with a hiss" (p. 165).

The young Ishmael, too, we learn shortly after, had succumbed to Ahab's irresistibly persuasive rhetoric and, to anticipate, his "unerring" iron will: "I, Ishmael, was one of that crew; my shouts had gone up with the rest; my oath had been welded with theirs, and stronger I shouted, and more did I hammer and clinch my oath, because of the dread in my soul. A wild, mystical, sympathetical feeling was in me; Ahab's quenchless feud seemed mine. With greedy ears I learned the history of that murderous monster against whom I and all the others had taken our oaths of violence and revenge" (p. 179). I will return to Ishmael's enabling confession, especially to the "dread" he appeases by taking the oath of "violence and revenge" against the white whale; here it will suffice to say that the resonant contradictory intuitions—the "hints"—at play in Ishmael's free-floating meditation on the grandeur of the tragic hero come to surface. Under the magnetic influence of Ahab's supervisory "master-eye," the "*Isolatoes*" he celebrates against the continental landsmen (p. 121) are leveled and "welded" to the Same—the Heideggerian "*Das Man*" ("the They"), the Nietzschean "Herd," the Kierkegaardian "Crowd," the Ishmaelian "plebeian herds crouched abased before the tremendous centralization." *The centered circle*, the principle of self-presence, the still point in the turning world, the ideal figure of beauty/perfection/truth in the Western ontotheological tradition, especially in the post-Enlightenment (its anthropological phase)—and this, whatever the exceptionalist claims made for its "New Worldness," applies to America—turns logically into the figure of power and domination: this is the trope that tropes Ishmael's narrative about a whaling voyage intended to circumnavigate the globe.

In some degree at least, Ishmael realizes the paradoxical implications of the privileged figure of the centered circle for literary form. And as the chapter on "The Mast-Head"—which immediately precedes his retrieval of the moment the crew takes its oath of violence—suggests, he is also, however vaguely, aware of one significant aspect of this "Emersonian" comportment toward being: the ontological. The "very ancient and interesting business of standing mast-head" (p. 154)[62] authorizes a metaphysical perspective that, like "Emersonian," if not entirely Emerson's, transcendentalism,[63] finally *sees* the actual from after or beyond or above, and thus overlooks and even forgets the phenomenal world—the differences that temporality disseminates—at its own peril. In other words, this "Emersonian" perspective, even when it assumes an inside out, that is, immanentalist, movement, is fundamentally *theoretical* (in the etymological sense of the word: a seeing from a distance) and thus, in one of its permutations, dangerously oblivious to the differential and anxiety-provoking world of historicality. From this transcendental height—this "thought-engendering altitude" (p. 155)—everything in the world (in space and time, including language and historically specific history) resolves itself into an internalized and sublimated identity, a "Pantheistic one," thus neutralizing "'interest' in the voyage" and the "carking cares of earth" (p. 158): "There you stand, lost in the infinite series of the sea, with nothing ruffled but the waves . . . everything resolves you into languor . . . a sublime uneventfulness invests you; you hear no news; read no gazettes; extras with startling accounts of commonplaces never delude you into unnecessary excitements" (p. 157)[64] Thus "free-floating" (Heidegger) or "hovering" (Kierkegaard) in this infinitely negative internalized space, "with the problem of the universe revolving in [him]," (p. 158) the "dreamy meditative man" (p. 156), this "young Platonist" (p. 158) (by which Melville surely means Hegelian), forgets his differential identity and becomes oblivious to his occasion: the real and always threatening abyssal "identity" of the sea (of being), at the heart of which, like the vortices (the centerless circles) Ishmael refers to, is not Presence, but absence, not Something, but nothing:

There is no life in thee, now, except that rocking life imparted by a gently rolling ship; by her, borrowed from the sea; by the sea, from the inscrutable tides of God. But while this sleep, this dream is on ye, move your foot or hand an inch; slip your hold at all; and your identity comes back in horror. *Over Descartian vortices you hover.* And perhaps, at mid-day, in the fairest weather, with one half-throttled shriek you drop through that transparent air into the summer sea, no more to rise for ever. Heed it well, ye Pantheists! (P. 158; my emphasis)

THE AMERICAN ADAM AND THE NAMING OF THE WHITE WHALE

At this time in his forwarding narrative, Ishmael is not yet aware of the *affiliative relationship* between the implications of the privileged figure of the centered circle for the form of fiction and the form of being, indeed, for the relay of forms that being takes all along its lateral, historically specific continuum from the ontological through the epistemological, linguistic, and cultural to the sociopolitical sites. The remainder of Ishmael's errant narrative will, in fact, dis-cover—and in the process, de-stroy—this relationship. Despite his resonant intuition about the negative consequences for actual life of the metaphysical perspective and its privileged forms and figures, Ishmael, in other words, has not descended far on the Platonic ladder or, in Melville's rhetoric, dived deep enough, into the destructive element. To dis-close the being of being without fixing it once and for all in the eye's Medusan light, one must, Heidegger observes, "leap into the [destructive] 'circle,' primordially and wholly."

Ishmael's remembrance of his and the crew's "oath of violence and revenge" against the white whale in fact instigates a decisive estrangement of the sedimented discourse of the tragic vision and of Ahab's rhetoric of persuasion and a deeper dive into the destructive element. Appalled by his and his shipmate's self-abasement around Ahab's "tremendous centralization," he begins to rethink the events that reduced by inflating a whaling voyage into a cosmic battle between two Titanic identities. His retrieval first takes the form of a meditation on the differences between Ahab's and his own understanding of the white whale. In response to Starbuck's accusation that his unrelenting desire for "vengeance on a dumb brute" is madness, indeed, blasphemous, Ahab had replied:

"All visible objects, man, are but pasteboard masks. But in each event—in the living act, the undoubted deed—there, some unknown but still reasoning thing puts forth the mouldings of its features from behind the unreasoning mask. If man will strike, strike through the mask! . . . I see in [the white whale] outrageous strength, with an inscrutable malice sinewing it. That inscrutable thing is chiefly what I hate; and be the white whale agent, or be the white whale principal, I will wreak that hate upon him." (P. 164)

In thus taking Starbuck down a "little lower layer," Ahab, as Donald Pease has shown in *Visionary Compacts*, "takes rhetorical control of the situation" by justifying a profounder and more inclusive indignation and rebellion than Starbuck's:

By diving for a deeper religious motive than Starbuck can command . . . Ahab implicitly chastens Starbuck for the comparatively shallow purposes to which he puts his indignation. If Starbuck is willing to kill whales only for the capital their oil will accrue back in Nantucket, he is not willing to see them as representive of any purpose deeper than the profit motive. His profit motive compels him to see whales as dumb brutes. Ahab, in informing the whale with purposes involving a cosmic *enantiodrama*, turns Starbuck into an implicit blasphemer. For in treating the whale as nothing but a "pasteboard mask" for his vainglorious profit motive, Starbuck confirms Ahab's moral judgment. As a Christian whose faith is equi-primordial with a profit motive, Starbuck can interpret whaling only in a market context. To remind Starbuck of a deeper motive, Ahab speaks with all the rage of a man who can no longer remain satisfied with a religion based on marketplace values. So instead of responding to Starbuck's charges, Ahab condemns Starbuck's context and does so with all the rage of a man who experiences Starbuck's marketplace religion as only an example of a further justification for his own revenge quest. (P. 237)

This is acute and persuasive commentary. But what it overlooks in order to later implicate Ishmael in Ahab's totalizing "scene of persuasion" is—and I use this word advisedly—the *occasion* of *Ishmael's* narrative. I mean, as I have been suggesting, his struggle to free himself from his inscribed self-present Self and its propensity to symbolize the cosmos—to read "the things themselves" as signatures of a preordained cosmic Book—the propensity, that is, which he has inherited from his American Puritan ancestors and which Ahab exploits to gain the consensus he needs to accomplish his singular mission in the wilderness of being.

To put it first in the general but crucial terms of ontology, Ishmael begins to realize that Captain Ahab's New World discourse of self-reliance betrays, in its encompassing and comprehensive anthropocentrism, its complicity with the "Old World's" logocentrism. Like his European prototype, that is, this American Adam would reify the Nothingness of being, level (in both philosophical and material senses) the proliferating differences its "errant" temporality disseminates to Identity, its multiplicity to the One (*Monos*), not simply to understand or comprehend its painfully disorienting ambiguities, but, as the resonant etymology of "comprehension" suggests, to "take hold of," "to grasp," "to manipulate" its elusive and dreadful mystery. The metaphysical objectification of dread transforms the nothing that activates it into Something and thus enables the practical "final solution":

No turbaned Turk, no hired Venetian or Malay, could have smote him with more *seeming* malice. Small reason was there to doubt, then, that ever since that almost fatal encounter, Ahab had cherished a wild vindictiveness against the whale, all the more fell for that in his frantic morbidness he at last came to *identify* with him, not only *all* his bodily woes, but *all* his intellectual and spiritual exasperations. The White Whale swam before him as the *monomaniac incarnation* of *all* those malicious agencies which some deep men feel eating in them, till they are left living on with half a heart and half a lung. That *intangible malignity* which has been from the beginning; to whose dominion even the modern Christians ascribe one-half of the worlds; which the ancient Ophites of the east reverenced in their statue devil;— Ahab did not fall down and worship it like them; but deliriously transferring its idea to the abhorred white whale, he pitted himself, all mutilated, against *it. All* that most maddens and torments; *all* that stirs up the lee of things; *all* truth with malice in it; *all* that cracks the sinews and cakes the brain; *all* the subtle demonisms of life and thought; *all* evil, to crazy Ahab, were *visibly personified*, and made *practically assailable* in Moby Dick. He piled upon the whale's white hump the *sum of all the general* rage and hate felt by his *whole* race from Adam down; and then, as if his chest had been a mortar, he burst his hot heart's shell upon it. (P. 184; my emphasis)

In Nietzsche's terms, Captain Ahab's single-minded pursuit of the white whale is ultimately motivated by the will to power over being that repeats Western logocentric Man's—the Old Adam's, as it were—resentful nihilistic obsession to revenge himself against the transience of time.[65] Captain Ahab's representation of the white whale as the "incarnation" of every thing and every event in the world that activates pain in human beings is indeed, as Ishmael insists, a madness. But this madness—this "monomania"—Melville seems to be saying is not Ahab's alone; it is Western civilization's at large, not least, as I will momentarily suggest, despite its self-representation as "the New World," antebellum America's. For, Ishmael implies, just as Ahab anthropomorphizes being into the single image of Moby Dick to make its duplicities "practically assailable" (p. 184), so Western philosophy, however various its supplements (including Emersonian transcendentalism), has as its representational end the recuperation of Identity from difference, Eternity from time, Stillness from motion. As Jacques Derrida puts it, following Heidegger, "[T]he entire history of the concept of structure . . . must be thought of as a series of substitutions of center for center, as a linked chain of determinations of the center. Successively, and in a regulated fashion, the center receives different forms or names. The history of metaphysics, like the history of the West, is the history of these metaphors and metonymies. Its matrix . . . is the determination of Being as *presence* in all sense of this word."[66] So also, however inadvertently, the logical economy of this One, perennially privileged by the West, has, as Heidegger has argued, justified the devastating, imperial singularity of Western technological *praxis*: the "enframing" and, through this, the reduction of *physis* to "standing reserve," the mastery and domestication or pacification—the cultivation and colonization—of the earth:

Man has already begun to overwhelm the entire earth and its atmosphere, to arrogate to himself in forms of energy the concealed powers of nature, and to submit future history to the planning and ordering of a world government. This same defiant man is utterly at a loss simply to say what *is*: to say *what* this *is*—That a thing *is*.

The totality of beings is the single object of a singular will to conquer. The simplicity of Being is confounded in a singular oblivion.[67]

Not least American Man: To put this Occidental logocentrism in terms of the historically specific occasion that Melville is addressing in *Moby-Dick* is to invoke the American Enlightenment allotrope of this abiding and determining Western center or principle of presence. I mean the self-identical Self that in large part had, or is represented by the Americanists who established the field-Imaginary of American literary studies in the 1940s and 1950s as having, its genealogical origins in the Puritans' errand in the wilderness to build the "city on the hill." And in so doing, it compels a "repetition" of the preceding analysis of Ishmael's ontological interrogation of Ahab's "tremendous centralization" and his representation of the white whale, this time in terms of its historically specific—American—origins and consequences for the America of Melville's time.

Understood in this historically specific context, Ahab's representation of the white whale in Man's image assumes the character of a *naming* that gathers being at large, in all its temporal and spatial multiplicity, into a *con-centrated* image—a single, undifferentiated, inclusive, and finally predictable "world picture," as it were—of universal Evil informed by the "insatiable malice" of "Moby Dick." This naming of the uncanny human predicament in an alien cosmos from his anthropocentric perspective not only enables Ahab's totalized trope but also empowers him to confront and manipulate its dislocating, "inscrutable," and intangible being as if it were a threatening object visible to his panoptic eye. In terms of this presiding biblical metaphorics resonating below the surface of Ishmael's representation of Ahab's anthropomorphization of a living creature of the deep, his imposition of a human identity on its elusive being, the captain of the *Pequod* becomes an inverted Adam: he would reenact the naming and pacification of the beasts in Genesis and, in so doing, exposes the hitherto "benign" Adamic impulse to name to be a will to master being. To put this theological estrangement in the more immediate terms of Melville's America, the American Ahab, the exponent of (the rights of) Man, reenacts the theologically or, more specifically, providentially ordained American Adam's errand in the wilderness in the name of the *anthropologos* and its secular logical economy, and, in so doing, discloses the continuity between the Puritan and the self-reliant "Emersonian" Adam. In thus disclosing the genealogical origins of the antebellum American principle of self-reliance in the Adamic discursive practices of the New England Puritans, not least the prefigurative (or typological) hermeneutics they adapted to their "New-World" purposes from the medieval Patristic Fathers, Melville, through Ishmael's disruptive errant narrative, also discloses the latent violence against difference informing the "benign" logic of the Emersonian myth of "Central" or "Representative" Man. Just as the Puritan *theologos* and its providential history compelled the American Adam's reduction of the anxiety-provoking differential forces of the "New-World wilderness" to the synecdochical image of the satanic "Salvage," and thus justified and facilitated the genocidal war against "It," so Ahab's anthropological principle of self-reliance enabled him to represent, to incarnate, the dreadful and pain-inflicting accidents—*all* that torments human being in the temporal or, more accurately, occasional, world—into the single and fixed, demonic image of "Moby Dick" and justified and facilitated its extinction. As in the case of the founding Puritan Fathers, the objectification—the naming— of dread transforms the nothing that activates it into Something and thus enables the practical "final solution."

Ahab's reduction of multiplicity in the name of the *anthropologos*—the end of Representative Man—exemplifies what Heidegger, in his genealogy of modern humanism, calls the "representational-calculative thinking" that brings the logical economy of the ontotheological tradition to it contradictory (mad) fulfillment (end).[68] For this reduction and assimilation of difference to the *Monos* (being to Being)—this "technologization" of thinking, as it were—which is also an acquisition of total "knowledge," is accompanied not simply by a facilitation of decisive action, but by the ability to act with an enormous and concentered power unavailable to the person who dwells among ambiguities:

But, as in his narrow-flowing monomania, not one jot of Ahab's broad madness had been left behind; so in that broad madness, not one jot of his great natural intellect had perished. That before living agent, now became the living *instrument*. If such a furious trope may stand, his special lunacy stormed his general sanity and carried it, and turned all its concentred canon upon its own mad mark; so that far from having lost his strength, Ahab, to that one end, did now possess a thousand fold more potency than ever he had sanely brought to bear upon any one reasonable object. (P. 185; my emphasis)

Despite the substitution "of one center for another," the "Emersonian" *anthropologos* for the Puritan *theologos*, the continuity between the trajectory of Puritan representation and practice in the face of the dreadful occasion of being and Ishmael's summation of Ahab's becomes strikingly manifest in this and the preceding passages, especially if we retrieve in this context, as we are clearly intended to do, the *exhortatio* of the Jeremiad on the Jonah text delivered by Father Mapple, the "pilot of the living God":

"But oh! shipmates! on the starboard hand of every woe, there is a sure delight; and higher the top of that delight, than the bottom of the woe is deep. Is not the main-truck higher than the kelson is low? Delight is to him—a far, far upward, and inward delight—who against the proud gods and commodores of this earth, ever stands forth *his own inexorable self*. Delight is to him whose strong arms yet support him, when the ship of this base treacherous world has gone down beneath him. Delight is to him, who gives no quarter in the truth, and kills, burns, and destroys all sin though he pluck it out from under the robes of Senators and Judges. Delight,—top-gallant delight is to him, who acknowledges no law or lord, but the Lord his God, and is only a patriot to heaven. Delight is to him, whom all the waves of the billows of the seas of the boisterous mob can never shake from this sure Keel of the Ages. And eternal delight and deliciousness will be his, who coming to lay him down, can say with his final breath—O Father!—chiefly known to me by Thy rod—mortal or immortal, here I die. I have striven to be Thine, more than to be this world's, or mine own." (P. 48)

The difference that Melville, through Ishmael's errant narrative, is focusing, I suggest, is the difference between the Puritan Adam's more overt and visible practice of power and the indirect and invisible practice of power of the secularized, "American Renaissance" Adam. As the movement that bears witness to the transformation of the "inexorable self" into an utterly passive and obedient agent of God, the Father, in Mapple's sermon suggests, what Melville discloses, in thus pressing the benign symbolic logic of self-reliance—the sovereign individual—to what Thomas Pynchon, not incidentally, would call its "paranoid" conclusion,[69] is the violence latent in this logic: the will to power informing the American discourse of individual freedom manifests itself only when it is in crisis. We have borne witness to this self-destruction of the logic of the sovereign subject, which Melville prophetically discloses, over and over again in modern American history, not least, as I will suggest in the conclusion of this book, in Vietnam and, more recently, in the Middle East.

ISHMAEL AND THE UNNAMING OF MOBY DICK

All this concerning the American will to name is precisely, if not in any final way, what Ishmael realizes in the following chapter, which he significantly entitles "The Whiteness of the Whale" in sharp contrast to the previous meditation on the genealogy of Ahab's ontological monomania, which he entitles "Moby Dick." Whereas Ahab pursues Moby Dick in the inexorable name of Mankind's vengeance against the dreadful force of being, the young Ishmael's impulse, if not his resolute decision, is to accept the white whale as a manifestation of being's unspeakable mystery. He resists reducing and converting the unnameable excess that spills across the circumscribing boundary of his imagination and terrifies him into something he can comprehend and pacify. Through his retrieval of his lapse before Ahab's concentered and concentering "master eye," the older Ishmael comes to understand that his oath was a temporary, however fateful, capitulation to that publically inscribed impulse, so magnified by the symbolizing totalitarian consciousness, to find a single, all-encompassing object for dread—a scapegoat—and thus to familiarize and contain the uncanny. His deepest instinct, however, is to acknowledge the dread activated by the terrible "whiteness" of the whale, the dread, which according to Heidegger, has no thing as its object, the Nothingness or absence of presence that reminds him of his thrownness in-the-world:

What the white whale was to Ahab, has been hinted. What, at times, he was to me, as yet remains unsaid.

Aside from those more obvious considerations touching Moby Dick, which could not but occasionally awaken in any man's soul some alarm, there was another thought, or rather vague, nameless horror concerning him, which at times by its intensity completely overpowered all the rest; and yet so mystical and well nigh ineffable was it, that I almost despair of putting it in a comprehensible form. It was the whiteness of the whale that above all things appalled me. But how can I hope to explain myself here; and yet, in some dim, random way, explain myself I must, else all these chapters might be naught. (P. 188)

In Ishmael's stuttering meditation on the whiteness of the whale, there is no uncertainty about the function of naming the whiteness that pervades being. As his long participial catalogue of various temporal and geographical cultural representations—writing or figuration—suggests, the naming is driven by the impulse to reify "it" for purposes of domesticating its threat, whether this domestication takes the form of utility, aesthetic repose, or enhancement of power:

Though in many natural objects, whiteness refiningly enhances beauty, as if imparting some special virtue of its own, as in marbles, japonicas, and pearls; and though various nations have in some way recognized a certain royal pre-eminence in this hue; even the barbaric, grand old kings of Pegu placing the title "Lord of the White Elephants" above all their other magniloquent ascriptions of dominion; and the modern kings of Siam unfurling the same snow-white quadruped in the royal standard; and the Hanoverian flag bearing the one figure of a snow-white charger; and the great Austrian Empire, Caesarian heir to overlording Rome, having for the imperial color the same imperial hue; and though this pre-eminence in it applies to the human race itself, giving the white man ideal mastership over every dusky tribe; and though, besides all this, whiteness has been even made significant of gladness, for among the Romans a white stone marked a joyful day; and though in other mortal sympathies and symbolizings, this same hue is made the emblem of many touching, noble things—the innocence of brides, the benignity of age. . . . (Pp. 188–89)

As the "conclusion" of this long catalogue suggests, however, Ishmael is also aware that these inscriptions (like "the surface stratified on surface" of Pierre's "geological" quest for identity) are re-presentations—in Derrida's term, *suppléments*—that finally defer what they would domesticate: "[Y]et for all these accumulated associations, with whatever is sweet, and honorable, and sublime, there yet lurks an elusive something in the innermost idea of this hue, which strikes more panic to the soul than that redness which affrights in blood" (p. 189).

Ishmael must, as he says, explain—verbally interpret—his unsayable "understanding" of the dread-provoking whiteness of the whale. But unlike Captain Ahab, who uses a comprehensive rhetoric of naming, of presence, to bring "it" to stand, Ishmael consciously and insistently—and in deference to (the ontological) difference—substitutes sign for sign for sign and thus defers the meaning of whiteness in a resonantly "playful" rhetoric of absence—"pale," "pallid," "pall," "palsied," "appalling" (pp. 188–95)—in keeping with his abyssal occasion. As in the encounter with Elijah, Ishmael's impulse is to refuse to take "seeming malice" (p. 184) as real, to refuse to "name," "to grasp," to "identify," to "capture," to "color," as it were, the "nameless" (p. 188), the "intangible" (p. 184), the "ineffable" (p. 188), the "elusive" (p. 188), the "muteness" (p. 193), the "dumb blankness" (p. 195), the "visible absence of color" (p. 195). Ishmael, that is, must thematize his earlier intuitions about the dreadful whiteness of the whale in writing, for his very narrative is at stake. Otherwise there is only blank silence. But, unlike Ahab, he "presents" the unpresentable in such a "dim, random way" that he lets the whale's ineffable being be.

By understanding Ahab's "monomaniac incarnation of all those malicious agencies" as a mad obsession to make an *end* of time and thus to bring time to its end, Ishmael comes, by contrast, to acknowledge his thrownness in a decentered universe (*die unheimliche Welt*) without beginning or end as his occasion, and accordingly, the temporal errancy of this open-ended "universe" as the measure of his occasion. To put this provisionally in terms of the discourse of "the postmodern condition," Ishmael/Melville's interrogation of the "Emersonian"/Coleridgean symbolizing impulse as practiced by Captain Ahab anticipates the postmodernist critique of Modernism—which is to say, the presentational discourse on which the Americanists' field-Imaginary is founded. His thematization of the self-destructive logic of the inclusive Imagination, that is, constitutes a dis-closure not simply of the will to power over being informing its spatializing practice, but a dis-closure of the "unpresentable" sublime it futilely would contain:

Here, then lies the difference: modern aesthetics is an aesthetics of the sublime, though a nostalgic one. It allows the unpresentable to be put forward only as the missing contents; but the form, because of its recognizable consistency, continues to offer to the reader or viewer matter of solace and pleasure. Yet these sentiments do not constitute the real sublime sentiment, which is in an intrinsic combination of pleasure and pain: the pleasure that reason should exceed all presentation, the pain that imagination or sensibility should not be equal to the concept.

The postmodern would be that which, in the modern, puts forward the unpresentable in presentation itself; that which denies itself the solace of good forms, the consensus of a taste which would make it possible to share collectively the nostalgia for the unattainable; that which searches for new presentations, not in order to enjoy them but in order to impart a stronger sense of the unpresentable. A postmodern artist or writer is in the position of a philosopher: the text he writes, the work he produces are not in principle governed by preestablished rules, and they cannot be judged according to a determining judgment, by applying familiar categories to the text or to the work. Those rules and categories are what the work of art itself is looking for. The artist and the writer, then, are working without rules in order to formulate the rules of what *will have been done*. Hence the fact that work and text have the characters of an *event*; hence also, they always come too late for their author, or, what amounts to the same thing, their being put into work, their realization (*mise en oeuvre*) alway begin too soon. *Post modern* would have to be understood according to the paradox of the future (*post*) anterior (*modo*).[70]

More specifically, Ishmael-Melville's "story" will be one intended precisely to destroy that generic determination of American literature constituted by the American field-Imaginary of the post–World War II American literary critics in opposition to the sociopolitically progressive "realism" of the Parringtonian tradition for purposes of establishing the American canon and, not least, of finding a place for Melville's recalcitrant—"loose, baggy monster"—*Moby-Dick*. I am referring, of course, to the (American) "romance," or, rather, to that allotrope, the novelistic "tragedy," which, according to Lionel Trilling, in the hands of writers like Nathaniel Hawthorne and Henry James, epitomizes its perfection.[71] I mean, to be more specific, that form, derived from the New Critics (especially T. S. Eliot's influential notion of the "objective correlative"),[72] privileged by F. O. Matthiessen and, above all, Trilling, and institutionalized by Richard Chase, Charles Feidelson, and the other founding fathers of American literary studies. As Pease and other New Americanists have shown, it is the literary form enabled by an "end of ideology" perspective that undertakes the internalization and sublimation of the external conflicts of its occasion into an inclusive, balanced, and self-contained artistic object, a "world elsewhere," and in the process conceals its ideological complicity with the massive postwar effort to establish and provide the cultural grounds for the reproduction of an imperial national consensus, specifically the Cold War scenario.

ISHMAEL, THEORY, AND PRACTICE

From the moment Ishmael tells his audience that Ahab's concealed purpose was to redirect or, more accurately, reprogram, the goal (and course) of the intended voyage—that "with the mad secret of his unabated rage bottled up and keyed in him, Ahab had purposely sailed upon the present voyage with the one only all-engrossing object of hunting the White Whale" (p. 186)—Ishmael's narrative of the *Pequod*'s vengeful pursuit of Moby Dick should begin to move more rapidly and undeviatingly toward the prescribed "denouement" the captain envisages. But Ishmael continues to resist the linear imperative of traditional fiction by interpolating into the "story line" what appear to be random digressions on cetology, whaling, philosophy, and the history and character of "peripheral" figures in the narrative. In fact, his "resistance" to the immune *logos*—"the center elsewhere," as it were—of traditional fiction is so pronounced that one might say his story constitutes an act of mutiny against its mystified "concen-tered" authority. The narrative continues to pursue, that is, "repeats," though now and increasingly in a deepening and more self-conscious way that implicates practice with theory, a double, or duplicitous, movement. It is a movement in which the "errant" impulse—and the discoveries it "charts" on the way (his *periplus,* as it were), not simply about ontology, but also, and crucially, as I will show, about other regions along the indissol-uble continuum of being—destroys what the tradition would call Ahab's grand and untouchable hubris and the consolatory tragic action it precipi-tates by disclosing this hubris to be a metaphysical monomania and the tragic action an unerring disciplinary movement that end in a catastrophe that no "secret cause" can accommodate.

From the emergent, occasional perspective of Ishmael's estrangement, Ahab's Adamic eye has become a coercive gaze that gathers the dreadful multiplicity of the errant energies of being—of the "Naught," as it were—that renders the human situation, man's being-in-the-world, intolerable, into a single, totalized dedifferentiated, visible, and identifiable trope. Thus, like his counterpart, the fallen but still "central" man in the Ameri-can tradition established by the Puritans, whose end "in the fullness of time" is promised in the beginning, Ahab is enabled to fulfill—in prac-tice—his monistic project (his story) without digressing or de-viating from the linear (circular) course it projects, without "swerving" from the pre-scribed way. In a delirious soliloquy that refers to his anthropological vision as a prophecy in which the "prophet [seer] and the fulfiller [are] one," in which, that is, *theoria* becomes *praxis,* the panoptic gaze, a total-itarian "politics," Ahab projects his fierce yet calculative purpose in terms of the metaphorics of the railroad, that technological instrument, not incidentally, precipitated by and for the rationalizing "sovereign subject" that was to play a decisive role in the leveling and domestication of the American earth—and the extermination of its native inhabitants: "Come, Ahab's compliments to ye [the malicious 'great God'] come and see if ye can swerve me. Swerve me! ye cannot swerve me, else ye swerve your-selves! man has ye there. Swerve me? The path to my fixed purpose is laid with iron rails, whereon my soul is grooved to run. Over unsounded gorges, through the rifled hearts of mountains, under torrents' beds, *unerringly* I rush! Naught's an obstacle, naught's an angle to the iron way!" (p. 168; my emphasis). Henceforth, it is this fierce, calculative inflexibility authorized by his monolithic, ontological leveling of alterity—this tech-nologizing of being—that Ishmael will insistently emphasize in referring to Ahab's direction of the *Pequod*'s unerring itinerary through the "un-hooped," labyrinthine seas. The ship's technological instruments become an extension of Ahab's "methodical" monomania (p. 200). Not unlike the "tables" of the natural and physical scientists of the Enlightenment, which, in their spatialization and classification of being, according to Foucault, paved the way for the panopticism of modernity, the harnessing of knowl-edge to power, to the task of transforming the hitherto amorphous, invisible, and threatening human collective into the modern disciplinary society, the ship's charts, for example, become an extension of Ahab's "master eye" in his unrelenting effort to track down the elusive white whale:

But it was not this night in particular [which preceded "that wild ratification of his purpose with the crew"] that, in the solitude of his cabin, Ahab thus pondered over his charts. Almost every night they were brought out; almost every night some pencil marks were effaced, and others substituted. For with the charts of all four oceans before him, *Ahab was threading a maze of currents and eddies, with a view to the more certain accomplishment of the monomaniac thought of his soul.*

Now, to any one not fully acquainted with the ways of the leviathan, it might seem an absurdly hopeless task thus to seek out one solitary creature in the unhooped oceans of this planet. But not so did it seems to Ahab, who knew the sets of all tides and currents; and thereby calculating the driftings of the sperm whale's food, and, also, calling to mind the regular, ascertained seasons for hunting him in particular latitudes; could arrive at reasonable surmises, almost approach-ing to certainties, concerning the timeliest day to be upon this or that ground in search of his prey. (Pp. 198–99; my emphasis)

Whenever, on its inflexibly steered course, the *Pequod* meets another whaling vessel, Ahab's first and only question to the captain, no matter what the vessel's occasion, is invariably whether he has seen the white whale.[73] Like his Puritan ancestors, he will not tolerate *wasting time* for "peripheral" purposes. Thus, for example, while Stubb is extracting the rich ambergris from a sick whale, Ahab impatiently commands him "to desist, and come on board, else the ship would bid them goodbye" (p. 407).

Even the diversions in the *Pequod*'s course are diversionary, covert acts of mastery calculated to appease—indeed, to neutralize by instrumentalizing—the potentially disruptive uneasiness of Ahab's sublunar, human crew, especially Starbuck's volatile abhorrence of Ahab's vengeful purpose and his desire to "disintegrate himself from it." Since the passage I am referring to is important for what it suggests not only about Ishmael's emergent attitude toward Ahab's "subtle insanity respecting Moby Dick" but also about his own narrative art, it warrants quotation at length:

> *To accomplish his object Ahab must use tools; and of all tools used in the shadow of the moon, men are most apt to get out of order.* He knew, for example, that however magnetic his ascendency in some respects was over Starbuck, yet that ascendency did not cover the complete spiritual man any more than mere corporeal superiority involves intellectual mastership; for to the purely spiritual, the intellectual but stands in a sort of corporeal relation. Starbuck's body and Starbuck's coerced will were Ahab's, so long as Ahab kept his magnet at Starbuck's brain; still he knew that for all this the chief mate, in his soul, abhorred his captain's quest, and could he, would joyfully *disintegrate himself from it,* or even frustrate it. It might be that a long interval would elapse ere the White Whale was seen. During that long interval Starbuck would ever be apt to fall into open relapses of rebellion against the captain's leadership, *unless some ordinary, prudential, circumstantial, influences were brought to bear upon him.* Not only that, but the subtle insanity of Ahab respecting Moby Dick was noways more significantly manifested than in *his superlative sense and shrewdness in foreseeing that, for the present, the hunt should in some way be stripped of that strange imaginative impiousness which naturally invested it; that the full terror of the voyage must be kept withdrawn into the obscure background (for few men's courage is proof against protracted meditation unrelieved by action); that when they stood their long night watches, his officers and men must have some nearer things to think of than Moby Dick.* . . . [W]hen [sailors] retained for any object remote and blank in the pursuit, however promissory of life and passion in the end, *it is above all things requisite that temporary interests and employments should intervene and hold them healthily suspended for the final dash.* (P. 212; my emphasis)

Indeed, *calculation*—the mental act of manipulating the elusive differential phenomena of temporality (the "nearer things," the "temporary interests and enjoyments") to achieve a preconceived (and preexistent) end—becomes the solar Ahab's essential measure in gaining "ascendency" over the essential mutability of his "sublunar" crew: "that protection [from the 'unanswerable charge of usurpation' to which his private purpose laid him open] . . . would only consist in his predominating brain and heart and hand, backed by a heedful, closely calculating attention to every minute atmospheric influence which it was possible for his crew to be subjected to" (p. 213). Accordingly, just as Sameness underlies the minute spatial particulars of Ahab's cosmos, so it underlies the minute temporal particulars of his understanding of time; just as Ahab's commitment to the ontology of the One levels spatial differentiation (in this case, the reduction and pacification of the differentiated crew of American *Isolatoes* into technologized, that is, docile and efficient bodies), so his commitment to an absolutely linear (circular) concept of time levels temporal differentiation. Like Father Mapple's prefigurative, exegetical method, Ahab's calculative measure will allow no thing or event to be superfluous. To recall a telling metaphor that Ishmael uses in the passage quoted above from "The Chart," Ahab's calculative measure, like the Athenian Theseus's, is positively capable of threading the maze of the oceans of being and to and from the lair of the "monstrous" Leviathan at its core.

In the last phase of the voyage, of course—as many Americanists since Matthiessen have observed—Ahab shows signs of relenting to his "natural" human impulses. Ishmael's attentive documentation of this emergent antithetical claim on Ahab's being—this disruption of his monolithic ideology, as it were—has been invoked by traditional Americanists to justify their representation of Ishmael/Melville's story as a narrative determined, not by ideology, but, in the terms Lionel Trilling appropriates from Henry James, by the "imagination of disaster,"[74] the "dialectical" or "liberal" imagination, he reiteratively tells us, by which "the world [is] *raised* to the noblest expression."[75] In the following passage, Trilling is referring to James's *Princess Casamassima*, but what he says by way of his analysis of Hyacinth Robinson's story about James's "imagination of disaster" is, in its exemplary resistance to the hegemony of the progressive, that is, ideologically driven, "realism" of the Parringtonian tradition, clearly intended as a generalization that applies to the American romance extending from Hawthorne through Melville to James.[76] And whether or not Trilling would, in fact, include *Moby-Dick* in this generalization, it is certainly the case that the Americanists who appropriated his enabling binary opposition between the romance and the realist novel, between the former's complex and "aware" "moral realism" and the latter's reductive and blind ideological realism would:

By the time Hyacinth's story draws to its end, his mind is in a perfect equilibrium, not of irresolution but of awareness. His sense of the social horror of the world is not diminished by his newer sense of the glory of the world. On the contrary, just as his pledge of his life to the revolutionary cause had in effect freed him to understand human glory, so the sense of the glory quickens his response to human misery—*never, indeed, is he so sensitive to the sordid life of the mass of mankind as after he has had the revelation of art.* And just as he is in an equilibrium of awareness, he is also in an equilibrium of guilt. . . .

Hyacinth's death, then, is not his way of escaping from irresolution. It is truly a sacrifice, an act of heroism. He is a hero of civilization because he dares do more than civilization does: *embodying two ideals at once,* he takes upon himself, in full consciousness, the guilt of each. He acknowledged both his parents. By his death he instructs us in the nature of civilized life and by his consciousness he *transcends it.*[77]

But Ishmael does not understand Ahab's emergent uncertainty, love, generosity, guilt, and even remorse in these clearly Richardsian/New Critical tragic terms. Despite the Shakespearian context in which it is imbedded, his invocation of Ahab's emergent "humanity" or moral sense is not intended to balance, to bring into equilibrium, Ahab's noble nature with his destructive monomania. It is not intended, that is, to enact the tragic paradox that Man's hubris—what is both grand and destructive about him—is, despite his historically specific occasion, his essential condition and, through this aesthetic paradox—" 'this *imagination* of disaster' "—to precipitate in his contemporary and future audiences a "civilizing" *catharsis* of the dread of being-in-the-world. I mean an analogous equilibrium or "balanced poise"—a static "dialectic," to qualify an essential term in Trilling's (and other Americanists', most notably R. W. B. Lewis's, critical vocabulary)[78]—between pity and terror: the kinetic (active) energies—desire and loathing, sympathy and repulsion, admiration and horror, and so on—that, despite the "moral realism" this equilibrium instills, leaves the unequal strife or rather the injustices of the world intact.[79] To put this more specifically in the terms at stake in Melville's novel, Ishmael's intention in attending to Ahab's emergent "humanity" is not the sublimation (*Aufhebung*) of the murderous consequences of the American Adam's absolute freedom and the historically specific "monomaniac" American practices he represents: westward expansion, Indian removal, laissez-faire capitalism, slavery, and even fanatic abolitionism. It is not, that is, the different but mutually ruthless (mono)logics that were to culminate in the 1860s in the vengefully contradictory return of the repressed, the disintegration of the One—which is to say, the American Civil War. His ultimate purpose, rather, is to thematize the blinding seductiveness of the "tragic vision," its magnetic power to draw us up and away not simply from this world and the *actual* imbalances of power that always inform its history, but from attention to the worldliness of its "world elsewhere."

Nor, on the other hand, as a certain version of phenomenological criticism claims, does Ishmael read Ahab's gestures of uncertainty primarily as manifestations of the "trial" of a Kierkegaardian "religious hero," who, like Abraham or Father Mapple's truly religious saint, must act out his violent, divinely "mad" calling "by virtue of the absurd," by "teleologically susp[ending] the ethical":

Despite his inner division, like a saint he wills one thing; like Father Mapple's religious hero, Ahab "stands forth his own inexorable self" in that he is willing to kill, burn, and destroy in the name of that possessing vision of truth which he has become, a vision which nevertheless dimly seems to see "some unsuffusing thing beyond" (xix) the fire-god to which all their "eternity is but time" and all their creativeness mechanical—some unsuffusing thing, it should be added, which might be placing Ahab on trial, a trial of the existence of which neither Ishmael nor we nor even Ahab could yet be aware. Like Abraham's, Ahab's temptation away from heroism is the ethical, as Pip and Starbuck, embody it.[80]

Given his destructive interrogation of naming and his emergent *ontological* willingness to remain in uncertainties without trying to objectify them (I emphasize the ontological dimension in anticipation of distinguishing Ishmael's "negative capability" from that which Trilling and others have attributed to the "moral realism" of the American "imagination of disaster"), Ishmael must, rather, understand Ahab's human gestures primarily as the measure of his *monomania*, which is to say, his dehumanization and its terrible consequences in the world. Having been reified into an instrument of lethal power, Ahab's "sovereign self" manifests itself as radical contradiction: it can no longer be located, let alone invoked, to modify its instrumentality or to alter the course of action. Ahab's grave, calculative strategy, in other words, has achieved an autonomy that precludes the play of difference and the possibility of human agency.

It is this unerring logic of the American Adam's "own inexorable self," in which errant time and its disseminations are reduced to an inexorable linearity, that, I submit, Ishmael finally, if implicitly, points to in the crucial chapter entitled "The Pequod Meets the Rachel." Answering the rhetoric of the Golden Rule with a rhetoric of mathematical precision only highlighted by his wavering, Ahab refuses—says a thunderous "No" to—the agonized plea of the *Rachel*'s captain to help him search for his two small sons, lost in the whale boats during the chase after Moby Dick:

> "I will not go," said the stranger, "till you say *aye* to me. Do to me as you would have me do to you in the like case. For *you* too have a boy, Captain Ahab—though but a child, and nestling safely at home now—a child of your old age too—Yes, yes, you relent; I see it—run, run, men, now, and stand by the squares in the yards."
>
> "Avast," cried Ahab—"touch not a rope-yarn," then in a voice that prolongingly moulded every word—"Captain Gardiner, I will not do it. Even now I lose time. Good bye good bye. God bless ye, man, and may I forgive myself, but I must go. Mr. Starbuck, look at the binnacle watch, and in three minutes from this present instant warn off all strangers; then brace forward again, and let the ship sail as before. (Pp. 532–33)

Before the first day of the chase, and encouraged by Ahab's softening in the face of his poignant recollection of his young wife and child and of the heavy burden of his Adamic past, Starbuck pleads: "Oh, my Captain! my Captain! noble soul! grand old heart, after all! let us fly these deadly waters! Let us home! . . . Away! let us away!—this instant let me alter the course!" (p. 444). Speaking more to himself than in response to Starbuck, Ahab asks: "What is it, what nameless, inscrutable, unearthly thing is it; what cozening, hidden lord and master, and cruel remorseless emperor commands me; that against all natural lovings and longings, I so keep pushing, and crowding, and jamming myself on all the time; recklessly making me ready to do what in my own proper, natural heart, I durst not so much as dare? I Ahab, Ahab? Is it I, God, or who that lifts this arm?" (p. 545). In this last sequence, in which he invokes the question of his free will, Ahab even searches for an external power as origin and determining force informing his monomaniacal action, oblivious to what Ishmael has earlier half-perceived but highlighted: that it is the internalized, unerring, and all-encompassing logic of his "own proper heart"—"his own inexorable self"—and its ontology of the One, of Presence, that drive him on toward the murderous and catastrophic end. And it is Ahab's focusing of this "contradiction" between Ahab's "natural heart" and his violent action—the self-present American self and the practice of domination—that finally focalizes for Ishmael the terrible continuity of the contradiction and, as I will suggest, precipitates a radical rethinking of the (American) self.

Indeed, the last phase of Ishmael's narrative "repeats" the disclosure that Ishmael's earlier juxtaposition of Ahab's and his own interpretation of the whiteness of whale had precipitated, but now decisively. Whereas, that is, in the earlier sequence the two aspects of the disclosure—that which thematized the American Adam's reification of being, on the one hand, and that which thematized the nothingness of being, on the other—were not conjoined in Ishmael's consciousness, the "repetition" Ishmael undertakes in the last phase of his narrative brings these into indissoluble relationship.

In his account of Ahab's revelation of his secret purpose to the crew, Ishmael, we recall, had marked the captain's reference to his "unerring" soul as a locomotive that disregards the various faces of nature in its iron-bound rush to its pre-tracked destination, and, in a remarkable anticipation of Michel Foucault's analysis of the Enlightenment's disciplinary machinery that turned living human beings into docile and useful bodies, Ahab's tendency to see and to convert his volatile crew of "renegades, castaways and mariners" into the tools necessary "to accomplish his object." In pointing to Ahab's calculative effort to "discipline" Starbuck's body—to increase "the forces of the body (in economic terms of utility)" and, at the same time, to diminish "these same forces (in political terms of obedience)"[81]—which otherwise would constitute a threat to his sovereignty and purpose, Ishmael, I suggested, was intuiting the implications of Ahab's ferociously monistic ontology not simply for philosophical discourse and narrative form but also for the economic and sociopolitical aspects of the voyage.

Now, in the culminating moments of his representation of the fiery chase, Ishmael's half-perception becomes conscious awareness and decisive in its underscoring of Ahab's reduction of difference into (a murderous) Identity. Under the aegis of the anthropocentric *Monos*, everything and everyone (as in Father Mapple's exegesis of the Jonah text)—the diverse instruments of navigation, the weapons, the *"Isolatoes"* who make up the *Pequod's* crew, the very materials of the ship itself—*all*, Ishmael remarks, are transformed not simply into a technological extension of what he had earlier referred to as Ahab's "delirious but still methodical scheme" (p. 200), but "welded" into *one* "unerring" collective harpoon (which, not incidentally, is a phallus) aimed at the "heart" (matrix) of the white whale.[82] Nor should Ishmael's rhetoric be overlooked: it repeats the rhetoric he used to articulate Ahab's tremendous reduction of "all that maddens and torments" man in the world to that "malign intelligence" of "Moby Dick," which made its invisible and intangible absence "practically assailable":

They were one man, not thirty. For as the one ship that held them all; though it was put together of *all contrasting things*—oak, and maple, and pine wood; iron, and pitch, and hemp—yet *all these* ran into each other in the one concrete hull, which shot on its way, both balanced and directed by the long central keel; even so, all the *individualities* of the crew, this man's valor, that man's fear; guilt and guiltlessness, *all varieties were welded into oneness, and were all directed to the fatal goal which Ahab their one lord and keel did point to.* (P. 557. My emphasis.)

But Ishmael's discovery does not end in his recognition of Ahab's monomania as a madly calculative, rational obsession to convert the erratic and duplicitous dynamics of being (the whiteness of the whale) into still life (*nature morte*) or dead *One*. For this disclosure, in turn, precipitates his awareness of the contradiction lurking in the corner of his eye: the Something into which Ahab's symbolizing imagination has, in its finality, transformed being exposes its origin in the Nothing, the absence of presence. To make this clearer, let me put Ishmael's discovery in the ontological terms of his privileged contemporaries—the terms, borrowed by the American exponents of the New Adam from the "Old World" German metaphysicians, that Melville, everywhere in his texts unrelentingly interrogates. The *comprehensive vision* enabled by Ahab's ontology of the One comes to be understood by Ishmael, not simply as an instrument of power as such, but as an instrument of power over the variety and play of differential being. I will amplify later on Ishmael's awareness of the etymology of the word "comprehension," whose privileged status in the Western philosophical tradition reaches its fulfillment in Hegel's *Er-innerung*[83] and its American equivalent (mediated by English and Scottish philosophers and poets) in the "Emersonian" effort to accommodate the things of this world to the "talismanic secret." (I am referring, of course, to the "preposterous rabble of Muggletonian Scots and Yankees, whose vile brogue," it will be recalled from *Pierre*, "still the more bestreaks the stripedness of their Greek or German Neoplatonic originals.") Here it will suffice to say that Ishmael's remarking of New Adamic Man's will to name—to comprehend—the meaning of being now, in the culminating moments of his narrative, takes the form of a significant revision, without effacement, of the metaphorics of instrumentality. In Ishmael's eyes,

Ahab's effort to comprehend being involves the transformation of the comely hand idealized by the classical Greeks into a monstrous claw. Having "located" "Moby Dick"—having, that is, "forced" him out of the obscure deep into the light of his gaze, Ahab, he writes, cries out triumphantly: "Stern all! Oh Moby Dick, I *clutch* thy heart *at last*" (p. 515, my emphasis). But where Ahab "grasps" most, the "comprehensive" elusiveness of language implies he "manages" least. Earlier in the narrative, Ishmael had recorded Ahab's certainty that no thing could swerve his locomotive soul from its fiercely willed end: "Naught's an obstacle, naught's an angle to my iron way!" Now, in the midst, as it were, he realizes the grimly ironic resonance—the duplicity—of this triumphant sentence, fired like a mortar shell out of his chest. In and through the explorative process of the narrative, he comes to know what he (and Ahab) unknowingly knew: that the Naught *is* an obstacle in his "unerring" iron way. Ahab's trope tropes. For at precisely the moment when the unerring logic of the self-present self comes to its end—when the *Pequod* as instrument/weapon of Ahab's monomania locates "Moby Dick"—the white whale not only eludes Ahab's "clutch," but becomes a sublimely retaliatory force that destroys the agent that would circumscribe and contain—comprehend—"it."

To this troping, this swerving which transforms nothing into Something, Something into nothing, seer into seen, seen into seer, eyer into eyed, eyed into eyer, Ishmael bears increasing vertiginous witness in the doubling narrative of the three days of "the chase." When on the first and second of these "vortextual" occasions, Ahab calls to the lookout in the mast-head, "What d'ye see?" the response is, "Nothing, nothing sir." And at that precise moment the white whale surfaces: "There she blow! [Ahab shouts]—there she blows! A hump, like a snow-hill. It's Moby Dick!" (Pp. 546, 55, with slight variations). The contradictory identification of Moby Dick and Nothingness (or the destructive reversion of Moby Dick to white whale)—and the reversal of the pursuer/pursued opposition—becomes explicit in Ishmael's narrative of the third and last day of the chase. For when the look-out answers Ahab's insistent question—"Nothing, Sir"—Ahab responds: "Nothing! and noon at hand! . . . How, got he start? Aye, he's chasing *me* now; not I, *him*—that's bad; I might have known it, too" (p. 564). Ahab continues to anthropomorphize the white whale, to ascribe "malicious intelligence to him" (p. 448). But if, as I think Melville intends, we put *"him"* under erasure, an inescapable metaphysical signifier that simultaneously "becomes" the excessive signified it cannot comprehend, the ontological implications of Ishmael's anxious meditation on the difference between Ahab's anthropomorphizing of the white whale into "Moby Dick" and his own *willingness* to let the mysterious whiteness of the whale be becomes explicit. The willful impulse, enabled by the logic of metaphysics, to master being drives "it" away: alienates the being it would comprehend or grasp.

As Charles Olson puts this correlation in *The Special View of History* (a text informed by the company of pre- and antimetaphysical writers—Heraclitus, Herodotus, Keats, Melville, Williams, Creeley, and possibly Martin Heidegger—with whom he claims a communal "relationship" as a postmodern or posthumanist poet), Man's will to power over being "estranges him from that with which he is most familiar."[84] Pushed to its logical conclusion, the anthropological will to name, to master, to subdue, to contain the ineffable and ungraspable be-*ing* of being (its whiteness in Melville's text) ends in a reversed metamorphosis: it "turns" being's energies into an "adversarial" ontological force. It ends, as I have suggested elsewhere in attempting to demonstrate the pervasiveness of this insight in the literature of postmodernism, in "ontological invasion."[85] Again to quote Olson:

If man chooses to treat external reality differently than as part of his own process, in other words as anything other than relevant to his own inner life, then he will (being a froward thing, and bound to use his energy willy-nilly, nature is so subtle) use it otherwise. He will use it just exactly as he has used it now for too long, for arbitrary and willful purposes which, in their effects, not only change the face of nature, but actually arrest and divert her force until man turns it even against himself, he is so powerful, this little thing. [The allusion is to the negative consequences of Odysseus's "triumph" over Polyphemus.] But what little willful modern man will not recognize is, that when he turns it against her he turns it against himself.[86]

Let me return to the spatial metaphor privileged by Olson's American contemporaries (and by the later Americanist field-Imaginary). Far from confirming the arrogantly willful effort of Central Man to comprehend and contain the sublime, the terrible mystery of being within the all-encompassing and enclosing circle projected by the metaphysical eye, Melville is interrogating it. For the circular movement ends contradictorily in a collision that breaches the circle, dis-closes the absence at its center. The "conclusion" of Ishmael's erratic "retrospective" ("circular") narrative, that is, reveals the circle idealized as the perfect *All* by Central Man's "transparent eyeball" to be, in fact, the radically imperfect *Zero* of Nothingness. Humanistic Man, the interrogator of being, now becomes the interrogated; the constituter, the constituted. The central panoptic eye (I) is dislocated; it becomes the marginal eyed, as it were. As his retrieval of the etymological resonances of the word "appalling" that he had thematized in "The Whiteness of the Whale" suggests, this inversion is what Ishmael struggles to articulate at the end of "The Chase—First Day," when, in a tremendously resonant visual figure that takes on planetary scope, he depicts the white whale wheeling concentrically around Ahab's central but now marginalized boat:

But soon resuming his horizontal attitude, Moby Dick swam swiftly round and round the wrecked crew; sideways churning the water in his vengeful wake, as if lashing himself up to still another and more deadly assault. The sight of the splintered boat seemed to madden him, as the blood of grapes and mulberries cast before Antiochus' elephants in the book of Maccabees. Meanwhile Ahab half smothered in the foam of the whale's insolent tail, and too much of a cripple to swim,—though he could still keep afloat, even in the heart of such a whirlpool as that; helpless Ahab's head was seen, like a tossed bubble which the least chance shock might burst. From the boat's fragmentary stern, Fedallah incuriously and mildly eyed him; the clinging crew, at the other drifting end, could not succor him; more than enough was it for them to look to themselves. For so revolvingly appalling was the White Whale's aspect, and so planetarily swift the ever-contracting circles he made, that he seemed horizontally swooping upon them. And though the other boats, unharmed, still hovered hard by; still they dared not pull into the eddy to strike, lest that should be the signal for the instant destruction of the jeopardized castaways, Ahab and all; nor in that case could they themselves hope to escape. With straining eyes, then, they remained on the outer edge of the direful zone, whose centre had now become the old man's head. (P. 551)

Again, even more decisively, this absence at the center—the "still point of the turning world," to appropriate the terms of T. S. Eliot's *Four Quartets*— is disclosed by Ishmael at the "end" of his narrative, when the white whale staves the *Pequod,* the very substantial instrument of Ahab's revenge, which goes down into the "yawning gulf," dragging the remaining whaleboat with it: "And now, concentric circles seized the lone boat itself, and all its crew, and each floating oar, and every lance-pole, and spinning, animate and inanimate, all round and round in one vortex, carried the smallest chip of the Pequod out of sight . . . [taking] a living part of heaven along with her" (p. 572). And, as we have been persistently prompted to believe, the (Adamic) American nation.

At the moment when the temporal circle is expected to close on itself, it dis-integrates. A generation ago, R. W. B. Lewis observed that Melville took his point of departure in the American "Matter of Adam" in its latest development: that which rejected the theme of the New Adam of the "party of Hope"—the innocent, solitary individual in the Edenic wilderness of America, who, in opposition to the Adam of the Calvinist "party of Memory" (irredeemably tainted by original sin), has liberately cut himself off from the [European] past—in favor of the Adam of the "Fortunate Fall." This was the Adam who, like Trilling's Hyacinth Robinson, is "transfigured" and dialectically raised above the conflicting partial claims of hopeful possibility and hopeless impossibility by the "experience" of fiery "trial" in the fallen world. It was the Adam, that is, of the "tragic" discourse of what Lewis, clearly with the New Critics in mind, calls "the party of Irony."[87]

It is true, of course, that Melville's matter in *Moby-Dick* is the narrative of the American Adam and that his intervention therein is activated by a profound disillusionment in the hopeful potentialities of America (if not exactly the New Adamic dream) he shares with others like Hawthorne, a disillusionment grounded in the social and political realities of what is metaleptically called the "antebellum" American experience. But it does not follow, unless one is blinded by the oversight of Lewis's Christian humanist version of the "Hegelian" logic, that Melville's "Adamic" novel exists to (partially) fulfill the historical dialectic of the Adamic Matter by bringing the tensions between the New Adam and the Adam of the *Felix Culpa* of nineteenth-century American writing into the peaceful ironic equilibrium of what he calls alternatively "drama," "narrative," "story," and most pointedly "the tragedy of hope." To put Lewis's interpretation of American cultural production in terms of the moral (and political) implications of this dialectical process, it does not follow that Melville's *Moby-Dick* would "transvalue the ["partial," that is, ideological] values" of the Adam of the "Puritans" and the Adam of the "Emersonians" into the morality of "communion," which, like Trilling's "moral realism," raises those who achieve it, despite its insistent reference to this world, into a universality where conflicting claims are *equal* and *in equilibrium*—which is to say, blinds them to the radically *unequal* balance of power that reigns in real history:

The party of Irony [the elder James, Horace Bushnell, Hawthorne, Melville, Henry James the younger, Francis Parkman] consisted of those men who wanted both to undermine and to bolster the image of the American as a new Adam. They urged their generation toward a communion—a renewal of contact—with moral reality and the traditional past, as the way to extend the range of contemporary life and letters. But they did so in the name of those same human and artistic possibilities that the hopeful were proclaiming; their mode of communion, therefore, was inevitably a kind of creative tussle with it object. For the perspective of their irony was not limited to the present; it extended to the past as well, and it threw its ambiguous light upon the sense of evil, as upon the feeling of innocence. Their irony, in short, was in the great tradition: inclusive and charitable, never restrictive. Their aim was to enlarge. The shared purpose of the party of Irony was not to destroy the hopes of the hopeful, but to perfect them.[88]

For, I suggest, Ishmael, under the pressure of the "naught" that is ontologically prior to the Something, now knows that this morality of communion and the ironic community—the national consensus—it would engender is finally no less suspect than the monolithic ethos of collectivity and the sociopolitical collective imposed by Ahab's imperial self, that the difference between the two is a matter of appearance, that, in the language made available to us by contemporary theory—and that Melville in so many remarkable ways anticipates—the one is totalitarian and the other hegemonic.

On the contrary, then, Melville's *Moby-Dick* takes the Adamic Matter into its structure in order to shatter that dialectic by treating the culturally produced myth, not as Lewis and others have done, in psychological or spiritual, but in material terms: in terms, that is, of its consequences for being-in-the-world. If the point of departure of his intervention in *Moby-Dick* is the later Adam who has experienced the disillusionment of serious "post-Emersonian" America, it is not to reject the Adam of "Emersonianism" in favor of the Adam of a Henry James Sr. or a Horace Bushnell or an Orestes Bronson. It is to "show" that these cultural narratives are not separate but, after all, continuous in two crucial and related senses: (1) They are both, despite the variations, internalized discourses ("imaginaries," as Althusser might say) determined by a *logos*—a principle of (self-)presence—

and its "future anterior" mode of interpretation;[89] and (2), as such, they overlook and/or conceal their indissolubly affiliated material consequences: their continuous imperative for a practice of coercion and domination, a practice justified by "a center elsewhere" that is beyond the reach of the freeplay of criticism, which is to say, of the uneven arena of historical struggle. Whether the Adamic Matter takes the form given it by Emerson and Thoreau or Bushnell or James the elder, Whitman and Cooper or (Lewis's version of) Hawthorne, Melville seems to be implying, they are both moments in the circular and darkly constraining history of the Adamic narrative in general.

When the "Matter of Adam" is thus understood as a "cycle," when the "dialectic" is seen as a process that closes back on itself, it can also be seen that the enactment of the Adamic action in its latest phase—one that traces the circular journey promised by the "fortunate fall" from an absolute origin—enacts as well its earlier phase. And in so doing, the narrative journey of the "masterpieces" of American literature, in fact, reenact the narrative journey of virtually all the "masterpieces" of the Western literary tradition. I mean the narrative journey that begins with Adam's naming of the beasts, has its middle in the violence against the naming *logos* and his (and Eve's) exile from the at-homeness (the canniness) of the Edenic fatherland into the uncanniness (the not-at-homeness) of *this (temporal) world*, and its end,—thanks to the trials (the radically differential or antithetical experience) of being-in-the-world and the pity and terror (the dread) that it precipitates—in the dialectical recuperation of the origin or center (however more complex, that is, "impervious to irony"), a recuperation that neutralizes the bite of differential time in the internalized equilibrium of its inclusive and now balanced and identical circle.

Ishmael's narrative indeed repeats this circular Adamic journey, but, as I have tried to suggest, it does not end according to the dictates of the Adamic action's dialectical logic. It ends *differently*, in the disclosure of a (the) difference that makes a difference. To put this in terms of Melville's formal purpose, the Adamic "narrative" of *Moby-Dick* in fact destroys the Adamic imagination and its romance of the American Adam, not simply that historically unfettered imagination that takes its point of departure in the New Adam, but also that "imagination of disaster" which takes its point of departure in the Fallen Adam.

As Ishmael had intuited after his account of the *Pequod's* meeting with the *Albatross*, "the first encountered ship,"[90] and is in the "end" at pains to emphasize, the circumnavigating voyage of the *Pequod* does not end, as Ahab had determined and his crew expected, with its return home, with the closing of the recuperative and all-inclusive circle. It ends, rather, in the empty center, in what one might call, borrowing from Thomas Pynchon (one of Melville's contemporary "offspring") and retrieving Ishmael's reference in "The Mast-head," the "zero zone" of the white Descartian vortext. It ends in the centerless and abyssal "middle," before which there is no beginning (*arché*) and after which there is no end (*télos*)—in both senses of the word: "Now small fowls flew screaming over the yet yawning gulf; a sullen white surf beat against its steep sides; then *all* collapsed, and the great shroud ["pall"] of the sea rolled on as it rolled five thousand years ago" (p. 572, my emphasis).

If this catastrophe, this destruction of an entire community of human beings in the name of Ahab's Adamic nominative principle of self-reliance or absolute freedom, is tragic, it is tragic neither in the Aristotelian, nor, more immediately, in the New Critical or Trillingian sense of the term. The dynamics of Ishmael's errant narrative emphasizes neither the consolatory grandeur of Ahab's terrible hubris nor the equilibrium of antithetical psychic/aesthetic impulses/tensions or the dialectically synthesized ethical antithesis—the "moral realism"—of "the imagination of disaster." It focalizes rather the appalling destructiveness of Ahab's—and, by extension, American Man's—"tremendous centralization" and its practical imperatives. Whatever the degree of Melville's conscious affiliation with the tragic literary tradition, what *Moby-Dick* in fact "accomplishes" is the destruction of the privileged ontology of the principle of presence, the spatializing eye (I) it empowers, and the centered circle into which it structures *all* things in space and *all* events in time—*and* their American Adamic allotropes—and in so doing, the "tragic vision." For, as the analogy between Aristotle's definition of tragedy and his metaphysics of the unmoved mover makes clear, it is the ontology of presence and the figuration of its operations in the centered circle that has authorized and empowered the *Idea* of tragedy and given it the privileged status, whatever the variations in the form it has taken and the names by which it has been called, that it has enjoyed in the literary/critical tradition, not simply of the Old World but of the "New."

At this point, a New Americanist might object that my destruction of the tragic representation of the Ahabian action and the consequent precipitation of a "political" or ideological reading that involves Ishmael's self-critique of his vow and dissociation from Ahab and his murderous ontological/political monism reinscribes the Old Americanist discourse in even a more overtly ideological way. More specifically, it might be said that my reading affiliates itself with that earlier displacement of the center of critical attention from Ahab to Ishmael, which, in privileging Ishmael's struggle for his freedom against the otherwise irresistible power of Ahab's totalitarianism, appropriated Melville's novel for the cause of the Cold War national consensus: with the reading, according to Donald Pease, most clearly formulated by Walter Bezanson, that represents Ishmael's dissociation from Ahab as the triumph of the American principle of the organic sovereign self over the mechanized collective state, individual freedom over totalitarian tyranny.

But this, as my emphasis on Ishmael's discovery that the Oneness of being, mechanical or organic, is a construct, that behind the center of the representational circle there is nothing, should make clear, is precisely what the destruction of the representation of *Moby-Dick* as tragedy does not do. What it does, in thematizing Ishmael's discovery of the absence of (self-)presence, is, rather, to focalize (1) the intuition of the complicitous continuity between the self-reliant self and the totalitarian self (in Pease's terms, between individual freedom and absolute freedom). And (2), in so doing, it precipitates an e-mergence from that relay, one which, as I will show, renders Ishmael's narrative neither a story that internalizes and reconciles oppositional forces (as in tragedy or romance) nor a story about individual salvation in the face of an utterly indifferent universe, but a social text that resonates, however unevenly actualized, all across the indissoluble continuum of being, from the ontological through the cultural to the economic and sociopolitical sites. As social text, it anticipates the difficult posthumanist search for a collective sociopolitical counterhegemonic project that is "grounded" in an absent cause. But before we can take this leap from the preceding focus on Ishmael's "individual" disaffiliation from Ahab's will to the emergent sociopolitical implications that Ishmael is attempting to think, it is necessary to "dive deeper" into the "conclusion" of Ishmael's narrative at the site that he and we have over-determined: the ontological.

Like the Heideggerian hermeneutic project, Ishmael's errant narrative constitutes a simultaneous de-structive/projective—an e-mergent—act, not simply a negative critique of the New Adamic will to power informing Ahab's ontological monism, but also and even more important, a retrieval and affirmation of what the logocentric structure of the Adamic narrative closes off and eventually forgets: the "Naught," which is to say, temporality or, more precisely, the differences that temporality disseminates, and the temporal/differential measure of the human occasion. "But to bury the past in nullity," we recall from Heidegger, "is not the purpose of the destruction; its aim is essentially positive." This positive phase of Ishmael's destructive text, which has been more or less underdeveloped or, rather, latent until this "climactic" point, suddenly discloses itself, however indefinitely, in the chapter following Ishmael's account of Pip's abandonment by Stubb, in which he anticipates "what like abandonment befell myself." Pip "dives" into the "wondrous depths, where strange shapes of the unwarped primal world glided to and fro before his passive eyes; and the miser-merman, Wisdom, revealed his hoarded heaps," a kind of uncanny primordial knowledge which "to reason, is absurd and frantic" (p. 414). In the next chapter ("A Squeeze of the Hand"), perhaps precipitated by the memory of a plunge similar to Pip's into the depths of the destructive element, Ishmael recalls the gratuitous moment when, while squeezing sperm he effectively abjures the terrible oath of violence he took against the white whale:

As I sat there at my ease, cross-legged on the deck, after the bitter exertion of the windlass; under a blue tranquil sky; the ship under indolent sail, and gliding serenely along; as I bathed my hands among those soft, gentle globules of infiltrated tissues, woven almost within the hour; as they richly broke to my fingers, and discharged all their opulence, like fully ripe grapes their wine; as I snuffed up that uncontaminated aroma,—literally and truly, like the smell of spring violets; I declare to you, that for the time I lived as in a musky meadow; I forgot all about our horrible oath; in that inexpressible sperm, I washed my hands and my heart of it; I almost began to credit the old Paracelsan superstition that sperm is of rare virtue in allaying the heat of anger: while bathing in that bath, I felt divinely free from all ill-will, petulence, or malice, of any sort whatsoever. (P. 416)

In thus retrieving his renunciation of the oath of violence, Ishmael begins to perceive that this crucial gesture of remembrance disengages him from the centralized and integrated crowd, which can only do violence in that instrumentalized capacity. Simultaneously, Ishmael opens up the possibility of a different kind of relationship with such a polyglot crew, a relationship not of an effective solidarity grounded in the principle of essential identity, but of a care-ful generosity—what Heidegger calls *Mitsein* (being-with) in *Being and Time*—activated by the recognition of the absence of (self-)presence.

What Ishmael actually articulates at this point is, as he well knows, both sentimental and unattainable in this world, and so he does not take it seriously. But it does anticipate the ultimate disclosure that comes in Ishmael's "Epilogue," which, as *epi-logos*, a word that is "beside" or "against" the Word, "upwards bursts," as it were, from the "vital center" of his troping narrative. Despite the familiarity of its terms, the "Epilogue" demands full quotation for the dislocation of the received meanings of its parts activated by the recognition of the "post-ultimacy" of this moment in Ishmael's text:

> The drama's done. Why then here does anyone step forth?—Because one did survive that wreck.
>
> It so chanced, that after the Parsee's disappearance, I was he whom the Fates ordained to take the place of Ahab's bowsman. When that bowsman assumed the vacant post; the same, who, when on the last day the three men were tossed from out the rocking boat, was dropped astern. So, floating at the margin of the ensuing scene, and in full sight of it, when the half-spent suction of the sunk ship reached me, I was then, but slowly, drawn towards the closing vortex. When I reached it, it had subsided to a creamy pool. Round and round, then, and ever contracting towards the button-like black bubble at the axis of that slowly wheeling circle, like another Ixion I did revolve. Till, gaining that vital centre the black bubble upward burst; and now, liberated by reason of its cunning spring, and, owing to its great buoyancy, rising with great force, the coffin life-buoy shot lengthwise from the sea, fell over, and floated by my side. Buoyed up by that coffin, for almost one whole day and night, I floated on a soft and dirge-like main. The unharming sharks, they glided by as if with padlocks on their mouths; the savage sea-hawks sailed with sheathed beaks. On the second day, a sail drew near, nearer, and pick me up at last. It was the devious-cruising Rachel, that in her retracing search after her missing children, only found another orphan. (P. 573)

"The drama's done. Why then here does anyone step forth?" Why, then, this epi-*logos* or supplement? this stepping forth across the bounding line of the traditional narrative determined by the "talismanic secret" or "Transcendental Signified"? In the temporal process of "re-telling" his "ancient mariner's" tale to the landsman listener, Ishmael does not come home again like the hero of the romance or more subtly of tragedy. He does not discover the still point in the turning world that certifies his fathered centrality in the cosmic scheme of things, in *physis*. At the end of his narrative journey he discovers the centerlessness of being, and that discovery de-centers him, renders him marginal. His "proper self"—the self-present (male) self of the self-reliant "Central Man" of the humanistic tradition whom Emerson and Thoreau and Whitman and Cooper would reinscribe into the romance of American culture—or the more complex but affiliated self-present self of Tragic Man of a certain Hawthorne or Henry James the elder—becomes the "ec-centric," or "ex-orbitant," self. I mean the self that, according to Nietzsche, Heidegger, Lacan, Irigaray, Derrida, Foucault, and many contemporary novelists and poets, the Western tradition at large has existed to discipline and reform in and for its symbolic order.

At the "end" of his narrative, Ishmael, as we have noted, comes to perceive the centered circle as a vortex, the All as zero. But as the declaration and the disruptive question that follows it in the "Epilogue" suggests, it is only now, by way of his "stepping forth"—his "ek-sisting"—that he realizes that the destruction of the circle as All is what has precipitated his "saving" errant "book." "Disintegrated from the One," as Starbuck could not be because of his commitment to the enterprising self of the "Nantucket market," by his recognition of metaphysics as a broken instrument (a recognition underscored by his ironic repetition of the metaphor of the Fates he had called into question in the beginning of his story) and his renunciation of violence against the white whale, Ishmael now understands and acknowledges mortality (Queequeg's coffin) as the absence of presence at the center of being. He thus liberates himself from whatever remaining hold the "abiding" patriarchal Word has on him. (It should not be overlooked that Ishmael is picked up by the "devious-cruising Rachel," a whaling ship of males hitherto on Man's [phallic] business, but now acting under the sign of women.)[91] And he divests himself of the vestigial remains of the coercive patriarchal genetic structure— the inclusive circle and its symbolic order that the patriarchal Word actualizes—which is the geo-metric measure legitimized by the American landsmen's philosophy of (Adamic) "Presence." Having "leaped in the circle primordially and wholly," as it were, Ishmael's circular story has precipitated not identity but difference.

To put this dislocation positively, an e-mergent Ishmael acknowledges his "orphanage," his being "at sea," as it were, concerning his "parentage," as the permanent condition of men and women in the world. But this orphanage, it is important to point out, is emphatically not to be understood as, say, R. W. B. Lewis does in appropriating Alexis de Tocqueville's analysis of American culture: as that rejection of the European Father in behalf of the American Adam, who, whether celebrating his lack of a patriarchal past like the Adam of Emerson and Thoreau, or, disturbed by its ambivalence, like the Adam of the "Fortunate Fall," will father himself. As orphan, Ishmael, in other words, does not perpetuate the American romance of the "saving remnant":

'Twas a most heavy Trial of their Patience, whereto they were called the first Winter of this their *Pilgrimage,* and enough to convince them, and remind them, that they were but *Pilgrims.* . . . But what a wonder was it that all the Bloody Salvages far and near did not cut off this *little Remnant!* If he that once muzzled the *Lions* ready to devour the Man of Desires, had not *Admirably,* I had almost said, *Miraculously* restrained them, *These* had been all devoured! But this People of God were come into a *Wilderness* to *Worship Him,* and so *He* kept their Enemies from such Attempts, as would otherwise have soon *annihilated* this Poor Handful of Men, thus far already diminished.[92]

I am referring to that fundamentally conservative allotrope of the Adamic story that has its origins in the Puritan narrative and extends down to the present in, for example, the cultural discourse of the dominant traditionalists of the post–Vietnam War decades, in their concerted campaign to represent exponents of contemporary critical theory—feminists, black critics, poststructuralists, genealogists, neo-Marxists, and so on—not simply as having taken over the Academy but as having imposed a "politically correct" orthodoxy that has marginalized the bearers of the remains of "Our Heritage."[93] This, more specifically, is the Hebrew/Roman mythic narrative that represents the disintegration of the Patriarchal City—the national consensus—by ungodly/irrational/ evil forces and the escape and the journey of a handful of "orphaned" relic- or seed-bearers, who, in the face of adversity, hardship, deprivation, and massive resistance, are destined not only to rebuild the city but extend its circumference, its sway over others, in the name of the seed or relic.

In an earlier meditation on being-in-the-world, Ishmael suggests the importance he attributes to the metaphor of ontological orphanage:

Would to God these blessed calms would last. But the mingled, mingling threads of life are woven by warp and woof: calms crossed by storms, a storm for every calm. There is no steady unretracing progress in this life; we do not advance through fixed gradations, and at the last one pause:—through infancy's unconscious spell, boyhood's thoughtless faith, adolescence' doubt (the common doom), then scepticism, then disbelief, resting at last in manhood's pondering repose of If. But once gone through, we trace the round again; and are infants, boys, and men, and If's eternally. Where lies the final harbor, whence we unmoor no more? In what rapt ether sails the world, of which the weariest will never weary? Where is the foundling's father hidden? Our souls are like those orphans whose unwedded mothers die in bearing them: the secret of our paternity lies in their grave, and we must there to learn it. (P. 492)

In this passage, which invokes the myth of the American Adam in terms of the theme of maturity, Ishmael (like his domestic counterpart, Pierre) acknowledges the absence of presence this side of the grave and dislocates and disseminates its genetic/dynastic metaphorics: that privileged (ontological, cultural, and sociopolitical) imaginary which posits maturation as a process of gestation in which the seed, by way of cultivation, becomes fruit. Or, rather, he shows it—as Melville will again in *Pierre*, though with far greater force—to be an always unstable "as if," an ideological construct, a "supreme fiction" in Wallace Stevens's terms, that always already defers Identity.

At this point in his narrative, Ishmael's insight into this deferral of the Father, the principle of Presence that renders Man a foundling or prodigal who can never *arrive*, can never complete the circuitous, recollective journey back to the prelapsarian "haven" of the fatherland, is accompanied by a profound pessimism. In his "Epilogue," however, after the "drama is done," Ishmael's dark recognition of the absolute, anxiety-provoking uncanniness of being-in-the-world paradoxically assumes a more positive resonance. Indeed, it becomes the projection of his de-structive narrative: an affirmation of his divestment, his carpetbagging, or, in Heidegger's terms, his mortal "poverty": his thrownness in the not-at-home (*Unheimlichkeit*). Ishmael's own rhetoric not only interrogates the romance tradition beginning with Plautus and the Greek "Sophist" romances of the second century A.D. and extending through Fielding's *Tom Jones*, to James Fenimore Cooper's *The Pioneers*, Mark Twain's *Puddin'head Wilson*, and James's *The Princess Casamassima*, in which the foundling or orphan turns out at the end of a circuitous journey through the "devious" world to be "legitimate." It also becomes a celebration, however necessarily dark, of his orphaned marginality. Having, like Bulkington and Pip, immersed himself totally in the destructive element, the realm of "accident," as it were, Ishmael has explicitly acknowledged orphaned errancy—the decentered self and its "as if"—as the measure of his occasion, of *being there* (*Da-sein*). If we recall the complex etymological resonance of the word "occasion," we realize that Ishmael/Melville destroys the sedimented Idea of the Occident sponsored in the name of the New Adam by his landsmen contemporaries—and those modern American critics who are their filial heirs—and retrieves its original living intensities.

Ishmael becomes a wester(n)er, not in the sense of the American frontiersman, who, in the name of a Manifest Destiny enabled by the Puritan errand in the wilderness, ruthlessly colonized and pacified the American continent, but in the sense of an American fully conscious of his orphaned status as "eternal If" with its anxieties and risks, yet able not only to dance a seaman's jig over the always present abyss, but in the transgressive process to call into question all the practices empowered by the Adamic principle of presence. Ishmael, in short, becomes the living "voice" of the American "seaman," Bulkington—the American who has never been—and his sprawling and digressive destructive chronicle, the epitaph to Bulkington's memory, which earlier in his narrative, Ishmael could only inscribe in a "six-inch chapter" (p. 106), a "well-wrought turn," as it were.[94] In addressing the question of the "disappearance" of Bulkington from Melville's novel, Richard Chase observes:

Bulkington disappears from *Moby-Dick* because if he had been more a part of the story it would have been inevitable that he should do what Starbuck can only try to do: oppose the command of Ahab and save the ship. But there is another reason why we do not see more of Bulkington. Melville himself does not see much of him. We know that he is a Promethean figure, who can save man from catastrophe and lead him safely through the creative rhythms which constitute growth, just as Bulkington's career is run to the rhythm of his repeated passages to sea and back to land again. But Bulkington eludes exact description. He is the stuff and energy of personality in the act of setting forth toward fulfillment. To employ the image of withdrawal and return, we see Bulkington just as he emerges on the returning beat—just as he is setting forth to sea. We know that he is the hope of the world because he is the heroic American—the Handsome Sailor, as Melville calls this heroic figure in *Billy Budd*. He is the titanic body of America (as the word 'Bulkington' suggests) stirring out of the uncreated night and passing ponderously into motion and consciousness.[95]

Disappear Bulkington does, indeed. But not, I am suggesting, because Melville did not see him quite clearly enough to monumentalize him in this narrative, did not, that is, consciously recognize him as the symbol of a future America that was to shape mankind in its Promethean image and in the process save it from the tyranny of (Communist) totalitarianism. Melville, like Nietzsche and Foucault, knew too much about monuments, as *Pierre* and especially *Israel Potter* strikingly testify in their profound solicitation of the monumentalizing American Cultural Memory. On the contrary, Bulkington's disappearance from *Moby-Dick* is a disappearance from history enacted by a "monumental history" that "bar[s] access to the actual intensities of creative life."[96] He is the differential American who, given the power over the American experience wielded by the "suprahistorical" historical perspective enabled by the prefigurative providential history of the New England Puritans, could never be. Or, rather, to put it in terms of Michel Foucault's critical genealogy, he is an image of the disinherited "Americans"—the "renegades, castaways, mariners"—who have no history, because American history, from Puritanism (its practice of preterition) to the present, has existed to obliterate their differential presence—and their disconcerting and threatening unfilial force.

At the "end" of his explorative, we might say now, genealogical, narrative, then, Ishmael achieves an ontological Repetition. By refusing the archival metaphysical imperative to begin from the end, or, put positively, by "leaping into the [hermeneutic] circle primordially and wholly," Ishmael in the "end" discovers not presence, but difference: the "meaning" of the name he has substituted for the patronym he has refused and has asked his listeners to call him in the "beginning" of his periplus. "Call me Ishmael": as thrown being-in-the-world he is called to be a nameless orphan, an eternal exile, an errant wanderer, a nomad at the margin, saying the un-Word—the eternal as if—in the face of "every man." Against those pious landsmen (*das Man*) who will call him "a wild man" in their gravely monolithic effort to secure the Paternal Word, its binarist logic, and its encompassing genetic/dynastic Adamic measure, he will assert the dislocating and irreverent freeplay of his careful errancy. Or, to invoke the other central metaphor he destroys in the "end," Ishmael is "vomited out" of the bottomless maw of the Leviathanic deep, not to become the subdued, docile, and obedient "anointed pilot-prophet of God," the Father, who will reproduce and perpetuate the circular lineage, but the errant, even devious, antiprophet (antiseer) of the Zero Zone, the eccentric who thinks temporality and the differences it disseminates and tells, not the original and abiding Word, but always already erring *words*. His "free and easy sort of genial" affirmation of the decentered self is, indeed, a "desperado philosophy," as Ishmael says early in his narrative ("The Hymn," p. 226), one reminding us of Nietzsche's corrosive laughter echoing across the abyss. But it is more than that, or, at any rate, something more than what the phrase means according to the demonizing binary logic of landsmen. For in acknowledging his orphanage, Ishmael also discovers the ontological difference that temporality disseminates, the difference that, in always already deferring presence, makes things-as-they-are in the world make a difference. In "washing his hand and heart of the oath of violence" as an act of ontological carelessness, as complicity with nihilism, Ishmael discovers *care* (the essential existential structure of *Dasein*, according to Heidegger) in the face of being, a care that, unlike Ahab's ontologically validated Adamic will to name, lets mystery be, a care that precipitates what Heidegger calls *Gelassenheit* as *Dasein's* appropriate comportment towards being. This "letting be" is not a quiescent passivity, it should be emphasized, but an active passiveness—a de-structive/projective measure that manifests itself as simultaneously negational and emancipatory. Like the "devious-cruising Rachel," which, in the midst, abandons the end (the whole) for the sake of the part, even at the expense of mastery and finality, so in the face of Ahab's "unerring" ontological monomania, Ishmael learns the positive implication of deviance (from the Latin, "to stray from the [right] way") that the American Adamic tradition in its "unswerving" rage for an accumulative order has not simply concealed and forgotten, but subdued and pacified in the name of the Word.[97]

To appropriate the language of *Pierre*, the "shock of his extraordinary emergency" precipitates Ishmael's emergence.[98]

ISHMAEL AND NEGATIVE CAPABILITY

In thus renouncing the impulse to master, Ishmael, it might be said, discovers what Keats called "Negative Capability":

& at once it struck me, what quality went to form a Man of Achievement, especially in Literature & which Shakespeare possessed so enormously—I mean *Negative Capability*, that is when man is capable of being in uncertainties, Mysteries, doubts, without any irritable reaching after fact & reason—Coleridge, for instance, would let go by a fine isolated verisimilitude caught from the Penetralium of mystery, from being incapable of remaining content with half knowledge.[99]

At this point, no doubt, both Old and New Americanists will be quick to point out that my invocation of Keats's paradoxical phrase confirms rather than delegitimates the Old Americanists' representation of the American romance in general and *Moby-Dick* in particular—and, as in the case of Lionel Trilling, justifies their negative evaluation and marginalization of a body of American writing that either rejects the aesthetic/moral imperatives of negative capability in favor of an "irritable" ideological "reaching after fact and reason" or is, in its confusion of idea with ideology, incapable of it:

There is a traditional and aggressive rationalism that can understand thought only in its conscious, developed form and believes that the phrase "unconscious mind" is a meaningless contradiction in terms. . . . But the extreme rationalist position ignores the simple fact that the life of reason, at least in its most extensive part, begins in the emotions. What comes into being when two contradictory emotions are made to confront each other and are required to have a relationship with each other is . . . quite properly called an idea. Ideas may also be said to be generated in the opposition of ideals, and in the felt awareness of the impact of new circumstances, upon old forms of feeling and estimation, in the response to the conflict between new exigencies and old pieties. And it can be said that a world will have what I have been calling cogency in the degree that the confronting emotions go deep, or in the degree that the old pieties are firmly held and the new exigencies strongly apprehended. In Hemingway's stories a strongly charged piety towards the ideals and attachments of boyhood and the lusts of maturity is in conflict not only with the imagination of death but also with that imagination as it is peculiarly modified by the dark negation of the modern world. Faulkner as a Southerner of today, a man deeply implicated in the pieties of his tradition, is of course at the very heart of an exigent historical event which thrusts upon him the awareness of the inadequacy and wrongness of the very tradition he loves. In the world of both men the cogency is a function not of their conscious but of their unconscious minds. We can . . . regret the deficiency of consciousness, blaming it for the inadequacy of both our American writers of the talent for generalization. Yet it is to be remarked that the unconscious minds of both men have wisdom and humility about themselves. They seldom make the attempt at formulated solution, they rest content with the 'negative capability.' And this negative capability, this willingness to remain in uncertainties, mysteries, and doubts, is not, as one tendency of modern feeling would suppose, an abdication of intellectual activity. Quite to the contrary, it is precisely an aspect of their intelligence, of their seeing the full force and complexity of their subject matter.[100]

This is not the place to interrogate the structural binary logic that determines Trilling's distinction between a discourse of ideas and a discourse of ideology. Suffice it to say that such an interrogation would ask whether the deep, originating emotions that are prior to conscious thought are natural (the expression of a self-present subject) or are themselves the product of social determination, whether the "unconscious" he posits as the proper origin of the idea against a traditional "aggressive rationalism" is not itself, however more complex, inscribed by the ideology of the dominant culture. It would ask, that is, whether Trilling's binarism does not preclude an understanding of conscious thought that is both existential and structural, simultaneously active and passive and, in so doing, contribute to the formation of an insidious discourse of hegemony. What for my purposes needs comment has to do with Trilling's assertion against those "ideological" critics who criticize "negative capability" thus defined as "an abdication of intellectual activity" that "it is precisely an aspect of [his writers'] intelligence, of their *seeing* the full force and complexity of their subject matter." For, however forceful his warning against an intellectual activity that reduces the complexities of the occasion, to represent negative capability this way is to authorize the displacement of the active intelligence from the world of action, to internalize the conflicts of this world in the individual subject, which, as a seer above the scene of struggle, enables the equalizing of the unequal forces at play in the world. Trilling names this elevated perspective "wisdom and humility." In so doing he is, of course, appealing to the discourse of the Western humanistic tradition—"the best that has been thought and said in the world"— which has universalized and sanctified them. But in the context of the retrieved world they come to mean something different: not simply withdrawal from the *agora*, nor active resistance to those who contribute their intellectual practice to struggles of liberation, but also tacit support of the dominant force in the unequal balance of power relations.[101]

To read Ishmael's achievement of negative capability in this Trillingian way, I submit, is to lend *Moby-Dick* to such a complicitous end. And this, as I have been at some pains to suggest in putting Ishmael's self-disclosure in terms of Heidegger's destructive hermeneutics, is not simply what Melville does not want to do; indeed, it is what he is actively resisting in *Moby-Dick*. The attribution of Keats's phrase to the self-destruction of Ishmael's "American" self, in other words, is appropriate only if we think its oxymoronic resonance, which is to say Keats's definition of negative capability—the creative perspective of the "Man of Achievement"—in its entirety: not simply the adjective but also and *simultaneously* the noun, as Trilling, in his effort to privilege a Modernist—and "end-of-ideology"—American literature does not. Given his Godwinian addressee (Dilke) in his epistolary account of his conversation to his brother, George, one would expect Keats to invoke, say, Godwin after naming the "irritable reaching after fact and reason" as that which negative capability is not. Instead—and, not incidentally, he gives the example of Coleridge. In other words, Keats posits negative capability not merely against a "liberal," ideological writing, powered by an "aggressive rationalism that can understand thought only in its conscious, developed form." He also and above all posits it against a certain Romantic/symbolist writing, which, in privileging the reconciling powers of the "esemplastic imagination," Keats implies, is not simply blinded to "a fine verisimilitude caught from the Penetralium of mystery" by its insight. In accommodating difference to the circle of the anthropological self (the "primary Imagination"), in repeating "in the finite mind . . . the eternal act of creation in the infinite I Am,"[102] this Coleridgian imagination represses "it." Keats also posits negative capability, that is, against a writing that informs the critical/cultural discourse of Emerson and, according to the Old Americanists, the writers of the "American Renaissance" at their best.

To think Ishmael's discovery (and the art of *Moby-Dick*) as negative capability is to transvalue both its terms—and to understand it, not as a precursor of Modernism, but postmodernism: the negative aura of *"negative"* is thus infused with a positive, and the positive aura of *capability* with a negative. Negative capability is certainly not, as Trilling rightly implies, an ideological practice understood in its vulgar sense, but it is also not a passive mode of "active" intellection. Admittedly, Keats does not thematize what negative capability *liberates* from the inclusive circle in which it has been colonized by the esemplastic imagination, but the definition as such does sanction such a project.

The negatively capable or destructive-projective process that I am attempting to elucidate, it is important to emphasize, is a simultaneous practice, but for the sake of analysis it becomes necessary to separate its oneness out into two phases. Unlike Coleridge's esemplastic imagination or Emerson's American version of it, which in fulfilling the imperatives of its logical economy, ends, as in the case of Captain Ahab, in a violent will to power that alienates the very being it would comprehend, Ishmael/Melville's negative capability brings being near, not in the sense of closing a distance but of activating awareness of what he was hitherto not aware.[103] His *act* of de-structuring or, in Derrida's resonant term, of "soliciting" the Coleridgian/Emersonian anthropological ontology, that is, both exposes the contradictory phenomena that the will to power of the latter represses and contains all along the continuum of being, and renders him capable of thinking them *as* difference, in terms of the measure of their occasion. Negative capability precipitates presencing (*An-Wesen*).

This interested "wresting [of the difference that temporality disseminates] by violence" from the comprehensive circle of metaphysical denomination, to put it in Heidegger's terms, explains Ishmael's communal relation to—his being-with—the "wholly other" Queequeg and, more inclusively, his "being-with" being in all its particular manifestations, a relationship not of abasement to a "tremendous centralization" *but one grounded in the acknowledgment of the absence of presence.* In the introductory chapter of his narrative, we recall, Ishmael contrasts the landsman's socially inscribed and sedimented indifference to the pull of mystery with his own inexplicable explorative impulse: "But as for me, I am tormented with an everlasting itch for things remote. I love to sail forbidden seas, and land on barbarous coasts. Not ignoring what is good, I am quick to perceive a horror, and could still be social with it—would they let me—since it is but well to be on friendly terms with all the inmates of the place one lodges in" (p. 7). In his recollective reading of *Moby-Dick*, Richard Sewall, following the lead of R. W. B. Lewis, interprets this passage as a manifestation of Ishmael's "shallow [American] optimism" against which Melville will pit his "tragic vision." Reading *Moby-Dick* temporally, however, we, like Ishmael, come to understand the "meaning" of this not-so-evident passage, like the name "Ishmael," for the first time. If Ishmael's expression of sociability is shallow, it is not in Sewall's sense of the word: an easy, innocent, and unearned affirmation of a prelapsarian Adam that is grounded in the incarnate *logos* of the tragic vision of the "fortunate fall." It is, rather, an intuition into a relationship with being that refuses the consolations of the tragic *logos*. In the corrosive process of his destructive narrative, in other words, Ishmael discovers and acknowledges the nameless and dreadful uncertainties—the ontological difference, as it were, which is the groundless ground of temporality and the differences it disseminates—that a tremendously centralized "they" (including himself) had suppressed—leveled to Identity—in behalf of alleviating its anxieties in the face of the dreaded whiteness of the whale. And if Ishmael does not adequately think the multisituated differences thus disclosed by his destruction of the "shallow" representation of being posited by the Adamic myth of the "fortunate fall," it at least prepares the way for such a thinking.

What I am suggesting about the overdetermined question of being is this. Melville's destruction of the anthropomorphic will of "Central Man," specifically, his disclosure of human being's ontological orphanage, constitutes a remarkable anticipation, not of the "negative capability" that Trilling, and other Old Americanists, by way of the dialectic or irony of the New Critics, attribute to that American tradition inaugurated by Emerson and Thoreau, deepened by Hawthorne and Melville, fulfilled by Henry James, and, after a rupture, recuperated in part—as a mnemonic and promissary relic—by a "saving remnant" of Modernists, consisting primarily of F. Scott Fitzgerald (*The Great Gatsby*), Ernest Hemingway (the Nick Adams stories), William Faulkner (*The Bear*), and, for some, T. S. Eliot. Rather Melville's destruction of the *anthropologos* prepares the ground for the "negative capability" of the "loose and baggy" company of postmodern American writers, whose open-ended or, rather, opening (doubling) texts are informed by an ontological understanding of being intended to destroy the metaphysics—the monumentalizing perception of *physis* from the end or above—that determines the representation of being in the American canonical tradition. To put this differentiation in the terms of Foucault's Nietzschean critical genealogy, in retrieving human being's ontological orphanage—its marginality, its accidental status, its thrownness in the world—as measure, the negative capability of Melville's text does not manifest itself in the privileging of an Origin whose (patriarchal) "story is always sung as a theogony," but in a irony-propelled demystification of the Origin that manifests itself as "effective history," as a mockery of the high seriousness of the Adamic narrative in behalf of retrieving man's "lowly" occasion, of liberating the "actual intensities and creations of life" to which the high theogonic song has barred access:

[Effective] history also teaches how to laugh at the solemnities of the origin. The lofty origin is no more than "a metaphysical extension which arises from the belief that things are most precious and essential at the moment of birth." We tend to think that this is the moment of their greatest perfection, when they emerged dazzling from the hands of a creator or in the shadow night of a first morning. The origin precedes the Fall. It comes before the body, before the world and time; it is associated with the gods, and its story is always sung as a theogony. But historical beginnings are lowly: not in the sense of modest or discreet like the steps of a dove, but derisive and ironic, capable of undoing every infatuation. "We wished to awaken the feeling of man's sovereignty by showing his divine birth: this path is now forbidden, since a monkey stands at the entrance."[104]

It is not to James or Fitzgerald or Hemingway or Faulkner or Eliot that Melville's negatively capable ontology speaks; it is rather to American postmodernists as diverse as the Wallace Stevens of "An Ordinary Evening in New Haven," the Charles Olson of *The Maximus Poems,* the Thomas Pynchon of *Gravity's Rainbow,* the Robert Coover of *The Public Burning,* and the Michael Herr of *Dispatches,* even the Kathy Acker of *Blood and Guts in High School,* all of whose writing in some degree or other has its condition of possibility in the absent cause and, to invoke the instance of Stevens, exists to deconstruct the "Omega," which is to say, to render the *story* of the Alpha, like Melville's *King Lear* or *Hamlet,* always already different:

Reality is the beginning not the end,
Naked Alpha, not the hierophant Omega,
Of dense investiture, with luminous vassals.

It is the infant *A* standing on infant legs,
Not twisted, stooping, polymathic *Z,*
He that kneels always on the edge of space

In the pallid perceptions of its distances.
Alpha fears men or else Omega's men
Or else his prolongations of the human.

These characters are around us in the scene.
For one it is enough; for one it is not:
For neither is it profound absentia.

Since both alike appoint themselves the choice
Custodians of the glory of the scene.
The immaculate interpreters of life

But that's the difference: in the end and the way
To the end. Alpha continues to begin.
Omega is refreshed at every end.[105]

This (unstable) affiliative bond with Melville is, in fact, one to which
Charles Olson insistently refers in the prose which articulates the enabling tendencies of his postmodern poetry. Thus, for example, in an
important essay-review of Milton K. Sterns's tellingly entitled study of
Melville's fiction, *The Fine Hammered Steel of Herman Melville*, he invokes
Melville's statement (in his letter to Hawthorne) that "[b]y visible truth,
we mean the apprehension of the absolute condition of present things,"
and suggests that Melville was interrogating not only the idealistic ontology informing the Symbolist literature of the American romance tradition,
but also its binary opposite, the naturalism Sterns attributes to Melville,
the naturalism, not incidentally, which Trilling identifies with the ideology of Parrington and Dreiser. Both in ontology and language, according
to Olson, Melville was, in fact, attempting to retrieve "quantity as intensive" from the "rigidities of the discrete"—the modern, especially American, allotrope of the metaphysical "universe of discourse" established by
the classical Greeks[106]—and the will to power that informs them. In doing
so, according to Olson, Melville was contributing to the postmodern
project, which Keats "initiated" when he derailed Hegel's unerring "Ahabian" metaphysical engine, by which, it should be remarked, he means in
part, the dialectics of the *Aufhebung* that, according to the Old Americanists, constitutes the essence of the American romance:

Two years before Melville was born John Keats, walking home from the mummers'
play at Christmas 1817, and afterwards, he'd had to listen to Coleridge again,
thought to himself all this irritable reaching after fact and reason, it won't do. I
don't believe in it. I do better to stay in the condition of things. No matter what it
amounts to, mystery confusion doubt, it has a power, it is what I mean by *Negative
Capability*.

Keats, without setting out to, had put across the century the inch of steel to
wreck Hegel, if anything could. Within five years, two geometers, Bolyai and
Lobatschewsky, weren't any longer satisfied with Euclid's picture of the world, and

they each made a new one, independently of each other, and remarkably alike. It took thirty-one years (Melville's age when he wrote *Moby-Dick*) for the German mathematician Riemann to define the real as men since have exploited it: he distinguishes two kinds of manifold, the discrete (which would be the old system, and it includes discourse, language as it had been since Socrates) and, what he took to be more true, the continuous.

Melville, not knowing any of this but in it even more as an American, down to his hips in things, was a first practicer . . . of the new equation, quantity as intensive.[107]

Here as elsewhere in his writing, Olson, it is true, could be read as reaffirming the ontology of the American Adamic myth and/or confirming the representation of negative capability posited by Trilling and other Old Americanists—especially if one chooses to remain within the terms of the differentiation Olson articulates in the first paragraph. If, however, one attends to what follows, to the decisively epochal metaphorics recalling Ahab's mechanization of his "unerring" will informing Olson's representation of the scene of Keats's discovery, one cannot but retrieve his qualification of "mystery confusion doubt"—"it has a power"—and thus perceive Keats's and Melville's and his own negative capability as a revolutionary act of critical violence that is simultaneously intended to liberate temporal being—"quantity as intensive" (the "actual intensities and creations of life"?)—from the reified Being of the Western philosophical tradition: from the "*picture* of the world" (my emphasis) that has its origins in Euclid's geometry and its consummation in the dialectics of the Hegelian *Aufhebung*.

Clearly, however, Olson's affiliation of his postmodern ontology with Melville's does not entirely fulfill the imperatives of the negative capability I am attributing to *Moby-Dick*. Remaining in "mystery confusion doubt" and *thinking* them *as* difference are not exactly the same thing. For a more adequate American postmodernist manifestation of Melville's negatively capable ontology we must turn to the fiction of Thomas Pynchon, especially to his remarkably Melvillean *Gravity's Rainbow*, which, in telling the "story" of Tyrone Slothrup, the contemporary American Adam, massively and "encyclopedically" evokes the cultural and sociopolitical history of America, not least, the origins of its representation of being in the Puritan theology of "preterition," in order to demystify the presiding truth discourse (symbolized by the "all"-destroying phallic rocket) of contemporary America (which is to say the America of the Vietnam decade). It is, of course, impossible to convey the continuity of this "other" tradition concerning the interpretation of reality that affiliates Melville and the American postmodernists. But some sense of the scope and depth of it may be suggested by quoting, necessarily at length, what I take to be that resonant moment in this magnificent, carnivalesque novel (its locus is Melville's Berkshires and its "logic" similar to that Ishmael uses to justify his participation in Queequeg's "savage" rite), analogous to the moment of what I have been calling Ishmael's discovery of negative capability, the moment that thinks the hitherto unthought, that brings to awareness for the first time what it has known but not known from the beginning:

William Slothrup was a peculiar bird. He took off from Boston, heading west in true Imperial style, in 1634 or -5, sick and tired of the Winthrop machine, convinced he could preach, as well as anybody in the hierarchy even if he hadn't been officially ordained. The ramparts of the Berkshires stopped everybody else at the time, but not William. He just started climbing. He was one of the very first Europeans in. After they settled in Berkshire, he and his son John got a pig operation going—used to drive hogs right back down the great escarpment, back over the long pike to Boston, drive them just like sheep or cows. By the time they got to market those hogs were so skinny it was hardly worth it, but William wasn't really in it so much for the money as just for the trip itself. He enjoyed the road, the mobility, the chance encounters of the day—Indians, trappers, wenches, hill people—and most of all just being with those pigs. They were good company. Despite the folklore and the injunctions in his own Bible, William came to love their nobility and personal freedom, their gift for finding comfort in the mud on a hot day—pigs out on the road, in company together, were everything Boston wasn't, and you can imagine what the end of the journey, the weighing, slaughter and dreary pigless return back up into the hills must've been for William. Of course he took it as a parable—knew that the squealing bloody horror at the end of the pike was in exact balance to all their happy sounds, their untroubled pink eyelashes and kind eyes, their smiles, their grace in cross-country movement. It was a little early for Isaac Newton, but feelings about action and reaction were in the air. William must've been waiting for the one pig that wouldn't die, that would validate all the ones who'd had to, all his Gadarene swine who'd rushed into extinction like lemmings, possessed not by demons but by trust for men, which the men kept betraying . . . possessed by innocence they couldn't lose . . . by faith in William as another variety of pig, at home with the Earth, sharing the same gift of life. . . .

He wrote a long tract about it presently, called *On Preterition*. It had to be pub-lished in England, and is among the first books to've been not only banned but also ceremoniously burned in Boston. Nobody wanted to hear about all the Preterite, the many God passes over when he chooses a few for salvation. William argued holiness for these "second Sheep," without whom ther'd be no elect. You can bet the Elect in Boston were pissed off about that. And it got worse. William felt that what Jesus was for the elect, Judas Iscariot was for the Preterite. Everything in the Creation has its equal and opposite counterpart. How can Jesus be an exception? could we feel for him anything but horror in the face of the unnatural, the extra-creational? Well, if he is the son of man, and if what we feel is not horror but love, then we have to love Judas too. Right? How William avoided being burned for heresy, nobody knows. He must've had connections. They did finally 86 him out of Massachusetts Bay Colony—he thought of Rhode Island for a while but decided he wasn't that keen on antinomians either. So finally he sailed back to Old England, not in disgrace so much as despondency, and that's where he died, among memories of the blue hills, green maizefields, get-togethers over hemp and to-bacco with the Indians, young women in upper rooms with their aprons lifted, pretty faces, hair spilling on the wood floors while underneath in the stables horses kicked and drunks hollered, the starts in the very early mornings when the backs of his herd glowed like pearl, the long, stony and surprising road to Boston, the rain on the Connecticut River, the snuffling good-nights of a hundred pigs among the new stars and long grass still warm from the sun, settling down to sleep. . . .

Could he have been the fork in the road America never took, the singular point she jumped the wrong way from? Suppose the Slothrupite heresy had had time to consolidate and prosper? Might there have been fewer crimes in the name of Jesus, and more mercy in the name of Judas Iscariot? It seems to Tyrone Slothrup that there might be a route back—maybe that anarchist he met in Zurich was right, maybe for a little while all the fences are down, one road as good as another, the whole space of the Zone cleared, depolarized, and somewhere inside the waste of it a single set of coordinates from which to proceed, without elect, without preterite, without even nationality to fuck it up. . . . Such are the vistas of thought that open up in Slothrup's head as he tags along after Ludwig.[108]

REPRESENTATION AND ERRANCY: THE ART OF NARRATION

From the Melville revival in the 1920s to the establishment of American literary studies in the 1940s under the aegis of New Critical hegemony, criticism of *Moby-Dick*, as we have seen, concerned itself primarily with the light the novel shed on Melville's biography or, when it addressed the novel as such, with matters of content. It paid little, if any, attention to Melville's realization of its "form," or, rather, its formal being. Even those Americanists, who, following in the wake of the New Critics, refocused their commentary on the autonomous text, cannot be said to have addressed the question of the novel's ontological "structure" except in the very broadest generic terms, and this, as in the criticism of Richard Chase, Leslie Fiedler, and R. W. B. Lewis, in order to relate the genre of *Moby-Dick* to the development of American cultural self-representation. For all its insistence (against the Parringtonian ideologues) on putting aesthetic and formal considerations back into the discourse on the American novel in general and *Moby-Dick* in particular, this criticism slighted the concrete and differential dynamics of Melville's narrative art in favor of an ideologically motivated cultural project intent on identifying its genre as a significant moment in the dialectical development of the American imagination. This, it seems to me, is the historically specific critical context that precipitated R. P. Blackmur's New Critical critique of the "carelessness" of Melville's "craft" in *Moby-Dick* and *Pierre*.

There is no question that Melville overdetermined the ontological thematics of *Moby-Dick*—Ahab's self-reliant monistic and teleological metaphysics and its implications concerning being—and that, in relation to this overdetermination of the question of being, the novel's linguistic/structural articulation is underdeveloped. But as I have suggested from the beginning, especially in distinguishing between the errant narrative implications of his temporal ontology of absence and the unerring imperatives of Father Mapple's spatial ontology of presence, Melville's novel is also, and even, despite his projection of ontology as a base to the linguistic/formal superstructure, primarily, about fictional art. For just as the transgressive phenomenological story Ishmael is telling gradually precipitates what he knows but does not *know* about his ontological status as a being-in-the-world at the "beginning" (already in the wake of the catastrophe)—that he is a nameless orphan, a centerless self in a Fatherless and decentered world—so this discovery of his ontological orphanage makes simultaneously explicit what he knows and does not know at the "beginning" about his status as author of the book he is writing to represent this experience: that nameless orphanage in a decentered world calls for an errant art that enacts the destructive/projective measure of its occasion.

From the first sentence of his narrative, we are compelled by the "end" to recall, Ishmael intimates an acute, if vague ("preontological") understanding of the relationship between the event he and the crew have suffered and the textual process of retelling or representing it. After bearing witness to the terrible contradictory consequences of the *Pequod*'s pursuit of the white whale, Ishmael can no longer be certain of the privileged truth of unity, causal or symbolic, or of the heretofore self-evident validity of the patriarchal/filial comportment of the writer: of the idea of the dynastic author as (re-)Creator of the world or as saving remnant, passing on the Word, monumentalizing the memory of its fullness, in the context of disintegration. Nor can he be certain any longer of the "instrument" of storytelling to which the representational tradition, since Aristotle, has given archival status: neither the linear empirical reason of realism or naturalism, nor the dialectical reason of romance or tragedy, neither, in T. S. Eliot's terms, "narrative method" nor "mythic method."[109] Indeed, it might even be said that Ishmael in some degree realizes that these hegemonic "methods" are socially constituted to serve the dominant culture. This is especially the case if we proleptically invoke Melville's identification in *Pierre* of "Young America in Literature" with the monumental patriarchal values of the Saddle Meadows presided over by Pierre's mother: the consensual ethics that not only reduces the young Pierre to "sweet and docile" body, but eventually renders him, first, another Ishmael and finally destroys him for transgressing them (pp. 16–20).[110]

Ishmael indicates from the "beginning" a disillusioned awareness, however emergent, that his experience on board the *Pequod* has rendered representational art, like Ahab's ontological monism, a broken instrument. As we have seen, this awareness of the disintegration of the unified world picture of the *logos*—of the "rupture of the referential surface"[111] its spatializing economy articulates—opens up and estranges the sedimented familiarity of traditional American narrative form to existential questioning, to "care," in Heidegger's terms. And, in so doing, it instigates the destructive process through which Ishmael will *repeat* the events of his past and, thereby, know them and his spontaneous way of retelling them for the first (but not the last) time. As W. B. Macomber says of Heidegger's hermeneutics of "disillusionment":

Things only appear to man's vision when the instrument breaks down and he stumbles upon a void in the world in which he lives. Now for the first time we have the presuppositions of theoretical knowledge which the traditional notion of truth [as *adaequatio intellectus et rei*] simply takes for granted, divorcing knowledge from its roots in life and rendering it original and autonomous. Now there are the subject and object [as there were not, so long as the work was in progress] and a distance between them rooted in the void. The negative has emerged as the basis of determination and intelligibility. And man is now predisposed—indeed compelled—to "stop and look."[112]

Given this preontological awareness of representational narrative as broken instrument, it is an inevitable consequence of Ishmael's explorative errancy in the void and the "careful disorderliness" of his "method" that he should write a playfully serious, meditative "cetological chapter," "Of the Monstrous Pictures of Whales." Here, the seaman discovers that the representational art of landsmen necessarily fails to picture the living whale accurately or, to use his own resonant words, to "hit the mark with any very considerable degree of exactness":

But these manifold mistakes in depicting the whale are not so very surprising after all. Consider! Most of the scientific drawings have been taken from the stranded fish; and these are about as correct as a drawing of a wrecked ship, with broken back, would correctly represent the noble animal itself in all its undashed pride of hull and spars. Though elephants have stood for their full-lengths, the *living* Leviathan has never yet fairly floated himself for his portrait. The *living* whale, in his full majesty and significance, *is only to be seen at sea in unfathomable waters; and afloat the vast bulk of him is out of sight, like a launched line-of-battle ship; and out of that element it is a thing eternally impossible for mortal man to hoist him bodily into the air, so as to preserve all his mighty swells and undulations.* And, not to speak of the highly presumable difference of contour between a young sucking whale and a full-grown Platonian Leviathan; yet, even in the case of one of those young sucking whales hoisted to a ship's deck, *such is then the outlandish, eel-like, limbered, varying* shape of him, *that his precise expression the devil himself could not catch. . . .*

For all these reasons, then, any way you may look at it, you must needs conclude that the great Leviathan is that one creature in the world *which must remain unpainted to the last.* True, one portrait may hit the mark much nearer than another, *but none can hit it with any very considerable degree of exactness.* So there is no earthly way of finding out precisely what the whale really looks like. And the only mode in which you can derive even a tolerable idea of his living contour, *is by going awhaling yourself; but by so doing, you run no small risk of being eternally stove and sunk by him.* (Pp. 263–64; my emphasis)

Let us be as clear as possible about what Melville is saying here, lest his solicitation of representation be interpreted, as a Derrida might, to proffer a recuperated metaphysics. Despite his privileging of "the living whale" against representations of it, Melville's "thought diving" does not finally posit a real Reality that representation covers up or veils, a hermeneutics, in other words, that would penetrate surfaces in behalf of radical illumination or, as Derrida insistently puts it against Heidegger's "phenomenology," of "unveiling or development":

[T]he process of disengaging or of elaborating the question of Being, as a question of the *meaning* of Being is defined as a *making explicit* or as an interpretation that makes explicit. The reading of the text *Dasein* is a hermeneutics of unveiling or of development. . . . If one looks closely, it is the phenomenological opposition "implicit/explicit" that permits Heidegger to reject the objection of the vicious circle, the circle that consists of first determining a being in its Being, and then of posing the question of Being on the basis of this ontological predetermination. . . . This style of a reading which makes explicit, practices a continual bringing to light, something which resembles, at least, a coming into consciousness, without break, displacement, or change of terrain.[113]

Nor, on the other hand, does Melville deny the Real (as poststructuralists tend to) in favor of an interpretive practice that is always already simply free-floating inscription ("without positive terms"). To put it in Heidegger's technical terms, Melville does not *separate* the ontic ("common sense," "the way things are publically interpreted": socially constituted "reality") from the ontological (the unsayable "essence" of being) in the act of interpretation. It should not be overlooked that in privileging the "living whale" Ishmael in the above passage, and elsewhere in Melville's text, paradoxically relies on a metaphorics that, in its carnivalesque exaggeration, focalizes the distance (the difference) between the word/image and the "thing itself." In so doing, he implies an understanding of metaphor the function of which is not, as in the tradition, that of discovering the identity or essence that lies behind the surface of differential phenomena, but of thematizing the difference which is the condition for the possibility of identity: its differential and deferring dynamics. Remarkably like Heidegger, that is, the act of interpretation in Melville's text is neither ontic nor ontological but always already ontic/ontological:

Is there not . . . a definite ontical way of taking authentic existence, a factical ideal of Dasein, underlying our ontological interpretation of Dasein's existence? That is so indeed. But not only is this fact one which must not be denied and which we are forced to grant; it must also be conceived in its *positive necessity*, in terms of the object which we have taken as the theme of our investigation. Philosophy will never seek to deny its "presuppositions", but neither may it simply admit them. It conceives them, and it unfolds with more and more penetration both the presuppositions themselves and that for which they are presuppositions.[114]

As in the case of Heidegger, that is, the act of interpretation in Melville is not intended to break through representation to an ontological essence, to bring pure Being into immediate view in the sense of closing the distance between the perceiving subject and the being it would re-present. Rather, it is to thematize—to bring to *awareness*—the *absent* Real that is always already historically specific inscription (textual), and thus always already deferred by writing as re-presentation. As simultaneously ontic/ontological, interpretation is not "theoretical" as such—a viewing from the distance of an end—nor a "practice" as such, but, as I suggested earlier, a "theoretical practice," an act of intellection that is always tethered to the concrete historical occasion, which always entails risk, the "stoving," as it were, of one's mediating representation. It is worth retrieving at this point that moment in *Pierre* (quoted in chapter 2) where, in response to his other Ishmael's emergent awareness of the mediated character of the "Reality" of his previous "world" (above all, of the portraits of his father), Melville proffers his definitive account of representation:

But not now to consider these ulterior things, Pierre, though strangely and very newly alive to many before unregarded wonders in the general world; still, had he not yet procured for himself that enchanter's wand of the soul, which but touching the humblest experiences in one's life, straightway it starts up all eyes, in every one of which are endless significances. . . . Ten million things were as yet uncovered to Pierre. The old mummy lies buried in cloth on cloth; it takes time to unwrap the Egyptian king. Yet now, forsooth, because Pierre began to see through the first superficiality of the world, he fondly weens he has come to the layered substance. But, far as any geologist has yet gone down into the world, it is found to consist of nothing but surface stratified on surface. To the axis, the world being nothing but superinduced superficies. By vast pains we mine into the pyramid; by horrible gropings we come to the central room; with joy we espy the sarcophagus; but we

lift the lid—and no body is there!—appallingly vacant is the soul of a man!
(Pp. 284–85)

There is, then, no avoiding representation for Melville: every "truth"
mined from a stratified representation is always another stratified representation. But for him it will be a representation-of-what-cannot-be-
represented: the ontological difference. The difference between representation understood by Emerson or Thoreau or "the preposterous rabble of
Muggletonian Scots and Yankees, whose vile brogue still the more bestreaks the stripedness of their Greek or German Neoplatonical originals"
(*Pierre*, p. 128) (and the Americanists who would invoke it to establish the
American canon) and representation understood by Melville is the difference between an interpretation assumed to be the final truth about reality
and one that *knows* it to be an imaginary (and thus always destructable)
real.

Coming at the mid-point in his narrative (after Ahab has galvanized his
crew into a deadly weapon), Ishmael's destructive reading of the paintings
that attempt to "capture" the "living whale" does not draw out the analogy
between graphic (spatial) and verbal (temporal) representation nor between "being there" and the concealing/unconcealing "essence" of being.
But, as we have seen, the narrative context—his emergent awareness of
the relationship between *what* he is saying and *how* he is saying it—
suggests that the deeper implications of these analogies are now latent
possibilities. Indeed, the remainder of his narrative gradually brings these
analogies to virtual explicitness. More, the erratic process discovers that,
like the representational paintings he refers to here, representational
narrative, whether empirical or symbolist, realist or romance, has as its end
the *re-presentation* of the temporal ec-stasies or, what is the same thing, the
spatialization of time in a linear or circular simultaneous epiphany.[115]

In the "end," Ishmael discovers *why* he has from the beginning resisted
the teleological structural imperatives of traditional narrative and *how* he
has, in fact, broken out of the enclosure into which these imperatives had
compelled the writers of the "New World." Put negatively, his destructive
narrative discovers that representational narrative is affiliated with metaphysics: like metaphysics, the representational method, mimetic (linear)
or symbolic (dialectical), is ultimately circular. It is willfully intended from
the beginning to bring absence ("the darkness of whiteness," as it were) or
difference (the temporal kinetics of being) into presence as a single,

totalized, and miniaturized object of knowledge, before the concentering imperial authorial eye (I). Ishmael's "dive" into the destructive element discloses to him that the imperative to use language logocentrically—as an agency of recollecting the diaspora of words into the One Word, of reifying process, of spatializing or structuralizing temporality—authorized by the myth of Adamic Man as namer makes language a disciplinary instrument of Man's will to power over the differential and threatening "Other." Understood from the interrogative perspective of "poststructuralist" genealogy, what Claude Lévi-Strauss says about the reversed and reductive operations of the structuralist imagination in general applies as well to Ishmael's insight into the American imagination that would lay claims on his narrative art:

What is the virtue of reduction either of scale or in the number of properties? It seems to result from a sort of reversal in the process of understanding. To understand a real object in its totality we always tend to work from its parts. The resistance it offers us is overcome by dividing it. Reduction in scale reverses this situation. Being smaller, the object as a whole seems less formidable. By being quantitatively diminished, it seems to us qualitatively simplified. More exactly, this quantitative transposition extends and diversifies our power over a homologue of the thing, and by means of it the latter can be grasped, assessed and apprehended at a glance. A child's doll is no longer an enemy, a rival or even an interlocutor. In it and through it a person is made into a subject. In the case of the miniature, in contrast to what happens when we try to understand an object as a living creature of real dimensions, knowledge of the whole precedes knowledge of the parts. And even if this is an illusion, the point of the procedure is to create or sustain the illusion, which gratifies the intelligence and gives rise to a sense of pleasure which can already be called aesthetic on these grounds alone.[116]

For the decentered Ishmael, the linear circularity of representational narrative becomes, like the *Pequod* and its de-differentiated crew of *Isolatoes* under the centralizing and assimilative gaze of Captain Ahab, an unerring "harpoon" aimed by the American cultural imagination at the heart of the threatening and recalcitrant American wilderness, an instrument of "fine hammered steel," as it were, designed, as Ishmael knows but does not know in his meditation on graphic representations of the whale, to "hit the mark." But this is not all. For, we recall, Ahab's monomaniacal instrument finally alienates the being it would track down, indeed, transforms its energies into a retaliatory force. Similarly, Ishmael discovers, in its effort to reify the "elusive" motion of being, the representational instrument alienates the very phenomena it is intended to bring to stand, "to capture," as the innocent rhetoric of this tradition has it. The re-presentational instrument not only "cannot hit [the mark] with any considerable degree of exactness," it also precipitates the contradictions that will break it. I am not simply referring to Melville's fiction and that of the postmodern American writers who have turned their art against the American canon; I am also referring to all those hitherto marginalized or accommodated "others"—women, blacks, homosexuals, ethnic minorities, and so on—who have emerged to challenge the hegemony of the American cultural identity this canon has constructed.

Put positively, though the two movements of disclosure occur simultaneously, Ishmael's discovery of his ontological marginality—his "improper self"—also makes explicit at the end the "meaning" of his preontological impulse to "be there" and, thus, to err artistically in the face of the literary proprieties of American landsmen. Ishmael's errant narrative is activated by an impulse to liberate what the metaphysical circle closes off, subdues, and eventually forgets, to de-colonize, as it were, what the imperial narrative colonizes: the temporality of being and its differentiations or, on another level, the idea of truth, not as dis-interested *adaequatio intellectus et rei*, but as interested *a-letheia*.

I have tried to suggest throughout this reading of *Moby-Dick* how Ishmael/Melville as American writer in fact breaks out of the impasse— the *circulus vitiosus*—in which the representational narrative of the American tradition imprisons itself, so extended discussion is unnecessary. But the resonant rhetoric of the epi-logue insists that we retrieve both Ishmael's insistent, if unthematized resistance to the "immune" *logos* of Father Mapple's undeviatingly panoptic exegesis of the Jonah text and the quite different "dim, random way," he spontaneously adopts to "explain" himself concerning the "mystical well nigh ineffable" nature of the white whale, where he despairs "of putting it in comprehensive form."

Committed to the Word, as a Transcendental Signified that is out of reach of the freeplay of criticism, Father Mapple, we recall, is thus certain of the Adamic power of language to name. He narrates his story from above or beyond the scene of Jonah's (and his audience's) occasion, ruthlessly selecting "significant" and repressing "duplicitous" particulars to point to his linear/symbolic story's preconceived/ordained end. Empowered by his transcendental perspective, nothing—no differential entity or event—can escape his leveling panoptic gaze. Every detail necessarily takes its *proper* place in his unerring and disciplinary narrative that moves inexorably to its intended closure, to the fulfillment of God's "hard command": that the errant Jonah become the bearer of the Word, a "saving remnant" in a disintegrating world. Father Mapple's art is a teleological art of confirmation and, in this sense, tremendously circular. As such, his story, despite its antithetical theology, becomes a literary equivalent of Ahab's ontological monomania.

As foundling, on the other hand, Ishmael in the "end" is no longer certain, if he ever was, of the positive capability of language to name. Having borne witness to the devastatingly contradictory consequences of Captain Ahab's ontological monomania, he understands now that this Adamic certitude about language's positive capability to name is, in fact, not merely a socially constituted instrument designed to domesticate or pacify being, including the being of the congregation of "fallen" seamen, but one that in carrying out this project estranges and defers its "talismanic secret." Activated, on the one hand, by his awareness of the relay between Captain Ahab's ontology of the *Monos* and Father Mapple's unerring story, and, on the other, by the American literary tradition's obsessive effort to bring the being of the American wilderness to presence, Ishmael, we can now say (if we understand it in the terms of its oxymoronic resonance), becomes fully conscious of the negatively capable imaginative stance that he has in fact spontaneously practiced in the process of "representing" the ineffable "living" reality of the "American event" to which he had borne witness. Simultaneously outside and inside the "drama" that is now "over," he celebrates an act of representation that is *at once* and *continuously* an action and a passion, a criticism and affirmation, or in Heidegger's terms, a "wresting [of being] by violence" which is simultaneously a "letting be" (*Gelassenheit*).[117] Unlike Father Mapple—indeed, unlike all the "representational" writers in the European and American tradition—who rests assured of the positively capable instrumentality of language to "capture" or "grasp" the thing itself, Ishmael/Melville acknowledges its ambiguity, its duplicity, and appropriates it to interrogate the certain discourses of representation. If he must use language, he will use it courageously and generously: not to bring the being of *physis* to stand within a structure, to presence "it" as fixed and permanent object before his and his reader's "master eye," as a *nature morte,* but precisely to call language as naming into question and to activate a careful awareness of the elusive and disruptive mystery—the "absent cause," the ontological difference—always concealed in the disciplinary structures it elaborates.

As we have seen, Ishmael achieves this understanding of language in the enabling chapter on "The Whiteness of the Whale," where, we recall, his effort to articulate the difference between Ahab's representation of the white whale and what it meant to him manifests itself not simply as a refusal of the name, "Moby Dick." It also shows itself to be a discursive process that we might call after Derrida "supplementarity," if we understand Ishmael's supplementary discourse as a naming that is simultaneously a disclosive unnaming: not a penetration of the illusory veil of the name to the essential thing, but a solicitation of naming itself, which, in disclosing the differential play of naming, also dis-closes the absent differential being that naming would annul. More specifically, Ishmael's "naming" takes the form of an extended relay of analogous metaphors or tropes on whiteness, which in the process of repetition always already postpones taking a final measure of the whale, always already defers its presence,[118] thus *letting* the whale in its differential being be: to go on *living*, in the very act of representing it. To his understanding of difference as deferral of the presence of being, we must add deference. This de-structive representation—this interrogation of naming which is simultaneously an unconcealing concealment that lets the mystery of being be—becomes increasingly, as I have been suggesting, the essential characteristic of the rhetoric or style of Ishmael/Melville's text.

So, too, the narrative movement of *Moby-Dick* at large. Whereas Father Mapple tells his story from the "impregnable Quebec" afforded by the archival (Protestant) Word, Ishmael/Melville tells his from in the midst, *interesse*, from the in-sistent, ek-sistent stance of *being there (Dasein)*. Unlike Mapple's, therefore, Ishmael's narrative is not an Ahabian re-presentation of the catastrophic journey of the *Pequod* from the certain vantage point of an end that dialectically resolves the contradictions in a larger and higher whole. Rather, Ishmael's insistently disruptive narrative tropes: moves exploratively back and forth, like the "devious-cruising" *Rachel* in search of her orphaned sons, between event and meditation, willing to let the "irrelevant," the accidental, "play" in the process and, in so doing, undermining symbolic readings. It thus dis-places the commanding anthropomorphic eye of the landsman reader as it always already swerves away from the point of contact between beginning and end demanded by the unerring, viciously circular geometry of the traditional narrative. The itinerary of orphaned Ishmael's narrative, in short, does not, as Father Mapple's allegorical romance does, reflect a memory that, in "recollecting backwards" forgets the historicity of its history in the process of confirming its *arché*. Rather, Ishmael's narrative "repeats forward," in Kierkegaard's and Heidegger's sense of the phrase, and thus activates a remembering of the temporality that the disciplinary recollective memory levels and forgets.

Melville, not incidentally, was to focalize and extend the ideological implications of this differentiation between what I am calling Recollection and Repetition in *Pierre*, where, we recall, he mocks the "countless tribe of [American] novels" for their "their false, inverted attempts at systematizing eternally unsystemizable elements; their audacious, intermeddling impotency, in trying to unravel, and spread out, and classify, the more thin gossamer threads which make up the complex web of life." But it is at the "end" of *Billy Budd* that this disclosure of the ideology of narrative structure achieves its definitive "statement." Here, we recall, Melville parodically juxtaposes the complex narrative that ends in the politically determined hanging of a common seaman with the official documentary "account of the affair,"—"doubtless for the most part written in good faith"—published after the event in "a naval chronicle of the time, an authorized weekly publication."

"On the tenth of the last month a deplorable occurrence took place on board H.M.S. *Bellipotent*. John Claggart, the ship's master-at-arms, discovering that some sort of plot was incipient among an inferior section of the ship's company, and that the ringleader was one William Budd; he, Claggart, in the act of arraigning the man before the captain, was vindictively stabbed to the heart by the suddenly drawn sheath knife of Budd.

"The deed and the implement employed sufficiently suggest that though mustered into the service under an English name the assassin was no Englishman, but one of those aliens adopting the English cognomens whom the present extraordinary necessities of the service have caused to be admitted into it in considerable numbers. [This, perhaps needless to say, is how the reporter's ideological frame of reference compels him to represent impressment.]

"The enormity of the crime and the extreme depravity of the criminal appear the greater in view of the character of the victim, a middle-aged man respectable and discreet, belonging to that minor official grade, the petty officers, upon whom, as none know better than the commissioned gentlemen, the efficiency of His Majesty's navy so largely depends. His function was a responsible one, at once onerous and thankless, and his fidelity in it the greater because of his strong patriotic impulse. In this instance as in so many other instances in these days, the character of this unfortunate man signally refutes, if refutation were needed, that peevish saying attributed to the late Dr. Johnson, that patriotism is the last refuge of a scoundrel.

"The criminal paid the penalty of his crime. The promptitude of the punishment has proven salutary. Nothing amiss is now apprehended aboard H.M.S. *Bellipotent*."[119]

Unlike this author's violently amnesiac, secular recollection of the events on board the *Bellipotent*, Ishmael's retrieval of the events on board the *Pequod* is simultaneously a destruction of that Ahabian mode of memory and a resolutely anticipatory process of discovering, a projective activity that lets the differential and deferring measure of the event he is representing be. As such, it allows him (and those reading his story) to "know" and to "represent" its being dialogically, as "*Auseinandersetzung*," without succumbing to the leveling and finalizing causal or dialectical imperatives of the retrospective metaphysical problematic:

Arising, as it does, from a resolute projection of oneself, repetition does not let itself be persuaded of something by what is "past", just in order that this, as something which was formerly actual, may recur. Rather, repetition makes a *reciprocative rejoinder* to the possibility of that existence which has-been-there. But when such a rejoinder is made to this possibility in a resolution, it is made *in a moment of vision; and as such,* it is at the same time a *disavowal* of that which in the "today", is working itself out as the "past." Repetition does not abandon itself to that which is past, nor does it aim at progress.[120]

Unlike the recollective narrative of Father Mapple's sermon and, for that matter, of the secular and admittedly more complex, but no less metaphysical narratives of the American Adamites (and those Americanist critics who would canonize its structure in behalf of a national consensus), Ishmael's, finally, takes the form of a Repetition that makes it possible for him (and his readers) to always already know the being of his text "for the first time." It is a Repetition, in other words, that, in retrieving the difference that representation as Recollection contains and forgets (renders indifferent), makes a difference in the contemporary world.

In the "end," then, to return one last time to the subsuming metaphorics of his discourse, Ishmael realizes that all along the way in his "circular" narrative, he has dislocated the circle into a vortex, destroying the centered circle of the traditional Adamic narrative and calling into question the will to power over the being of being informing its reductive geometry. Returning to the beginning in the "Epilogue," to the question of his name, his parentage, and his homeland, Ishmael discovers, not the center, but the absence of a center at the still point of the moving narrative circle. And this, as I have been suggesting, precipitates the saving "coffin," as it were: the literary text that measures and is measured by its decentered and temporary (mortal) occasion. The Ishmael who survives the catastrophe of the "fifth act" is not the choric Fortinbras who symbolizes the restorative forces of being that recuperate the health of a rotten Denmark, the harmonious order of the shattered *polis*, nor the foundling of romance, who, in turning out to be the legitimate heir, recuperates and reaffirms the temporarily disintegrated Symbolic Order. He is, rather, the author as mortal being-in-the-world who, having borne witness to death and nothingness, to the thrownness of the human occasion, will tell his story against the grain of all those representational forms that would persuade us that, finally, "whatever is, is right."

Understood as a deliberate deferral of presence, as a refusal to fulfill the inscribed expectation of closure and the sublated psychological equilibrium its dialectic promises, to satisfy Adamic Man's archival impulse to "stage" being in a distancing "drama" or, to appropriate Heidegger, to "enframe" the temporal occasion,[121] the errant art of *Moby-Dick* becomes an art of estrangement and entanglement. In breaking down the binary logic and the hierarchical structure of the Adamic *anthropologos*, it displaces not only the Author but the reader as "Central Man" to the anxiety-provoking margins. Turning the piercing gaze of differential being against the Adamic spectator by calling Captain Ahab's self-reliant anthropomorphization of the white whale into question, Melville not only focuses the American reader/viewer's complicity with Ahab's violent will to power, but in so doing also dislocates his/her central and centering panoptic eye and its anthropologocentric measure. Whereas the symbolic/mythic author in the American romance tradition that a Trilling or a Lewis or a Chase would valorize accommodates the spatializing eye of the American reader/spectator, rendering his/her art an agency that confirms, legitimizes, and reproduces its Adamic self-reliance, the author of *Moby-Dick* alienates it and, thus, like the reversal of the relationship between the whale and Ahab in the temporal process of his narrative, renders the

American reader the read, the interpreter, the interpreted, the questioner, the questioned: the see-er, the seen. Liberating the difference subdued by and to the American cultural identity, the troping force contained by American meaning, Melville's novel turns the self-reliant Adamic Man the Measurer into man the measured. This indirect strategy of subversion—this dislocating reversal of the roles prescribed by the logocentric problematic of "American" justice—will, not incidentally, manifest itself in a definitive and politically suggestive, but yet to be fully understood, way in Melville's great short story, "Bartleby the Scrivener."

In "The Craft of Herman Melville: A Putative Statement," which seems in part to be a response to the Americanist cultural critics of his day who would overlook Melville's erratic art in their concerted effort to endow *Moby-Dick* with canonical status, R. P. Blackmur, we recall, concludes that Melville failed to influence the "direction of the art of fiction," because he was "careless" of the tools of his craft:

[I]t is astonishing, when you consider the magnitude of his sensibility, that he never affected the modes of apprehension, the sensibilities, of even the ablest of his admirers. He added nothing to the novel as a form, and his work nowhere showed conspicuous mastery of the formal devices of fiction which he used. Unlike most great writers of fiction, he left nothing to those who followed him, except the general stimulus of high devoted purpose and the occasional particular spur of an image or a rhythm. It is not that he is inimitable, but that there was nothing formally organized enough in his work to imitate or modify or perfect. It is easy enough to say on this score that Melville was a sport, and unique . . . ; but it would be more useful if we were able to say that Melville's lack of influence at least partly arose from a series of technical defects in persuasive craft—from an inefficient relation between writer and the formal elements of his medium. None of us would want to recommend his ware along the lines of Melville's strategy.[122]

Insofar as Blackmur's criticism is intended to challenge the reading of American literary critics such as Matthiessen, Trilling, Lewis, Chase, and Fiedler, who would harness certain aspects of the New Criticism to an end-of-ideology cultural criticism directed against the progressivist ideology of the Parringtonian tradition, he is absolutely right in reminding them that Melville "had no sure rule," that his "rule was vagary." Where the blindness of Blackmur's Jamesian insight manifests itself is in his representation of Melville's formal errancy in negative terms, in his failure in the mid-1950s to see that vagary was indeed his "rule." Despite Blackmur's remarkably prescient recognition of the coercively reductive moral (and political) economy of the modern "Puritan" imagination in a critic like Irving Babbitt, he remained, like James and the theorist of the Jamesian novel Percy Lubbock, inscribed by a supervisory Puritan economy of literary production (the binary logic of which demonized all forms of artistic deviation from the logocentric aesthetic Norm), an economy that represented and evaluated literary texts in terms that privileged thrift over waste, what counts over what doesn't count, wholeness over superfluity, regularity over unruliness, controlled directionality over errancy.[123] Retrieving Blackmur's critique of Melville's "craft" in the context of the philosophical and literary discourses of the posthumanist moment, what it tells us, I suggest, is that far from "add[ing] nothing to the novel as form," Melville's "rule of vagary" was far in advance of his time. It tells us that Blackmur's New Critical measure, as well as that of the Americanists who appropriated it for their cultural criticism, was, even then, obsolete: inadequate, in its equation of craft and dramatized closure, to the task of sounding the innovative—and sociopolitically suggestive—turn Melville gave to the craft of American fiction. Before its apotheosis by James, Lubbock, and Trilling, Melville dethroned the imperial supervisory gaze of the dialectical/dramatic novelist. In so doing, he bore witness not only to the aesthetic contradictions inhering in the American Adamic form of his day and the possibilities of a new or different—a posthumanist— American fiction, but also to the ideological contradictions inhering in the self-representation of the American cultural identity and the possibility of projecting a multicultural "American" "identity" that never was.

It is not, I submit, because Melville was careless about his craft that accounts for his failure to influence his contemporaries. It was, rather, as the concerted effort to domesticate by monumentalizing the subversive force of his writing by the American critics of the Cold War era suggests, his measure of "care," the deviant and transgressive measure which, grounded in its occasion, errs in behalf of the play of difference: the measure, in short, that the grave imperial measure of the American Adam was and continues to be constructed to subdue. And it is precisely this "old measure of care," as Charles Olson calls it,[124] that, in the wake of the self-destruction of the American cultural identity during the years of the Vietnam War, was retrieved by a new generation of American writers— the late William Carlos Williams, Charles Olson, Robert Creeley, Edward Dorn, Denise Levertov, Amiri Baraka, and more recently, the

L=A=N=G=U=A=G=E group in poetry and, Thomas Pynchon, Norman Mailer, Robert Coover, Donald Barthelme, Joseph Heller, Stanley Elkin, E. L. Doctorow, Ishmael Reed, Michael Herr, Don DeLillo, Paul Auster, Kathy Acker in fiction—in behalf of thinking a post-Adamic American literature and a post–Cold War American City.

I think also of the Wallace Stevens of "Notes Towards a Supreme Fiction":

And we enjoy like men, the way a leaf
Above the table spins its constant spin.
So that we look at it with pleasure, look

At its spinning its eccentric measure. Perhaps,
the man-hero is not the exceptional monster,
But he that of repetition is most master.

Or, at least, the Stevens who is struggling to be born in these lines, so remarkably Melvillean in their tenor, that pit an ec-centric measure and a poetics of repetition against the tremendously centered measure of the monstrous self-reliant representative American Man and his all-comprehending and dominating design. I mean, to anticipate the last chapter of this book, the Stevens whose "Anecdote of the Jar" could, according to Frank Lentricchia's brilliant reading of his poetry as American social text, offer Michael Herr a generation later a startlingly exact language in behalf of an otherwise impossible effort to convey his appalled Ishmaelian sense of the insane, imperial—and, I would add, Ahabian—"New Frontier" logic of the American adventure in Vietnam:

Had Wallace Stevens lived through our Vietnam period he might have had the right answer to the question posed by Norman Mailer in 1967: *Why Are We in Vietnam?* Had he forgotten what he knew, long before our military intervention in Southeast Asia, he would have been . . . reminded by Michael Herr who at the end of his book *Dispatches* . . . wrote: "Vietnam Vietnam Vietnam, we've all been there." Herr maybe in part knew what he knew because he had read Stevens, who taught him about where we've all been, all along: "Once it was locked in place, Khe Sanh became like the planted jar in Wallace Stevens' poem. It took dominion everywhere."[125]

In returning to "first things," Melville was fully aware that, as Charles Olson puts it, "we are the last first people." But it was never his intention—

at least after *Moby-Dick*—as it was in some degree for so many of his American predecessors and contemporaries (and for the modern American literary critics who would historize this project in the post–World War II period), to recollect a narrative form that reflected a cultural initiative dedicated to the recuperation in the present of the Origin (and the national consensus it promises) that a decadent Europe had betrayed. On the contrary, Melville's return to first things was intended, as I suggested earlier by invoking Pynchon's Puritan heretic in *Gravity's Rainbow*, to retrieve the measure and the way not taken by the custodians of the myth of the American Adam: precisely the errant measure of the American occasion and the errant "way" of ec-centric forwarding, which the Adamic *logos* and its dialectics precluded.

In his commitment to this interested literature of Repetition, which is both destructive and projective, Melville bore prophetic witness to the return of the repressed in the years of the Civil War. And if his corrosive witness was itself first repressed by his contemporaries and the generation that followed and then accommodated to one form or another of the myth of the American Adam in the wake of the revival of interest in his work in the 1920s, what he had said in *Moby-Dick* about the unsaid in the discourse and practice of the American Cultural Memory was too powerful to remain in the dormant and pacified state to which it had been reduced. His saying of this unsaid irrupted as the cultural contradiction it fundamentally was when the principle of self-reliant individualism—the (new) frontier spirit—perennially reproduced by American cultural production, "high" and "low," manifested itself contradictorily in the self-appointed monomaniacal American mission to "save" Vietnam for the "Free World." I will attempt to think the relationship between Melville's fiction and the Vietnam occasion in the last chapter of this book. Here, it will suffice to say that it is *Moby-Dick*, more clearly than any other text in the American literary tradition, that speaks the awful truth of the American intervention in Vietnam. I am not simply suggesting that it constitutes a proleptic disclosure of the genealogical origins of the national ethos that could justify the near destruction of the Vietnamese earth (*Xa*) and its culture by high-technology fire power in its madly rational effort to bring to light, into the open, a "malignly" invisible and elusive "enemy." I am also suggesting that it points the way to a mode of cultural production that, like the elusive Vietcong enemy, applies the postmodern lesson contradictorily taught by the self-exposure of the complicity of the free subject with the inclusive cultural imperialism of the logocentric Western narrative and with the sociopolitical imperialism of Western history.

In implicating self-reliance with an arrogant anthropocentric will to power over a recalcitrant being that, in turn, fulfills its "false, inverted" representational logic in an technologized Ahabian monomania, in showing that the American Adamic eye (I) will, when resisted, finally manifest itself in the reification of being, a forcible bringing of the essentially invisible and ungraspable to light, that renders it "practically assailable," Melville, in short, like Lentricchia's Stevens after him, proleptically enabled both a profound genealogical understanding of the American cultural identity (its self-representation) produced and reproduced by its cultural monuments and a profoundly devious, that is, postmodern, way of subverting its imperial work. It is no accident, I would suggest in a provisional way, that Thomas Pynchon's antiencyclopedic *Gravity's Rainbow* "ends" in the "gap" between the falling all-consuming Rocket and a human world reduced by American culture to theater, a gap out of which floats a song "They never taught anyone to sing," an uncanonical "hymn by [the heretical American Puritan] William Slothrup, centuries forgotten and out of print," to the "Pret'rite," to, that is, the differential being suppressed by the American Cultural Memory in the name of the (s)election warranted by the American Myth of Adam. Nor is it an accident that Robert Coover's *Public Burning*, which takes the McCarthy years of the Cold War period as its *mise-en-scène*, should end in a carnivalesque auto-da-fé intended to remind an American body politic that was justifying something perilously close to the genocide of the Vietnamese people in the name of the global American mission of the Salem witch burnings. I am, of course, referring to that early moment in American history, retrieved by Melville by way of his implicit identification of Father Mapple's *exhortatio* with Captain Ahab's monomania, which, however shameful to a later American psyche, established an all-too-familiar pattern of American historical practice in crisis, continuing through the Vietnam War to the war against "Saddam Hussein": the practice characterized by the American national psyche's reduction of the "threatening" complex "Other"—"the sum of all the general rage and hate felt by his whole race from Adam down"—to an utterly demonized One upon which it could "turn all its ["hot heart's"] concentered cannon." Nor, finally, as I will show at some length in the last chapter, is it an accident, that Michael Herr's *Dispatches*, a remarkably Melvillean text the genre of which, like *Moby-Dick*, recalcitrantly refuses determination, takes the point of departure of its devastatingly carnivalesque genealogy of the American "Mission's" representation and conduct of the war in Vietnam during the year of the Tet Offensive from the synecdochical example of the madly rational Adamic/frontiersman logic of the American major who, "in a successful attempt at attaining history," said in the aftermath of a search and destroy mission, "We had to destroy Ben Tre in order to save it."[126]

CETOLOGY AND DISCIPLINE

In the preceding sections, I have focused my commentary primarily on the ontological origins of the Adamic (meta)narrative structure that Melville's text is interrogating. This, it is of primary importance to point out, is because it is, in fact, the Adamic representation of being that Melville overdetermines in *Moby-Dick* in his genealogy of Ahab's monomaniac practices. At the crossroads of Melville's post-Jacksonian historical occasion—when the metamorphosis of the Puritan theology into a democratic bourgeois/capitalist anthropology is virtually completed—Melville, that is, chose to interrogate, not the sociopolitical history of his occasion as such, but, by way of his awareness of the emergent contradictions made historically visible by the metamorphic process, the ontological agency that in some fundamental way was a significant, if not the essential condition for the possibility of the Ahabian "sociopolitics" of this history: the rhetoric of persuasion, the technologization of knowledge production, the politics of spoils, westward expansionism, Indian removal, land speculation, the mass production of labor and capital, the harnessing of the question of slavery to the expedience of civil and political power, and so forth. It was, in other words, *American history*, not some "universal" or "transcendental" idea associated with the tradition of literary expression, that precipitated Melville's decision to overdetermine interrogation of the ontology of the American Adamic discursive practices. Which is to say that this overdetermination of the ontological site did not preclude his interrogation of the relay of more "practical," more visibly, "historical" or "real" sites—cultural production, economics, technology, sociopolitics, for example—on the indissoluble continuum of being, as this continuum was represented in and by the American culture of his day.

The story I have retrieved from the canonical discourse of American literary studies is, therefore, by no means the whole story. Indeed, were one to limit Melville's destructive project in *Moby-Dick* to his disclosure of the Ahabian will to power informing the Adamic *logos* and its reified and totalized representation of being and to the projection of Ishmael's ontological orphanage—to his decentered self/world—such a delimitation would quite rightly be exposed to the New Historicist/Americanist charge that such a story simply reinscribes another, albeit more complex, version of the Cold War discourse. This, in fact, is what Donald Pease anticipates when, in a telling slide from an earlier identification of Ishmael's anti-Ahabian discourse with "the pure persuasion of Emerson's rhetoric," he attributes something like a deconstructionist textuality—the operations of *différance*—to it:

In speaking with the force of Ahab's demand for a world indistinguishable from his human will, but free of the consequences of that will, Ishmael can discover pleasure not quite in another world but in a prior world, in which the endless proliferation of possible deeds displaces the need for any definitive action. The pleasure in this prior world results from the endless delay of a conclusion to the pleasure-inducing activity. The capacity to experience this delay as pleasure (rather than frustration) also derives from Ahab. The fate befalling Ahab's decisive conversion of words into deed determines Ishmael's need for a realm, in which the indeterminate play of endless possible actions overdetermines his indecision.[127]

The slide to which I refer above does, indeed, implicate a certain deconstructive textual criticism in the subtextual Cold War project of the founders of the Americanist field-Imaginary. But, as I have been suggesting in thematizing the *errant forwarding* of Ishmael's "retrospective" story—its "endless delay of a conclusion"—his narrative, playful as it is, is precisely not a "pleasure-inducing activity" of the private mind as such, one, that is, which "displaces the need for any definitive action." Such a reading rests on the assumption that its temporal *mise-en-scène* is the past experience itself, an assumption, that is, which circumvents the question of representation, the mediation of event by language. On the contrary, Ishmael's errant narrative, I submit, is precisely a social *praxis*. Indeed, it is a social *praxis* that does not confine its disciplinarity to the site of ontology—to the disclosure of a highly abstracted and vague totalitarian "politics" that informs the "Emersonian" representation of being—but, however underdeveloped in relation to the latter, extends indissolubly into other, more historically immediate regions of American representation and practice.

To make this relay clearer it will be necessary to briefly repeat what I said in chapter 2 about my extension of the "meaning of being" which I take to be implicit in Heidegger's insistence that "phenomenological" inquiry is always ontic/ontological, not a matter of a hierarchical binary between (mere) appearance and being, but of a belongingness in strife: an *Auseinandersetzung*.

The "Heideggerian" destructive project that has guided my "reading"— my inquiry into the "being"—of Melville's *Moby-Dick* to this point has been broadly (though not exclusively) limited to the interrogation of the metaphysical imperative to name that informs the Adamic (anthropological) discourse of self-reliance. But naming is also and simultaneously a process of *classification* determined by the enabling ontological principle of metaphysics—that Identity is the condition for the possibility of difference and not the other way around—and its disciplinary optics. It is a process, in other words, which, in *differentiating* being into *specific* and locatable categories within a larger comprehensive, gridded, and subsuming whole (a structured Identity), obscures their determined common essence. Admittedly, Heidegger by and large limited his destruction of the metaphysics of the ontotheological tradition to the site of ontological representation (*Vorstellung*) at the tremendous cost of blinding himself to or even misrepresenting the modern sociopolitical implications of his disclosures about the relation between being and time in this tradition.[128] Nevertheless, he went far to establish the discursive context for the recognition by postmodern or poststructuralist or, as I prefer, posthumanist thinkers, especially those critical genealogists identified with Michel Foucault's interrogation of the post-Enlightenment representation of the power/knowledge nexus,[129] of the arbitrariness (the social constitution) of knowledge classification and of the continuous will to power over difference that informs its specific differentiations.

In dislocating Man, in disclosing *Dasein's* being as an ineluctable being-in-the-world (its ontic/ontological disposition), Heidegger's ontological investigations disclosed that the ontotheological tradition's compartmentalization of being into "autonomous" categories—the ontological, linguistic, cultural, economic, social, and political, and so on— within the comprehensive framework of Being has existed to obscure being as it is experienced by *Dasein* as being-there: as, that is, an *indissoluble temporally lateral and unevenly developed relay or continuum of forces* that history always already transforms *en masse*. The representation of being as Being by the ontotheological tradition constrains inquiry to disciplinary (ontic) study—ontology, linguistics, anthropology, literary criticism, sociology, economics, political science, and so on—or, at any rate (as in orthodox Marxism), to a base/superstructure model in which the privileged discipline understands the other disciplines as epiphenomenal. In collapsing the arbitrary distinction between the so-called disciplines of knowledge production into an indissoluble relay of lived forces that are unevenly developed in history, Heidegger, on the other hand, enabled (if he himself failed to realize it in his practice) the possibility of an antimetaphysical mode of inquiry that is radically transdisciplinary in its interrogative operations, one that brings back into play (retrieves) the regions of being that the disciplinary study of the ontotheological tradition is blind to or leaves unsaid. According to this "Heideggerian" model, wherever one situates inquiry on the diachronic lateral continuum, whether he/she overdetermines the site of being, or language, or understanding or culture or economics or sociopolitics, one is always already addressing in some uneven degree the other sites (and their historical occasion). Understood in this way, literary inquiry into a particular text, for example, becomes an interested *praxis*: a historically situated interrogation of a historically situated literary text whose being is simultaneously ontological, epistemological, legal, sociological, sexual, cultural, and political in its affiliations. As the successive exposures of the historically specific ideological subtexts of their disciplinary procedures have made clear, this is even the case not only of the New Criticism (its commitment to the autonomy of the poetic text) and Old Americanist cultural criticism (its commitment to an end-of-ideology dialectics), but also of the deconstructive criticism that assumes its work to be "apolitical" (its commitment to the "textuality" or "literariness" of the text).

What I am suggesting in thus thinking what is taken to be its more "practical," that is, sociopolitical, implications, is, in short, that the ontic/ontological operation of Heidegger's existential analytic *vis à vis* being enables a model of critical inquiry capable not only of addressing the relations between power and knowledge *in general* (in the Western tradition at large), where Heidegger all too blindly confined it, but also in particular, in its historically specific determinations. More specifically, I am suggesting that it enables a mode of inquiry that, in its ability to thematize the relay between the more or less visible center determining the discursive practices of pre-Enlightenment and the invisible "center elsewhere" of post-Enlightenment discursive practices, is more adequate than any model heretofore to the task of interrogating the particular allotrope of power/ knowledge relations that has informed the discourse and practice of modernity since the Enlightenment. I am referring, of course, to what might be called—if it is understood to include the ontological site, which all to often and disablingly it is not—the discourse and practice of hegemony: the practice of power, not as direct domination (indoctrination) but (as in the "end-of-ideology" cultural criticism of Lionel Trilling and the founders of the Americanist field-Imaginary) as the production of spontaneous consent:

The concept of hegemony often, in practice, resembles [definitions of ideology as consciously practiced systems of coercion], but it is distinct in its refusal to equate consciousness with the articulate formal system which can be and ordinarily is abstracted as 'ideology'. It of course does not exclude the articulate and formal meanings, values and beliefs, which a dominant class develops and propagates. But it does not equate these with consciousness, or rather it does not reduce consciousness to them. Instead it sees the relations of domination and subordination, in their forms as practical consciousness, as in effect a saturation of the whole process of living—not only of political and economic activity, nor only of manifest social activity, but of the whole substance of lived identities and relationships, to such a depth that the pressures and limits of what can ultimately be seen as a specific economic, political, and cultural system seem to most of us the pressures and limits of simple experience and common sense. Hegemony is then not only the articulate upper level of 'ideology', nor are its forms of control only those ordinarily seen as 'manipulation' or 'indoctrination'. It is a whole body of practices and expectations, over the whole of living: our senses and assignments of energy, our shaping perceptions of ourselves and our world. It is a lived system of meanings and values—constitutive and constituting—which as they are experienced as practices appear as reciprocally confirming. It thus constitutes a sense of reality for most people in society, a sense of absolute because experienced reality behind which it is very difficult for most members of the society to move, in most areas of their lives. It is, that is to say, in the strongest sense a 'culture', but a culture which has also to be seen as the lived dominance and subordination of particular classes.[130]

In invoking here a critical theory that extends Heidegger's ontological destruction to incorporate the critical genealogy of contemporary cultural criticism, my intention is not to impose this model on Melville's *Moby-*

Dick. I have invoked it cautiously, rather, to provide a context which, I hope, will suggest, against the American cultural critics who rendered the novel a monument of the authentic American national psyche, that the affiliative disclosures of Melville's errantly "encyclopedic" narrative collectively constitute a remarkable anticipation in the form of fiction—however undeveloped in scope—of the transdisciplinary disclosures *vis à vis* knowledge/power relations enabled by this posthumanist criticism.

As we have seen, Ishmael/Melville situates his fictional "inquiry" primarily at the site of ontology, as this site is represented in the anthropological discourse of American Adamic Man: it is the ontological significance of naming the white whale "Moby Dick" that he overdetermines. In a fundamental way Ishmael's decision to retell his experience aboard the *Pequod* as story is motivated by his need to think the difference between Ahab's Adamic representation of the whiteness of the whale and his own far more ambiguous understanding of it. But as I have shown at length in differentiating Father Mapple's inexorably linear/circular narrative method with Ishmael's unmethodical "method," this inquiry into ontology becomes simultaneously an inquiry into literary form: the interpretation of being, then, subtly, inexorably, and pervasively determines the formal "shape," the "texture," of the literary text. Further, as we have seen (by way of the striking similarity between the violent moral imperatives of Father Mapple's prefigural, Puritan, exegetical method and Ahab's utter reduction of the *Pequod*'s crew to instrument of violence against being, which he justifies by his representation of the white whale as Moby Dick), Ishmael's ontological inquiry also opens out to implicate the political order in this relay. But the relay does not end here. However underdeveloped in relation to the ontological, the narrational, and the political, it extends into at least two other intermediate regions of the lateral continuum of being as it manifests itself specifically in the America of Melville's antebellum day: the regions of scientific knowledge production and economic production. It is to these that I want to turn in the last sections of this chapter, not as afterthought, but to think a certain relay of motifs that have been at work throughout the novel but which I have held in abeyance because of the exigencies of analysis.

One of the persistent "problems" that modern critics of Melville's novel have had to confront in their effort to monumentalize it has been, of course, the so-called cetological chapters interspersed erratically throughout the text. Insistently, Melville critics refer to these chapters—if, as in the case of Father Mapple's sermon, they do not entirely overlook them—as digressions (or even transgressions) that disrupt the narrative line, thus distracting from the suspense of the *Pequod*'s dialectical literary "adventure," as embarrassments, which nevertheless are more than compensated for by the imaginative power of Melville's tragic or romance narrative. Even those critics who assert that Melville's excursions into cetology are integral moments of the work do not adequately explain how this is so. Read in the context opened up by a reading that discloses ontological decentering as the "center" of Melville's novel, however, the "purpose" of the cetological chapters achieves explicitness: they exist, to put it generally, to call into question all "disinterested" or "objective" epistemological efforts to name or classify the "living" Leviathan. They become, that is, an asymmetrical equivalent, at the site of knowledge production, of Melville's interrogation of the nineteenth-century American allotropes of the totalizing, reductive, and pacifying imperatives of the Adamic ontology and of the teleological Adamic narrative structure. More specifically, they constitute, like Melville's repeated subversion of the authority of realistic paintings of the whale, a destruction of the secondary and derivative empirical mode of inquiry (which is, in its commitment to objectivity, assumed to be primary) informing the emergent natural sciences. I mean that calculative technological mode of knowledge production (reflecting the transformation of Puritanism—its divinely sanctioned "rationalization of the world [the '*lex naturae*']"[131] in all its detail—into bourgeois capitalism) that was increasingly becoming in mid-century America the privileged instrument for comprehending being, which is to say, for subduing and exploiting the American wilderness. In other words, the cetological chapters disclose that the empirical method of the emergent natural sciences is, precisely in its distanced "objectivity," also re-presentational, an allotrope of, not a radical departure from, the prefigurative Puritan and idealist Emersonian modes of knowledge production. It is a *supervisory* anthropologocentric instrument of power over being, a disciplinary technology the leveling imperatives of which take the form of dedifferentiating differentiation. As such, the cetological chapters of Ishmael's narrative implicate the knowledge production of the emergent natural sciences with the violence of Father Mapple's theological and Captain Ahab's anthropological monomania: it, too, despite its investment by the language of amelioration, which pits truth against power, renders the being it would bring to light "practically assailable." At the same time, these chapters point to or, rather, enact a more original mode of inquiry, remarkably analogous to Heidegger's ontic/ontological phenomenology in *Being and Time*, a mode of inquiry as *Auseinandersetzung*, that, like Ishmael's *interested* narrative "method" itself, "returns to the things themselves" in the sense of a representational discourse that is always already aware of the "absent cause."

There is no need to undertake an extended justification for these assertions. Given the context out of which they have arisen, their viability should by this time be rather self-evident. When, for example, after recalling Captain Ahab's declaration of his hidden monomaniac purpose, and before his meditation on power ("The Specksynder"), Ishmael/Melville writes that "the classification of the constituents of a chaos, nothing less is here essayed" (p. 134) and goes on to project a "ground-plan" (p. 137), "the draught" of a "systematization of cetology" (p. 136) that "shall comprehend them all both small and large" (p. 137) in terms of the metaphor printers use to classify the size of books ("I. The Folio Whale; II. The Octavo Whale; III. The Duodecimo Whale") (p. 137), it is not the natural science of the American Enlightenment or Renaissance he is celebrating. On the contrary, Ishmael's invocation of this system of classification is intended as a carnivalesque parody (one that, not incidentally, recalls Bakhtin's genealogy of the disruptive polyglossic novel in the "degraded" folk imagination) of the high imperial Linnaean ground and the schematizing methodological imperatives of natural science: its distanced and certain archival stance in the face of being and its unerring project to *visualize*—to *spatialize* or *re-present*—living being. Its purpose is to undermine the "objectivity" of natural science by showing that its "truth" is gained by the disciplinary transformation of being's elusively differential —and threatening—force into a structure of classification in which, like Father Mapple's narrative or Captain Ahab's representation of "all that torments . . . ; all the subtle demonisms of life and thought" (though far more complexly), no thing—no detail—is superfluous, in which every thing and event, even those which are missing, take their *proper* place: a fixed and graded ground plan of regularities, a blue print, a grid, a map, determined by the ontological priority of Identity over difference, that can be *comprehended* by the imperial gaze of the master eye of the "objective" natural scientist.[132] Indeed, what Ishmael's parody discloses in invoking Linnaeus's system of classification is remarkably similar to what Foucault's genealogy of the "regime of truth" of modernity makes explicit: its origins in the Enlightenment's projection of the disciplinary "table," that multivalent panoptic economy of temporal phenomena—nature, human being, monetary exchange—that reduced their ambiguous and threatening force to living pictures of "ordered multiplicities":

The first of the great operations of discipline is . . . the constitution of 'tableaux vivants', which transform the confused, useless or dangerous multitudes into ordered multiplicities. The drawing up of 'tables' was one of the great problems of the scientific, political and economic technology of the eighteenth century: how one was to arrange botanical and zoological gardens, and construct at the same time rational classifications of living beings; how one was to observe, supervise, regularize the circulation of commodities and money and thus build up an economic table that might serve as the principle of the increase of wealth; how one was to inspect men, observe their presence and absence and constitute a general and permanent register of the armed forces; how one was to distribute patients, separate them from one another, divide up the hospital space and make a systematic classification of diseases: these were all twin operations in which two elements—distribution and analysis, supervision and intelligibility—are inextricably bound up. In the eighteenth century, the table was both a technique of power and a procedure of knowledge. It was a question of organizing the multiple, of providing oneself with an instrument to cover it and to master it; it was a question of imposing upon it an 'order'.[133]

This parodic subversion of the natural scientific problematic and the will to power informing it should be evident in the mock-serious stance and the travestying rhetoric of miniaturization, regulation, and mastery Ishmael employs, for example, to "argue" his antiscientific/disciplinary case against Linnaeus's Genesis-inspired pronouncement of the conclusion he draws from his "objective" scientific research:

There are some preliminaries to settle.

First: . . . In his System of Nature, A.D. 1766, Linnaeus declares, "I hereby separate the whales from the fish." . . .

The grounds upon which Linnaeus would fain have banished the whales from the waters, he states as follows: "On account of their warm bilocular heart, their lungs, their moveable eyelids, their hollow ears, penem intrantem feminam mammis lactantem," and finally, "ex lege naturae jure meritoque." I submitted all this to my friends Simeon Macey and Charley Coffin, of Nantucket, both messmates of mine in a certain voyage, and they unite in the opinion that the reasons set forth were altogether insufficient. Charlie profanely hinted they were humbug.

Be it known that, waiving all argument, I take the good old fashioned ground that the whale is a fish, and call upon holy Jonah to back me. This fundamental thing settled, the next point is, in what internal respect does the whale differ from other fish. Above, Linnaeus has given you those items. But in brief, they are these: lungs and warm blood; whereas, all other fish are lungless and cold blooded.

Next: how shall we define the whale, by his obvious externals, so as conspicuously to label him for all time to come? To be short, then, a whale is *a spouting fish with a horizontal tail*. There you have him. However contracted, that definition is the result of expanded meditation. A walrus spouts much like a whale, but the walrus is not a fish, because he is amphibious. But the last term of the definition is still more cogent, as coupled with the first. Almost any one must have noticed that all the fish familiar to landsmen have not a flat, but a vertical, or up-and-down tail. Whereas, among spouting fish the tail, though it may be similarly shaped, invariably assumes a horizontal position. (Pp. 136–37)

Any lingering doubt that Ishmael/Melville's cetology is fraught with a genealogical irony intended to expose the supervisory will to power informing an increasingly powerful form of knowledge production grounded in the regulating Linnaean table should be dispelled by recalling the "conclusion" of his "cetological System." Unlike the masterful natural scientist, the assured end of whose anthropological system sustains his assured and undeviating course despite the resistance of contradictions in the process of naming/regulating, Ishmael finally "submits" (like the builders of the cathedral of Cologne to the corrosive dynamic of time) to "the constituents of chaos":

Finally: It was stated at the outset, that the system would not be here, and at once, perfected. You cannot but plainly see that I have kept my word. But now I leave my cetological System standing thus unfinished, even as the great Cathedral of Cologne was left, with the crane still standing upon the top of the uncompleted tower. For small erections may be finished by their first architects; grand ones, true ones, ever leave the copestone to posterity. God keep me from ever completing anything. This whole book is but a draught—nay, the draught of a draught. Oh, Time, Strength, Cash, and Patience! (P. 145)

We are not, here, far, despite the chronological distance, from the taxonomy of "a certain Chinese encyclopedia" imagined by Borges, which, according to Michel Foucault, "shattered . . . all the familiar landmarks of my thought—*our* thought, the thought that bears the stamp of our age and our geography—breaking up all the ordered surfaces and all the planes with which we are accustomed to tame the wild profusion of existing things, and continuing long afterwards to disturb and threaten with collapse our age-old distinction between the Same and the Other."[134]

Ishmael has, of course, delimited his project in the beginning to a "draught of a systematization of cetology" (p. 136), and his rhetoric in the above passage, repeating this delimitation, apparently anticipates the completion and fulfillment of his "system" in some future time. But a crucial difference emerges in the last sentence that undermines the anticipation of finality, not to say the authority of his "originating" text: like the book he is writing, which will deliberately defer the presence—the "talismanic secret"—it ostensibly is searching for, his cetological system is not simply a draught, but "the draught of a draught" or, in Derrida's phrase "a supplement of a supplement." As in the case of his narrative, what Ishmael is suggesting here is that the more precise, the more "finely hammered," the (techno)logical instrument that would measure being, the more acutely aware one must become of its inadequacy to comprehend its elusive "object." Whatever its degree of seriousness, Ishmael's cetology, in fact, ironically discloses the antithesis of what, as instrument of knowledge production, it is "designed" to bring to light: his representation does not unveil presence but the absence of presence at the "center" of differential being. Indeed, whenever Ishmael's cetological representation precipitates the possibility of revealing the Origin—the answer to the riddle of the whale—to his "mastering" gaze, it invariably disrupts and defers it:

The more I consider this mighty tail, the more I deplore my inability to express it. At times there are gestures in it, which, though they would well grace the hand of man, remain wholly inexplicable. . . . Nor are there wanting other motions of the whale in his general body, full of strangeness and unaccountable to the most experienced assailant. Dissect him how I may, then, I but go skin deep; I know him not, and never will. But if I know not even the tail of this whale, how understand his head? much more, how comprehend his face, when face he has none? Thou shalt see my back parts, my tail, he seems to say, but my face shall not be seen. But I cannot completely make out his back parts; and hint what he will about his face, I say again he has no face. (Pp. 178–79)

In thus displacing the inscrutability of the divine face to the inscrutable and illegible "face" of the whale, Ishmael's cetological discourse shows itself, in fact, to be a strategy intended to provoke the American landsman's inscribed expectation of a conclusive end to the process of inquiry only to confound it. It shows itself, in other words, to be a destructive mode of knowledge designed to activate the archival reader's self-conscious awareness of the heretofore unquestioned source of his/her anticipation of a final comprehension and mastery and of the inevitable consequence of its unerring logic of dissection: the alienation of what it seeks to *know*. The "objective" logic of the objective natural sciences, Ishmael's "cetology" implies, is informed by a will to power that estranges us from that with which we are most familiar.[135] In the end the probing logic of classification "accomplishes" its paradoxical self-destruction in the sense of betraying "reading" to be a mode of representation which is a writing that always already defers the presence of the being it would grasp. What Melville says in *Pierre* about the science of geology in his commentary on Pierre's futile effort to penetrate the "superinduced superficies" to the "unlayered substance"—to uncover the "talismanic secret" that would explain the mystery of his identity and the world in which it is thrown— applies as well to the analogous self-destructive disciplinary logic of the cetology that would penetrate the surface to the essence of the whale.

Ishmael's cetological discourse, that is, is informed by a strategy intended to disempower ceto-logy by thematizing its function as instrument of an "experienced assailant," by showing that its "truth" is complicitous with, not an adversary of, power. Put projectively, it is a strategy intended to empower that living force that cetology would "kill," that is, reduce to knowledge—and utility. However dislocating, the "impasse" at which it arrives is no cause for regret. Indeed, it is, as suggested by the Rabelaisian or, better, Borgesian tone with which he confronts the "appalling" mystery of the whale his cetology discovers, a cause for celebration. For what is a logical impasse to the natural scientist is for him an opening of the repressive metaphysical circle: "God keep me from ever completing anything."[136]

To recognize this destructive/projective import in the cetological chapters is to recognize their relevance to the novel at large. If they have a certain gratuitous autonomy, it is not the result of carelessness but precisely of a care that is deferent to historical specificity within the relay of specificities constituting what I have called the lateral continuum of being.

Thus, just as Ishmael calls into question the archival ontology of the American Adam, which assumes a presiding *logos* that renders the cosmos a symbolic picture, and the archival Adamic narratology, which assumes a presiding End that determines the beginning and the dialectics of the middle, so, too, however underdeveloped its articulation in *Moby-Dick,* his errant "cetological" discourse calls into question the archival rules of discursive formation of the natural sciences coming to maturity in mid-nineteenth-century America in the form of a technological instrument designed to complete the American errand in the wilderness: the conquest of nature. Over and over again, Ishmael mocks the ontological and literary "landsmen," who filially accept received opinion about being and the literary text (including the text of literary history), never going "to the things themselves," never plunging into the destructive element, in their anxiety that such a dive might disintegrate the assimilated and com-prehensive order that grants repose in the faceless face of and/or power over the uncanny and dislocating world.

Over and over again, it is, as in the case of the exegesis of the Jonah text, the witness of "seamen" (who, because they are interested and engaged, put their prejudices at risk) that Ishmael invokes as a more reliable authority in his meditations on the representation of the being of being and the being of the literary text. So also in his excursions into the representation of natural history. Like the landsman metaphysician or artist who is far removed—both literally and figuratively—from the occa-sion he would represent, the natural scientist (the Linnaeus of the above passage, for example) maps out his system of classification on the basis of "hearsay"—the (secondary or derived) Word of the Archive.[137] From this immune archival perspective which is beyond the reach of the freeplay of criticism—he becomes, as in the case of Linnaeus, who "would fain banish the whales from the waters," positively capable of disciplining (and com-modifying) difference, of rendering its differential force docile and useful by *including* it within a totalized design in which everything has its proper place. Melville, it will not be an imposition to proleptically recall, will carnivalize the disciplinary logic of Linnaeus's banishment of the whale from the distance of his scholarly study in *The Confidence-Man,* where he invokes the fate of the Australian "duck-billed beaver" at the hand of the English naturalists half a world away from its occasion: "When the duck-billed beaver of Australia was first brought stuffed to England, the natural-ists, appealing to their classifications, maintained that there was, in reality, no such creature, the bill in the specimen must needs be, in some way, artificially stuck on" (p. 70).

In thus parodically drawing our critical attention to the panoptic disciplinary perspective and its "center elsewhere" from which the natural scientist represents the living denizens of the deep, Melville compels us to recall the "impregnable Quebec" from which Father Mapple delivers his Jonah sermon, not only the providential Adamic ontology and the teleological Adamic narrative it enables, but also their imperatives of violence. In so doing, he also compels us to recognize the continuity between the three historical moments in the development of the American cultural identity and its interpretation of American space: the Puritan origin (its providential errand), the New England Renaissance (its anthropological errand), the Jacksonian expansion (its bourgeois capitalist errand, which harnessed an instrumental natural science to the task of rationalizing and exploiting its resources). Nor should my invocation of this polyvalent imperial trope be read as imposing a weight of significance it cannot bear. For this figure is reiterative in Melville's texts and serves a similar function, not least in *The Confidence-Man*, where the "Cosmopolitan"—the figure whom Melville derives from the Satan of the Book of Job (the Satan who, unlike God in his distant heaven, walks to and fro in the world) to expose the confidence of all manner of confidence men, not simply theologues but anthropologues (like Emerson and Thoreau)—"advises" the "good man" against "cavilers" who would introduce the disconcerting voice of the hitherto spoken-for "other":

In short, with all sorts of cavilers, it was best, both for them and for everybody, that whoever had the true light should stick behind the secure Malakoff of confidence, nor be tempted forth to hazardous skirmishes on the open ground of reason. Therefore, he deemed it inadvisable in the good man, even in the privacy of his own mind, or in communion with a congenial one, to indulge in too much latitude of philosophizing, or, indeed, of compassionating, since this might beget an indirect habit of thinking and feeling which might unexpectedly betray him upon unsuitable occasions. (P. 66)

Like the metaphysical distance of the Adamic philosophers of being and the aesthetic distance of Adamic literary artists and critics, the archival distance of American natural scientists, Ishmael implies, is the "objective" agency of spatialization, miniaturization, comprehension, and domination. Like the *Pequod* itself, natural science becomes a regulative instrument of the will to power over being. But in the "end" this landsman's instrument, like that of the Adamic philosopher and literary artist or critic, not only fails to contain and grasp the temporal being it would comprehend—the whale's physical amplitude and "his pre-Adamic traces"—and detemporalize. Its willful effort to reduce the many into a system of the One also, like Captain Ahab's self-reliant monomania, alienates the "wondrous" magnitude of the living reality. In fact, Ishmael/Melville makes precisely this point in the consecutive cetological chapters entitled "Measurement of the Whale's Skeleton" and "The Fossil Whale," where he parodically destroys the disciplinary "measure" of the natural scientist. Fully aware of the etymology of the Hegelian word "comprehend," which resonates insistently in these chapters, he invokes the living whale's uncomprehendable spatial and temporal magnitude, which defies the natural scientists' and geologists' efforts to "compress," "comprehend," and thus to "manhandle this Leviathan." Indeed, his parodic project to liberate the whale's ineffable size and geological age from the reductive circle of metaphysical comprehension—the "all-grasping Western world" (p. 381)—manifests itself as a remarkable anticipation of a characteristic poststructuralist gesture in taking the form of an imperial logical economy that ends in infinite regress. It is as if Ishmael/Melville were a Foucauldian genealogist directly responding to Lévi-Strauss's apotheosis of structuralist miniaturization as an agency of achieving power over the threatening Other of being. Only extended quotation can convey the full force of this liberating or, better, decolonizing parodic operation, in which the expanding outward and encompassing movement of the prose "ends" in a sublimely "unsourced" and "incalculable" spatial and temporal endlessness that "displaces" Man's presumptuous centrality and discloses his imperial panoptic gaze to be a minutely narrow and impotent blindness:

From his mighty bulk the whale affords a most congenial theme whereon to enlarge, amplify, and generally expatiate. Would you, you could not compress him. By good rights he should only be treated of in an imperial folio. . . .

Since I have undertaken to manhandle this Leviathan, it behooves me to approve myself omnisciently exhaustive in the enterprise; not overlooking the minutest seminal germs of his blood, and spinning him out to the uttermost coils of his bowels. Having already described him in most of his present habitatory and anatomical peculiarities, it now remains to magnify him in an archaeological, fossiliferous, and antideluvian point of view. . . .

One often hears of writers that rise and swell with their subject, though it may seem but an ordinary one. How, then, with me, writing of this Leviathan? Unconsciously my chirography expands into placard capitals. Give me a condor's quill! Give me Vesuvius' crater for an inkstand! Friends, hold my arms! For in the mere act of penning my thoughts of this Leviathan, they weary me, and make me faint with their outreaching comprehensiveness of sweep, as if to include the whole circle of the sciences, and all the generations of the whales, and men, and mastodons, past, present, and to come, with all the revolving panoramas of empire on earth, and throughout the whole universe, not excluding its suburbs. Such, and so magnifying, is the virtue of a large and liberal theme! . . .

When I stand among these mighty Leviathan skeletons, skulls, tusks, jaws, ribs, and vertebrae, all characterized by partial resemblances to the existing breeds of sea-monster; but at the same time bearing on the other hand similar affinities to the annihilated ante-chronical Leviathans, their incalculable seniors; I am, by flood, borne back to that wondrous period, ere time itself can be said to have begun; for time began with man. Here Saturn's grey chaos rolls over me, and I obtain dim shuddering glimpses into those Polar eternities; when wedged bastions of ice pressed hard upon what are now the Tropics; and in all the 25,000 miles of this world's circumference, not an inhabitable hand's breadth of land was visible. Then the whole world was the whale's; and, king of creation, he left his wake along the present lines of the Andes and Himmalehs. Who can show a pedigree like Leviathan? Ahab's harpoon had shed older blood than the Pharaohs'. Methuselah seems a schoolboy. I look round to shake hands with Shem. I am horror-struck at this antemosaic, unsourced existence of the unspeakable terrors of the whale, which, having been before all time, must needs exist after all human ages are over.

But not alone has this Leviathan left his pre-adamite traces in the stereotype plates of nature, and in limestone and marl bequeathed his ancient bust; but upon Egyptian tablets, whose antiquity seems to claim for them an almost fossiliferous character, we find the unmistakable print of his fin. (Pp. 455–57)

No wonder, then, that Ishmael should conclude by deriding the "untravelled"—the archival—inquirer's arrogant assumption that the mystery of the whale is positively capable of objective scientific measurement: "How vain and foolish, then, thought I, for timid untravelled man to try to comprehend aright this wondrous whale, by merely poring over his dead attenuated skeleton, stretched in this peaceful wood. No. Only in the heart of quickest perils; only when within the eddying of his angry flukes;

only on the profoundest unbounded sea, can the fully invested whale be truly found out" (p. 453).

As the juxtaposition of this and the preceding passage suggests, then, authentic scientific inquiry demands *"being there"* (*Da-sein*), at sea, as it were, not in the sense of an immediate, primal Origin, but of a lack, an absence, that always already "informs" all mediation. It demands, that is, a comportment toward the object of inquiry that is always ontic/ontological, one in which the inquirer is always willing to risk his/her prejudices in the encounter. It is not to think *about* the being of entities to an anthropological measure, but to *think* them in the measureless measure of thinking's occasion. Thus understood, Ishmael/Melville's "cetology," both in its relation to the living whale and to the derivative representations of the natural scientists, is analogous to his "ontology" and his "narrative art." This continuity between ontological and scientific inquiry (thinking) and *poiesis* that risks archival "truths" by "being there" is underscored if we retrieve the passage quoted earlier from Ishmael's meditation on the artistic representation of the living whale: "For all these reasons, then, any way you may look at it, you must needs conclude that the great Leviathan is that one creature in the world which must remain unpainted to the last. . . . So there is no earthly way of finding out precisely what the whale really looks like. And the only mode in which you can derive even a tolerable idea of his living contour, is by going awhaling yourself; but by so doing you run no small risk of being eternally stove and sunk by him" (p. 264).

Unlike the scholarly (landsmen) cetologists, who like Linnaeus, *were not there*, who, that is, appeal to the mediated authority of the Archival Book as measure in their production of objective scientific knowledge, these seamen cetologists, like Juan de la Cosa, *had been there* in immediate/mediate relationship with the living Leviathan, risking their presuppositions in the destructive/phenomenological *process* of "measuring" the living whale. Like the measure of his narrative art, in other words, the measure of Ishmael's mode of inquiry is the interested measure of his being-in-the-world, of his occasion. Being there, in a de-centered and uncanny world—mortal (temporal) and orphaned (thrown)—calls not only for a negatively *capable* "errant art," but for a negatively *capable* thinking, a thinking praxis that simultaneously interrogates the received names of being and is interrogated by the endlessly differential being these names cannot finally contain. It will not be inappropriate to invoke here Charles Olson's version of the occasional thinking/practice in *The Special View of History* to gloss Ishmael's. As in the case of Heidegger's discourse on measure, Olson invokes the "pre-Socratic" Heraclitus and the pre-Thucydidian Herodotus, "the first and instantly the last [Western] historian,"[138] as the immediate sources of his postmodern American epistemology. But it is clear from the context of Olson's writing on the question of knowledge production that Melville too is one of his antitheoretical or occasional "authorities":

It is literally true that you *have* to know everything. And for the simplest reason, that you do, by being alive. [This is Olson's equivalent of Heidegger's understanding of the hermeneutic circle.] It is this which Heraclitus meant when he laid down the law which was vitiated by Socrates [the metaphysician] . . . that man is estranged from that which is most familiar, that . . . we treat ourselves cheap.

I see history as the one way to restore the familiar to us—to stop treating us cheap. Man is forever estranged to the degree that his stance towards reality disengages him from the familiar. *And it has been the immense task of the last century and a half to get back to what he knows.* I repeat the phrase: *to what he knows.* For it turns out to coincide exactly with that other phrase: *to what he does.* What you do is precisely defined by what you know, *which is not reversible, and therein lies the reason why context* [i.e., occasion] *is necessary to us;* it is only that when one can say either (if it is the person's life) here is a perfect thing or (if it is a created thing—what every art is, by its very source as rising from one of us) here is form.[139]

For Melville, in short, the function of *interested* inquiry into natural phenomena is finally to wrest the difference from the classificatory tables into which Central Man's panoptic will to know—to comprehend, reduce, and domesticate—has coerced it. Or, rather, it is to name being in such a way as to preserve its tremendous, sublime mystery. To invoke one final passage from Ishmael's meditations on cetology, it is to represent being, give "it" a face, that, in its illegibility, undermines the Occidental master eye's re-presentation and will to meaning: "Champollion deciphered the wrinkled granite hieroglyphics. But there is no Champollion to decipher the Egypt of every man's and every being's face. Physiognomy, like every other human science, is but a passing fable. If, then, Sir William Jones, who read thirty languages, could not read the simplest peasant's face in its profounder and more subtle meanings, how may unlettered Ishmael hope to read the awful Chaldee of the Sperm Whale's brow? I but put that brow before you. Read it if you can" (p. 347). It is this refusal of interpretation, this interrogation of the empirical reason's will to closure, which is simultaneously an acknowledgment of the ineffable multiplicity of being, that is insistently enacted in Ishmael's numerous "digressions" on cetology.[140]

To put this refusal of meaning positively, the function of Ishmael's occasional mode of "scientific" inquiry is, like his general ontology and narrative art, to always already instigate *opening*: the *strife*, to appropriate the terms Heidegger develops in "The Origins of the Work of Art"—a text, not incidentally, that, like Melville's, relates thinking (*Denken*) with *poiesis* (*Dichtung*)—between that discourse which would "world" the American earth and the nameless earth (*Erde*) that resist being worlded. For Ishmael, as I have said, the potent impotence of the instrumental reason coming to dominate knowledge production in mid-nineteenth-century America to name or comprehend—to world—the "Leviathan," the finally uncontainable sublimity of the American continent, is, however disconcerting and anxiety-provoking, not a cause for regret. Indeed, the self-destruction of the Adamic epistemological instrument which, we can now say, like the Adamic novel, is precipitated by the "false inverted attempts at systematizing eternally unsystemizable elements," opens up a different, more original, way of thinking nature, one that simultaneously brings the being of the American earth near, in the sense of estranging its sedimented and "self-evident" familiarity, and always lets its differential mystery be. The truth about the whale to which Ishmael's cetological discourse bears witness[141] is not the *veritas*—the adequation of the mind's eye and the thing it observes—of the learned Linnaeus, the arrogant metaphysical natural scientist who "would fain have banished the whales from the waters" from the panoptic distance of his library. Nor, finally, is it the immediate or expressive truth of the Old Sag Harbor or Charlie Coffin, who refute the Linnaeuses on the basis of their experience, though their testimony is preferable. It is, rather, the mediate/immediate "truth" of the very learned "simple seaman," the *a-letheia* which brings the ontological difference colonized by the imperial gaze of instrumental reason back into play in discourse: the concealing/unconcealing that is instigated by *being there*. It is in this sense of instigating the rift between the name and the unnameable, of demystifying the Adamic eye and opening a horizonal dialogue—an *Auseinandersetzung*—between the inquirer and the interminably differential and incomprehensible "earth," that Ishmael's transgressive cetological discourse becomes a significant, if underdeveloped moment in a *de-structive* chain that overdetermines the ontological and the narrative sites.

Melville's genealogy of the dominant culture of mid-nineteenth-century America is not limited to tracing the origins of the emergent natural sciences back through the Emersonian representation of the subject or "self-reliant" self to the discourse and practice of the divinely ordained Puritan errand in the wilderness. It also implicates the emergent realignment of the American economic and political social order with this discursive history. More specifically, Melville, in a remarkable anticipation of Michel Foucault's genealogy of what he calls the post-Enlightenment "disciplinary society," extends the knowledge/power relations enabled by the classificatory table of the natural sciences to the differentiated world of the *Pequod*, which, not incidentally, he insistently represents as a factory that, at the same time, is a political community: a (capitalist) ship of state. What I want to suggest in this section, in other words, is (1) that the "digressions" on the practice of whaling are indissolubly affiliated with the "digressions" on cetology, in the sense that they disclose "the classificatory table" as the model of its organization, and (2) that, like the latter, they are, however asymmetrical the relation, integral to the Adamic ontology and the Adamic narrative that his interrogation overdetermines. More specifically, I want to suggest that, despite a certain residual ideological resistance, Ishmael/Melville's discourse on whaling practice constitutes a critical genealogy of the whaling industry, which, in turn, serves as a synecdoche for a sociopolitical economy that was reorganizing agrarian America into an industrial society. It is a genealogy that exposes this new productive economy's reliance on the differentiated dedifferentiating— disciplinary—table and its origins in a cultural history extending back through the constitution of the "self-reliant" (anthropological) Emersonian self to the "elected" Puritan self, its divinely ordained responsibility for rationalizing the smallest detail in time and space, and its corollary work ethic.

Admittedly, Melville's account of the historically specific economy of whaling practice appears to be less conscious of its affiliative relationship to the restricted economy of the Puritan *logos* and its work ethic than his account of the economy of the natural sciences. This blindness, I think, is the consequence of his vestigial attraction to the romance of whaling. Indeed, on the surface, he appears in these chapters to be contradictorily celebrating the American Adam's will as a positively capable instrument to master and exploit nature by domesticating its sheer rawness, by transforming its anarchic forces into a beautiful and opulent civil order, into a New Canaan, a City on the Hill. What he says very early in the novel about the whaling town, New Bedford, it would seem, applies as well, in its echoes of the Puritan providential narrative, to the American wilderness:

Had it not been for us whalemen, that tract of land [New Bedford] would this day perhaps have been in as howling condition as the coast of Labrador. . . . It is a land of oil, true enough: but not like Canaan; a land, also, of corn and wine. The streets do not run with milk; nor in the spring-time do they pave them with fresh eggs. Yet, in spite of this, nowhere in all America will you find more patrician-like houses; parks and gardens more opulent, than in New Bedford. Whence came they? how planted upon this once scraggy scoria of a country?

Go and gaze upon the iron emblematical harpoons round yonder lofty mansion, and your question will be answered. Yes; all these brave houses and flowery gardens came from the Atlantic, Pacific, and Indian oceans. One and all, they were harpooned and dragged up hither from the bottom of the sea. Can Herr Alexander perform a feat like that? (P. 32; see also "The Advocate," pp. 108–12)

Despite this apparent encomium to the whaling industry, the force of Melville's disclosure of the will to power inhering in the American Adam's representation of being, his literature, and his science, I submit, carries over into the economic/sociopolitical site of the continuum of the text's being. Given the constraints of space, it is not possible here to bring this relay of the "political unconscious" of Melville's text to full explicitness. But it may be suggested by invoking the resonant ambiguity in the above passage, not least the synedochal reduction of the whaling industry to the harpoon, with those aspects of the affiliative relationship between knowledge and power already thematized in the foregoing "reading" of *Moby-Dick*.

We have seen that Ishmael's narrative discovers Ahab's monomania—his reduction of the being of being to an identifiable One—to be a ruthlessly monistic ontology which enables the transformation of the *Pequod* and its crew into a devastating instrument of practical power over the white whale, indeed, into a metaphorical harpoon aimed at its heart. When, now, we "repeat" the process and recall the textual context in which this fetishization of the whale and instrumentalizing of the crew is articulated—the numerous chapters on the economic sources and ends of whaling, the nature of labor aboard the whaling ship, the methodology of pursuit, the technological means employed, the legal codes of whaling, and the process of transforming the raw material into marketable commodity—we begin to realize that the *Pequod* is not simply a technological instrument extending Adamic man's "grasp" of being or, in Nietzsche's deeper formulation, enabling him to "gain vengeance against the transience of time." It simultaneously becomes a historically specific economicopolitical instrument modeled on the classificatory table of empirical science and intended to domesticate and exploit nature—for the "benefit of [the American Adam's] estate," material and financial.

No matter how obscured by his attraction to the romance of whaling, in other words, Melville's insistent descriptions and analyses of the economics, labor relations, and production and consumption processes of whaling make it overwhelmingly clear that whaling is an American capitalist industrial enterprise and the whale ship an American capitalist factory, which converts the power relations of the *"tableaux vivants"* of the natural sciences thematized in the cetological chapters to material practice. And, as such, they enact the economicopolitical equivalent of Captain Ahab's anti-Puritan, Puritan, self-reliant monomania. Although Charles Olson does not make this last connection explicit, it is no accident, given his phenomenological effort to retrieve the Melville who was "down to his hips in things" from a canonical reading that implied his complicity with an American version of the Hegelian "Man of Power," that he should identify whaling with the emergence of "big business" in mid-century America and the Pacific as the extension of the American frontier: "So if you want to know why Melville hailed us in *Moby-Dick*, consider whaling. Consider whaling as FRONTIER, and INDUSTRY. A product wanted men got it: big business. The Pacific as sweat-shop. Man, led, against the biggest damndest creature nature uncorks. The whaleship as factory, the whaleboat the precision instrument. The 1840's: the New West in the saddle and Melville No. 20 of a rough and bastard crew. Are they the essentials?"[142]

Once this affiliative relay between the whaleship as ontological instrument of the America Adam's will to power over being and as economicopolitical instrument of the industrial pacification and exploitation of the American wilderness is recognized, Melville's latent interrogation of the developing imperial capitalism of Jacksonian America begins to achieve explicitness all along the economic and political spectrum—its historical origins, its relation to empirical science, its representation of wealth, its

organization of labor, wages, production, and consumption, its legal justification, its social relations, and its conceptualization of the state.[143] For
brevity, I will limit my commentary to two related areas that, more than
the others in this enumeration, resonate beyond the disciplinary boundaries in which traditional inquiry separates and contains them: the justifying origins of the American whaling industry and the constitution of labor
on the whaling ship.

From the outset, Melville clearly suggests—if he does not make it
explicit—that the *Pequod*'s murderous voyage is not determined simply by
Captain Ahab's "idealistic" monomania. It is also determined by an apparently far more "prosaic" cause which, however asymmetrically related to
Captain Ahab's monomania, is in the end no less murderous: the economy
of the capitalist spirit authorized and legitimated by the New England
Protestant theology and its work ethic and refined by the classificatory
table enabled by its mandated attention to detail. To recall Donald Pease's
commentary on the quarterdeck scene, Ahab's silencing of Starbuck's
appeal to the "Nantucket market" is not legitimized by positing a radically
different rationale for his revengeful pursuit of Moby Dick, but by penetrating more deeply than Starbuck into the scheme of things, by invoking a self-reliant self which is ontologically prior to but finally continuous
with Starbuck's laissez-faire self. Ishmael will hint at, if he will not finally
thematize, this complicity in his account of the economy of the whaling
industry.

Indeed, Ishmael's retrieval of his and Queequeg's "signing on" and, in the
process, his carefully articulated satirical portrayal of the "well-to-do"
Quakers (p. 74), Captains Peleg and Bildad, who are the major shareholders and thus "principal proprietors" of the *Pequod* (p. 76), constitute a
remarkable anticipation of Max Weber's classic analysis of the Protestant
origins of the "liberal" "capitalist spirit"—its ruthlessly rational and undeviating progress toward the achievement of an "iron-caged" imperial
economic world order—in the equally ruthless (however divinely sanctioned) Protestant "work ethic."

Justified by its assumption of an inscrutable God who refuses to reveal
His elections (the Calvinist doctrine of predestination), the Protestant
work ethic, we recall, demands a "worldly asceticism"[144] characterized by a
justified disdain of play, spontaneity, idleness, prodigality, and wayward-
ness—what earlier I summarized as waste—in favor of the virtues and
rewards of gravity: discipline, method, industry, thrift, and duty, which

alone can rationalize the raw and proliferating natural world. In the terms I have used to focus the ideological stakes of this book, the Protestant work ethic demands an end-oriented praxis in the material world, a praxis governed by a normative measure that glorifies efficient and productive labor and demonizes errancy and waste (of time) in the name of an unerring utilitarian economy sanctioned by divine dispensation. On the analogy of the Protestant God who is "beyond the reach of human understanding"—a center elsewhere, as it were—but who is understood to have "decided the fate of every individual and regulated the tiniest detail of the cosmos from eternity" (pp. 103–4), this economy, we recall, will not tolerate superfluity, anything in space or event in time to be wasted, (or, on another register, ultimately different) in the pursuit and fulfillment of its religiomaterialistic end. In other words, it establishes a binary logic in which the unrationalized, the unsocialized, the wasteful, and so on are not simply subordinated to the rationalized, the socialized, the useful, but become the very necessary means of determining and maintaining the identity of the latter. The Puritan Richard Baxter, for example, objected not to the accumulation of wealth *per se* in his charac-teristic ascetic warning against it: "the real moral objections," according to Weber, "is to relaxation in the security of possession, the enjoyment of wealth with the consequences of idleness and the temptations of the flesh, above all of *distraction* from the pursuit of a righteous life. In fact, it is only because possession involves this danger of relaxation that it is objection-able at all. . . . Waste of time is thus the first and in principle the deadliest of sins. The span of human life is infinitely short and precious to make sure of one's own election. Loss of time through sociability, idle talk, luxury, even more sleep than is necessary for health . . . is worthy of absolute moral condemnation" (pp. 158–59). In this assimilation of waste of time and money with distraction from the Way, the unerring way from the Puritan Baxter to the prototypical bourgeois capitalist Benjamin Franklin is, according to Weber, an easy and inevitable one: "'Remember, that *time* is money. He that can earn ten shillings a day by his labour, and goes abroad, or sits idle, one half of the day, though he spends but sixpence during his diversion or idleness, ought not to reckon *that* the only expense; he has really spent, or rather thrown away, five shillings besides'" (p. 48). This, not incidentally, is the same Benjamin Franklin speaking whom Melville will satirize in *Israel Potter* by focalizing this monumentalized American's discarding and forgetting—his "preterition," as it were—of his fellow

American, whose roots, too, are Puritan and typologically Israelite, when his use value has been utterly used up.[145]

This paradoxical Calvinist/Franklinian "calling," which, in the name of the liberty of the sovereign individual, authorizes the methodical, calcula-tive, and relentless pursuit of the "organization of our social environment" in behalf of God's "utilitarian" purpose—and His elected owners of the means of production (pp. 108–9)—is, in fact, thematized in Ishmael's satirical portrayal of the *Pequod*'s major shareholders, the highly irascible and vocal Peleg and the austere and tight-lipped Bildad, whose "own person was the exact embodiment of his utilitarian character. On his long gaunt body, he carried no spare flesh, no superfluous beard, his chin having a soft economical nap to it, like the worn nap of his broad-brimmed hat" (*Moby-Dick*, p. 75). It is no accident that Ishmael introduces his and Queequeg's initiation to the whaling expedition that the captains sponsor by satirically focusing the elaborately staged, which is to say, repeatable, "dialogue" between the two: it serves to foreground the circu-lar, calculative logic—the unerring, instrumental rationality designed to get in the end the answers it wants in the question it poses in the beginning—that lies behind their "generous" argument. Thus the captains' "thou," from the Protestant rhetoric of brotherly love, becomes, in fact, a contractual instrument, an efficient agency for minimizing the outlay of the voyage (especially the wages of labor) and for maximizing the possi-bilities of material production (especially the output of labor).[146] Thus, also, the "stingy old Bildad['s]" exegesis of the passage from the New Testament he "happens" to be reading (Matthew 6:19–21) "justifies" to the apparently outraged Captain Peleg the minimal wage ("lay") he is deter-mined to give Ishmael for his labor. This Dickensian passage is worth quoting at length, because it both focalizes the Protestant origins, how-ever secularized by this time in American history, of the *Pequod*'s capitalist enterprise, with its rationalization of exploitation in a scenario that pits the virtue of thrift against a lax generosity, and, however different the tone, recalls the coercive moral economy of Father Mapple's Puritan, figurative exegesis:

But one thing, nevertheless, that made me a little distrustful about receiving a generous share of the profits was this: Ashore, I had heard something of Captain Peleg and his unaccountable old crony Bildad; how that they being the principal proprietors of the Pequod, therefore the other and more inconsiderable and scattered owners, left nearly the whole management of the ship's affairs to these two. And I did not know but what the stingy old Bildad might have a mighty deal to say about shipping hands, especially as I now found him on board the Pequod, quite at home there in the cabin, and reading his Bible as if at his own fireside. Now while Peleg was vainly trying to mend a pen with his jack-knife, old Bildad, to my no small surprise, considering that he was such an interested party in these proceedings; Bildad never heeded us, but went on mumbling to himself out of his book, "'*Lay* not up for yourselves treasures upon earth, where moth—'"

"Well, Captain Bildad," interrupted Peleg, "what d'ye say, what lay shall we give this young man?"

"Thou knowest best," was the sepulchral reply, "the seven hundred and seventy-seventh wouldn't be too much, would it?"—'where moth and rust do corrupt, but *lay*—'" . . .

"Why, blast your eyes, Bildad," cried Peleg, "thou dost not want to swindle this young man! he must have more than that."

"Seven hundred and seventy-seventh," again said Bildad, without lifting his eyes; and then went on mumbling—"'for where your treasure is, there will your heart be also.'"

"I am going to put him down for the three hundredth," said Peleg, "do ye hear that, Bildad! The three hundredth lay, I say."

Bildad laid down his book, and turning solemnly towards him said, "Captain Peleg, thou hast a generous heart; but thou must consider the duty thou owest to the other owners of this ship—widows and orphans, many of them—and that if we too abundantly reward the labours of this young man, we may be taking the bread from those widows and those orphans. The seven hundred and seventy-seventh lay, Captain Peleg." (Pp. 76–77)

Ishmael feigns uncertainty about the origins of this paradoxical religious/economic "calling." But the juxtapositions he projects to articulate a general portrait of the "pious" and yet "sane and sensible" Bildad clearly suggest his source in the Protestant God, who coerces men's "labour in a calling which serves the mundane life of the community" (*Protestant Ethic*, p. 108) Bildad, in other words, imitates in this world the supervisory deity who, in compelling men to rely on material success as measure of election, justifies the austere, methodical, undeviating, and, finally, ruthless exploitation of man (labor) and nature (resources):

Though refusing, from conscientious scruples, to bear arms against land invaders, yet himself had illimitably invaded the Atlantic and Pacific; and though a sworn foe to human bloodshed, yet he in his straight-bodied coat, spilled tuns upon tuns of leviathan gore. How now in the contemplative evening of his days, the pious Bildad reconciled these things in the reminiscences, I do not know; but it did not seem to concern him much, and very probably he had long since come to a sage and sensible conclusion that a man's religion is one thing, and this practical world quite another. This world pays dividends. Rising from a little cabin-boy in short clothes of the drabbest drab, to a harpooneer in a broad, shad-bellied waistcoat; from that becoming boat-header, chief-mate, and captain, and finally a ship-owner; Bildad . . . had concluded his adventurous career by wholly retiring from active life at the goodly age of sixty, and dedicating his remaining days to the quiet receiving of his well-earned income. (P. 74)

The Protestant proprietors of the *Pequod*, Ishmael seems to imply, justify their capitalist enterprise by assuming, on the basis of its material success, that they serve God's rationalizing purpose, bringing to utilitarian fruition (their reading of) the *"lex naturae,"* the "wonderfully purposeful organization and arrangement of [His] cosmos" (p. 109). As the hyperbolical metaphors of invasion and bloodshed here (and elsewhere in his text) suggest, however, Ishmael understands this capitalist appeal to a divinely sanctioned social and legal domestication of nature to be a rationalization. Like the "rationalization" of the American wilderness by the Jacksonian democracy of Melville's day, it is finally a rhetoric of persuasion that excuses the systematic reification and violent plundering of nature's "wealth" at the expense of the laborer and in behalf of an "elected" few.

The disciplinary economy of the Protestant/capitalist work ethic, further, determines the spatial geometry of the *Pequod* and, by extension, the nature of labor aboard the whaling vessel. As Ishmael makes insistently and increasingly clear in his genealogical accounts of the whaling industry and its legal codes ("Fast and Loose Fish," p. 395–96), the whaling ship (including the whaleboats) are spatially organized like the tables of the natural sciences. Just as these last, according to Foucault, were appropriated by the bourgeois/capitalist "reformers" of the post-Enlightenment in behalf of extending knowledge/power over an emergent multiplicity of wasteful and threatening underclasses, so the spatial economy of the whaling ship is intended to achieve maximum efficiency of production and thus maximum efficiency of capital returns at the least economic and political expense. Its geometry has *that productive end in view* from the beginning. Like Linnaeus's system of classification or Mendeleev's periodical table, or

Boissier de Sauvages's nosology, all vertical space, from masthead to hold, and all horizontal space, from bowsprit to fantail, is divided, arranged, and used to facilitate the successful pursuit of the whale, from the lowering of the kill, and the transformation of the raw material into essential and valuable product, from cutting in, through baling the case, to trying out. In this sense, the whaling ship is not simply a factory, but, as Olson says of the whaleboat, a "precision instrument" of technological disciplinary power shaped to get the "product wanted." It is no accident, I think, that Ishmael's detailed and technical accounts of labor aboard the *Pequod* are generalized and convey the sense of a disciplined, systematic, frictionless, and efficient production process performed by "hands" that has its *prescribed* and undeviating sequence:

One of the attending harpooneers now advances with a long, keen weapon called a boarding-sword, and watching his chance he dexterously slices out a considerable hole in the lower part of the swaying mass. Into this hole, the end of the second alternating great tackle is then hooked so as to retain a hold upon the blubber, in order to prepare for what follows. Whereupon, this accomplished swordsman, warning all hands to stand off, once more makes a scientific dash at the mass, and with a few sidelong, desparate, lunging slicings, severs it completely in twain; so that while the short lower part is still fast, the long upper strip, called a blanket-piece, swings clear, and is all ready for lowering. The heavers forward now resume their song, and while the one tackle is peeling and hoisting a second strip from the whale, the other is slowly slackened away, and down goes the first strip through the main hatchway right beneath, into an unfurnished parlor called the blubber-room. Into this twilight apartment sundry nimble hands keep coiling away the long blanket-piece as if it were a great live mass of plaited serpents. And thus the work proceeds; the two tackles hoisting and lowering simultaneously; both whale and windlass heaving, the heavers singing, the blubber-room gentlemen coiling, the mates scarfing, the ship straining, and all hands swearing occasionally, by way of assuaging the general friction. (p. 304)

More important, it does not escape Ishmael that Peleg's and Bildad's Protestant/capitalist work ethic constitutes the origin of this peculiar spatial economy of the whaling vessel. For all his eulogizing of the *Isolatoes* aboard the *Pequod*, his descriptions of the whaler insistently suggest that its spatial geometry is also and simultaneously designed to complement the disciplinary "forms and usages of the sea" that Ahab cunningly exploits to gain mastery over his diverse crew. Like Mapple's sermon to the congregation of errant seamen, though in a more complicated way, this design minimizes the "natural" propensities to errancy, idleness, wastefulness—and, not least, mutiny—of this underclass of multiethnic laborers, while maximizing their efficiency and utility in behalf of the American God's earthly projects—and the American owners' material wealth. In Michel Foucault's terms, which, as I have suggested, derive in some degree from the genealogical connection he perceives between the all-seeing invisible Calvinist deity and Jeremy Bentham's Panopticon, the Protestant/capitalist work ethic transforms the American whaleship/factory into a "disciplinary space" that, like the prison, the hospital, the classroom, the factory of the "Age of the Enlightenment," is spatially designed to re-form (by super-vising) always deviant human beings into docile and materially useful bodies, that is, to gain knowledge and power over the "inmates"; indeed, to render them willing agents of their own incarceration:

In the factories that appeared at the end of the eighteenth century, the principle of individualizing partitioning became more complicated [than it was in the model coastal naval hospital at Rochefort in France]. It was a question of distributing individuals in a space in which one might isolate them and map them; but also of articulating this distribution on a production machinery that had its own requirements. The distribution of bodies, the spatial arrangement of production machinery and the different forms of activity in the distribution of 'posts' had to be linked together. . . . By walking up and down the central aisle of the workshop, it was possible to carry out a supervision that was both general and individual: to observe the worker's presence and application, and the quality of his work; to compare workers with one another, to classify them according to skill and speed; to follow the successive stages of the production process. All these serializations formed a permanent grid: confusion was eliminated: that is to say, production was divided up and the labour process was articulated, on the one hand, according to its stages or elementary operations, and, on the other hand, according to the individuals, the particular bodies, that carried it out: each variable of this force—strength, promptness, skill, constancy—would be observed, and therefore characterized, assessed, computed and related to the individual who was its particular agent. Thus, spread out in a perfectly legible way over the whole series of individual bodies, the work force may be analysed in individual units. At the emergence of large-scale industry, one finds, beneath the division of the production process, the individualizing fragmentation of labour power; the distributions of the disciplinary space often assured both.[147]

More specifically, as the above passage suggests, the mid-century American whaling ship/factory Ishmael painstakingly describes reflects an elementary stage of the emergent mass production process that was to transform not simply the economy, but the culture and political organization of America in the post–Civil War era, a process in which the division of labor, like the anatomical divisions of the classificatory tables of natural science, is the chief disciplinary agency of an efficient and highly productive economy.[148] For, as on the *Pequod*, it is essentially the specialization of labor, the rote repetition of a partial task in a particular space, that above all facilitates the essential ends of the Protestant work ethic: the supervision and mechanization of labor and the transformation of the potentially time-wasting and disruptive force of the human body into a regulated and utilitarian energy. In short, the divinely mandated division of labor, which, by individuating a confused mass within an ontologically prior whole makes the regulation and leveling—the de-differentiation and domestication—of human being easier, thus renders the individual laborer a willing function of the larger productive machine and his/her labor a partial contribution to an unerring, purposeful, and value-producing collective action without wastage of time (and money). As Weber observes in *The Protestant Ethic*:

True to the Puritan tendency to pragmatic interpretations, the providential purpose of the division of labor is to be known by its fruits. On this point Baxter expresses himself in terms which more than once directly recall Adam Smith's well-known apotheosis of the division of labour. . . .

[T]he characteristic Puritan element appears when Baxter sets at the head of his discussion the statement that "outside of a well-marked calling the accomplishments of a man are only casual and irregular, and he spends more time in idleness than at work," and when he concludes it as follows: "and he [the specialized worker] will carry out his work in order while another remains in constant confusion, and his business knows neither time nor place . . . therefore is a certain calling the best for everyone." Irregular work, which the ordinary labourer is often forced to accept, is often unavoidable, but always an unwelcome state of transition. A man without a calling thus lacks the systematic, methodical character which is . . . demanded by worldly asceticism. (p. 161)

Indeed, in pointing insistently to the affiliative relationship between the Puritan concern for detail, the Protestant work ethic, the classificatory tables of the natural sciences, and the spatial arrangement of the whaleship as factory, Melville in 1851 "prefigures," however incipiently, the American equivalent of that "enlightened" moment in Western economicopolitical history which, according to Foucault, produced the essential instrument of power of the modern disciplinary society:

The historical moment of the disciplines was the moment when an art of the human body was born, which was directed not only at the growth of its skills nor at the intensification of its subjection, but at the formation of a relation that in the mechanism itself makes it more obedient as it becomes more useful, and conversely. What was then being formed was a policy of coercions that acted upon the body, a calculated manipulation of its elements, its gestures, its behaviour. The human body was entering a machinery of power that explores it, breaks it down and rearranges it. A "political anatomy", which was also a "mechanics of power", was being born; it defined how one may have a hold over others' bodies, not only so they may do what one wishes, but so they may operate as one wishes, with the techniques, the speed, and the efficiency that one determines. Thus discipline produces subjected and practical bodies, "docile" bodies. Discipline increases the forces of the body (in economic terms of utility) and diminishes these same forces (in political terms of obedience). In short, it dissociates power from the body; on the one hand, it turns it into an "aptitude", a "capacity", which it seeks to increase; on the other hand, it reverses the course of the energy, the power that might result from it, and turns it into a relation of strict subjection. If economic exploitation separates the force and the product of labour, let us say that disciplinary coercion establishes in the body the constricting link between an increased aptitude and an increased domination.[149]

Once it is recognized that Melville's interrogation of the anthropological ontology of the American Adam in *Moby-Dick* is an overdetermined instance of an interrogation that extends, however unevenly thought, all along an indissoluble lateral continuum that includes knowledge production, cultural production, economic production, and sociopolitical production, Ishmael's apparently romantic celebration of the heroic exploits of his "mariners, castaways, outcasts"—the Starbucks, Stubbs, Flasks, Queequegs, Tashtegos, Daggoos, Pips, and Fedallahs—gives way to a deeper and more somber image of the crews of the American whaling fleet: an individuated collective body simultaneously charged to accomplish individual feats of production in behalf of the industry (what is normally called heroism) and reduced to docility by a ruthlessly rational and economy-oriented work ethic and the spatial geometry this ethic imposes. To counter the all-too-easy tendency, admittedly sanctioned by certain prominent gestures in *Moby-Dick*, of the founders of American literary studies to aestheticize the reality that was whaling—to represent a highly competitive, bloody, violent, exploitative American industry in the image of romance or symbol—it is worth recalling here, as Charles Olson does in *Call Me Ishmael*, that "of the 18,000 men employed by the American whaling industry in 1840, *one-half* ranked as green hands and more than *two-thirds* deserted every voyage. . . . Melville himself is a case in point. He deserted the *Acushnet*, his first whaleship, at the Marquesas. He was one of eleven mutineers aboard his second, a Sydney ship the *Lucy Ann*, at Tahiti. Nothing is known of his conduct on the third, except that he turned up after it, alone, at Honolulu."[150]

I have said that Ishmael becomes acutely aware in the process of his narrative that Ahab's "tremendous centralization," enhanced by the "paramount forms and usages of the sea," reduces the ethnically differentiated crew of the *Pequod*—"*Isolatoes* . . . not acknowledging the common continent of men, but each *Isolato* living on a separate continent of his own" (p. 121)—to a violent, indeed, demonic instrument of his monomaniacal will to power over the white whale: "[A]ll varieties were welded into oneness, and were directed to that fatal goal which Ahab their one lord and keel did point to" (p. 557). What I have suggested about the economicopolitical site of *Moby-Dick* might seem, then, to contradict the ontological interpretation of Ahab's transformation of the crew into his willing instrument. For the question will inevitably arise: How can the reduction have its origin in both Ahab's monistic ontology and the protocapitalist economicopolitics of the proprietors of the *Pequod*? If, however, the ontological and the economicopolitical are understood, not as radically separate disciplinary sites, but as different and, in terms of their historical specificity, unevenly developed phases of a totalized construction of being, the contradiction disappears.

In the context of the Protestant/capitalist economy and its normative measure that Ishmael/Melville is at great pains to provide, the *Isolatoes'* capitulation to Ahab's "irresistible dictatorship" (p. 147) becomes easier to perceive. By leveling the temporal and differential being of beings-in-the-world into a differentiated/assimilated function of a larger technological instrument, the division of labor on the whaleship alienates the members of the crew, not simply from the products of their labor, but also from being, understood as an indissoluble continuum, itself, thus reducing their *care*—the time-induced sense that things make a difference in the world, which Heidegger posits as the basic existential structure of *Dasein* as temporal being-there—to a care-less, which is to say calculative, free-floating, instrumental activity. In thus alienating the *Isolatoes* of the *Pequod* from being or, what can now be understood as the same thing, in thus reducing their differentiating care to indifference in the face of being, the disciplinary division of labor renders them docile material, as pliant to the materialistic purposes of the corporate owners of the means of production, who would exploit them and the earth ruthlessly for the sake of capital gain, as to the grotesquely vindictive purposes of the "idealistic" mono-maniac, who would wreak vengeance against the uncentered be-ing of being for the sake of justifying the anthropological Adamic *logos*, the integrity of the absolute (American) Self. In other words, it is not Ahab's ontological monomania alone that reduces the *Isolatoes'* "play of mind" to predictable and murderously efficient docility before his grave, demonic *end*; it is also the disciplinary imperatives of Captains Peleg and Bildad's austere American Protestant/capitalist ethos.

Indeed, as I have earlier suggested in following Pease's reading of Ahab's invocation of "the little lower layer" against Starbuck's appeal to the "Nantucket market," Ahab's ontological instrument and the *Pequod's* own-ers' economic/political instrument are not oppositional in their relation-ship but continuous and complicitous in this process of reifying and instrumentalizing living beings. This, I suggest, is what the multiple and apparently incommensurate discourses of *Moby-Dick* (we should recall here Evert Duyckinck's still unchallenged assertion that "there are evi-dently two if not three books in Moby Dick rolled into one") persuade us to entertain when, at the penultimate moment of his narrative of the *Pequod's* disastrous voyage, Ishmael's returns to—we can say "repeats"—the leveling and instrumentalizing power of Ahab's awesome "central eye":

As the unsetting polar star, which through the livelong, arctic, six months' night sustains its piercing, steady, central gaze; so Ahab's purpose now fixedly gleamed down upon the constant midnight of the gloomy crew. It domineered above them so, that all their bodings, doubts, misgivings, fears, were fain to hide beneath their souls, and not sprout forth a single spear or leaf.

In this foreshadowing interval, too, all humor, forced or natural, vanished. Stubb no more strove to raise a smile; Starbuck not more to check one. Alike, joy and sorrow, hope and fear, seemed ground to finest dust, and powdered, for the time, in the clamped mortar of Ahab's iron soul. Like machines, they dumbly moved about the deck, ever conscious that the old man's despot eye was on them. (Pp. 536–37)

Given the scientific and economicopolitical meditations that, in accompanying his narrative, provide a context for it, it is no accident that Ishmael conflates—points to the complicity between—the industrial and ontological instrumentalization of the *Pequod* and its crew into a single image which turns the enabling terms of the sacred errand in the wilderness inside out in his appalled account of that ultimate phase of the mass-production process. I am referring, of course, to the chapter entitled "The Try-Works," which, not incidentally, is coincident with the beginning of the ultimate phase of the fiery, ontological pursuit. Taking their lead from the end, not the beginning, of this chapter, traditional Americanists have insistently read its structure as a kind of synecdoche of the symbolic meaning of *Moby-Dick* at large, more specifically of Melville's developing moral attitude toward the human condition in general. Thus for example, R. W. B. Lewis invokes Ishmael's concluding warning—"Look not too long in the face of fire, O man!"—to accommodate Melville's not quite perfected text to the dialectical narrative plot of the "party of Irony," that constituency of the American Adamic tradition that reconciled and raised the innocence of the "Emersonian" "party of Hope" and the despairing knowledge of evil of the "Edwardsian" (Puritan) "party of Memory" into the higher (dramatic) synthesis of "tragic hope":

There occur (as Ishmael sees it) two dangerous alternative conditions. On the one hand: an empty innocence, a tenacious ignorance of evil, which, granted the tough nature of reality, must be either immaturity or spiritual cowardice. On the other: a sense of evil so inflexible, so adamant in its refusal to admit the not less reducible fact of existent good that it is perilously close to a love of evil, a queer pact with the devil. Each alternative is a path toward destruction; the second is the very embrace of the destroying power.

Now these two conditions have affinities with the contemporary moral visions of the party of Hope and the party of Memory. They could be grasped and expounded only by someone who had already by an effort of will and intelligence transcended them both. By the time he wrote *Moby-Dick*, Melville had dissociated himself in scorn from what he now regarded as the moral childishness of the hopeful. But he was not blind to that hypnosis by evil which a bankrupt Calvinism had visited upon the nostalgic. . . .

Melville, that is to say, had penetrated beyond both innocence and despair to some glimmering of a moral order which might explain and order them both, though his vision remained slender, as of that moment, and the center of light not yet known, but only believed in—and still ambiguously at that. But, like the elder Henry James, Melville had moved towards moral insight as far as he had just because he had begun to look at experience dramatically. He had begun to discover its plot; and Melville understood the nature of plot, plot in general, better than anyone else in his generation.[151]

If, however, we put the beginning of the try-works chapter, which, given his ruthlessly teleological problematic, Lewis is compelled to conveniently overlook, back into play, a different reading asserts itself. It is a reading that, without negating the ontological terms Lewis thematizes, nevertheless radically undermines the universalized metaphysical ("Hegelian") conclusion he draws from them: it brings Melville's dialecticized novel, that is, back into the world to render it a social text. If, in other words, we attend to the fact that "The Try-Works" begins, like so many other chapters devoted to the whaling industry, with a technical description of its composition and function in the mass production process that gradually modulates into a terrific language of hallucination that estranges the sedimented original terms of rational efficiency, everything that follows, including the final passage that Lewis invokes, comes to be understood as a powerful critical/genealogical commentary on this culminating phase of the productive process aboard the *Pequod*. In its gradual transformation of an empirically represented space and action into a grotesquely ritualized scene—specifically, the productive trying of the oil into something like a fiery demonic ceremony around an alchemical alembic—Ishmael's account of the final phase of the mass production process, in which laborers finally reduce and distill by fire the impure raw material—the living, the differential, the ineffable whale's body—to the pure, essential, and wealth-making product, cannot but suggest the continuity between the whaleship as factory with Captain Ahab's monomaniac reduction of "all that maddens and torment; all that stirs the lea of things" to a "practically assailable" essence: "then the rushing Pequod, freighted with savages, and laden with fire, and burning a corpse, and plunging into that blackness of darkness, seemed the material counterpart of her monomaniac commander's soul" (p. 423). It cannot but also suggest the continuity of the whaleship as factory with the American Puritans' fanatically monistic exegetical instrument that reduced the differential dross of temporal history into the pure and abiding narrative of the Word of their Calvinist God to justify and positively enable their worldly errand in the wilderness.

Besides her hoisted boats, an American whaler is outwardly distinguished by her try-works. She presents the curious anomaly of the most solid masonry joining with oak and hemp in constituting the completed ship. It is as if from the open field a brick-kiln were transported to her planks. . . .

By midnight the works were in full operation. We were clear from the carcase; sail had been made; the wind was freshening; the wild ocean darkness was intense. But that darkness was licked up by the fierce flames, which at intervals forked forth from the sooty flues, and illuminated every lofty rope in the rigging, as with the famed Greek fire. The burning ship drove on, as if remorselessly commissioned to some vengeful deed. . . .

The hatch, removed from the top of the works, now afforded a wide hearth in front of them. Standing on this were the Tartarean shapes of the pagan harpooneers, always the whale-ship's stokers. With huge pronged poles they pitched hissing masses of blubber into the scalding pots, or stirred up the fires beneath, till the snaky flames darted, curling, out of the doors to catch them by the feet. The smoke rolled away in sullen heaps. To every pitch of the ship there was a pitch of the boiling oil, which seemed all eagerness to leap into their faces. Opposite the mouth of the works, on the further side of the wide wooden hearth, was the windlass. This served for a sea-sofa. Here lounged the watch, when not otherwise employed, looking into the red heat of the fire, till their eyes seemed scorched in their heads. Their tawny features, now all begrimed with smoke and sweat, their matted beards, and the contrasting barbaric brilliancy of their teeth, all these were strangely revealed in the capricious emblazonings of the works . . . as to and fro, in their front, the harpooneers wildly gesticulated with their huge pronged forks and dippers; as the wind howled on, and the sea leaped, and the ship groaned and dived, and yet steadfastly shot her red hell further and further into the blackness of the sea and the night, and scornfully champed the white bone in her mouth, and viciously spat round her on all sides; then the rushing Pequod, freighted with savages, and laden with fire, and burning a corpse, and plunging into that blackness of darkness, seemed the material counterpart of her monomaniac commander's soul. (Pp. 419–23)

If, after this solicitation of Ishmael's discourse on the American whaling industry, we repeat the beginning, where he seems to celebrate the Protestant/capitalist spirit of the Bildads and Pelegs, which "planted" New Bedford "upon this once scraggy scoria of a country," the passage undergoes a *Verfremdungseffekt* that resists a positive reading:

Had it not been for us whalemen, that tract of land would this day *perhaps* have been in as howling condition as the coast of Labrador. . . . The town itself is perhaps the *dearest place to live in,* in all New England. *It is a land of oil,* true enough; *but not like Canaan;* a land, also, of corn and wine. *The streets do not run with milk;* nor in the spring-time do they pave them with fresh eggs. Yet, in spite of this, nowhere in all America will you find more *patrician-like houses;* parks and gardens, *more opulent,* than in New Bedford. Whence came they? how planted upon this scraggy scoria of a country?

Go and gaze upon the *iron emblematical* harpoons round yonder *lofty mansion,* and your question will be answered. Yes; all these *brave houses* and *flowery* gardens came from the Atlantic, Pacific and Indian oceans. One and all, they were *harpooned and dragged up hither* from the bottom of the sea. Can Herr Alexander perform a feat like that? (P. 32; my emphasis)

What has emerged in the interim, as we have seen, is a body of counterknowledge about the whaling industry that brings to explicitness the disruptive details in this passage, which are all too easily overlooked by assimilative Americanists like Lewis seeking confirmation of the inspiring Adamic romance they would read into the American cultural and sociopolitical tradition. More specifically, this counterknowledge brings into openness its differential or aporetic rhetoric, which, in turn, defamiliarizes and thus puts into question the archival representation of America as "enlightened" democratic/capitalist *polis* that, mediated by the American Revolution, fulfills the sociopolitical promise announced by the Puritan saving remnant or seed-bearers: their "Israelite" errand in the wilderness to *plant* the City on the Hill. To put it another way, it reveals this Adamic rhetoric to be, in fact, an anthropological discourse that privileges and naturalizes the etymologically cognate abstractions, circle, culture, and colonization, which is to say, a seminal rhetoric of plantation, cultivation, growth, and maturation (and, correlatively, of vision and enlightenment) that has authorized and legitimized the plundering and exploitation of the wilderness by the elected few. It reveals, in short, not simply the ideology of material privilege but also the technological instrument of violence against man and nature (being) that it shaped to achieve its end: the privilege and instrument of violence concealed in the "enlightened" City on the Hill coming to fruition in the New Eden of mid-century America. As for the "romance" of whaling:

As the boats now more closely surrounded him [the exhausted whale harpooned by the *Pequod's* boats in chauvinistic competition with the German *Jungfrau*], the whole upper part of his form, with much of it that is ordinarily submerged, was plainly revealed. His eyes, or rather the places where his eyes had been, were beheld. As strange misgrown masses gather in the knot-holes of the noblest oaks when prostrate, so from the points which the whale's eyes had once occupied, now protruded blind bulbs, horribly pitiable to see. But pity there was none. For all his old age, and his one arm, he must die the death and be murdered, in order to light the gay bridals and other merry-makings of men, and also to illuminate the solemn churches that preach unconditional inoffensivess by all to all. (P. 357)

The light shed by the Jacksonian phase of the American "Enlightenment" on the darkness of the human condition becomes, in this context, the exclusive "light" of a material, middle-class, capitalist opulence sanctioned by the light of the "solemn churches [of the Bildads] that preach unconditional inoffensiveness by all to all"—the light that glows inside the few "patrician-like houses," the "lofty" mansions, of New Bedford. This *polis*, we recall, is the New "Canaan" barbarously "harpooned and dragged up hither from the bottom of the sea" in the name of the Puritan's divinely mandated duty to "rationalize" the "New World."

Melville's invocation of the Israelite's journey through the wilderness to Canaan in this "celebration" of New Bedford recalls the famous passage in *White-Jacket* about America's "predestinated" mission in the world. I mean, of course, the one that both the makers of the modern American canon and those "New Americanists," like Bercovitch and Dimock, who would call it into question by thematizing the "ritual of socialization" or the imperial project inscribed in the restrictive economy of its bipolar "jeremiadic" structure, have made pivotal not only to any understanding of the ideological significance of Melville's writing, but of American cultural history at large:

Escaped from the house of bondage, Israel of old did not follow after the ways of the Egyptians. To her was given an express dispensation; to her were given new things under the sun. And we Americans are the peculiar, chosen people—the Israel of our time; we bear the ark of the liberties of the world. Seventy years ago we escaped from thrall; and, besides our first birth-right—embracing one continent of earth—God has given to us, for a future inheritance, the broad domains of the political pagans, that shall yet come and lie down under the shade of our ark, without bloody hands being lifted. God has predestinated, mankind expects, great things from our race; and great things we feel in our souls. The rest of the nations must soon be in our rear. We are the pioneers of the world; the advance-guard, sent on through the wilderness of untried things, to break a new path in the New World that is ours. In our youth is our strength; in our inexperience, our wisdom. At a period when other nations have but lisped, our deep voice is heard afar. Long enough have we been skeptics with regard to ourselves, and doubted whether, indeed, the political Messiah had come. But he has come in *us*, if we would but give utterance to his promptings. And let us always remember that with ourselves, almost for the first time in the history of earth, national selfishness is unbounded philanthropy; for we cannot do a good to America but we give alms to the world. (Pp. 150–51)[152]

This famous passage clearly recapitulates the "exceptionalist" history of "America" that, according to the "classic" writers of the "American Renaissance," was announced (prefigured) and promised by the New England Puritans' appropriation of the figural interpretation of providential history to their historically specific context: specifically, their representation of their identity as a "saving remnant" and their spiritual/worldly mission as the divinely ordained task of planting/building a City on the Hill in the "New World," of transforming the wilderness by cultivation into a New Canaan of milk and honey. This celebration of "America" in *White-Jacket*— which, whatever its reservations, is also in some sense a celebration of the historically specific, messianic America of the Jacksonian period—has more or less been universally taken to be Melville's. Given the fictional context that is its occasion—a savage critique of the authoritarian legal code of the American navy and the totalitarian sociopolitical organization of a United States navel vessel insistently referred to as a ship of (the American) state—I am not at all convinced that the issue is that simple.

Whether or not such an interpretation of *White-Jacket* is justified, it should be now clear that the "America" Ishmael/Melville thinks in the interim between the "encomium" to the romance of whaling in "The Street" (p. 32) and the "high and mighty business of whaling" in "The Advocate" (p. 108), on the one hand, and the grimmer view of this business enterprise in "The Pequod Meets the Virgin" (p. 357), on the other, both of which invoke this sacred/secular—Protestant/capitalist—paradigm, does not constitute a fulfillment of the Puritan promise. Or, rather, it constitutes a "fulfillment" of a promissary logic that self-destructs. Like the history of Western philosophy which, in fulfilling the potential promise of the beginning, according to Heidegger, precipitates in the end what its metaphysical economy necessarily represses, it discloses the radical contradiction inhering in the self-confirming American exceptionalist paradigm. The synecdochal New Bedford "is a land of oil . . . but not like Canaan, a land, also, of corn and wine. The streets do not run with milk; nor in the spring-time do they pave them with fresh eggs." The Puritan City on the Hill, the fulfillment of the American Puritan promise, turns out in the end, to be, not a generous democratic city, in which the "political Messiah . . . has come in us," the bearers of "the ark of the liberties of the world." It is rather the ruthless Capitalist City "harpooned and dragged up from the bottom of the world's oceans," the city in which a rich merchant elect presides over a vast preterite class of dispossessed ("the town is perhaps the dearest place to live in, in all New England"), who are the docile and dispensable instruments of this "civilized" opulence. Like Walter Benjamin's historical materialist, Ishmael has come in the process of writing *Moby-Dick* to view "[what] are called cultural treasures . . . with cautious detachment. For without exception the cultural treasures he surveys have an origin that he cannot contemplate without horror. They owe their existence not only to the efforts of the great minds and talents who have created them, but also to the anonymous toil of their contemporaries. There is no document of civilization which is not at the same time a document of barbarism."[153]

Ishmael, in other words, is not, as Donald Pease claims against the liberal, humanist, Cold War critics such as F. O. Matthiessen, Lionel Trilling, and Richard Chase, who identified him with the sovereign American self in the struggle against Nazism and then Stalinist Communism (Ahab), the flip, parasitic, side of Ahab's totalitarian problematic of persuasion. He is not the internalizing subject "who turns virtually all events in the narrative into an opportunity to display the power of eloquence capable of taking possession of them," who "can discover pleasure not quite in another world but in a prior world in which the endless proliferation of possible deeds displaces the need for any definitive action."[154] Such a reading, I submit, is gained by identifying the time of Ishmael's narrativization with the actual events of the voyage of the *Pequod*. If, however, we read Ishmael's narrative as a contemporary improvisatory—and projective—hermeneutic struggle to make critical sense of that cataclysmic chain of events in the past in which he was inextricably implicated, another interpretive situation offers itself. We are permitted to sympathize with Pease's effort in *Visionary Compacts* to liberate *Moby-Dick* from its representation by the Cold War critics, which, according to its logic, "turn[ed] to Ishmael, who, in surviving [the "total destruction"] *must* . . . have survived as the principle of American freedom who hands over to us our surviving heritage" (p. 270). But we are, at the same time, permitted to refuse our assent to his claim that, in exposing "Ahab's and Ishmael's narrative relation as a single self-conflicted will, instead of letting Ishmael remain in opposition to Ahab, [Melville] reveals the way in which Ishmael's obsession depends on Ahab's compulsion" in order to "ask us if we can survive the free world Ishmael has handed down to us" (p. 274).

We are invited, rather, to understand Ishmael as something like a proto-American theorist of what Antonio Gramsci, in the wake of the transformation of capitalism into fascism—and against the essentialism of Stalinist Marxism—called the "historical bloc": the affiliative solidarity of historically specific, differential or "organic" constituencies in their local struggles against oppression, which he posited against the dedifferentiated and universal collectivity supervised by the "Party."[155] For Ishmael's multiply situated narrative cannot be represented as a discourse informed by "a will capable of moving from one intellectual model to another—to seize each, invest each with the subjunctive power of his personality, then, in a display of restlessness no eloquence can arrest, to turn away from each model as if it existed only for this ever-unsatisfied movement of attention" (*Visionary Compacts*, p. 271). As I have shown, rather, Ishmael's discourse is motivated by the *critical* will of a deliberately organic or specific (as opposed to general or universal) intellectual.[156] I mean an intellectual whose discourse is a discursive practice instigated belatedly not simply by his "obsession" with his own earlier "victimization" (his fatal succumbing to the powerful lure of Ahab's totalitarian rhetoric), but by his recognition that this specific victimization is simply the overdetermined instance in an uneven relay of discrete but affiliated victimizations that traverse the continuum from the construction of being as such (nature), through the production of the self and knowledge, to the constitution of the sociopolitical formation.

In other words, Ishmael's discourse is informed by an engaged will activated by his discovery *as* teacher/intellectual of what Gramsci has called "the discourse of hegemony" and Foucault, "the repressive hypothesis": that "truth"—the truth of, say, American providential history (Father Mapple's sermon) or Linnaean natural science (the cetology chapters) or Smithsonian capitalism (Starbuck's Nantucket market) or New England transcendentalism (Ishmael's meditation on the mast-head) or Emersonian self-reliance (Captain Ahab on the quarter-deck)—is not external to and thus the privileged agent of deliverance from power (Ahab's sultanism), but productively complicitous with it.[157] It is not, then, the pleasure-inducing indeterminate freedom that allegedly resists, but in fact, like that of the Cold War Americanists, needfully locks itself into the orbit of the Ahabian will to power that characterizes Ishmael's discourse. It is, rather, this insight into the relations between truth and power: that Ahab's violent practice is not incommensurate with, but latent in, the relay of differential truth discourses that ostensibly constitute digressions in the narrative. And it is this insight that distinguishes Melville's Ishmael from the figure of Ishmael represented by the Cold War critics. Indeed, it is this essential disclosure of the complicity between truth and power in antebellum America that proleptically invalidates the appropriation by the founders of American literary studies of Ishmael as the triumphant voice of the sovereign individual of American democracy against Ahabian totalitarianism for their Cold War project.

REPETITION AND THE INDISSOLUBLE CONTINUUM OF BEING: MELVILLE'S *POLIS*

The Puritan figural paradigm in *White-Jacket*, which celebrates America's global mission, does not constitute the inclusive scenario within which *Moby-Dick* (and the novels that follow) is contained and measured. To assume it does is to betray the hermeneutic violence done to the thought "margins" ("digressions") of Melville's "diabolic book." More specifically, it betrays a disabling blindness to the distinction between two, seemingly similar, but in fact antagonistic modes of circular interpretation that, I submit, is fundamental, however undeveloped, in Melville's fictional art: what, for convenience, I have called, after Kierkegaard and Heidegger, Recollection (*Er-innerung*) and Repetition (*Wiederholung*). I mean the distinction between a logocentric or teleological hermeneutics that begins from the end (this is the vicious "Puritan" circularity that Melville is destroying) and a decentered hermeneutics that, if it begins from the end, understands the end in ontic terms: as a *forestructure* that is put at risk in the face of historicity. (This is the postlogical circular economy that Melville is discovering in the process of structuring Ishmael's narrative.) Whereas Recollection is informed by a logic of self-confirmation, Repetition is informed by a logic of self-contradiction or difference.

What I have tried to show in the foregoing "reading" of *Moby-Dick* is that its errant structure of Repetition discloses the narrative of American identity to proceed according to a coercive, circular logic at a number of sites—ontology, *poiesis*, science, labor—in the indissoluble field of forces I have called "American" being, a logic in which the pursuit of its end in the face of the resistance of the differences that time disseminates eventually manifests itself in an imperial violence that contradicts its initial, allegedly benign purpose. But I have also shown that this violent logic precipitates an uneven relay of "identities"—ontological difference (temporality), poetic difference (*aporia*), natural difference (the whale), sociopolitical difference (the multicultural crew)—which it tries to contain or colonize but finally—in the end—cannot. Indeed, we might say, after Michel Foucault, that the structure of Repetition disclosed by my thematization of the relay of digressions as a relay of transgressions is intended to retrieve the history of those constituencies of being to which History has denied a history. Or, to remain within the American context, we might say, after Thomas Pynchon, that this structure of Repetition becomes the means by which Melville would rehabilitate the differential continuum of "preterites"—those constituencies of being that the American History constructed by Puritanism had passed over and forgotten. The agenda implicit in the structure of Repetition in *Moby-Dick*, in other words, is an alternative *polis*, if by the word we mean not simply a political space, but this relay of unidentical (decentered) identities[158] dis-closed by (Melville's thematization of) the self-destruction of the American identity.

Since, as I have said, Melville does not completely work out the affiliative relationship between his economic-political discourse and the destructive ontology informing Ishmael's narrative of Ahab's "unerring" pursuit of Moby Dick, there is, of course, little in his text to suggest the specific nature of the decentered *polis* that would replace the Protestant/capitalist (disciplinary) City on the Hill. Nevertheless, the force of specific disclosures or decolonizations at the sites of ontology, art, and scientific inquiry carry over implicitly in some degree into the site of political economy. Since, by this time, these disclosures have emerged as manifestations of the groundless ground of Melville's errant art—the worldly art of *being there*—there is no need to retrieve them here. It will suffice to say that Melville clearly is not pointing toward something so simple as liberal reform—the amelioration of specific injustices in labor relations and production in the whaling industry, for example—nor, as in the case of Thoreau, for a nostalgic retreat from the emergent indus- trial/urban city that is the inevitable consequence of the closure of the Adamic frontier.[159] What Melville's witness to institutional power in ante- bellum America does symptomatically espouse, rather, is the abandon- ment or overcoming of the privileged idea of Central Man—of (Self- reliant) Man as measure—and the systematic exploitation of nature, human and material, it justifies in the name of the "benefit of man's estate." The *polis* latent in his discourse on the whaling industry is a *polis* of "*Isolatoes*" (understood as social constituencies), each of whom, unlike John Donne's nostalgic continentalists (or American exceptionalist versions of them), does not acknowledge the preordained "common continent of men," but lives—and dies—"on a separate continent of his own" (p. 121). This *polis* consists of different human beings—mortals—who are "yet federated," not into a national consensus—a technological instrument of power used and used up by a privileged class to plunder the wealth of nature or to retaliate against the "malice" of being. In terms of its ontologi- cal perspective, it is, rather, a horizonal or improvisational and, therefore, *care*-ful—negatively capable—community of errant ec-centrics (orphans, in Melville's metaphorics) that gives to as well as takes from nature. In its improvisational relationship to being, this community of *unidentical identities* always already instigates the unconcealing/concealing strife—the *Ausein- andersetzung*—between world and earth, knowledge and mystery, named and unnamed, which forestalls the reductive dynamics of totalization, or, as Heidegger puts it, constitutes authentic "dwelling on this earth."[160] In terms of its sociopolitical perspective, it is a multicultural social democ- racy, in which the different and differential (non-self-present) constituen- cies or subject positions and their practices are determined, not by a privileged accommodational principle of presence, but by the historically specific conditions—the (im)balance of power relations as they actually exist—that obtain in any particular present.[161] Melville's *polis*, in other words, is the dis-integrated or an-archic City, the scattered gather, of occasional men and women, who, like the Ishmaelite writer and thinker, in *being there* (as opposed to the invisible author and thinker immured in his impregnable Quebec), acknowledge the diaspora as their case and labor in-the-world according to an agonic, dialogic measure that is "no mere geo-metry,"[162] but a measure that keeps the boundary—no frontier for colonization—the "*horismos* . . . the horizon" always open and forwarding.[163]

In the novel's terms, Melville's ship of state is not, then, the *Pequod*, in which the *Isolatoes* are "federated along one keel": neither a polyglot crew melted down, in fact, by the supervisory American work ethic into a finely tempered and powerful imperial instrument/weapon designed to drag the "wealth" of the seas into the privileged neighborhoods of New Bedford, nor an "Anacharsis Clootz deputation from all the isles of the sea, and all the ends of the earth, accompanying Old Ahab . . . to lay the world's grievances before that bar from which not very many of them came back" (p. 121). Melville's state-ship is, rather, a destroyed *Pequod*: the "errant" *polis* that emerges from the self-destruction of the polyvalent logic that propelled the *Pequod* in its fiery, undeviating pursuit of the One in the deviating All. It is something like Queequeg's saving coffin, which he wanted modeled on the Nantucket canoe, "all the more congenial to him, being a whaleman, that like a whale-boat these coffin-canoes were without a keel, though that involved but uncertain steering, and much lee-way adown the dim ages" (p. 478). It is also, like the very book he writes (its narrative mode, its ontology, and its cetology), the "devious-cruising Rachel," "yaw[ing] hither and thither at every dark spot, however small, in the sea," recognizing orphanage, even in the pursuit of business, as the human occasion, and adjusting its praxis (its keel, as it were) to that errant and careful measure.

What, then, of that all-too-limited motif in the otherwise variously productive Melville criticism of the New Americanists, which, in its effort to disclose the repressive (Cold War) ideology imbedded in the end-of-ideology field-Imaginary of the Old Americanists, identifies Melville's sociopolitics with the imperial discourse of American exceptionalism? What, in other words, of the revisionist criticism that reads *Moby-Dick* as either subscribing to the naturalized (capitalist) founding myth of America and its (imperial) mission in the wilderness (Wai-chee Dimock and Paul Royster, for example)[164] or as reinscribing itself in this disabling discursive practice even as it tries to break out of its confines (Sacvan Bercovitch)?

Collapsing the distinction between Ishmael's narrative and the "imperial folio" that Melville invokes as the only space capable of accommodating the "vast bulk" of the whale, Dimock, we will recall, "demonstrates" *Moby-Dick's* complicity, by way of "blaming the victim" (Ahab and the native Americans), with antebellum America's imperial project:

> Spatialized time is . . . what *Moby-Dick* invokes to make Ahab's fate legible. Reading that fate, Melville's prophets turn Ahab too into a doomed figure, spatializing his temporal endeavor into a timeless script. Melville's "imperial folio," then, logically shares the same temporal economy with its imperial environment, for a structure of dominion is inseparable from a structure of time. . . . Fate in *Moby-Dick* and Manifest Destiny in antebellum America are kindred constructs. . . .
>
> Of course, the relation here cannot be anything other than *mirroring*, for if Ahab and America are in one sense kindred, kindred in their timelessness, in another sense they are also diametrically opposed. The destiny that afflicts Ahab is, after all, nothing like the destiny that awaits America. It resembles rather the fate of those whose "doom" America dictates [the native Americans, for example]. But even here, America's destiny and Ahab's are not so much opposed as complementary. One exists as the companion to the other, the necessary condition for the other's possibility. Putting this another way, we might say that America and Ahab represent the two poles in a single narrative of spatialized time, a narrative that (not surprisingly) also has two contrary provisions: for sovereignty as well as for subjection, the doom of the one being no more than a measure of the other's fated ascendancy.[165]

Given the massive evidence pointing to Melville's destruction of the totalizing/panoptic/imperial gaze I have brought to bear in the foregoing reading of the novel, it is not too difficult to see that Dimock's "demonstration" of the complicity of Melville's discursive practice with antebellum American expansionism constitutes, in fact, an instance of the very spatializing imperial discourse that she attributes to Melville.

Unlike Dimock, however, Bercovitch reads *Moby-Dick* as Melville's effort to decenter the ever-expanding imperial circumference. It is not so easy, therefore, to perceive in what sense Melville's novel provides precisely, if in an underdeveloped way, for an alternative discursive practice that is not determined by the discourse of American exceptionalism, that is, for a counterhegemonic practice that, according to Bercovitch, remains unavailable to Melville, caught, as he is, within the discourse of the American jeremiad. For Bercovitch, we will recall, Ishmael's narrative is an American "anti-jeremiad," and since "both the jeremiad and anti-jeremiad foreclosed alternatives,"[166] offers no way out of this cultural double bind: "[T]he novel offers no hope whatever. Melville's options, given his commitment to America, were either progress towards the millenium or regression towards doomsday. He simply could not envision a different set of ideals—an antinomian self-sufficiency, a non-American course of progress—beyond that which his culture imposed."[167] Bercovitch's representation of American exceptionalism at large in terms of the discourse of the jeremiad (and anti-jeremiad), needless to say, constitutes a groundbreaking contribution to American literary studies. But this should not obscure a curious and limiting paradox: that his critique of the hegemonic discourse of American exceptionalism reinscribes the discourse of American exceptionalism into his reading of American literature, not least of *Moby-Dick*. The insight afforded by his problematic into the leveling (consensus-making) operations of the American jeremiad, that is, forecloses the possibility of seeing that Melville is working precisely toward the articulation of an alternative, "non-American," agenda "beyond that which his culture imposed." To put it differently, the negative conclusion he draws is the inevitable consequence of a totalizing Americanist problematic, the unerring imperialist interpretive logic of which must render the deliberately alien and alienating *aporias*—the parodic destruction or carnivalizing of Father Mapple's prefigural hermeneutics and the providential American history it enables and of the structuralist classificatory tabling of cetology, for example—invisible in the pursuit of its preestablished end.

In retrieving the parodic function, above all, of Father Mapple's Jonah text—in revealing the repressive cultural and sociopolitical imperatives of the "benign" logic of his panoptic American exegetical method (not least, its complicity with the violence authorized by Captain Ahab's monomania)—I have shown otherwise. These retrievals have revealed, on the contrary, that Melville's decentering of the imperial metaphysical ontology determining the cultural discourse of "American Renaissance" writers constitutes an overdetermined moment in an indissoluble, however unevenly developed, relay of decenterings that includes the scientific site (the discursive practices of positivist science), the economic and social sites (the *Pequod* as capitalist factory and *socius*), and the political site (the self-reliant subject whose fulfillment is Ahab's totalitarianism) of the antebellum American world picture.

If, further, Melville's parodic disclosure of the complicity of Father

Mapple's interpretive practice with the interpretive practice of the natural sciences—their prophetic/capitalist imperial project—is understood as a critical genealogy of the indissoluble relay of values privileged by Jacksonian democracy, it will also be seen that his digressive narrative, by contrast, constitutes an indissolubly multisituated, negatively capable critique of "America." Or, to use the enabling terms of the "foreign" discourse I have used in this book to think Melville's novel, the decentered and "errant" narrative constitutes a de-structive project that *escapes*—indeed, exists to undermine—the totalizing hegemonic American discourse. I mean, specifically, the discourse that operates within the comprehensive and abstracting parameters of the binary opposition between individual freedom and absolute freedom, American democracy and totalitarianism, liberty and empire: that is, within the closed but always accommodating (Thomas Pynchon would call it "paranoid") circle of the discourse of the American jeremiad—and the anti-jeremiad. Such a recognition, in other words, will reveal that Melville's decentering of the American *logos* discloses the possibility of, if it does not fully develop, a counter*hegemonic* discourse and practice: precisely the alternative "set of ideals—an antinomian self-sufficiency, a non-American [American] course of progress"[168]— that Bercovitch's curiously "Americanist" scenario of the American jeremiad (and, in a different if no less disabling way, Wai-chee Dimock's "empire for liberty") forecloses to *Moby-Dick* in the name of his antiimperial "New Americanist" project.[169]

MOBY-DICK AS DIABOLIC BOOK

"This is the book's motto [the secret one]—Ego, non baptiso te in nomine—but make out the rest yourself." The rest, of course, is "Patris et Filii et Spiritus Sancti—sed in Nomine Diaboli." Thus Melville, invoking the diabolic rhetoric Ahab incants in baptising the harpoon he will hurl at in order to kill—to bring to permanent presence—the elusive white whale, characterizes his "wicked book," *Moby-Dick* in his letter to Nathaniel Hawthorne.[170] On the basis of Melville's dramatic invocation of the name of the *Diabolos*, it has become dully customary for liberal humanist critics to refer to his fiction as a "diabolic art" in the sense that, as artist, he was, like Shelley, Byron, and Blake, "of the Devil's party" against the vulgar God of the American moral majority:

There is little doubt about the nature of the enemy in Melville's day. It was the dominant ideology, that peculiar compound of puritanism and materialism, of rationalism and commercialism, of shallow, blatant optimism and technology, which proved so crushing to creative evolutions in religion, art, and life. In such circumstances every "true poet," as Blake said, "is of the Devil's party," whether he knows it or not. . . . Melville, anyhow knew that *he* belonged to the party, and while writing *Moby-Dick* so glorified in his membership that he baptized his work *In Nomine Diaboli.*[171]

There is, of course, some justification in thus naming *Moby-Dick* (though too often critics, like Murray, identify Melville's "diabolic" purposes too exclusively with Ahab's). But finally it is a liberal, humanist representation that, like the elitist humanism of the revivalist critics of the 1920s, obfuscates rather than brings the e-mergent being of Melville's transgressive fictional art near. This is not simply because the adversarial use of the word "diabolic," as in the above passage, is restricted to and determined by the sedimented moral sense constructed and handed down by the discourse of the Christian theological tradition. It is also, and above all, because, in pitting the word against the party that crushes creativity and "every true poet," this usage reinscribes Melville's diabolism within the constraining framework of the discourse of (self-)presence. Despite its emancipatory intentions, this critical convention thus fails to thematize the word's more originative (repressed) ontological resonances that carry over into the multisituated errant *art* of *Moby-Dick*, which, as I have suggested in responding to R. P. Blackmur's criticism, is as primary for Melville as its ontology.

Understood in the context opened up by my destructive reading of *Moby-Dick*, the word *"Diabolos"* suggests a more primordial meaning that radically differentiates Melville from the liberal humanist "Satanists" of the Romantic tradition with which the Old Americanists, as saving remnant, would identify him. And it makes the novel's implications for literary form and American literary history explicit. *Diabolos:* ultimately from the Greek *dia* (or *di*, the form of *dia* used before a vowel), "through," "during," "across," but also "apart," "asunder," which itself is related to *duo*, "two"; that is, the double or duplicitous that ensues from the sundering of the One; and *bolos*, "a throw" or *ballein*, "to throw." Hence *Diabolos:* that nonentity which throws the One apart, dis-integrates the Integral, scatters Identity into difference, the Word in words. Or, to invoke an important affiliated metaphorics, that which precipitates *diaspora*, dis-*semination*. If we understand the One, the

The Errant Art of *Moby-Dick*   **233**

Integral, the Identical, the Seminal, the Word as Permanent Presence or the Being of being, the *Diabolos* undergoes a resonant estrangement. It comes to be recognized as that astonishingly comprehensive personification of the ontological difference or centerlessness, which like Don Quixote's "enchanter," is the hermeneutic principle of last resort for the Christian imagination in its willful effort to justify, comprehend, and domesticate "evil" in the world, that is, to incorporate the utterly contradictory and recalcitrant be-*ing* of being into its totalized cosmic romance. As such it shows itself as the (non)agent of an an-archic temporality and, by extension, of differentiation and deferral. For time—even prior to writing (*écriture*), which for Derrida is the "agency" of dissemination—in always already destroying the structurations of presence (breaking up and deferring the end), is that nonprinciple of inter-ference which precipitates difference (from the Greek *diapherein*, "to tear asunder," "to draw apart," "to differ"); that is, "to carry [what is dispersed] over, across, or through" time, in the sense of differentiating/deferring presence.[172] Finally, then, as "agent" of time and the dissemination of difference, the *Diabolos* also makes the world make a difference, that is, activates dis-inherited (orphaned) human being's *care*, its *interest*, in the question of being. Significantly, the Greek word meaning "to interest in," "to make a difference," is *endiapherein*, a corollate of *diapherein*. It is difference as ontological spatial/temporal phenomenon—differentiation/deferral/deference—that engages men and women in what Heidegger calls *die Seinsfrage*: the forgotten question of what it means to be.[173] It is not by chance that in *Billy Budd*, long after *Moby-Dick*, but in keeping with the figure of the confidence-man and his abiding contempt for the "false inverted attempts [of American novelists] at systematizing eternally unsystemizable elements," Melville identified the *Dia-bolos*—the (non)agency of dissemination—as the "arch interferer, the envious marplot of Eden," who, like the Satan of the Book of Job, would disrupt the *story* of the Creation and the authority of its Author by reminding us of the differential realities of temporal being-in-the-world, in this case, more specifically, the fatal stutter that disrupts the allegory of good and evil, signifier and signified, knowledge and practice, and the authority that authorizes this privileged form:

[T]here was just one thing amiss in him [Billy Budd]. No visible blemish indeed . . . ; no, but an occasional liability to a vocal defect. Though in the hour of elemental uproar or peril he was everything that a sailor should be, yet under sudden provocation of strong heart-feeling his voice, otherwise singularly musical, as if expressive of the harmony within, was apt to develop an organic hesitancy, in fact, more or less of a stutter or even worse. In this particular Billy was a striking instance that the arch interferer, the envious marplot of Eden, still has more or less to do with every human consignment to this planet of Earth. In every case, one way or another he is sure to slip in his little card, as much as to remind us—I too have a hand here.[174]

Understood in its originative ontological sense, the "Diabolic" can—if we put the pejorative binary status assigned to the word by late Greek and Roman metaphysics, Christian theology, and post-Enlightenment anthropology under erasure—be represented as the antithesis of the "Symbolic": ultimately from the Greek prefix *sym* (which is the counteressence of *"dia"*), "together," "united," "at one," and *ballein*: hence "pertaining to the harmonious and inclusive centripetal unity (*sum*) which has been thrown together from discordant multiplicity." The *Symbolos*, it then might be said, is the "deity" of the ontotheological tradition—Being (Greco-Roman), God (medieval), Logic (Enlightenment)—whose function, from a center elsewhere, is to "redeem the time" or to reveal itself "in the fullness of time." He is the "monomaniacal," patriarchal *logos*—the *principium* of presence—whose meta-physical light shows/compels errant man—the prodigal and deviant son—the unerring way through the dis-orienting duplicities of difference to the recuperative prelapsarian Adamic state, the integral, mature, and well-lighted realm of permanent presence, of the imperial *Monos*. Hence, the symbolist writer is he (or she) who imitates in language the *Symbolos's* structuring of temporality, recollects—*sums* up, as it were—and levels the scatter, the *dia-spora*, into a comprehensive or, better, synoptic spatial structure, the many in the One, words into the Word. It is not by chance that Samuel Taylor Coleridge's seminal definition of the symbolic imagination is taken over not only by Emerson and the Emersonians of the "American Renaissance," whose poetics Melville is calling into question, but also by those Modernist American critics like F. O. Matthiessen, Charles Feidelson, Lionel Trilling, and Richard Chase, who, by way of the mediation of the New Critics (most notably I. A. Richards), appropriated this internalizing, comprehensive, and imperial imagination in behalf of the Cold War against Communism:

The IMAGINATION then, I consider either as primary, or secondary. The primary IMAGINATION I hold to be the living power and prime Agent of all human

Perception, and as a repetition in the finite mind of the eternal act of creation in the infinite I AM. The secondary imagination I consider as an echo of the former, co-existing with the conscious will, yet still identical with the primary in the *kind* of its agency, and differing only in *degree*, and in the *mode* of its operation. It dissolves, diffuses, dissipates, in order to recreate; or where this process is rendered impossible, yet still at all events it struggles to idealize and to unify. It is essentially *vital*, even as all objects (as objects) are essentially fixed and dead.[175]

Read in the ontological context opened up by this etymology, Melville's baptism of his "wicked book" *in Nomine Diaboli*, it turns out, is not simply intended to announce a thematic strike against conventional antebellum Christian morality. It is also, and far more importantly, intended to signal a destruction of the de-differentiated and, for Melville, in-different "Symbolist" art sponsored by his American transcendentalist contemporaries and their "Greek and German Neoplatonical originals."

To put this differentiation in terms of the current critical debate over the identity of American literature, Melville's baptism of his novel in the name of the *Dia-bolos* announces a *poiesis* that proleptically calls into question the kind of art it became more or less customary, until quite recently, to call *Moby-Dick*, ever since the founders of the Americanist field-Imaginary identified the cultural dominant of the "American Renaissance" as the Symbolic imagination and the dominant novelistic form as the romance in their effort to extricate the American literary tradition from the politically liberal critical/historical line established by V. L. Parrington and embodied in "realistic" fiction by Theodore Dreiser: from, that is, what these founders took in the period of the Cold War to be a disastrous turn from *American*— "dialectic"—reality, to an artistically disabling and politically threatening doctrinaire social realism. As Trilling puts it:

Parrington's characteristic weakness as a [liberal] historian is suggested by the title of his famous book, for the culture of a nation is not truly figured in the image of the current. A culture is not a flow, nor even a confluence; the form of its existence is struggle, or at least debate—it is nothing if not dialectic. And in any culture there are likely to be certain artists who *contain a large part of the dialectic within themselves, their meaning and power lying in their contradictions; they contain within themselves, it may be said, the very essence of the culture,* and the sign of this is that they do not submit to serve the ends of any one ideological group or tendency. It is a significant circumstance of American culture, and one which is susceptible of explanation, that an *unusually large proportion of its notable writers of the nineteenth century were repositories of the dialectic of their times*—they contained both the yes and no of their culture, and by that token they were prophetic of the future. Parrington said that he had not set up shop as a literary critic; but if a literary critic is simply a reader who has the ability to understand literature and to convey to others what he understands, it is not exactly a matter of free choice whether or not a cultural historian shall be a literary critic, nor is it open to him to let his virtuous political and social opinions do duty for percipience. . . . [To write negatively, as Parrington does of Poe, Hawthorne, Melville, and James] is not merely to be mistaken in aesthetic judgment; rather it is to examine without attention and from the point of view of a limited and essentially arrogant conception of reality the documents which are in some respects the most suggestive testimony to what America was and is, and of course to get no answer from them.

Parrington lies twenty years behind us. . . . Yet [he] still stands at the center of American thought about culture because, as I say, he expresses the chronic American belief that there exists an opposition between reality and mind and that one must enlist oneself in the party of reality.[176]

By invoking Melville's *Diabolos* against the *Symbolos* and the Symbolic novel, I do not mean to imply that *Moby-Dick* should be identified with the Parringtonian tradition: that, as Milton Stern puts the case against the tradition established by Trilling and others, Melville, in his commitment to "rationalism, empiricism, objectivity, and relativity," is a literary natural-ist who takes his patriarchal place "at the head of a tradition that extends (with basic modifications) through Twain, Dreiser, Hemingway, and Faulkner in distinction to the transcendental continuum."[177] For, as I have shown, naturalism is the binary opposite—the counteressence—of ideal-ism (Symbolism or romance) in the discourse of the ontotheological tradition. It simply substitutes Man (the *anthropo-logos*) for God (the *theo-logos*), naturalizes the supernatural; God, the naturalist claims, is made in Man's image. Thus Stern, blind to Melville's deliberately errant art—and to his own initial insight—believes that "Melville's God is time—the physical, infinite reality of eternity—nothing more and nothing less. He agrees that the universe offers physical pattern and material cycle. But as far as man is concerned, it is ethically blind, morally patternless. Limited living man must exchange blindness for planning and impose his own patterns of morality upon history by controlling his own fate, for beyond the physical facts of creation, empty time will not do this for him."[178]

In thus identifying the "fine hammered steel" of Melville's art (presumably in the image of a deadly harpoon aimed at the heart of a personified Nothingness) with human(istic) planning in an ontological void, Stern's "naturalist" representation of *Moby-Dick* does, indeed, reduce the novel to a supervisory and calculative agency of the *ratio* as *adaequatio intellectus et rei* and, by extension, to the kind of ideological apparatus that, according to Trilling, characterizes the sociopolitical, liberal, Parringtonian critical tradition. Whatever Stern's conscious intention, his reduction of Melville's dia-bolic art to a "straightforward" technological instrument of the will to power over the differential being of being is simply the obverse face of Symbolic interpretation in its willful relegation of potentially disruptive difference to oblivion. And what Melville thought about this forgetful, positivist, "recollective" mode of representation is made devastatingly clear, as I have noted, in the carnivalesque "conclusion" of *Billy Budd*, where he offers a "historiographical" example of the kind of "inverted" narration that he castigates in *Pierre* for "trying to unravel, and spread out, and classify, the more than thin gossamer threads which make up the complex web of life." Following the "inside" account of the events "leading up to" the execution of Billy (and a report of Captain Vere's last estranging words "Billy Budd, Billy Budd"), Melville, we recall, brings his narration to an "unfinished" and "ragged" close with the reproduction of an "outside" re-presentation of the events on board the *Bellipotent* published in an official "naval chronicle of the time." In its disciplined clarity, cogency, and efficiency, this eminently straightforward narrative reduces by violence the differential complexity of that terrible history—the preceding "inside narrative" that, in thematizing the violence of "the law," undermines the authority of the historically constructed, ideological narrative that compels Captain Vere's judgment against Billy—to a grotesque misrepresentation of the truth. In thus fulfilling the benign "outside" logic of planning in an act of violence, it self-destructs in a way that is reminiscent of the self-destruction of Father Mapple's providential narrative. It is not simply that this historical narrative discloses its "truth" to be a justification and enforcement of the official ideology of the British navy ("The criminal paid the penalty of his crime, the promptitude of the punishment has proved salutary. Nothing amiss is now apprehended aboard H.M.S. Bellipotent"). Even more important, it discloses itself as the undeviating determinant of (the truth of) "history." To repeat the insistent Melvillean motif that recalls the loud silences of the American history enabled by the

Puritan doctrine of election and anticipates not simply Thomas Pynchon's revisionary American history but Michel Foucault's genealogy of Western historiography at large, what gets remembered and what gets forgotten, what History gives and denies a history to, "[t]he above, appearing in a publication now long ago superannuated and forgotten, is all that hitherto has stood in human record to attest what manner of men respectively were John Claggart and Billy Budd."[179]

Melville's "diabolic" art, in other words, will not be contained within the binarist problematic that has determined the philosophical and literary discourses of the ontotheological tradition at large and the American philosophical and literary tradition in particular. Its recalcitrant errancy compels us, rather, to understand it as the art of the "middle" excluded by the binary, logical oppositions of this tradition: a de-structive (/projective) art that retrieves the diachronic—temporality, difference, words, freeplay, errancy—from the coercive "Symbolic" imagination and its "Naturalist" or "Realist" allotrope and from the logocentric archive and culture these have elaborated.

In thus invoking a "poststructuralist" rhetoric against Feidelson's "Symbolism" or Trilling's "dialectic" or Chase's "romance" and Stern's "Naturalism," I do not, on the other hand, want to suggest that Melville's "diabolic" fiction is a purely verbal art that deconstructs its pretentions to meaning and worldly *praxis*—a free-floating art of *différance*—as it has been called in recent, brilliantly revisionary, but finally too parochially (and institutionally), situated essays by such deconstructive critics as Barbara Johnson, Rodolphe Gasché, Edgar Dryden, and Joseph Riddel:

At the end of a series of reflections, which began in the figure of the "book" as an "atoll," or the sedimentation of skeletal forms into the shape of a mountain, the narrator [of *Pierre*, which extends and radicalizes the problematic of original writing, indeed, of the possibility of American literature broached by *Moby-Dick*] elaborates yet another figure of the book, this time as the exterior of the "soul" of man, cast in the architectural shape of the pyramid, itself a composition of heterogeneous elements, a tomb that is produced to house the body of the King, the "mummy [which] lies buried in cloth on cloth." The explorer or reader of the pyramid or book seeks its center, moving through and re-moving layer upon layer, seeking the "unlayered substance." But a stratified reading does not uncover the unstratified. The "central room . . ." is empty, "no body is there!" Neither the King nor the author. The pyramid, which Melville elsewhere notes is made on a model of natural mountains, represents instead the "atoll." Neither nature nor its representation is anything more than a representation; neither house their origin. Neither atoll nor pyramid is natural. The "book," then, is not a representation of nature, but a text, the texture of a representation, of nature as always already an architecture, a technic, a text, a construct. And it is interesting that in the one paragraph separating these opposing yet complementary metaphors of the "book" (as circle upon circle, as atoll) and the "sarcophagus," Melville poses the figure of the traveller in Switzerland, who can never see, let alone achieve, the peak of his Alps. . . . It is just this natural origin that is never beheld, except in a belated image that can never represent it fully but can only stand for its absence, like a textual construct.[180]

This is, as far as it goes, a persuasive thematization of the essential differing/deferral dynamics that always disrupt representation in *Pierre*. But the difference in Melville's fiction, especially in *Moby-Dick* and the novels that follow, is not finally "*différance*," that is, a difference restricted to the "scene of writing," as it tends to be for the American followers of Jacques Derrida (if not for Derrida himself). As the passage from Riddel's text—which is intended to stand for the whole, not simply of *Pierre*, but *Moby-Dick*, indeed, for all of American literature[181]—suggests, such a limited, I am tempted to say, disciplinary, view of difference, however subversive in the face of traditional certainties about the decidability of literary works, all too easily neutralizes the ontological difference: the difference that Melville's destructive novel *also* makes *in the temporal world*. Just as the concrete historical pyramid, explorer, and sarcophagus are reduced to abstract and reiterated "book," "reader," and "absence of meaning," so *Pierre*, *Moby-Dick*, and American literature at large are taken up and leveled to an infinitely negative transcendental: a universal, invariable, and adiaphoristic textual *différance* that reinscribes in reverse the Old Americanist internalization and annulment of historically specific contestation. Such a view of difference applied to *Pierre*, for example, overlooks Melville's exposure of the sociopolitical violence of a textuality understood as the socially constituted American *discourse of hegemony*. I mean this discourse's representation of the American truth—from the subject (Pierre's identity), through the family (Pierre's relationship to his mother, who monumentalizes the memory of his father and his grandfather, "grand old" Pierre, the "hero" of the Revolutionary War), to culture (the classist,

"Revolutionary" American Identity)—in such a way as to construe Pierre's act of resistance to these self-evident communal values as an act of madness, a construction that eventually and inexorably will destroy him. It is, in fact, Pierre's "e-mergency"—the estrangement from the monumental truth of his early idyllic life in Saddle Meadows—precipitated by the letter from Isabel that not only discloses this (horological) truth to be an illusory construction, but unleashes the violence hitherto concealed in its benign semblance: the violence that relentlessly pursues and finally corners and destroys the Pierre who has refused his mother's representation of him as "a noble boy, and docile" (p. 19–20) and those he would emerge from the oblivion (mergence) to which this "American" truth relegates them:

In the joyous young times, ere his great grief came upon him, all objects which surrounded him were concealingly deceptive. Not only was the long-cherished image of his father now transfigured before him from a green foliaged tree into a blasted trunk, but every other image in his mind attested the universality of that electrical light which had darted into his soul. Not even his lovely, immaculate mother, remained entirely untouched, unaltered by the shock. . . . Wonderful, indeed, was that electric insight which Fate had now given him into the vital character of his mother. She well might have stood all ordinary tests; but when Pierre thought of the touchstone of his immense strait applied to her spirit; he felt profoundly assured that she would crumble into nothing before it.

She was a noble creature, but formed chiefly for the gilded prosperities of life, and hitherto mostly used to its unruffled serenities; bred and expanded, in all developments, under the sole influence of hereditary forms and world-usages. Not his refined, courtly, loving, equable mother, Pierre felt, could unreservedly, and like a heaven's heroine, meet the shock of his extraordinary emergency, and applaud, to his heart's echo, a sublime resolve [to acknowledge Isabel as his sister], whose execution should call down the astonishment and jeers of this world.

My mother!—dearest mother!—God hath given me a sister, and unto thee a daughter, and covered her with the world's extremest infamy and scorn, that so I and thou—*thou*, my mother, mightest gloriously own her, and acknowledge her, and,—Nay, nay, groaned Pierre, never, never, could such syllables be one instance tolerated by her. Then, high-up, and towering, and all-forbidding before Pierre grew the before unthought of wonderful edifice of his mother's immense pride;— her pride of birth, her pride of affluence, her pride of purity, and all the pride of high-born, refined, and wealthy Life, and all the Semiramian pride of woman.

Then he staggered back upon himself, and only found support in himself. Then Pierre felt that deep in him lurked a divine unidentifiableness, that owned no earthly kin. Yet was this feeling entirely lonesome, and orphan-like. Fain, then, for one moment, would he have recalled the thousand sweet illusions of Life; tho' purchased at the price of Life's Truth; so that once more he might not feel himself driven out an infant Ishmael into the desert, with no maternal Hagar to accompany him.

... He too plainly saw, that not his mother had made his mother; but the Infinite Haughtiness had first fashioned her; and then the haughty world had further molded her; nor had a haughty Ritual omitted to finish her.

... Well may this head hang on my breast,—it holds too much; well may my heart knock at my ribs,—prisoner impatient of his iron bars. Oh, men are jailers all; jailers of themselves; and in Opinion's world ignorantly hold their noblest part a captive to their vilest. (Pp. 88–91)

Applied to *Moby-Dick,* a deconstructive version of difference such as Riddel's, precipitates a reading that neutralizes the novel's historically specific occasion: its contestation of the Puritan/transcendentalist legacy of the expansionist post-Jacksonian (or antebellum) period and its releasement of ideological alternatives this relay precludes. More specifically, it overlooks, in its universalization of "writing in general," the *historicity* of Melville's "diabolic" interrogation of the logocentric eye. I mean its disclosure of the gaze to be one that affiliates the ontological (Emersonian transcendentalism), the epistemological (the sovereign subject and its positivist science), the literary/critical (the recollective/amnesiac *poiesis* of the American cultural memory), and the economicopolitical (capitalist democracy) in a continuous and total, however uneven, discursive practice of hegemony, or, to put this disclosure positively, its liberation or decolonization of a relay of identityless "others" potentially capable of reconstituting itself as the counterhegemonic practice of a "historical bloc."

In other words, the interpretive practice incumbent on a textualized *différance* too often becomes a formalism turned inside out, a new New Criticism that substitutes undecidability for certain meaning and the aesthetic pleasure of perceiving the unweaving for the weaving of the textual fabric, but goes on reading Melville's historically contestatory novel as a free-floating ahistorical text at the "scene of writing." Melville becomes "Melville" and American literature becomes "American Literature" just as Rousseau becomes "Rousseau" in the early texts of Jacques Derrida: internalized and practically, if not theoretically, resolved images or *simulacra* whose original reference to historically specific praxis has receded into oblivion. In this way, such an *aestheticized* interpretive practice finally becomes complicitous with the American ideology it would subvert.[182]

This Kierkegaardian conclusion, to return to the New Americanist revisionary initiative, is, in fact, the implicit one Donald Pease draws in eliding the self-reliant or self-identical American subject of the Old Americanists and the subject of the deconstructionists, which is always not self-present or self-identical, in the process of liberating *Moby-Dick* from the "modern scene of persuasion . . . popularly designated as the Cold War." This is the scenario, according to Pease, into which "a lineage of commentators from F. O. Matthiessen to the present"—the founding fathers of the field-Imaginary of American literary studies—incarcerated Melville's novel when, "as if to supply the opposition to Ahab the crew [including Starbuck] could not," they "found an alternative figure of dissent," when, that is, they "set Ishmael's subversive narrative energies against the totalitarian will at work in Ahab's policy." Against this "canonical reading and . . . the ongoing placement of *Moby-Dick* within the narrative context F. O. Matthiessen called the American Renaissance," Pease observes:

In speaking with the force of Ahab's demand for a world indistinguishable from his human will, but free of the consequences of that will, Ishmael can discover pleasure not quite in another world but in a prior world, in which the endless proliferation of possible deeds displaces the need for any definitive action. The pleasure in this prior world results from the endless delay of a conclusion to the pleasure-inducing activity. The capacity to experience this delay as pleasure (rather than frustration) also derives from Ahab. The fate befalling Ahab's decisive conversion of words into deed determines Ishmael's need for a realm in which the indeterminate play of endless possible actions overdetermines his indecision.

We can understand the dynamics of this relationship better when we turn to the crucial distinctions which critics during the Cold war have drawn between Ishmael and Ahab. In their view, Ishmael, in his rhetoric, frees us from Ahab's fixation by returning all things to their status as pure possibilities. What we now must add is that Ishmael has also invested all the rest of the world of fact with possibility, then invests possibility with the voice of conviction. And when all the world turns out to be invested with the indeterminate interplay of possibility, it does not seem free but replicates what we call boredom (the need for intense action without any action to perform), and what Ishmael called the hypos, the "drizzly November in the soul" that made him feel attracted to Ahab in the first place. This interpolation of an excess of indeterminacy between motive and act displaces Ahab's fixation, but in doing so causes Ishmael to develop a need for Ahab. In short, Ishmael's form of freedom does not oppose Ahab but compels him to need Ahab—not only as the purification of his style, but as the cure for a boredom verging on despair. Only in Ahab's final act can the Ishmael who has in his rhetoric converted the external world into an exact replica of the restless displacements of endlessly mobile energies of attention find a means to give all these energies a final, fatal discharge. Ahab's fatal, decisive deed permits Ishmael to feel the excessive force of Ahab's decision overdetermine his exercises in indecision. Put more simply, Ahab's compulsion to decide compels Ishmael not to decide. (*Visionary Compacts*, p. 273)

Pease's argument is persuasive in its brilliant diagnosis (very reminiscent of Kierkegaard's critique of the [German] aesthetic sensibility)[183] of Cold War criticism as the parasitic relationship of indeterminacy to decisiveness. And it constitutes a momentous contribution not simply to our understanding of Melville's writing, but to American literary studies in general—if, as he does not, we read his reading of Ishmael as a critique of the Ishmael represented by the Cold War critics and, in the last analysis, of *their deconstructionist heirs*. But, as I have tried to suggest, by way of distinguishing the chronology of the "telling" from the chronology of the event, Ishmael, the narrator of *Moby-Dick* (and Melville), is not a deconstructionist in the narrow or disciplinary, i.e., rhetorical, sense subsuming both Riddel's positive and Pease's negative readings. It is true that for Ishmael, as for the deconstructionists, the enabling event is the de-centering of the *logos*. But for Ishmael, both spatial and temporal differentiation/deferral is a matter of the ontological difference, of the de-structive force of being *vis à vis* Being, or, to draw out a certain underdeveloped motif in Heidegger's *Being and Time*,[184] of the very originless be-ing of being understood as an indissoluble and equiprimordial, however asymmetrical, lateral relay of disruptive forces, not simply of the originlessness of a particular (disciplinary) region of being, namely writing. It is not *written signs* per se, but the endless or atelic temporality of being that always already disseminates differences and defers the traces of presence: even writing takes time. As such this "absent cause" of dissemination, as it were, does its corrosive work all along the lateral continuum of (structured or re-presented) Being from ontology as such through language ("writing in general") to culture and sociopolitics. It is precisely Ishmael's increasingly self-conscious enactment of this extended version of the ontological difference in the form/content of *Moby-Dick*—his demystification and dispersion of the summary One (of Being *as* [one] Thing: *Summum Ens*) inscribed as a deep structure of the American allotrope of the Western consciousness *and elaborated* all along the lateral continuum of being—that *breaks through* textuality and, to appropriate Derrida's rhetoric against his American followers, generates the historical "force" of his text.[185] To be more historically specific, it is (1) its breaching of the privileged circle of American Adamic ontology and its narrative, scientific, economic, and sociopolitical allotropes *and* (2) its releasement of a multiplicity of unidentical identities potentially capable of becoming a counterhegemony—a multicultural discursive practice, to invoke a currently much-abused term—that, despite its "iterability" or its "endless delay of a conclusion," makes Ishmael's "story" a "social text": not simply different (novel), but one that makes a difference both in American literary history and the American world. It is, in other words, the multisituated de-structive/projective practice that renders Ishmael/Melville's *Moby-Dick* a "narrative" that breaks out of the reinscriptive binarist terms of all the affiliated discursive formations or, more accurately, allotropes, of the American problematic, not least the American jeremiad and the Cold War scenario. Whatever Melville thought he intended in his letter to Hawthorne, it is this alternative discourse that *Moby-Dick* discloses Melville to have meant in baptizing his bastard, prodigal, and errant book, *"non in Nomine Patris et Filii et Spiritus Sancti sed in Nomine Diaboli."*

THE QUESTION OF ISHMAEL'S NAME: A REPETITION

"Call me Ishmael." This indefinite *and* different and always inaugural, improper, and troping, "voice," we discover at the end for the "last" first time—at the term of the hermeneutic circle—is the impious, improper, and troping multisituated voice of the *dia-bolos*—disseminator of the seminal word, dissimulator of the same, the assimilated, and the simultaneous—the finite, eccentric voice that, by way of his agonistic dialogue, his *Auseinandersetzung* (in Heidegger's resonant word) with being, repeats and retrieves the (community of) the *dia-spora*: human beings' always orphaned ("thrown") and exiled ("estranged" and "uncanny") occasion from the oblivion in which the panoptic "Symbolic" imagination of the ontotheological tradition in general and the American Adamic tradition in particular have all but buried it. As such it is a voice that not only repeats and retrieves the errant or diabolic voices of such eccentric but accommodated *European* writers as Herodotus, Petronius, Euripides, Rabelais, Cervantes, Diderot, and Sterne. In so doing—and despite Blackmur's blind but heuristic assertion that Melville "never influenced the direction of the art of fiction"—it is also a voice that, as I have been suggesting, opens up the space of American literature colonized and exploited ideologically by the American Adamic consciousness up to the Cold War critics to the radical—decentered, but positional—postmodern or, as I prefer, posthumanist imagination: to the occasional and "forwarding" measure of the fiction of Thomas Pynchon, John Barth, Robert Coover, Donald Barthelme, William Gaddis, Stanley Elkin, Don DeLillo, and Kathy Acker and of the poetry of William Carlos Williams, Charles Olson, Robert Creeley, Ed Dorn, Denise Levertov, to invoke only a few more or less obvious examples. As Charles Olson put it, "Melville went back to discover us, to come forward."[186]

"Call me Ishmael": would it be too fanciful to suggest that the seaman's voice addressing the "landsman" reader in the opening sentence of *Moby-Dick* is also the voice of the Occident—the evening land—re-calling American *being-there* to its original and originative agonistic/dialogic "calling"? Could it be, in other words, that Ishmael embodies Melville's intuition at an epochally critical moment in American history—the period bearing witness to the establishment of the hegemony of Jacksonian America—not simply of the multisituated contradictions in the New Adamism precipitated by the "fulfillment" of its logical economy, but also of its polyvalent positive possibilities? Is he the transgressive and productive trace of the originative voice that the Westering momentum has repressed but never finally silenced in the "undeviating wake" (*Moby-Dick*, p. 516) of its increasingly insistent retrospective, monologic, and imperial exceptionalist "errand in the wilderness": its "progressive" circuitous voyage back to "Rome," to that inclusive realm of the Absolute Truth, in which time—its mortal sting—is transformed into Icon or Circle and the differences it disseminates into Empire?

There's another rendering now; but still one text.

Stubb, in *Moby-Dick*

It has become a commonplace of canonical Melville criticism that *Moby-Dick* is, in the "richness of its human vision," capable of accommodating as many interpretations as the Ecuadorean doubloon Ahab nailed to the mast does for the crew of the *Pequod.* This cliché of traditional Americanist criticism is, of course, a manifestation of its humanist "pluralism": its tolerance of different points of view. But it is also symptomatic of a pluralism that, in its "benign" disinterestedness—its calculated disdain for "ideological" reading—conceals a complexly effective ideological agenda. For a pluralism that allows for a multiplicity of "incommensurable" readings of *Moby-Dick*—is grounded in the assumption that all the positions informing these differential readings, in so far as they are adequately argued, are equal and thus negotiable. This pluralism, in which power is represented as equally distributed, that is, takes place *nowhere*: in a free-floating zone beyond the reach of history. As Melville is at great pains to show in *Moby-Dick* and his later novels, however, power relations in history are not equal; they are characterized by injustice, conflict, and contestation: by the uneven struggle for power. In thus transforming worldly conflict to the value-free arena of debate, the dominant pluralist tradition has produced an identical *Moby-Dick,* despite the apparent diversity of its interpretations of Melville's novel. This criticism, in other words, is informed by an undeviating commitment to the monumentality of a novel that, like the fiction that followed, was dedicated to the subversion of the American will to monumentalize "America." To be more specific, this criticism is informed by a commitment to permanentize the status of *Moby-Dick* as a memorial to a pluralist American value system against an Old World authoritarianism and/or its ideological criticism that reflects, confirms, and enhances the hegemony of its pluralist ideology: its authoritarianism by deception.

It is to counter this deceptive authoritarianism that I have undertaken this "ideological" or "interested" reading of *Moby-Dick*: to put back into play the unjust, external, American Adamic world—the relay of historically specific injustices I have claimed Melville is contesting in *Moby-Dick*—that the until recently dominant field-Imaginary of American literary studies has put off limits in the name of the disinterested inquiry of humanist pluralism.

It will, of course, be objected that in invoking worldly phenomena such as injustice and the uneven balance of power, in opting for a contestory reading against pluralist "disinterest," to appropriate *Moby-Dick* in behalf of the struggle against the injustice masquerading as a just "New World Order" in the present historical occasion, such a gesture recuperates a logocentric principle of identity and the will to power it authorizes and thus contradicts my interpretation of the novel as a decentered and de-centering narrative. In response to this objection, I will simply invoke my reading of *Moby-Dick*: What Ishmael learns in the process of repeating the dreadful events culminating in the destruction of the *Pequod* and its crew is that the struggle against injustice simply reinscribes injustice if it is determined by the (ontological) principle of identity; that, in other words, this struggle must not be carried out in terms of a politics of identity; that it must be determined by the imbalance of power all along the indissoluble (however uneven) continuum of being *as* that imbalance exists in history or, more accurately, in the historically specific occasion.

This "paradoxical" relation between undecidability (theory) and practice (sociopolitics), not incidentally, has yet to be thought not only by the body of postmodern criticism that, in its commitment to textual un-decidability, re-inscribes itself into the ideology of the pluralism it ostensibly opposes. It has also yet to be thought adequately by the "New Americanists," who, having borne strong witness to the complicity of the pluralist tradition and literary deconstruction, have forcibly relocated Melville's text from a free-floating zone into the American *agora*, into the arena, not of "freeplay" as such but of the freeplay of *criticism*. However more preferable to literary deconstruction, this "New Americanist" field-Imaginary, in so far as it has failed to think its New History in terms not simply of decentering but of the de-centering of the indissoluble continuum of being, it privileges a practice that reinscribes precisely the disciplinary will to power that the multiply situated decentering has delegitimized.

To put this critique in more familiar and immediately specific terms, insofar as the New Americanist historicism employs one or another kind of totalizing disciplinary scenario that acts as base to epiphenomenal superstructures in the process of attempting to subvert its authority, it will be inadequate to the enormously difficult task of emancipation bequeathed to the radical Left by the failure of the traditional Left to track the transformation of power relations accomplished by an American democratic capitalism driven by an exceptionalist ontology since the Enlightenment. I am referring to the fulfillment of the historical process, brilliantly and decisively described by Michel Foucault, which has borne witness to the *realization* of the practical possibilities inhering in the Enlightenment logic of the "repressive hypothesis": the completed transformation of a vulnerable because overt practice of power into an invulnerable and effective practice in which truth (knowledge), which is always complicitous with power, has been naturalized as external to and the essential and decisive agency of emancipation from power at the end of this century. I mean specifically the process that has culminated in the advent of the "New World Order" and its representation as "the end of history": in, that is, the indissolubly related "triumph" of the principles of (American) democracy over Communism in the Cold War and the "triumph" of late capitalism, variously called "la societé de la spectacle," "the consumer society," "the society of simulacra," or, as I prefer, after Heidegger, "the age of the world picture." This—and the imperative of errancy— is Melville's proleptic witness in *Moby-Dick*.

4

MOBY-DICK AND THE CONTEMPORARY AMERICAN OCCASION

"Are you going to change yet again, shift your position according to the questions that are put to you, and say that the objections are not really directed at the place from which you are speaking? . . . Are you really preparing the way out that will enable you in your next book to spring up somewhere else and declare as you're now doing: no, no, I'm not where you are lying in wait for me, but over here, laughing at you?"

"What, do you imagine that I would take so much trouble and so much pleasure in writing, do you think that I would keep so persistently to my task, if I were not preparing—with a rather shaky hand—a labyrinth into which I can venture, in which I can move my discourse, opening up underground passages, forcing it to go far from itself, finding overhangs that reduce and deform its itinerary, in which I can lose myself and appear at last to eyes that I will never have to meet again. I am no doubt not the only one who writes in order to have no face. Do not ask who I am and do not ask me to remain the same: leave it to our bureaucrats and our police to see that our papers are in order. At least spare us their morality when we write."

Michel Foucault, *Archaeology of Knowledge*

"I would prefer not to."

Herman Melville, "Bartleby, the Scrivener: A Story of Wall-Street"

THE "VIETNAM SYNDROME"

As I suggested in the "final" comments of my "interpretation" of *Moby-Dick*, my "study" is not intended to be History: a retrospective reading from the point of view of the present which would put Melville's novel in its *proper* place in the inclusive table of American literary and cultural history. My de-structive reading, rather, has been intended as genealogy. It is meant, that is, to be a contribution to the "history of the present" place of *Moby-Dick* in the discourse of the American Cultural Memory, a history written from the perspective of the countermemory precipitated by the retrieval of the multiply situated relay of differences that "American History" has repressed in the process of constructing *Moby-Dick* as a monument to America's exceptionalist destiny: a monument that not only memorializes the "Revolutionary" past, but prophesies the end of the post–Cold War and the advent of the "New World Order."

The recent history of Melville criticism, in other words, has been shown to be a history reflecting, not, as it is assumed, impartial debate over the aesthetic greatness of Melville's fiction, but a struggle to appropriate it for present ideological purposes. And my text is no exception, although what distinguishes its problematic decisively from that of the "end-of-ideology" field-Imaginary of the founders of American literary studies—and, less certainly, from that of a particular version of the New Americanists—is its *interestedness:* my recognition that my reading *is* an imaginary. What, then, is at stake in my intervention in the ideological struggle over *Moby-Dick* characterizing the contemporary American critical occasion? What, more specifically, does my destructive reading have to say about the relation between Melville's fiction, especially *Moby-Dick,* and the representation of the end of the Cold War and the "decisive" defeat of Saddam Hussein in the Gulf War as the advent of the "New World Order" and the "end of history"?

To put my answer to this question provisionally, it has been my purpose to suggest that Melville's novel proleptically delegitimizes two massive and temporally related American cultural initiatives of the contemporary historical conjuncture: (1) It deconstructs the field-Imaginary that has harnessed *Moby-Dick* to American Cold War ideology and, by extension, to the justification of the massive American intervention in Vietnam in the 1960s and its sustained and brutal, multisituated conduct of the war. In *Moby-Dick,* that is, Melville anticipates the critique of the American involvement in Vietnam—the exposure of the genocidal violence informing the logic of its democratic mission to "save" the Vietnamese people from Communism—made by the body of critical discourse usually referred to as postmodern but which, in order to dissociate it from Fredric Jameson's influential and, in many ways critically disabling, characterization of post-modernism as a "cultural dominant" identifiable with late capitalism, I prefer to call posthumanist. (2) It proleptically undermines the systematic

effort of the American Cultural Memory to "forget" Vietnam by recollectively re-figuring that disturbing brutal history in the prolonged aftermath
of the defeat of the United States. I am referring to the project of the post-
Vietnam culture industry or what Althusser has more accurately called the
ideological state apparatuses—from its documentary histories, through its
films, plays, fiction, autobiographies, and even comic books to its repeated
staging of massive national ceremonies of cultural remembrance—to recuperate the national consensus that disintegrated during the Vietnam
War. I mean specifically the project to reaffirm the image of "America" that
self-destructed in the face of events that bore witness to the fulfillment of
the "benign" logic of "winning the hearts and minds" of the Vietnamese
people in the name of "the rights of man" in the unleashing of a technological firepower unparalleled in the history of nonatomic warfare, a
firepower that reduced (pacified) a traditional rice culture utterly at one
with the land and its history to an entire population of alienated and nomadic refugees.[1] I mean, to put it in the synecdochical terms of the American culture industry, the recuperative national project epitomized by the
binary metaphorics of health and (mental) sickness that was invented by
the dominant culture and that has saturated the discourse of the American
public sphere ever since the end of the war, but especially since the dedication of the Vietnam War Memorial in 1982. In its early—defensive—
stage this recuperative rhetoric took the form of "healing the wound" suffered by the American psyche (its cultural identity) during the Vietnam
decade. In the aftermath of the "revolutions" in Eastern and Central Europe and the former Soviet Union and, perhaps above all, of the Gulf War
(which "vindicated" and rehabilitated the American military machine), it
has taken the aggressive form of representing the healthy national self-
doubt activated by the war as "kicking the Vietnam syndrome." To explain
this answer to the question of the relationship between *Moby-Dick* and the
present historical conjuncture will require a detour into a textual space
that for the discourse of American canon formation is unimaginable.

FREDRIC JAMESON AND FRANK LENTRICCHIA:
READING MICHAEL HERR'S *DISPATCHES*

In a reference to Michael Herr's *Dispatches*, Fredric Jameson called the
Vietnam War "the first terrible postmodern war,"[2] without, however, artic-

ulating what kind of warfare such a war entails. Rather, he chooses to cite a justly well-known passage from Herr's text that, in its struggle to verbalize the "virtually unimaginable quantum leap in technological alienation" symbolized by the collective "metachopper" that Herr invokes to characterize the essential "motion" of the war and of covering it, suggests "the breakdown of all previous [narrative] paradigms . . . of a shared language" through which the experience might be conveyed: "In this new machine, which does not, like older modernist machinery of the locomotive or the airplane, represent motion, but which can only be represented *in motion*, something of the mystery of the postmodern space is concentrated."[3] Indeed, given the context of this passing but resonant observation, the postmodern war Jameson implies would (1) be restricted to the American side (as if the military strategy of the National Liberation Front and the North Vietnamese Army were not involved) and (2) partake of the conditions, logical economy, and rhetoric of late capitalism *as* Jameson, following Ernest Mandel, defines them; namely, the disarticulation of presence into "the well-nigh universal practice today of what may be called pastiche": a "blank parody" or "linguistic fragmentation of social life itself to the point where the norm itself is eclipsed" and thus the reduction of historical depth to radically heterogeneous and commodified surface of simulacra and the consequent "waning of affect."[4]

Jameson's diagnosis of contemporary cultural production in terms of the logic of late (or consumer) capitalism constitutes a significant, indeed, indispensable contribution to our understanding of the present age. But in its globalization of pastiche as the cultural dominant—and its affiliated overlooking of the unconventional, which is to say, *non-European*, military strategy of the Vietnamese insurgents—it can tell us little about the epochally real "postmodernity" of the Vietnam War. What Jameson leaves unsaid in his imperial identification of the Vietnam War with postmodernity—it is an unsaid that permeates his analysis of postmodernism at large: architecture, painting, fiction, video, and theory—is the *remembering* or *retrieval* of the *forgotten*, which is the necessary obverse face of the postmodern dis-integration—or de-centering—of (forgetful) monumental History and its annulment of historical depth. Or, at least, of a certain postmodern reading and practice of this de-centering, not least Michael Herr's. I am, of course, referring to the temporality or, alternatively, the differences that temporality disseminates, which it is the essential purpose of the (imperial) logical economy of metaphysical spatialization or, more immediately, of the technological reification of time, to obliterate. And the retrieval of this forgotten is an imperative of thinking—of any "cognitive mapping" of—the new postmodern space. To put this critique differently, Jameson's globalization of pastiche has the same disabling effect on his "vision" of postmodern space as Gerald Graff's similar representation of the modern American university as "something of a deconstructionist, proliferating a variety of disciplinary vocabularies that nobody can reduce to the common measure of a metalanguage."[5] It precludes perception of "the center elsewhere . . . which is beyond the reach of [free] play"[6]— more specifically the ontological principle of the self-present or sovereign self, the principle *par excellence* of American self-representation—that subsumes, indeed, as Foucault has persuasively shown, enables, the infinite proliferation *and accommodation* of the (apparent) fragmentation exploited by late capitalist culture. It also blinds him, I suggest, to the violence latent in the logic of this ontological principle, the violence, that is, which, as Gramsci observes in his momentous analysis of the relation between civil and political society, is held in abeyance until confronted by determined resistance.

Addressed in the context of this retrieval of what Jameson leaves unsaid in his identification of postmodernity with spatialized pastiche—the radical temporality that disintegrates the imperial will to spatialize being— the postmodernity of the Vietnam War is better explained by Frank Lentricchia, who has also in passing appropriated Herr's *Dispatches* to suggest the post-Modernity (if not the postmodernity) of the Vietnam War: that is, to expose the imperialist project informing the United States' intervention in Southeast Asia in the name of an "errand in the wilderness" intended to "save" the Vietnamese people from a Soviet- and Chinese-inspired Communism. Unlike Jameson, it is not, significantly, Herr's metachopper that Lentricchia invokes. It is, rather, Herr's appropriation of Wallace Stevens's "post-Modernist" Modernist poem "Anecdote of the Jar." The passage, quoted earlier in this book, bears repetition, and some amplification, not simply to recall its previous Melvillean context, but to focus the differential resonances it will take on in the commentary that follows.

None of it had happened yet when Khe Sanh became lost forever as a tactical entity. It is impossible to fix the exact moment in time when it happened, or to know, really, why. All that was certain was that Khe Sanh had become a passion, the false love object in the heart of the Command. It cannot even be determined which way the passion traveled. Did it proceed from the filthiest ground-zero slit trench and proceed outward, across I Corps to Saigon and on (taking the true perimeter with it) to the most abstract reaches of the Pentagon? Or did it get born in those same Pentagon rooms where six years of failure had made the air bad, where optimism no longer sprang from anything viable but sprang and sprang, all the way to Saigon, where it was packaged and shipped north to give the grunts some kind of reason for what was about to happen to them? In its outlines, the promise was delicious: Victory! A vision of as many as 40,000 of them, out there in the open, fighting it out on our terms, fighting for once like men, fighting to no avail. There would be a battle, a set-piece battle where he could be killed by the numbers, killed wholesale, and if we killed enough of him, maybe he would go away. In the face of such a promise, the question of defeat could not even be considered, no more than the question of whether, after Tet, Khe Sanh might have been militarily unwise and even absurd. Once it was all locked in place, Khe Sanh became like the planted jar in Wallace Stevens' poem. It took dominion everywhere.[7]

And Lentricchia invokes Herr's Stevens precisely to suggest the power of the American democratic/capitalist imaginary (its historically continuous self-representation) to construct a coherent and all-inclusive reality, specifically, the synecdochical reality of the "Siege of Khe Sanh" in the face of the absence of presence, which is to say, of an identifiable and visible enemy.

By thus focusing on Herr's appropriation of Stevens's jar—its inexorably inclusive centering/spatializing of the differential Tennessee wilderness—Lentricchia, in other words, discloses America's representation of the actuality of the synecdochical Khe Sanh to be both paranoidal (or monomaniacal) and imperial. As such, it suggests that the postmodernity of the Vietnam War has less to do with the "blank parody" of pastiche, as Jameson understands the postmodern occasion, as with the exposure of the *center elsewhere* of American late capitalism, the power of which is both positively capable of infinitely accommodating emergent (antagonistic) differences to its expanding circumference and also held in reserve until these emergent differences begin to resist the truth of its circumscribing gaze—to precipitate an emergency, as it were:

Had [Wallace Stevens] forgotten what he knew, long before our military intervention in Southeast Asia, he would have been (had he lived so long) reminded of Michael Herr who at the end of his book *Dispatches* (1970) wrote "Vietnam Vietnam Vietnam, we've all been there." Herr maybe in part knew what he knew because he had read Stevens, who taught him about where we've all been, all along: "Once it was all locked in place, Khe Sanh became like the planted jar in Wallace Stevens' poem. It took dominion everywhere." Herr's perversely perfect mixed metaphor of the "planted jar," if it might have struck Stevens as an incisive reading of his poem, might also have awakened in him an obscure memory of one of the powerful philosophical presences of his Harvard days, William James, writing out of the bitterness of his political awakening, writing on 1 March 1899 in the *Boston Transcript* against our first imperial incursion in the Orient: "We are destroying down to the root every germ of a healthy national life in these unfortunate people. . . . We must sow our ideals, plant our order, impose our God." James might have ended his letter: "The Philippines the Phillipines the Phillipines, we've all been there."

. . . I offer Herr, Stevens, and James (in that order, reading backward, which is always the way reading takes place: through our cultural formation) as three voices from a tradition of American anti-imperialist writing (a unified cultural practice) that cuts through the boundaries of philosophy, poetry, and journalism, a discourse of political criticism.[8]

Lentricchia's reading of Michael Herr's reading of Stevens's (and James's) proleptic postmodern reading of the Vietnam War is extraordinarily suggestive. But two points can be made by way of qualification: (1) in failing to consider the peculiar role emphatically underscored by Herr, played by the Vietnamese insurgents in the war, it is, like Jameson's, incomplete; (2) in restricting his historical reference to Stevens's "Anecdote," that is, to an American Modernist poem, and to James's bitterly anti-imperial comments in the *Boston Transcript*, it minimizes Herr's resonant insight into how deeply "backgrounded" the obsessive cultural—and violent—Imaginary these modern American writers critically focalize by estranging its "truth." I mean the continuity of this Imaginary with the entire history of American self-representation, from the Puritan errand in the wilderness through the post-Revolutionary Jeremiad and the expansionist discourse of Manifest Destiny to the Cold War scenario *vis à vis* the Third World (the "domino" hypothesis), indeed, into the coming full circle of this Imaginary's historical itinerary, which is to say, its self-destruction, in its practice in Vietnam:

You couldn't find two people who agreed about when it began, how could you say when it began going off? Mission intellectuals like 1954 [the fall of Dien Bien Phu and the collapse of the "decadent" French colonialism in Indochina] as the reference date; if you saw as far back as War II and the Japanese occupation you were practically a historical visionary. "Realists" said that it began for us in 1961 [when President Kennedy sent "military advisors" to Vietnam], and the common run of Mission flack insisted on 1965, post-Tonkin Resolution, as though all the killing that had gone before wasn't really war. Anyway, you couldn't use standard methods to date the doom; might as well say that Vietnam was where the Trail of Tears was headed all along, the turnabout point where it would touch and come back to form a containing perimeter; might just as well lay it on the proto-Gringos who found the New England woods too raw and empty for their peace and filled them up with their imported devils. Maybe it was already over for us in Indochina when Alden Pyle's body washed up under the bridge at Dakao, his lungs all full of mud; maybe it caved in with Dien Bien Phu. But the first happened in a novel, and while the second happened on the ground it happened to the French, and Washington gave it no more substance than if Graham Greene had made it up too. Straight history, auto-revised history, history without handles, for all the books and articles and white papers, all the talk and the miles of film, something wasn't answered, it wasn't even asked. We were backgrounded deep, deep, but when the background started sliding forward not a single life was saved by the information. The thing had transmitted too much energy, it heated up too hot, hiding low under the fact-figure crossfire there was a secret history, and not a lot of people felt like running in there to bring it out.[9]

Despite Lentricchia's profoundly resonant correlation of Herr, Stevens, and James as an affiliated triad of American writers whose interrogation of the logocentric Modernist aesthetic principle of order implicates this principle with political imperialism—as "three voices from a tradition of American anti-imperialist writing . . . that cuts through the boundaries of philosophy, poetry, and journalism"—his problematic remains vestigially disciplinary in its focus, not simply on the essentially political site of this American imaginary but on this American imaginary itself at the expense of the discursive practices of the "Other." It is, thus, blinded to a more fundamental, if not unrelated proleptic critique of the American imaginary that produced Vietnam. I mean, of course, Herman Melville's *Moby-Dick*.[10] This novel, I submit, despite its relative invisibility, is a determining presence in Herr's *Dispatches*.[11]

THE POSTMODERNITY OF THE VIETNAM WAR

The Vietnam War was, indeed, the first postmodern war. But what was postmodern about it cannot be determined simply by focusing on the essence of the American intervention, a gesture that, as a number of recent

Third-World critics have insisted, remains imperial.[12] The response of the "other" must *also* be taken into account. One must consider the way the National Liberation Front and, later, the North Vietnamese army under General Giap "confronted" this intervention, just as any reading of *Moby-Dick* must take into account the "whiteness of the white whale": their "refusal" to conform their military practice to the imperatives of the polyvalent Name imposed on "them" by their inexorably willful pursuers, just as the white whale "refuses" to conform to the demands of the affiliated relay of representations embodied in the discursive practices of the Linnaean table of classification through the Nantucket market to the inverted Puritan providentialism of Captain Ahab.

It was not the new, late-capitalist technology introduced by the United States in Vietnam as such that rendered the Vietnam War the first postmodern war. It was, rather, the "enemy's"—the "other's"—perfection of a guerrilla ("low-intensity") warfare integrally related to the land it would protect and be protected by; a kind of warfare, that is, more or less foreign to the "high intensity" and abstracted warfare practiced historically by the West from the campaigns of Alexander the Great and Julius Caesar through the Franco-Prussian War to World War II—and anticipated or hoped for by the American Military Command in Saigon.[13] To be more specific, the "other" insistently refused to act in terms of the logic of the Identity imposed on them not simply by the American Military Command but by the relay of commands encompassing the military and the ideological: the cultural, the economic, and the political.[14] To invoke the metaphorics I have disclosed as saturating *Moby-Dick*, it is as if the Vietnamese "other" had learned by their harsh experience of French colonialism and its *"mission civilatrice"* how profoundly inscribed as a deep structure the logocentrism—the Center/periphery, Capital/provinces—and its logical corollary, decidability, were in the Occidental consciousness and they had appropriated them to undermine their power. Whatever the viability of this hypothesis, it could be said that for all practical purposes the Vietnamese insurgents developed a "dia-bolic" strategy—a "careful disorderliness," as it were, intended to de-structure not simply the abstract imperial strategy of the perimeter, but the very metaphysical ontology—including the metaphorics of spatialization and light—that enabled it.

This destructive practice of the Vietnamese insurgents was accomplished, above all, by their refusal to make themselves visible—a "conventional" or "regular" army—to the much more formidable American military/technological machine. As it is well known, it was this uncanny ability of the "irregular" Vietnamese enemy to remain invisible (an absent presence, as it were) enabled by their integral relations to the land (*Xa*), that confounded the alienated American soldier in Vietnam, rendering his tour a sojourn in the dreadful realm of the uncanny: *die Unheimliche*. As Tim O'Brien puts this pervasive de-structured condition in which the privileged see(e)r in the discourse of Occidental hegemony becomes, like Captain Ahab and his crew, the seen, the helpless object of the gaze of the "Other":

From a distance, even seen through binoculars, a village was a thicket of vines and shrubs, and only behind the hedges did you see the true village. Guarding, but mostly concealing, the hedgerows in Quang Ngai sometimes seemed like a kind of smoked glass forever hiding what it was that was not meant to be seen. Like curtains, or like walls. Like camouflage. So where the paddies represented ripeness and age and depth, the hedgerows expressed the land's secret qualities: cut up, twisting, covert, chopped and mangled, blind corners leading to dead ends, short horizons always changing. It was only a feeling. A feeling of marching through a great maze; a sense of entrapment mixed with mystery. The hedgerows were like walls in old mansions: secret panels and trapdoors and portraits with moving eyes. That was the feeling the hedges always gave him, just a feeling.[15]

It was also this complexly articulated strategy of invisibility that confounded the American Military Command at large. Despite the early creation of the Special Forces (such as the Green Berets), which, according to the cultural discourse of President Kennedy's "New Frontier," was trained for insurgency combat, the American Military Command preferred the inscribed strategy of direct confrontation and, when that failed, of enticing the recalcitrant enemy into *decisive* battle, a strategy, I am suggesting, ultimately grounded in the Occidental ontology (metaphysics), its understanding of truth as *adequatio intellectus et rei* (*techne*), its retrospective or calculative spatial orientation, its panoptic ethnocentrism, and its imperial territorialization. This constellation of Western ideological constructs, for example, informed General Westmoreland's strategy in Vietnam as late as what came to be (mis)represented monumentally as "The Siege of Khe Sanh." And, as Herr observes, disclosed the astonishing blindness (to historical difference) of its "tremendously concentering" monologic gaze:

Tactically, [Khe Sanh's] value to the Command was thought so great that General Westmoreland could announce that the Tet Offensive was merely Phase

II of a brilliant Giap strategy. Phase I had been revealed in the autumn skirmishes between Loc Ninh and Dak To. Phase III ("the capstone," the general called it) was to be Khe Sanh. It seems improbable that anyone, at any time, even in the chaos of Tet, could have actually called something as monumental (and decisive) as that offensive a mere diversion for something as negligible as Khe Sanh, but all of that is on record.[16]

Indeed, so profoundly inscribed was this centered and centering Occidental/American problematic that its restricted economy determined the Military Command's representation of the events at Khe Sanh, *even after* history demonstrated its tactical irrelevance:

A great many people wanted to know how the Khe Sanh Combat Base could have been the Western Anchor of our Defense one month and a worthless piece of ground the next, and they were simply told that the situation had changed. . . . The Mission called it a victory, and General Westmoreland said that it had been "Dien Bien Phu in reverse." In early June engineers rolled up the airstrips and transported the salvaged tarmac back to Dong Ha. The bunkers were filled with high explosives and then blown up, the sandbagging and wire that remained were left to the jungle, which grew with a violence of energy now in the Highland summer, as though there was an impatience somewhere to conceal all traces of what had been left by the winter.[17]

This desperate yearning for the "set-piece battle" in fact pervades the documentary accounts of the Vietnam War. It is, for example, at the crux of Philip Caputo's autobiographical justification of his "murder" of two Vietnamese civilians, *A Rumor of War*, and his condemnation of America's intervention in Vietnam: "It was not warfare. It was murder. We could not fight back against Viet Cong mines or take cover from them or anticipate when they would go off. Walking down the trails, waiting for those things to explode, we had begun to feel more like victims than soldiers. So we were ready for a battle, a traditional, set-piece battle against regular soldiers like ourselves."[18] It is also poignantly central to Tim O'Brien's fictional account of the low-intensity warfare suffered by the utterly unprepared American soldier:

They did not know even the simple things: a sense of victory, or satisfaction, or necessary sacrifice. They did not know the feeling of taking a place and keeping it, securing a village and then raising the flag and calling it a victory. No sense of order or momentum. No front, no rear, no trenches laid out in neat parallels. No

Patton rushing for the Rhine, no beachheads to storm and win and hold for the duration. They did not have targets. They did not have a cause. They did not know if it was a war of ideology or economics or hegemony or spite. On a given day, they did not know where they were in Quang Ngai, or how being there might influence larger outcomes.[19]

As the sedimented metaphorics informing these representative passages suggests—the map or table, the regularity of the moves these afford, and the assumption of a decisive end to the game—the lack expressed by this yearning is determined by a profoundly Occidental, especially American, ocularcentrism: meta-physical vision, a spatializing that perceives being all at once in miniature, in which every differential thing and event in time and space has its *proper and identifiable place* in the larger identical whole.

The response of the Vietnamese insurgents to this culturally inscribed and blinding commitment to the "set-piece battle where he could be killed by the numbers, killed wholesale," and its "promise" that "if we killed enough of him, maybe he would go away,"[20] was to decenter it: to frustrate the power of its monolithic economy by fracturing the "front line" (perimeter) and volatilizing its willful directionality. As Herman Rapaport puts the consequences of this refusal in a brilliant Deleuzian/Guattarian interpretation of this transformation of a powerfully efficient military economy into a disarticulated and wasteful one:

Truong Son of the N.L.F. reports that the North Vietnamese took very much into account the American expectation that one ought to win "decisive battles" in Vietnam. "Though somewhat disheartened, the Americans, obdurate by nature and possessed of substantial forces, still clung to the hope for a military solution, for decisive victories on the battlefield." Truong Son's comments are based on the perception that an American view of an all-or-nothing victory can easily be converted to a tactic by which the "superior forces," anxious for quick victory, are by way of a certain fracturing, reduced to something less than victory. That is, the North Vietnamese immediately realized that a molecularization of its forces among those of the Southern resisters would force the United States to spread its resources thin. Son's assessment of the American strategy is that "it did not specifically center on anything" and that "the Americans and their puppets had no definite way of utilizing their mobile and occupational forces . . ." For this reason even when conflict was "head on," that conflict would be articulated in terms of passivity, since action did not necessarily lead to anything more than action itself. Moreover, the communists saw to it that the "corps" would be disarticulated along various mobile "fronts" all at the same time. In doing so they insured that "action" would be reduced to random or marginalized events which even if successfully won by the Americans would not mean victory. As so many soldiers said to themselves over and over again, "what a waste . . ."[21]

This decentering (and dispersion or dissemination of the power enabled by the panoptic gaze/center), which reduced not only the imperial American military machine to ineffectuality but the very seminal ontology of the *anthropologos* or centered circle on which it is founded, goes far to explain why it is appropriate to call the Vietnam War the "first postmodern war." But it is only a part of the story. The other has to do with the predictable practical response of the United States to the resistant "other's" fracturing strategy. It should be recalled that the United States justified its intervention in Vietnam in the benign name of the founding principles of liberal humanistic democracy—the sovereign individual, freedom, disinterestedness, and so on—and took the form of representing its end as "winning the hearts and minds" of the Vietnamese people. This representation remained a constant throughout the Vietnam War, from the Kennedy through the Johnson to the Nixon administration. But American practice changed radically as the recalcitrant "other's" de-centering strategy increasingly disrupted the frontal logic of the American Military Command and dispersed the concentrated power of its military machine by refusing its "proper" role in the American narrative. Rather than adjusting to the conditions imposed by the visibly invisible insurgent other, the American Military Command predictably—and, one is entitled by the actuality to say, monomaniacally—pursued the practical imperatives of the "logic" of the *anthropologos* to its self-destructive *telos*. In response to the frustration of its promised end by the "absence" of presence at the core of its self-definition, it unleashed a technological firepower *indiscriminately* at the Vietnamese people and their land—the B-52 bombings, the massive napalming of the jungles and forests (defoliation), the destruction of the rice paddies by spraying them with herbicides—that was epochal in its proportions. As such, this initiative (self-)disclosed the genocidal violence—as well as the madness—latent in the benign rationality of Occidental (humanist) democracy.[22] To invoke Nietzsche by way of Michel Foucault, the American response was something like an epochal instance in practice of that humanist economy of representation in which the terms of its "benign" identity (classical Greece) turn out to be the same as those demonic terms it imposed on the "other" (Egypt) in order to define itself and its enabling superiority:

Nietzsche's criticism, beginning with the second of the *Untimely Meditations*, always questioned the form of history that reintroduces (and always assumes) a suprahistorical perspective: a history whose function is to compose the finally reduced diversity of time into a totality fully closed upon itself; a history that always encourages subjective recognitions and attributes a form of reconciliation to all the displacements of the past; a history whose perspective on all that precedes it implies the end of time, a completed development. The historian's history finds its support outside of time and pretends to base its judgments on an apocalyptic objectivity. This is only possible, however, because of its belief in eternal truth, the immortality of the soul, and the nature of consciousness as always identical to itself. Once the historical sense is mastered by a suprahistorical perspective, metaphysics can bend it to its own purpose and, by aligning it to the demands of objective science, it can impose its own "Egyptianism."[23]

This self-exposed spectacle of the enormous distance—which is also a terrible proximity—between the representation and the practical reality of the American intervention in Vietnam was the essential testimony of the years of the Vietnam War—until the post–Cold War custodians of the American Cultural Memory began the calculative process of forgetting this appalling history. Like so much else about the dark underside of the American intervention in Vietnam, it is epitomized by Michael Herr's recurrent carnivalization—invoked earlier in reference to the violent imperatives of Father Mapple's hermeneutics—of official representations of the sublimely ineffectual and devastating violence of the American military machine:

At the end of my first week in-country I met an information officer in the headquarters of the 25th Division at Cu Chi who showed me on his map and then from his chopper what they'd done to the Ho Bo Woods, that vanished Ho Bo Woods, taken off by giant Rome plows and chemicals and long, slow fire, wasting hundreds of acres of cultivated plantation and wild forest alike, "denying the enemy valuable resources and cover".

It had been part of his job for nearly a year now to tell people about that operation; correspondents, congressmen, movie stars, corporation presidents, staff officers from half the armies in the world, and he still couldn't get over it. It seemed to be keeping him young, his enthusiasm made you feel that even the letters he wrote home to his wife were full of it, it really showed what you could do if you had the know-how and the hardware. And if in the months following that operation incidences of enemy activity in the large area of War Zone C had increased "significantly," and American losses had doubled and then doubled again, none of it was happening in any damn Ho Bo Woods, you'd better believe it. . . .[24]

And even more decisively: "We took space back quickly, expensively, with total panic and close to maximum brutality. Our machine was devastating. And versatile. It could do everything but stop. As one American major said, in a successful attempt at attaining history, 'We had to destroy Ben Tre in order to save it.'"[25]

By invoking Stevens's "Anecdote of the Jar" in order to suggest the complicity between American cultural production and American imperialism in Vietnam, then, Frank Lentricchia "corrects" Jameson's sense of the "postmodernity" of the Vietnam War. He shows, that is, that the apparently infinite fragmentation of the contemporary occasion—the simulacral "pastiche" or "blank parody" of the late capitalist world picture in Jameson's formulation—is informed by a center elsewhere immune to the freeplay of criticism. Nevertheless he fails to perceive (or at least to show) that Stevens's jar is not simply a Modernist poem, but also a figure (the centered circle) of meta-physical ontology. In other words, the complicitous continuity Lentricchia discovers between American cultural production and imperial politics is itself subsumed by the polyvalent principle of (metaphysical) principles: that Identity is the condition for the possibility of difference.[26] Or what is the same thing—if *principle* is understood in terms of its relation to *princeps*—by a will to power over the be-ing of being. Lentricchia, that is, fails to perceive that imperialism proper, as the liberation theologist Henrique Dussel has argued, has its condition of possibility in meta-physics.[27] What this means specifically is that the fulfillment of the logic of this principle of principles legitimizes and enables the forcible reduction of the differences time disseminates to the all-inclusive—and reified—One and thus to make "it" "*practically assailable.*" In other words, it necessarily ends, like the promise/fulfillment structure of Father Mapple's providential hermeneutics and Captain Ahab's monomania, in the material annihilation of everything ("All") that contradicts it. Herr's synecdochal invocation of Stevens's "Anecdote" bears repetition at this point for the subtle but decisive sea change, both of content and tone (toward parody in the genealogical mode), wrought on Lentric-chia's reading by placing it in its proper context.

In its outline, the promise was delicious. Victory! A vision of as many as 40,000 of them out there in the open, fighting it out on our own terms, fighting for once like men, fighting to no avail. This would be a battle, a set-piece battle where he could be killed by the numbers, killed wholesale, and if we killed enough of him, maybe he would go away. In the face of such a promise, the question of defeat could not even be considered, no more than the question of whether, after Tet, Khe Sanh might have become militarily unwise, and even absurd. Once it was locked in place, Khe Sanh became like the planted jar in Wallace Stevens' poem. It took dominion everywhere.

As a consequence of this ontological blindness of his New Historical or, perhaps more accurately, New Americanist insight, Lentricchia also fails to see (or at least to show) what Herr is on the edge of discovering/saying in his symptomatic invocation of Stevens's "Anecdote" and the "perversely perfect mixed metaphor of the 'planted jar'" to characterize the hold that the narrative of "America's (exceptionalist) promise" had on the possessed Americans fighting against an invisible enemy in Vietnam: that the self-destruction of the discourse of "the errand in the wilderness" or "the American Jeremiad" in the Vietnam War was not a local break, but epistemic in its proportions. Lentricchia fails to see, in other words, that the "fulfillment" of the promissary logic informing the American cultural identity in the violence of Vietnam was a decisive rupture in the dominant discourse of hegemony, one that once and for all foreclosed (theoretically, at least) its recuperation by the perennial appeal to the repressive hypoth-esis, to the argument that any violence perpetrated by America is always accidental, always the consequence of a *lapse* from or *betrayal* of its subsum-ing truth principles, rather than the necessary effect of its "American" (onto)logic. Put more specifically, Lentricchia and other New American-ists who have rehabilitated history in the critique of the (textuality of) literature fail to perceive that the United States' intervention in Vietnam and its brutal conduct of the war precipitated an epochal de-centering of the anthropological gaze (and the relay of imperial centers it enables—those grounding the sovereign subject, disinterestedness, the "liberal imagination," humanist pluralism, democracy, and so on)—that not only delegitimized the discourse of "America" but, in doing so, called for, if it did finally enable, a decentered discursive practice as a counterhegemonic alternative. I mean an oppositional discourse that, like the guerrilla strategy of the Vietnamese other *vis à vis* the polyvalent *monos*-oriented discourse and practice of the American Command, is not only adequate to the task of resisting domination and colonization by always already fracturing and disarticulating the relay of (disciplinary) centers of the dominant culture, but also envisions a (horizonal) thinking and *polis* of differential identities grounded in the (un)principle that difference is the condition for possibility of identity and not the other way around.[28]

MOBY-DICK AND THE VIETNAM WAR

And Indian-hating still exists; and, no doubt, will continue to exist, so long as Indians do.

Charles Noble, in Herman Melville, *The Confidence-Man*

This detour into a future ostensibly quite remote from antebellum America thus brings us back to Herman Melville and *Moby-Dick*. For, as I have tried to suggest, it is precisely this critique of the meta-physical discourse of "America," which is simultaneously a releasement or de-colonization of the multiple forces its spatial structure contained, that, however asymmetrically, *Moby-Dick* enacts. It is this de-structive project, in other words, that renders Melville's novel a proleptic delegitimation of the American intervention in Vietnam and justification of the multiple subject positions, hitherto repressed or spoken for, that e-merged spontaneously during the Vietnam decade as contradictions of the dominant order's "benign" logic. It is, finally, this double-faced e-mergent project announced in *Moby-Dick* that inaugurated an alternative or counterhegemonic initiative in the abyssal interstices of the American myth. Of course, it remains an initiative. For despite the advances in reading representation achieved with the advent of postmodern theory, Melville's inaugural project has, unfortunately, yet to be fully thought because of the increasing antagonism between those who resist theory (the ontological) in the (ostensible) name of practice (the ontic or historically specific) and those who resist practice in the (ostensible) name of theory. I mean specifically the failure to perceive the indissoluble relationship between the *Pax Metaphysica* and the *Pax Americana*.

Like the circular structure of the detour that "ends" in repeating Herr's invocation of Stevens's jar in Tennessee, we are thus compelled to retrieve (*wiederholen*) the preceding reading of *Moby-Dick* to appreciate the resonant transformation of "meaning" that accrues to the novel by thus forcibly dislocating it from its "proper" place in the American canon to which the custodians of the American Cultural Memory consecrated it at the outset of the Cold War period and by relocating it within the historically specific present, within, that is, the emergent alternative—post-American or counterhegemonic—tradition which, I am claiming, Melville "founded." This, of course, we cannot do here. But we can get a provocative glimpse of this extraordinary transformation simply by repeating what I have shown to be the synecdochical moment of the destructive/projective movement of Melville's novel, the moment, that is, which instigated the enabling crisis in Ishmael's narration of the cataclysm that befell the *Pequod*, its captain, and its crew of *Isolatoes*. I am referring to the moment when Ishmael discovers with the shock of recognition his complicity with Captain Ahab or, rather, the complicity of his Emersonian self-reliance with Ahab's absolute freedom. As Ishmael put it—in a way that cannot but activate an extraordinary historical resonance in the last lines of Michael Herr's *Dispatches*, "Vietnam, Vietnam, Vietnam, we've all been there":[29] "I, Ishmael, was one of that crew; my shouts had gone up with the rest; my oath was wedded with theirs; and stronger I shouted, and more did I hammer and clinch my oath, because of the dread in my soul. A wild, mystical, sympathetical feeling was in me; Ahab's quenchless feud seemed mine. With greedy ears I learned the history of that murderous monster against whom I and all the others had taken our oaths of violence and revenge" (p. 179). These sentences, in which Ishmael confesses that his vow of fealty to Ahab's monomaniacal, that is, *totalizing*, project is compelled by the need to objectify—to find an object for—his dread of nothing, are, of course, the opening sentences of the consecutive chapters entitled "Moby Dick" and "The Whiteness of the Whale," that diacritical place in Ishmael's narrative that opens out to radical *dis-closure:* to both a decisive critique of ontological naming and and, at least, the acknowledgment of the nothing—the ontological difference—it would subdue and the need to think "the nothing" positively.

Melville's proleptic anticipation of the "postmodern" destruction of the American errand in Vietnam, right down to its racist overtones, is astonishing in the exactness of its contours. This becomes remarkably clear when Ishmael's confessional retrieval of the Ahab to whom he had vowed allegiance is juxtaposed against Michael Herr's Stevensian demystification of the benign myth of American cultural identity: his disclosure of the totalizing violence—the ferocity of the monomaniacal will to dominate and subdue the elusive Vietnamese other—informing its exceptionalist logic:

No turbaned Turk, no hired Venetian or Malay, could have smote him with more seeming malice. Small reason was there to doubt, then, that ever since that almost fatal encounter [with the white whale], Ahab had cherished a wild vindictiveness against the whale, all the more fell for that in his frantic, morbidness he at last came to identify with him, not only all his bodily woes, but all his intellectual and spiritual exasperations. The White Whale swam before him as the monomaniac incarnation of all those malicious agencies which some deep men feel eating in them, till they are left living on with half a heart and half a lung. That intangible malignity which has been from the beginning; to whose dominion even modern Christians ascribe one-half of the worlds; which the ancient Ophites of the east reverenced in their statue devil;—Ahab did not fall down and worship it like them; but deliriously transferring its idea to the abhorred white whale, he pitted himself, all mutilated, against it. All that most maddens and torments; all that stirs the lees of things; all truth with malice in it; all that cracks the sinews and cakes the brain; all the subtle demonisms of life and thought; all evil, to crazy Ahab, were visibly personified, and made practically assailable in Moby Dick. He piled upon the whale's white hump the sum of all the general rage and hate felt by his whole race from Adam down; and then, as if his chest has been a mortar, he burst his hot heart's shell upon it. (P. 184)[30]

But Melville's proleptic anticipation of Herr's (and Lentricchia's) postmodern critique of America's intervention in Vietnam and its conduct of the war constitutes more than a mere parallel in at least two crucial ways. First, it makes *the ontological ground* of Herr's disclosure of the violence informing the imperial American will to power explicit. It shows that the *naming*—the production of knowledge about being that makes "it" *comprehensible* (totally "take-holdable")—is a mode of the will to power that involves a reification of its invisible and ineffable nothingness (the personification of its whiteness) that renders it "practically assailable." That is, it deepens the political critique of America's imperial project in Vietnam (the *Pax Americana*) by identifying it with the unrelenting annihilating logic of a paranoid representation of the being of being (the *Pax Metaphysica*). Secondly, and even more important, it also extends Herr's (and especially Lentricchia's) focus on the complicity of cultural production and political domination to include the entire indissoluble continuum of being—providing Ahab's monomania is understood, as I have suggested it should, as the *incarnation* of the will to power over being informing the Puritans' exceptionalist errand, the Emersonian principle of self-reliance, the classificatory tables of natural science, the division of labor of the factory, and the disciplinary organization of the *polis*.[31]

But this disclosure is only the negative phase of Melville's anticipation of the postmodernity of the Vietnam War. The positive or pro-jective phase, which is simultaneous with the negative, has to do with its prolepsis of the emergent comportment toward the being of being, which is grounded precisely in the de-centered space—the opening—disclosed by the (self-)destruction of the globalized structure of (American) being. This phase, not accidentally, is announced in the second of the two chapters I have invoked as a synecdoche of the "whole" of *Moby-Dick*, the chapter that, in direct opposition to the one it follows ("Moby Dick"), is entitled "The Whiteness of the Whale":

> What the whale was to Ahab, has been hinted; what, at times, he was to me, as yet remains unsaid.
>
> Aside from those more obvious considerations touching Moby Dick, which could not but occasionally awaken in any man's soul some alarm, there was another thought, or rather vague, nameless horror concerning him, which at times by its intensity completely overpowered all the rest; and so mystical and well nigh ineffable was it, that I almost despair of putting it in a comprehensible form. It was the whiteness of the whale that above all things appalled me. But how can I hope to explain myself here; and yet, in some dim, random way, explain myself I must, else all these chapters might be naught. (P. 185)

This acknowledgment of the "ineffable" or "vague, nameless horror" associated with the white whale—and Ishmael's way of confronting "it" in the extraordinary improvisational discourse that follows—constitutes, as I have suggested, a remarkable anticipation of the postmodern (or post-anthropological) diagnosis of the relation between language and being, signifier and signified. It is not only reminiscent of Martin Heidegger's inaugural acknowledgment (in "What is Metaphysics?") of the dreadful and appalling nothing repressed and forgotten by the Occidental philosophical tradition by naming or comprehending "it," but also of Jacques Derrida's acknowledgment of the dis-forming dynamic informing the hitherto transparency of language: the *différance* that, in naming, endlessly differentiates and defers the presence it would re-present. But taken in its immediate context, in terms, that is, of its opposition to a stridently vocal naming that is showing itself to be an annihilating violence against its "object" and of the quite different—and indirect or "poetic"—way of saying the whiteness of the whale, a way that is consciously "random," that "names" without naming, it is more than that. It becomes, in its appropriation of the elusive *silence* and *invisibility* of the whiteness of the white whale against the will to power of naming, an announcement of the nomadic and molecularizing subversive discourse which I have called the "errant art" of *Moby-Dick*. It becomes a discourse of "the other" that, like the practice of the Vietnamese insurgents in the face of the American military machine "which could do everything but stop," relies on the *predictability*—the ultimate *mono*glossia and *mono*mania—imbedded in the logical economy of the "benign" polyglossia of Occidental civilization to disarticulate and deterritorialize its in-clusive global ambitions, which is to say, to dis-empower the power that would colonize it in the name of the *anthropologos*. To show that this "posthumanist" interpretation of Ishmael's maddeningly elusive narrative strategy is not entirely arbitrary, it will suffice simply to invoke Melville's short story "Bartleby, the Scrivener," published only three years after *Moby-Dick*.[32] For this polyvalent molecularizing effect of Ishmael's errant narrative—this multisituated disarticulation and deterritorialization of the totalizing/spatializing logical economy of "American" "premises"— is precisely what is enacted in this justly celebrated, but still to be understood, text at the site of domestic urban American space. Just as Ishmael's carpetbagging refusal to consent and adhere to the disciplinary terms of the "benign" narrative of "America" in the end baffles, dislocates, and thus disempowers the hegemonic discursive practices of the dominant culture, so does Bartleby's "I prefer not to." Like Ishmael's errant narrative, which provokes the *self-destructive* compulsion to name and master it—to identify it with the (imperial) discourse of "America"—Bartleby's refusal to consent and adhere to the Wall Street "premises" of the "humanist" lawyer-narrator—the representative of liberal middle-class/capitalist American culture—provokes a relentless effort to win the "heart and mind" of his maddeningly elusive employee that ends in bafflement, dislocation, and finally disempowerment of his certain, finally monolithic "American" logic. I am, of course, aware of the sharp contrast between Ishmael's garrulousness and Bartleby's wordlessness. And this difference bespeaks an ideological difference that needs to be thought. But my representation of Ishmael's narrative should block a too-hasty dismissal of this affiliation. For it suggests that Ishmael's errant prolixity constitutes the obverse face of

Bartleby's unmovable taciturnity. They are both discourses of *silence*, discourses, that is, which, each in its own peculiar way, exist in their "invisibility" to resist—indeed, to baffle—a certain saying that, in its imperial assumption that being is visible and appropriable, cannot know or tolerate any other.

What remains to be added is that Ishmael's ontological differentiation between "Moby Dick" and the whiteness of the whale, between naming and silence, visibility and invisibility, is not to be understood as a disciplinary opposition that privileges being as such (the ontological or "chronometrical") as a base to cultural and political superstructures (the ontic or "horological"), as, for example, history is to writing in the discourse of deconstruction and ontology is to history in the discourse of the New Historicists and, all too frequently, of the New Americanists. This differentiation is to be understood, rather, as I have tried to suggest, as an ontic/ontological (chronometrical/horological) announcement that overdetermines the ontological site of an indissoluble relay of sites which, however unevenly, constitute the field of forces I have been calling being. As such, therefore, and despite his failure to adequately think the sociopolitical implications of his destruction of the discursive practices of the American Adam, Melville not only anticipates the postmodern insistence on thinking the positive possibilities of the manifold "other"—the relay of preterites—disclosed by the self-destruction of American modernity. He also proleptically surpasses it in so far as his announcement of a "devious" or "invisible"—decentered and de-centering—strategy of resisting the will to power of the Adamic One is also an announcement of the formation of what I have called after Gramsci the affirmative "historical bloc": a multiplicity of discrete but affiliated counterhegemonic identityless identities or collective subject positions—the displaced or migrant differential constituencies of the postcolonial world—which, each in its own way, have been the damaged victims of the imperial American will to name and assimilate authorized by America's inaugural and hegemonic Adamic errand in the wilderness.

In this multisituated strategy of ec-centric resistance—this refusal *to be answerable to* the reifying premises posited by the unerring logic of the "imperialist" American vision—one might say, the resonantly benign discourse of the *Pax Americana*—Melville, to situate this counterhegemonic strategy in a more chronologically immediate milieu, anticipates one of the most promising, if still to be adequately thought, of the admittedly minimal because damaged alternatives of resistance presently available against the polyvalent and all-incorporating Western (neo)colonial project. I am referring to that version of the "postcolonial" or "multicultural" initiative that, like the disarticulating strategy of the invisible and un-answering Vietnamese insurgents in the Vietnam War, has its origins in the effort to think the implications of the progressive self-*de-struction* of the benign logic of the discourse and practice of Western imperial rule in the last half of this century. More specifically, I am referring to the strategy of ec-centric resistance tentatively elaborated by Edward Said at the end of his (counter)monumental work *Culture and Imperialism* as a consequence of his thematization of the massive transformation of global demo-graphics—the radically destabilized "political map of the contemporary world"—incumbent on the progressively self-induced collapse of British imperial hegemony in India and the Middle East after World War II, of French colonialism in Southeast Asia and North Africa in the 1950s, and, above all, of American neocolonial hegemony in Vietnam in the 1960s. I mean the epochal historical occasion that has unhomed a vast portion of the world's population, not only in the sense of uprooting them from their respective cultural homelands but also of disaffiliating them from the affiliative bonds of the dominant culture and its "benign" discourse, which, in so doing, has suggested a "nomadic" or "errant" practice that, in its po-tential to disarticulate the lines of hegemonic force proceeding from the metropolis, promises an epochal reconfiguration of the global power rela-tions that have obtained throughout the history of Western hegemony. Since the proleptic parallel I am suggesting between Melville's refusal (Bartleby's "I prefer not to" as well as Ishmael's errant prolixity) and Said's refusal ("the emigré's eccentricity") is remarkably precise (and since the strategy of resistance Said has tentatively elaborated in *Culture and Imperial-ism* has been largely neglected in the commentaries, I will quote at length:

We can perceive this truth [the possibility in the postcolonial era of "a nomadic practice whose power . . . is not aggressive but transgressive"] on the political map of the contemporary world. For surely it is one of the unhappiest characteristics of the age to have produced more refugees, migrants, displaced persons, and exiles than ever before in history, most of them as an accompaniment to and, ironically enough, as afterthoughts of great post-colonial and imperial conflicts. As the struggle for independence produced new states and new boundaries, it also produced homeless wanderers, nomads, and vagrants, unassimilated to the emerging structures of institutional power, rejected by the established order for their intransigence and obdurate rebelliousness. And insofar as these people exist between the old and the new, between the old empire and the new state, their condition articulates the tensions, irresolutions, and contradictions in the overlapping territories shown on the cultural map of imperialism.

There is a great difference, however, between the optimistic mobility, the intellectual liveliness, and "the logic of daring" described by the various theoreticians on whose work I have drawn [above all Paul Verilio and Gilles Deleuze and Félix Guattari], and the massive dislocations, waste, misery, and horrors endured in our century's migrations and mutilated lives. Yet it is no exaggeration to say that liberation as an intellectual mission, born in the resistance and opposition to the confinements and ravages of imperialism, has now shifted from the settled, established, and domesticated dynamics of culture to its unhoused, decentered, and exilic energies, energies whose incarnation today is the migrant, and whose consciousness is that of the intellectual and artist in exile, the political figure between domains, between forms, between homes, and between languages. From this perspective then all things are indeed counter, original, spare, strange. From this perspective also, one can see "the complete consort dancing together" contrapuntally. And while it would be the rankest Panglossian dishonesty to say that the bravura performances of the intellectual exile and the miseries of the displaced person or refugee are the same, it is possible, I think, to regard the intellectual as first distilling then articulating the predicament that disfigures modernity—mass deportations, imprisonment, population transfer, collective dispossession, and forced immigrations.

"The past life of emigrés is, as we know, annulled," says Adorno in *Minima Moralia,* subtitled *Reflections from a Damaged Life.* . . . Why? "Because anything that is not reified, cannot be counted and measured, ceases to exist" or, he says later, is consigned to mere "background." Although the disabling aspects of this fate are manifest, its virtues or possibilities are worth exploring. . . . Adorno's general pattern is what in another place he calls the "administered world" or, insofar as the irresistible dominants in culture are concerned, "the consciousness industry." There is then not just the negative advantage of refuge in the emigré's eccentricity; there is also the positive benefit of challenging the system, describing it in language unavailable to those it has already subdued:

In an intellectual hierarchy which constantly makes everyone answerable, unanswerability alone can call the hierarchy directly by its name.[33]

In *Visionary Compacts*, Donald Pease concludes his strong reading not simply of *Moby-Dick*, but of the literature of the "American Renaissance," by opposing Melville's discourse (which he characterizes as being founded on "a shared covenant") against Ishmael's decentered and unhomed discourse, which, in annulling the possibility of decisive collective action, renders itself complicitous with the totalitarian Ahabian will to absolute freedom:

> In a way, Ishmael underscores the fundamental problem for a society which has lost sight of a shared covenant. Without a common basis for their judgments, a nation's citizens have nothing more enduring than their self-interest with which to reflect. . . .
>
> Unlike Ishmael, Melville, in his correspondence with Hawthorne [and presumably in the novel he dedicated to his friend], preserved the civil covenant he believed bound them together. Melville's correspondence with Hawthorne provided him with a visionary bond enabling him to oppose Ishmael's obsessive-compulsive attraction to Ahab with a friendship grounded in genuine fellow feeling. Since his letter of November 17, 1851, indicates the depth of his need for a visionary compact with Hawthorne, I will quote from it to end this book:
>
>> Whence came you, Hawthorne? By what right do you drink from my flagon of life? And when I put it to my lips—lo, they are yours and not mine. I feel that the Godhead is broken up like the bread at the Supper, and we are the pieces. Hence this infinite fraternity of feeling.[34]

In other words, Ishmael's erratic discourse, like the "undecidability" of deconstruction (and the "dissensus" of that form of New Historicist American criticism espoused by Sacvan Bercovitch),[35] is not simply incapable of achieving a counterhegemonic practical force, but is implicated with the self-interest of capitalist society in general and Cold War capitalism in particular.

Pease's enabling contribution to the struggle to free Melville—indeed, American literature at large—from the bondage of American Cold War discourse is precisely his decisive displacement of the question of its contemporary intelligibility from the domain of the sovereign subject to that of hegemony, more specifically, his reading of *Moby-Dick* as an announcement, not of the recuperation of a traditional discourse of consensus as such, but of the retrieval by the American countermemory of the possibilities for a counterhegemony. The question Pease does not clearly address, however—and this is typical of the New Historicist discourse of the New Americanists—is, what will constitute the ontological "ground" of this "visionary compact"? Indeed, his critique of Ishmael's discourse as decentered—as utterly dependent on Ahab's "master eye" and totalitarian will—suggests that, despite gestures to the contrary, the answer to this critical question involves a reversion to some sort of supervisory *logos* or other. And it is this refusal or overlooking of the positive possibilities of the decentered (postmodern) ontological occasion that I object to in his interpretation of Ishmael's role in the narrative of *Moby-Dick.*

Pease's exposure of the Cold War ideological agenda informing the representation of Ishmael by the founders of American literary studies is, indeed, decisive. But is his reading of Ishmael/Melville's? The answer I have tried to suggest is "no," if not in thunder. For, it seems to me, Pease's Cold War problematic (like Wai-chee Dimock's imperial and Bercovitch's jeremiadic problematic), even as it exposes the ideologically motivated blindness of its totalizing vision, blinds him to the "postmodernity" of Ishmael's narrative, understood precisely as the announcement of a groundless counterhegemonic discursive practice of collective resistance. I mean a "compact" whose justification resides not in a "visionary" but a "horizonal" comportment toward being:[36] not, that is, in an appeal to a universal principle, but to the historically specific occasion, which is to say, to the *imbalances of power*—the injustices—that obtain in any present conjuncture of the finite world. This decentered, yet counterhegemonic discursive practice—this *Auseinandersetzung*—is, I suggest, what Melville proleptically announces by way of what I have called the errant art of *Moby-Dick.*

If we insert the struggle over Melville's text into the context of the present historical occasion—I mean specifically the period inaugurated by the so-called revolutions in Central and Eastern Europe and the former Soviet Union and culminating in the Gulf War—it will be seen why the revisionary New Americanist interpretation of *Moby-Dick* is, however productive, inadequate as such to the task imposed by recent history on a criticism that would ask "us if we can survive the [Cold War representation of the] free world Ishmael has handed down to us."[37] The reading of *Moby-Dick* sponsored by the founders of American literary studies in the late 1940s would go far not only to legitimize the massive amnesiac project of the American Cultural Memory to forget Vietnam, to "heal the wound" opened up in the collective American psyche by the brutal American intervention (and defeat) in Vietnam (an amnesiac initiative the most recent moment of which is the rehabilitation of Richard Nixon at the time of his death in May 1994). It would also lend itself to the legitimation of the present representation of the recent global events in Central and Eastern Europe and the former Soviet Union as the dialectical "triumph" of (the principles of) liberal American democracy and the "fall" of communism, that is, as the advent of the "New World Order" or, as one highly visible exponent of this representation puts it, "the end of history," presided over by the United States.[38] In so far as the New Americanists would retrieve *Moby-Dick* as a social text from its incarceration in and by the "liberal imagination"—a text that proleptically delegitimizes the Cold War discourse and its recently foregrounded dialectical dynamics—their project synecdochically contributes to the task of retrieving a still-nascent critical American tradition capable of forestalling this Hegelian "end" of the Cold War. However, insofar as they neglect or overlook the ontological site—Melville's de-centering of the ontotheological *logos* privileged in and by the American Adamic tradition—in overdetermining historically specific sociopolitical conflict, they fail to perceive that Melville's focus on Ishmael's profound and fundamental concern with the question of the representation of being is not symptomatic of a disabling internalization and sublimation of historically specific conflict that in the end renders him complicitous with his antagonist. In eschewing the ontological site, to put it positively, the New Americanists are blinded by their sociopolitical insight to the possibility that Ishmael's engagement with the *Seinsfrage* constitutes the *overdetermination* of an ontological *praxis*: the emancipation of being from the *Pax Metaphysica* that opens out to include the other, more immediate, but indissolubly related sites of anti-imperialist *praxis*.

Insofar, that is, as these New Americanists resist the Old Americanist Cold War discourse in terms of the latter's reading, which "sets Ishmael's subversive narrative energies against the totalitarian will at work in Ahab's policy"[39] and in the process renders Ahab Ishmael's (or Melville's) victim, they fail to perceive that Ishmael's belated recognition of the will to power informing Ahab's American Adamic ontology inaugurates a de-structive or de-centering process in which he (and Melville) comes to recognize the indissoluble, however uneven, complicity of this ontological will to power and the will to power informing other apparently discontinuous American cultural, social, and political practices. And this failure of oversight is why, despite its critical promise, such a genealogical reading is finally and symptomatically inadequate as such to the task of countering the dominant American representation of the global events of the 1990s as the advent of the New World Order supervised by the United States—and, in Noam Chomsky's resonant phrase, of "deterring American democracy."[40] For no less than the Marxist overdetermination of economic struggle, the New Americanist overdetermination of the "Cold War" in its critical resistance against the discourse of American hegemony is precisely what these recent global events have rendered anachronistic and thus disempowered if not entirely delegitimized. It is not, in other words, American economic or political practice *as such* that is now being invoked by the spokesmen of the dominant culture as the determining agent of the epochal triumph of the "free world" against Communism. It is the founding American Adamic *principles* (the sovereign individual, equality among men, disinterested inquiry, the external and antagonistic relationship between truth and power, and so on), or, rather, these principles understood, like Ishmael/Melville's achieved disruptive understanding of the (American) world and time of the *Pequod*, as the base to the liberal democratic/republican/capitalist superstructure of the American *polis*. It is, in other words, precisely the Adamic *ontology* of democracy and democratic practices that Ishmael/Melville comes to discover in the process of writing *Moby-Dick*, not as independent of and irrelevant to technology (empirical science), the factory, and the state, but as a moment, if not the determining one, of an asymmetrical relay that includes them all. It is precisely, in short, the very epistemic order that America's intervention in Vietnam and its brutal conduct of the war decisively broke and delegitimized.

In *Moby-Dick*, Melville's effort to articulate an alternative discourse to that of Adamic America is by no means fully worked out. The traces of the latter manifest themselves insistently in the narrative—above all, in his ambivalence toward Ahab, toward the whaling industry, and toward the very form of the novel he is writing. And it is no doubt these traces of his vestigial adherence to the legacy of "America" that render this powerfully engaging novel a site of cultural and political struggle. But, as I have shown in my reading of *Moby-Dick*, these traces are not calculated adherences. They are precisely vestigial traces of the discourse from which Melville was struggling to emancipate himself in the context of a cultural milieu—a "young America"—that, as *Pierre* especially makes clear, was essentially hostile to his antihegemonic project.

Whatever its blindnesses, then, *Moby-Dick* speaks resonantly across the great divide of time not to (American) Man but to the present historical occasion. It is not, to extend a resonant motif in Michel Foucault, simply a genealogy, a "history of [Melville's] present": it is also a history of the American future, of the present historical occasion that we precariously inhabit. This, as I have argued, is not only because Melville proleptically delegitimized the Cold War discourse of the founders of American literary studies—whom we can now call the custodians of the American Cultural Memory. It is also and more importantly—if less discursively—because, in anticipating the self-destruction of the American *episteme* in the Vietnam War, it proleptically delegitimized the discourse of the New World Order. I mean the ontologically grounded and dialectically propelled discourse of the post-Cold War, the "end-of-history" discourse that is essentially beyond the critical reach of the New Historicism of the New Americanists, at least in its present—disciplinary—form. I offer this reading of Herman Melville's *Moby-Dick*, therefore, not as an alternative, but as a contribution to a New Americanist thinking that will make this insidious end-of-history discourse thinkable.

NOTES

1 *MOBY-DICK* AND THE AMERICAN CANON

1. See Sacvan Bercovitch, *The American Jeremiad* (Madison: University of Wisconsin Press, 1978). For a general but nevertheless significant study of the substantial role played by this cultural imaginary in the representation of the Vietnam War, before, during, and after, see John Hellman, *American Myth and the Legacy of Vietnam* (New York: Columbia University Press, 1986).

2. The term *problematic* derives from Louis Althusser and, except for the tendency to minimize agency, is intended to convey precisely the meaning he gives it in order to foreground the particular visual metaphorics that informs traditional (humanistic) inquiry (and to distinguish this situated "blindness of oversight," as it were, from Paul de Man's free-floating "blindness of insight"): "[Science] can only pose problems on the terrain and within the horizon of a definite theoretical structure, its problematic, which constitutes its absolute and definite condition of possibility, and hence the absolute determination of *the forms in which all problems must be posed,* at any given moment in the science.

"This opens the way to an understanding of the determination of the *visible* as visible, and conjointly, of the invisible as invisible, and of the organic link binding the invisible to the visible. Any object or problem . . . in the definite structured field of the theoretical problematic of a given theoretical discipline . . . is visible. . . . The sighting is thus no longer the act of an individual subject, endowed with the faculty of 'vision' which he exercises either attentively or distractedly; the sighting is the act of its structural conditions. . . . It is literally no longer the eye (the mind's eye) of a subject which *sees* what exists in the field defined by a theoretical problematic: it is this field itself which *sees itself* in the objects or problems it defines—sighting being merely the necessary reflection of the field on its objects. . . .

"The same connexion that defines the visible also defines the invisible as its shadowy obverse. It is the field of the problematic that defines and structures the invisible as the defined excluded, *excluded* from the field of visibility and *defined* as excluded by the existence and peculiar structure of the field of the problematic. . . . These new objects and problems are necessarily *invisible* in the existing theory, because they are not objects of this theory, because they are *forbidden* by it—they are objects and problems necessarily without any necessary relations with the field of the visible as defined by the problematic. They are invisible because they are rejected in principle, repressed from the field of the visible; and that is why their fleeting presence in the field when it does occur (in very peculiar and symptomatic circumstances) *goes unperceived*, and becomes literally an undivulged absence—since the whole function of the field is not to see them, to forbid any sighting of them. Here again, the invisible is no more a function of *a subject's sighting* than is the visible: the invisible is the theoretical problematic's non-vision of its non-objects, the invisible is the darkness, the blinded eye of the theoretical problematic's self-reflection when it scans its non-objects, its non-problems without seeing them, *in order not to look at them*" ("From *Capital* to Marx's Philosophy," *Reading Capital* [London: Verso, 1979], pp. 25–26).

3. See Henry Rosovsky, "Report on the Core Curriculum" (Cambridge, Mass.: Faculty of Arts and Sciences of Harvard University, February 15, 1978); Walter Jackson Bate, "The Crisis of English Studies," *Harvard Magazine*, vol. 85 (September–October 1987), pp. 46–53; Allan Bloom, *The Closing of the American Mind: How Higher Education Has Failed Democracy and Impoverished the Souls of Today's Students* (New York: Simon and Schuster, 1987); E. D. Hirsch, *Cultural Literacy: What Every American Needs to Know* (Boston: Houghton Mifflin, 1982); William J. Bennett, "To Reclaim a Legacy: Report on Humanities in Education," *Chronicle of Higher Education* (November 28, 1984); Wayne Booth, *The Company We Keep: An Ethics of Fiction* (Berkeley: University of California Press, 1988); Roger Kimball, *Tenured Radicals: How Politics Has Corrupted Our Higher Education* (New York: Harper and Row, 1990); Dinesh D'Souza, *Illiberal Education: The Politics of Race and Sex on Campus* (New York: Free Press, 1991); Frederick Crews, *The Critics Bear It Away: American Fiction and the Academy* (New York: Random House, 1992)—see especially, "Whose American Renaissance?" pp. 16–46, originally published in the *New York Review of Books*, vol. 35, no. 16 (October 27, 1988); and Crew's "Foreword" to *After Poststructuralism: Interdisciplinarity and Literary Theory*, ed. Nancy Easterlin and Barbara Riebling (Evanston, Ill.: Northwestern University Press, 1993), pp. vii–x.

4. I am not simply referring to the deliberate antitheory initiative of Steven Knapp and Walter Benn Michaels, articulated in the by now famous essay "Against Theory," in *Against Theory: Literary Studies and the New Pragmatism*, ed. W. J. T. Mitchell (Chicago: University of Chicago Press, 1985), pp. 11–30. See also Walter Benn Michaels, *The Gold Standard and the Logic of Naturalism* (Berkeley: University of California Press, 1987). It will become clear in what follows, that I am also referring to a certain tendency of the New Americanists, a tendency especially informing the New Historicism of Sacvan Bercovitch, but also, though less disablingly, of Donald Pease, Frank Lentricchia, and Wai-chee Dimock. For brilliant and decisive critiques of the ahistorical history of Steven Knapp and Walter Benn Michaels and of Bercovitch and his school,

see Paul Bové, "Introduction: In the Wake of Theory," pp. 1–24, and "Notes toward a Politics of 'American' Criticism," in *In the Wake of Theory* (Hanover, N.H.: Wesleyan University Press, 1992), pp. 48–66.

5. See *Approaches to Teaching Melville's "Moby-Dick,"* ed. Martin Bickman (New York: Modern Language Association of America, 1985) and *New Essays on "Moby-Dick; or, The Whale,"* ed. Richard H. Brodhead (Cambridge: Cambridge University Press, 1986).

6. I have developed this thesis at considerable length in the chapter entitled "Heidegger, Nazism, and the 'Repressive Hypothesis,'" in my *Heidegger and Criticism: Retrieving the Cultural Politics of Destruction* (Minneapolis: University of Minnesota Press, 1993), pp. 221–30. See also Éliane Escoubas, "Heidegger, la question romaine, la question impériale. Autour du 'Tournant,'" in *Heidegger: Questions ouvertes,* ed. Élaine Escoubas (Paris: Éditions Osiris, 1988), pp. 173–89.

7. Martin Heidegger, *Parmenides,* trans. André Schuwer and Richard Rojcewicz (Bloomington: University of Indiana Press, 1992), pp. 40–43. Translation modified.

8. Edward W. Said, "Traveling Theory," in *The World, the Text, and the Critic* (Cambridge, Mass.: Harvard University Press, 1983), pp. 226–47.

9. The continuity between Puritan New England and the post-Revolutionary Republic that I am pointing to is suggested by thematizing the common enabling term of the different discursive practices of Puritanism and American republicanism: Rome. This thesis is too complex to be argued here. It will suffice for my present purpose to cite Cotton Mather's *Magnalia Christi Americana,* as quoted (though for a different purpose) in Sacvan Bercovitch's *American Jeremiad,* a book tracing the genealogy of post–Revolutionary (i.e., republican) America—its imperial mission grounded in a national identity understood as the chosen "saving remnant"—back to the Puritans' divinely ordained "errand in the wilderness": "For Mather, of course, New England's story not only parallels but supersedes that of the founding of Rome, as his literary 'assistance' from Christ excels the inspiration of Virgil's muse, as the 'exemplary heroes' he celebrates resemble but outshine the men of Aeneas' band—not only as Christians but as seafarers and conquerors of hostile pagan tribes—and, most spectacularly, as the millennium toward which the Reformation is moving provides the far more glorious antitype of the Augustan *Pax Romana*" (p. 87). See also, Kenneth B. Murdock, "The *Magnalia*," in Cotton Mather, *Magnalia Christi Americana; or, The Ecclesiastical History of New England,* Bks. 1 and 2, ed. Kenneth B. Murdock with Elizabeth W. Miller (Cambridge, Mass.: Harvard University Press, 1977), pp. 44–45.

10. Since the word *relay* plays an important role, I should spell out the meaning I attribute to it at the start. I derive the idea that informs the term from Heidegger's discourse on being, an idea perhaps best suggested in his commentary on the Anaximander fragment, where he criticizes the traditional reading of pre-Socratics that claims their thought was "primitive" insofar as it fails to distinguish between metaphor and "truth," that is to say, for reading and evaluating it from a later—more maturely "scientific"—(and reductive) philosophical representation of being:

With the collapse of the presupposition that the [Anaximander] fragment strives after scientific knowledge concerning the demarcated realm of nature, another assumption becomes superfluous, namely, that at this time ethical or juridical matters were interpreted in terms of the disciplines we call 'ethics' and 'jurisprudence.' Denial of such boundaries between disciplines does not mean to imply that in early times law and ethicality were unknown. But if the way we normally think within a range of disciplines (such as physics, ethics, philosophy of law, biology, psychology) has no place here—if boundaries between these subjects are lacking—then there is no possibility of trespass or of the unjustified transfer of notions from one area to another. Yet where boundaries between disciplines do not appear, boundless indeterminacy and flux do not necessarily prevail: on the contrary, an appropriate articulation of a matter purely thought may well come to language when it has been freed from every oversimplification.

The words *dike, adikia, tisis* [from the Anaximander fragment] have a broad significance which cannot be enclosed within the boundaries of particular disciplines. 'Broad' does not mean here extensive, in the sense of something flattened out, but rather far-reaching, rich, containing much thought. For precisely that reason these words are employed: to bring to language the manifold totality in its essential unity. For that to happen, of course, thinking must apprehend the unified totality of the manifold, with its peculiar characteristics, purely in its own terms. (*Early Greek Thinking*, trans. David Farrell Krell and Frank A. Capuzzi [New York: Harper & Row, 1975], pp. 21–22)

It is my contention, following Heidegger, that the compartmentalization of being into distinct and (implicitly) unrelated sites (disciplines) by Plato and Aristotle and, following them, the philosophical discourse of the ontotheological tradition at large, has, besides reifying the force of being, rendered criticism of the "truth" of this tradition difficult, above all, by obscuring the indissoluble *relation* between these "disciplinary sites," by, in other words, an operation—similar to that which Foucault discloses in his analysis of the invention of the (disciplinary) subject (individualism) in the period of the Enlightenment—of divide and conquer. It is my further contention that, despite the theorization of the critically negative effects of such a disciplining of being, contemporary theorists of every stripe—whether deconstructionist or New Historicist—continue in some disabling degree to think being in disciplinary terms.

11. The meaning I attribute to this much abused concept of hegemony derives from Antonio Gramsci. See *Selections from the Prison Notebooks* ed. and trans. Quintin Hoare and Geoffrey Nowell Smith (New York: International Publishers, 1971), p. 12.

12. Michel Foucault, *Discipline and Punish: The Birth of the Prison*, trans. Alan Sheridan (New York: Pantheon, 1977), p. 194.

13. Michel Foucault, *The History of Sexuality*, vol. I, *An Introduction*, trans. Robert Hurley (New York: Pantheon, 1978), p. 10.

14. Ibid., pp. 88–89.

15. Foucault, *Discipline and Punish*, p. 205.

16. Ibid.

17. Foucault does not elaborate on this extension of the disciplinary machinery. That it is in principle intrinsic to his analysis of the disciplinary society is clearly suggested in "The Life of Infamous Men," in *Power, Truth, Strategy*, ed. Meaghan Morris and Paul Patton, trans. Paul Foss and Meaghan Morris (Sydney, Australia: Feral Publications, 1979). Here, Foucault observes in passing, the novel "forms part of the great [panoptic] system of constraint by which the [post-Enlightenment] West compelled the everyday to bring itself into discourse" (p. 91). For an extended application of the polyvalent, panoptic diagram to the site of literary criticism and history, see the chapter entitled "Percy Lubbock and the Craft of Supervision," in William V. Spanos, *Repetitions: The Postmodern Occasion in Literature and Culture* (Baton Rouge: Louisiana State University Press, 1987), pp. 149–88.

18. The "progress" from censorship to pluralist accommodation has, perhaps needless to say, been uneven. This uneven development can be seen, for example, in the accommodational literary discourses of humanists such as M. H. Abrams and of the New Critics. In the first instance we find the following: "The poet must win our imaginative consent to the aspect of human experience he presents, and to do so he cannot evade his responsibility to the beliefs and presuppositions of our common experience, common sense, and common moral consciousness. . . . The artist's cost of failure in this essential respect is demonstrated by the writing of accomplished craftsmen in which the substance is too inadequately human to engage our continuing interest, or which require our consent to positions so illiberal or eccentric or perverse that they incite counterbeliefs which inhibit the ungrudging 'yes' that we grant to masterpieces" (Abrams, "Belief and the Suspension of Disbelief," in *Literature and Belief*, English Institute Essays [New York: English Institute, 1957], pp. 28–29). In the second instance, we find the "fallacy of imitative form," according to which a text whose form reflects a content expressive of the theme of chaos is denied the status of literature. Both bear witness to the continuity between the older discourse of exclusion and the newer discourse of accommodation or inclusion.

19. See Jacques Derrida, "Force and Signification," in *Writing and Difference*, trans. Alan Bass (Chicago: University of Chicago Press, 1978): "For the sake of determining an essential 'Corneillean movement,' does not [Jean Rousset] lose what counts? Everything that defies a geometrical-mechanical framework—and not only the pieces which cannot be constrained by curves and helices, not only force and quality, which are meaning itself, but also *duration*, that which is pure qualitative heterogeneity within movement—is reduced to the appearance of the inessential for the sake of this essentialism or teleological structuralism. Rousset understands theatrical or novelistic movement as Aristotle understood movement in general: transition to the act, which itself is the repose of the desired form. Everything transpires as if everything within the dynamics of Corneillean meaning, and within each of Corneille's plays, came to life with the aim of final peace, the peace of the structural *energeia: Polyeucte*. Outside this peace, before and after it, movement, in its pure duration, in the labor of its organization, can itself be only sketch or debris. Or even debauch, a fault or sin as compared to

Polyeucte, the 'first impeccable success.' Under the word 'impeccable,' Rousset notes: '*Cinna* still sins in this respect'" (pp. 20–21).

20. This extension, if his comparative analysis of the "author function" in medieval and modern exegetical theory and practice is seen to include literary history, is the point Michel Foucault makes in "What Is an Author?" in *Language, Counter-Memory, Practice: Selected Essays and Interviews,* ed. Donald F. Bouchard, trans. Donald F. Bouchard and Sherry Simon (Ithaca, N.Y.: Cornell University Press, 1977), pp. 127–29. The remarkable parallel with Derrida's critique of structuralism in the previous note should not be overlooked. I will address the inevitable objection that Foucault and Derrida are confronting an ideological context very remote from the Protestant American matrix in which the struggle over Melville's fiction is imbedded. Suffice it to say here that the practice of Puritan exegetical tradition is no less grounded in typological or, more accurately, prefigurative exegetical theory than the practice of the great Catholic tradition that Foucault is invoking. See the section of chapter 2 entitled "Melville's Errant Measure," where the passage from Foucault's "What Is an Author?" is quoted at length.

21. Max Weber, *The Protestant Ethic and the Spirit of Capitalism,* trans. Talcott Parsons (New York: Charles Scribner's Sons, 1958).

22. I am indebted here and for much of what immediately follows about the early reception of *Moby-Dick* to James Cesarano Jr.'s unpublished dissertation, "The Emergence of *Moby-Dick:* An Archaeology of Its Critical Value," State University of New York at Binghamton, 1984.

23. *Southern Quarterly Review,* vol. 5 (January 1852), p. 262, reprinted in the Norton Critical Edition of *Moby-Dick,* ed. Harrison Hayford and Hershel Parker (New York: W. W. Norton, 1967), p. 619.

24. Evert A. Duyckinck, "Melville's *Moby-Dick;* or, *The Whale,*" *Literary World,* 9 November 22, 1851, pp. 403–4, reprinted in *Moby-Dick,* ed. Hayford and Parker, p. 615. My emphasis.

25. Friedrich Nietzsche, *"On the Genealogy of Morals" and "Ecce Homo,"* trans. Walter Kaufmann (New York: Vintage Books, 1969), pp. 36–37.

26. As James Cesarano observes, "Although this revival [of the 1880s] could not break free of its times' discursive formation, it began a discursive regularity, the theme of Melville's withdrawal, that eventually served as the point of leverage for the valuation of *Moby-Dick* as a masterpiece [in the 1920s]" ("The Emergence of *Moby-Dick,*" pp. 155–56).

27. See, for example, Lewis Mumford, *The Golden Day: A Study of American Experience and Culture* (New York: Boni and Liveright, 1926) and Harold Stearns, ed. *Civilization in the United States: An Inquiry by Thirty Americans* (New York: Harcourt, Brace, 1922). The latter includes essays by Lewis Mumford, H. L. Mencken, John Macy, Robert Morss Lovett, J. E. Spingarn, Van Wyck Brooks, Conrad Aiken, and George Jean Nathan. For a useful reading of the discursive regularity of these and other politically diverse critical voices of the Modernist avant-garde of the 1920s—their common representa-

tion of North American culture as disablingly Puritan/materialistic and their self-representation "as the embattled defenders of culture in a society hostile to spiritual values," i.e., as a saving humanist remnant, see Cesarano, "The Emergence of *Moby-Dick*," pp. 201ff. What Cesarano leaves unsaid in his analysis is the degree to which Matthew Arnold's English humanist discourse on Hellenism and Hebraism, culture and anarchy, is inscribed in this American discursive regularity and to which the narrative of their relation to American society repeats that of the founding Puritans.

28. Cesarano gives the following account of this regularized narrative: "The revival [of the 1920s] knew Melville as the author of *Moby-Dick*. In fact, throughout the criticism one finds comments that *Moby-Dick* is a unique book in Melville's oeuvre or that it is his only great novel. The same way that Melville's contemporaries interpreted all of his life and works by using *Typee* and *Omoo*, the revival structured the discourse about Melville through comments about *Moby-Dick*. In the words of one critic with a not untypical perspective [Peter Quennel], 'In writing of *Moby-Dick*, one comprises an entire life's work; for Herman Melville's other novels, whatever their various merits and notwithstanding the considerable interest which attaches to each of them, are by way of prologue and epilogue to that supreme effort.' Hence, the revival saw the novel as Melville's central work. When the modern critics talked about Melville's characteristics, most of them had formed their impression of him and his works from a valorization of *Moby-Dick* as Melville's 'supreme effort'" ("The Emergence of *Moby-Dick*," pp. 224–25). What needs to be added to this perceptive account of revival criticism is that the genetic metaphorics informing its discourse is symptomatic of its metaphysics: a perception of Melville's life/works from after or above (*meta*) their historically specific being (*physis*) that enables the mastery and pacification of the force of their differential elements. This retrospective or future anterior perspective, which excludes differences from or internalizes and accommodates them to its preestablished structure, is, according to Derrida and Foucault, we recall, the model of all canon formation. See notes 19 and 20.

29. See, for example, Lewis Mumford, *The Golden Day*: "In the bareness of the Protestant cathedral of Geneva one has the beginnings of that hard barracks architecture which formed the stone-tenements of Seventeenth Century Edinburgh, set a pattern for the austere meeting-houses of New England, and finally deteriorated into the miserable shanties that line Main Street. The meagerness of the Protestant ritual began that general starvation of the spirit which finally breaks out, after long repression, in the absurd jamborees of Odd Fellows, Elks, Woodmen, and kindred fraternities. In short, all that was once made manifest in a Chartres, a Strasbourg, or a Durham minster, and in the mass, the pageant, the art gallery, the theatre—all this the Protestant bleached out into the bare abstraction of the printed word. Did he suffer any hardship in moving to the New World? None at all. All that he wanted of the Old World he carried within the covers of a book. Fortunately for the original Protestants, that book was a whole literature; in this, at least, it differed from the later protestant canons, perpetrated by Joseph Smith or Mrs. Mary Baker Eddy. Unfortunately, how-

ever, the practices of a civilized society cannot be put between two black covers. So, in many respects, Protestant society ceased to be civilized" (quoted in Cesarano, "The Emergence of *Moby-Dick*," p. 210). This elitist—and nostalgic—representation of Mumford's America is (like that of most Modernist biographer/critics of the 1920s) the *mise-en-scène* of his narrative of Melville's artistic struggle and spiritual triumph (in *Moby-Dick*) over the alienating dessication of American civilization. Thus in the "Epilogue" to *Herman Melville* (New York: Harcourt, Brace, 1929), Mumford writes: "Herman Melville [unlike his younger contemporaries, who, as in the case of Henry Adams, had also experienced the disintegration and spiritual enervation of post–Civil War America] portrayed a human purpose, concentrated to almost maniacal intensity, in *Moby-Dick*; and in *Pierre* and *The Confidence-Man*, he showed the black aftermath, when he himself was deserted in his extremity, by contemporaries who neither understood nor heeded nor shared his vision. No single mind can hold its own against all that is foreign to it in the universe . . . such unity of spirit as one may possess, as philosopher or poet, must be sustained in the community itself. Now, a new culture, the product of two hundred and fifty years of settled life in America, had produced *Walden*, *Leaves of Grass*, Emerson's *Notebooks*, and *Moby-Dick*; but that culture, instead of supporting and carrying forward the integration of man and nature and society shadowed forth in those books, was completely uprooted by the Civil War, and a material civilization, inimical in many respects to the forms and symbols of a humane culture, was swept in by the very act of destruction" (Mumford, pp. 363–65).

30. I have demonstrated elsewhere the complicity of the definitive educational reform movement at this moment in American history—its "disinterested" establishment of the general education program as the national pedagogical model—especially at Columbia University in 1919—with an Americanism that identified itself not simply by demonizing Bolshevism but that exploited class of Americans most likely to embrace its un-American discourse and practice. See the chapter entitled "The Violence of Disinterestedness: A Genealogy of the Reform Initiative of the 1980s" in William V. Spanos, *The End of Education: Toward Posthumanism* (Minneapolis: University of Minnesota Press, 1993), pp. 118–61.

31. Matthew Arnold, *Culture and Anarchy*, ed. J. Dover Wilson (Cambridge: Cambridge University Press, 1960), p. 49.

32. Terry Eagleton, "The Rise of English," in *Literary Theory: An Introduction* (Minneapolis: University of Minnesota Press, 1983), p. 25. See also the chapters entitled "Humanist Inquiry and the Politics of the Gaze" and "The Apollonian Investment of Modern Humanist Education Theory: The Examples of Matthew Arnold, Irving Babbitt, and I. A. Richards" in William V. Spanos, *The End of Education*, pp. 25–65, 66–117.

33. Jacques Derrida, "Structure, Sign, and Play in the Discourse of the Human Sciences," *Writing and Difference*, p. 279.

34. Michel Foucault, "Revolutionary Action: 'Until Now'," *Language, Counter-Memory, Practice*, pp. 221–22.

35. The self-representation of "America" (the dominant culture) as "saving remnant" has its origins in the Puritan appropriation of Patristic biblical exegesis (typological or prefigurative hermeneutics): the affiliative chain relating Isaiah to Virgil to the Puritan "errand in the wilderness." Like the essential instrument of its cultural transmission, the "American Jeremiad," it has been and continues to be a deeply inscribed constant in the cultural discourse of "America." For a discussion of the use and abuse of this powerful figure in the crisis of American culture precipitated by the Vietnam War, see Spanos, "De-struction and the Critique of Ideology: A Polemic Meditation on Marginal Discourse," in *Repetitions*, pp. 280–84.

36. Donald E. Pease, "New Americanists: Revisionist Interventions into the Canon," in *New Americanists: Revisionist Interventions into the Canon* 1, a special issue of *boundary* 2, vol. 17 (Spring 1990), pp. 1–37. "By the term field-Imaginary," Pease writes, "I mean to designate a location for the disciplinary unconscious. . . . Here abides the field's fundamental syntax—its tacit assumptions, convictions, primal words, and the charged relations binding them together. A field specialist depends upon this field-Imaginary for the construction of her primal identity within the field. Once constructed out of this syntax, the primal identity can neither reflect upon its terms nor subject them to critical scrutiny. The syntactic elements of the field-Imaginary subsist instead as self-evident principles" (pp. 11–12). Pease's "field-Imaginary" is thus a version of Althusser's "problematic." See note 2. What is lacking in his brilliant insight is Althusser's emphasis on vision. He needs to think the unthought in his word "scrutiny."

37. Pease, "New Americanists: Revisionist Interventions into the Canon," pp. 7–8.

38. See Lionel Trilling, *Matthew Arnold* (New York: Meridian, 1969).

39. See especially, Donald E. Pease, "Visionary Compacts and the Cold War Consensus," in *Visionary Compacts: American Renaissance Writings in Cultural Context* (Madison: University of Wisconsin Press, 1987), pp. 3–48.

40. A particularly explicit example of this accommodation of continental theory to Americanist discourse can be found in Peter C. Carafiol, "In Dubious Battle: American Literary Scholarship and Poststructuralist Theory," introduction to *The American Renaissance: New Dimensions*, ed. Harry R. Garvin and Peter C. Carafiol (Lewisburg, Pa.: Bucknell University Press, 1983). Beginning with a critique of the xenophobia of traditional Americanists, the essay ends with a plea for a reconciliation (of incommensurable positions), in which poststructuralism becomes a tool of Americanist discourse: "The entrenched views did not and do not take kindly to the introspective self-scrutiny urged on them by the radical new comers. Preoccupied all along with their own status, they perceive dissent from within as a fifth-column movement, subversive agents of foreign powers, threatening the structures they have painfully (and newly) erected. Proponents of the 'New Views,' coming out of Concord or out of Baltimore and New Haven, were raised on an atmosphere of debate about authority and know no other vocabulary. In their zeal to reform the old order and distinguish themselves from it, they often forget how much they owe it, how deeply implicated in it they are, and consequently they often seem on the verge of demolishing themselves as well" (p. 13).

41. Paul Bové, "Notes toward a Politics of 'American' Criticism," p. 63.

42. Although the essays in the Cambridge volume occasionally invoke the "New Historicism" of American cultural critics such as Michael Paul Rogin and Sacvan Bercovitch, one looks in vain for reference to the postcolonial or postmodern continental intellectuals such as Spivak, Gramsci, and Foucault, who, in the terms quoted above from Paul Bové's "Notes toward a Politics of 'American' Criticism," have theorized the ground for a "being in and of one's locale while understanding its needs and hence one's projects in terms of a global or transnational set of interlocking perspectives."

43. Spanos, "The Intellectual and the Posthumanist Occasion," in *The End of Education*, p. 191.

44. William J. Bennett, "To Reclaim a Legacy," p. 19.

45. I am referring to Harvard's adoption of the "Harvard Core Curriculum Report," the "reform" initiative which was intended to restore the General Education Program in place since the end of World War II (the beginning of the Cold War), which, according to the report, had been "eroded" by "the proliferation of courses" in the Vietnam decade, that is, by the student protest movement's disclosure of the complicity between the core curriculum and the American intervention in Vietnam. See Spanos, *The End of Education*, particularly "The Violence of Disinterestedness: A Genealogy of the Educational Reform Initiative in the 1980s," pp. 118–61.

46. Edgar Dryden, "The Entangled Text: Melville's *Pierre* and the Problem of Reading," *boundary* 2, vol. 7, no. 1 (Spring 1979), 145–73; Henry Sussman, "The Deconstructor as Politician: Melville's *Confidence-Man*," *Glyph* 4 (Baltimore: Johns Hopkins University Press, 1978), pp. 32–56; Barbara Johnson, "Melville's Fist: The Execution of *Billy Budd*," in *The Critical Difference: Essays in the Contemporary Rhetoric of Reading* (Baltimore: Johns Hopkins University Press, 1980), pp. 79–109. See also, Rodolphe Gasché, "The Scene of Writing: A Deferred Outset," (on the chapter "Cetology" in *Moby-Dick*), *Glyph* 1 (Baltimore: Johns Hopkins University Press, 1977), pp. 150–71.

47. Antonio Gramsci, *Selections from the Prison Notebooks*, p. 12.

48. Raymond Williams, *Marxism and Literature* (New York: Oxford University Press, 1977), pp. 109–10. Since Gramsci imbeds what he means by hegemony within the necessarily indirect analysis of capitalist society compelled by his incarceration in fascist Italy, I have for convenience relied on Williams's definitive account.

49. Francis Fukuyama, *The End of History and the Last Man* (New York: Free Press, 1992), p. 45.

50. Jonathan Arac, "F. O. Matthiessen: Authorizing an American Renaissance," in *The American Renaissance Reconsidered: Selected Papers from the English Institute, 1982–1983*, ed. Walter Benn Michaels and Donald E. Pease (Baltimore: Johns Hopkins University Press, 1985), pp. 90–112.

51. Donald Pease, *Visionary Compacts*, pp. 10–11. As I will suggest, Pease's definition of Modernist symbolism as "open-ended" process needs to be modified by adding that its openness is *accommodational*, that is, determined by a *logos* or center that always already

reconciles novel differences precipitated by time. In this ontological paradigm, Identity is the condition for the possibility of difference and not the other way around. See especially my discussion of the *symbolos/diabolos* binary in the section "*Moby-Dick* as Diabolic Book" in chapter 3.

52. See Spanos, *The End of Education*, particularly the chapter entitled "The Violence of Disinterestedness," pp. 118–62.

53. Pease, *Visionary Compacts*, p. 235.

54. "Although [Matthiessen] mentions Hitler only in his account of Chillingworth, the figure whose totalitarian position Matthiessen wrote *American Renaissance* to oppose is everywhere present in his discussion of Ahab" (ibid., p. 257).

55. Ibid., p. 243.

56. Pease, "New Americanists," pp. 5–9.

57. Pease, *Visionary Compacts*, pp. 243–44.

58. For a telling—and yet self-parodic—example of this appropriation of the "end of the Cold War" in behalf of the recuperation of the "core curriculum" and the indictment of the multicultural initiative as "political correctness," see the remarks of Lynne Cheney, the director of the National Endowment for the Humanities during the George Bush administration, in an interview on the ABC news program "This Week with David Brinkley" (Sunday, January 6, 1991): "Well, I think education, not just in our schools, but in our colleges and universities, is the shadow on what might otherwise be a sunny prediction for the next century and America's role in it. If you look at culture from a global perspective, there is every reason to be optimistic. The events of Eastern Europe and the Soviet Union of the past year or so have, in many ways, been affirmations of American culture, not just of our political system and our economic system, but people have read our books and they've seen our films and they've listened to our music and they've liked what they've read and seen and heard. . . . I think perhaps the most serious symptom [that casts its shadow across the sunny future of the world and America's role in it] is this idea of political correctness, that there are some thoughts that it is now proper to express and some thoughts that it is improper to express. Perhaps the most worrisome aspect of political correctness to me is one that you [the politically conservative syndicated columnist, George Will] hit on a little bit in the earlier conversation. Somehow, Western civilization, that whole long story of human failure and triumph and thought and achievement has become politically incorrect in many places. It's become regarded as oppressive and indeed, it is the wellspring of those many, many attributes that we have as a country that people throughout the rest of the world envy. We saw students in Tiananmen Square, we saw students in Prague and in Budapest and Warsaw who know John Locke better than our students do because we don't teach John Locke as much as we used to, if we teach him at all."

59. Pease, *Visionary Compacts*, p. 271.

60. A scenario, as I have suggested elsewhere, is, like the table, a previsionary or teleological blueprint (a reduction and spatialization of the differential force of time)

to a miniaturized figure of totality that prefigures and thus determines or interprets (contains) future temporal events from the beginning (before they happen). See my reading of the abortive American interservice rescue mission staged against the Son Tay prisoner-of-war camp in North Vietnam in December 1970 in "The Detective and the Boundary: Some Notes on the Postmodern Literary Imagination," *boundary 2*, vol. 1, no. 3 (fall 1972), pp. 163–65; reprinted with revisions in *Repetitions*, pp. 38–43.

61. Pease, *Visionary Compacts*, p. 244.

62. Although Dimock harnesses the New Americanist problematic to a different purpose—the implication of Melville in the discourse of American imperialism—the contradictory consequences of its operation is even more startlingly visible in her influential and in many ways brilliant reading of *Moby-Dick*, entitled "Blaming the Victim" in *Empire for Liberty: Melville and the Poetics of Individualism* (Princeton: Princeton University Press, 1989), pp. 109–39. Dimock applies the very spatial problematic in reading *Moby-Dick* that she accuses Melville of using to victimize Ahab and to contribute to the cause of Manifest Destiny. In this reading, which refers to the novel as "Melville's 'imperial folio'" and which entirely overlooks the erratic structural process of Ishmael's narrative (not least, as we shall see, the "digression" of Father Mapple's Jonah sermon), Dimock represents Captain Ahab (and the "doomed," that is, *self*-destructive, American Indian with whom he is identified) as the victim of an imperial prophecy/fulfillment narrative—Melville's and that of the dominant American culture he represents. In the name of the sovereign individual and liberty, this prophetic narrative names/spatializes/colonizes temporality ("the potentialities of sequence") and the ontological and sociopolitical differences it disseminates: "Earlier, we spoke of personification as a procedure that spatializes time. In Ahab we see that procedure at work. Through him we also see, perhaps more clearly then anywhere else, the context as well as the function of such spatializations. For it is just this procedure that authorizes the category of 'fate' in *Moby-Dick*: authorizes it, in a temporal landscape in which the future appears, already inscribed, composed, demarcated, almost as a fact of geography. . . . Signs and omens hail from this region; prophets make their way into it, like so many venturous prospectors, mapping its terrain, claiming it as virtual property. [Dimock is referring specifically to Elijah, not, significantly, to Father Mapple, who, it should be remarked, does not appear in her text.] Prophecy in *Moby-Dick* is a territorial enterprise. To be a prophet one must survey the future, with an eye to ownership. . . .

Prophecy in *Moby-Dick* enlarges upon the past. But that too is what one should expect from a spatial ordering of time. Indeed, the future is knowable to the prophets only because it has been converted into a spatial category, part of a known design. Prophets are prospectors and colonizers because they are emissaries of the known, because their mission is to expand and assimilate, to annex the 'wilderness of untried things' into the domain of the existing. They can function as prophets only by reducing the potentiality of sequence to the legibility of design, only by reading time as space.

In that regard Melville's prophets are perhaps less prophets of the future than spokesmen for their own age, for spatialized time was the very condition for Manifest Destiny. . . . The familiar strategy for antebellum expansionists was to invoke some version of 'Providence,' whose plans for the future happened to coincide exactly with America's territorial ambitions. American expansion in space and providential design in time turned out to be one and the same. . . . Yet the same mechanism could just as easily victimize and destroy. For Indians too happened to be subjects of spatialized time. As much as America, they too were 'destined'—destined, that is, 'to melt and vanish.'

Spatialized time is also what *Moby-Dick* invokes to make Ahab's fate legible. Reading that fate, Melville's prophets turn Ahab too into a doomed figure, spatializing his temporal endeavor into a timeless script. Melville's 'imperial folio,' then, logically shares the same temporal economy with its imperial environment, for a structure of domination is inseparable from a structure of time. . . . Fate in *Moby-Dick* and Manifest Destiny in antebellum American are kindred constructs. Ahab and America, bearers both of a timeless destiny, mirror each other in familial likeness" (pp. 132–34).

63. Since the resonant word *occasion* plays an important role in my critical discourse, I hope I will be excused for quoting my etymological analysis in the essay on the poetry of Charles Olson, the "Melvillean" author of *Call Me Ishmael: A Study of Melville* (San Francisco: City Lights, 1947), in *Repetitions: The Postmodern Occasion in Literature and Culture:* "'occasion': immediately from 'occasus' ('the setting of the sun'), which ultimately derives from *cadere* ('to fall,' 'to drop,' as in the setting of heavenly bodies, and 'to fall,' 'to perish,' as in *de casibus virorum illustrium*, 'of the fall of great men'). A poetry that is the measure of its occasion, thus, is not a masterful and transcendent Euclidean 'geometry' having its ultimate model in the Platonic *mousike* of the spheres that Sir John Davies celebrates in *Orchestra*. Nor is it, to appropriate the rhetoric of the great paradigms of Modernist poetry, the 'oriental' measure of a golden bird singing 'Of what is past, or passing, or to come,' from the infinitely negative distance of eternity. It is, rather, the measure of 'Those dying generations—at their song,' a falling cadence (also from *cadere*) that acknowledges man's 'mortal dress' as his *case*. It is the measure of 'the local,' of being-in-the-world, of *being there—Da-sein*—'caught' in that which passes. It is the decentered or errant and fallible measure of mortality or, rather, of dwelling in the context of human being's temporal finitude. . . . As such a 'strange' measure-taking, 'which at no times clutches at the standard' [as Heidegger puts it in his celebration of Hölderlin], the measure of a poetry that is the measure of its occasion does not, therefore, derive from the 'Byzantium' of the nostalgic and sometimes imperial Modernist imagination. It is, rather—if we are careful to avoid reinscribing Orientalism into the terms—the primordial measure of the 'West' of the '*Abendland*,' forgotten in the increasingly virulent reaching after fact or reason of the metaphysical tradition. It is, in other words, a negatively capable *westering* measure that, like Olson's *Maximus Poems*, retrieves in its 'forwarding' . . . or forwards in its retrieval the Homer who precedes his re-construction by Virgil's 'oriental' perspective. . . . For another etymological root of

occasion is, we recall, the cognate *occidere* (which 'means' both 'to fall,' especially to 'set' or 'to wester,' as in the case of the movement of the sun; and 'to die,' 'to perish') from the present participle of which (*occidens*) the English word *Occident* comes" (p. 142). The German word for the English *Occident* is *Abendland*: Eveningland.

64. See Martin Heidegger, *An Introduction to Metaphysics*, trans. Ralph Manheim (New Haven: Yale University Press, 1959): "In the conflict [*Aus-einandersetzung*, setting apart] a world comes into being. It constitutes unity, it is a binding-together, *logos. Polemos* and *logos* are the same" (p. 62). Heidegger's term is a translation of Heraclitus's *polemos*. In focusing the paradoxical *belongingness* of the two oppositional forces *in strife*, it is, among other things, intended to distinguish the Greek from the modern European idea of the beautiful as the "repose" consequent on an imperial victory of the *logos* over being understood as "mere appearance" (p. 131).

65. F. O. Matthiessen, *American Renaissance: Art and Expression in the Age of Emerson and Whitman* (London: Oxford University Press, 1941), p. 448. In the process of his reading of *Moby-Dick*, Matthiessen shifts the relative tragic balance between Ahab's nobility and the destructive consequences of his *hubris*, first by transferring the tragic catharsis from the hero to Melville himself: "Even though he had composed a tragedy in-complete when judged by Shakespearean standards, he had eased his thoughts by the act of creating so prodigious an artistic structure. He had experienced the meaning of catharsis, even though his protagonist had not" (p. 458). This compensatory shift then prepares for the elevation of Ishmael's "democratic" consciousness to the central position in the text and thus the identification of Ahab's self-exaltation not simply with Emerson's self-reliant man but with the ruthless individualism of the mid-nineteenth-century American Self. And, as the imperfectly concealed jeremiadic rhetoric of the following passage suggests, with an antidemocratic collective will not only incapable of combatting totalitarianism but even dangerously similar to it: "And the captain's career is prophetic of many others in the history of later nineteenth-century America. Man's confidence in his own unaided resources has seldom been carried farther than during that era in this country. The strong-willed individuals who seized the land and gutted the forests and built the railroads were no longer troubled with Ahab's obsessive sense of evil, since theology had receded even farther into their backgrounds. But their drives were as relentless as his, and they were to prove like him in many other ways also, as they went on to become the empire builders of the post–Civil War World. . . . Without deliberately intending it, but by virtue of his intense concern with the precariously maintained values of democratic Christianity, which he saw everywhere being threatened or broken down, Melville created in Ahab's tragedy a fearful symbol of the self-enclosed individualism that, carried to its furthest extreme, brings disaster both upon itself and upon the group of which it is a part. He provided also an ominous glimpse of what was to result when the Emersonian will to virtue became in less innocent natures the will to power and conquest" (Matthiessen, p. 459). For Mumford's similar prewar reading of *Moby-Dick*, see his *Herman Melville*, pp. 185–87.

1. Jacques Derrida, "Force and Signification," in *Writing and Difference*, trans. Alan Bass (Chicago: University of Chicago Press, 1978), pp. 17–18.

2. Samuel Taylor Coleridge, *The Complete Works*, vol. 3, *Biographia Literaria*, ed. W. T. G. Shedd (New York: Harper, 1860), p. 363. It should not be forgotten that Coleridge's poetics derives in large part from the German idealist philosophers, who, by way of Coleridge and other English Romantics, influenced mid-nineteenth-century American writers, not least Emerson, and that this chain of influence is the overt object of Melville's satirical scorn, most notably in *Pierre*.

3. T. S. Eliot, "*Ulysses*, Order, and Myth," in *Selected Prose*, ed. Frank Kermode (New York: Harcourt, Brace, Jovanovich, 1975), p. 177. For Arnold's version see "On the Modern Element in Modern Literature," in *The Complete Prose Works*, vol. 1, ed. R. H. Super (Ann Arbor: University of Michigan Press, 1974), p. 20.

4. Raymond Williams, *Marxism and Literature* (Oxford: Oxford University Press, 1977), pp. 77–80. My emphasis, except "*relational*."

5. See Michel Foucault, "Nietzsche, Genealogy, History," in *Language, Counter-Memory, Practice: Selected Essays and Interviews*, ed. Donald F. Bouchard, trans. Donald F. Bouchard and Sherry Simon (Ithaca: Cornell University Press, 1977): "Nietzsche's criticism, beginning with the second of the *Untimely Meditations*, always questioned the form of history that reintroduces (and always assumes) a suprahistorical perspective: a history whose function is to compose the finally reduced diversity of time into a totality fully closed upon itself; a history that always encourages subjective recognitions and attributes a form of reconciliation to all the displacements of the past; a history whose perspective on all that precedes it implies the end of time, a completed development. The historian's history finds its support outside of time and pretends to base its judgments on an apocalyptic objectivity. This is only possible, however, because of its belief in eternal truth, the immortality of the soul, and the nature of consciousness as always identical to itself. Once the historical sense is mastered by the suprahistorical perspective, metaphysics can bend it to its own purpose and, by aligning it to the demands of objective science, it can impose its own 'Egyptianism'" (p. 152). This "Egyptianism," which Nietzsche and Foucault find to be essential to the Occidental perspective, is, of course, the name that the "Greek" West has given to the culture that it has perennially claimed it is not. I would suggest that Melville is using the term "sultanism" in precisely this ironic way.

6. Donald Pease, "The New Americanists," in *The New Americanists: Revisionist Interventions into the Canon*, a special issue of *boundary* 2, vol. 17 (Spring 1990), p. 8.

7. Matthew Arnold, "On the Modern Element in Modern Literature," p. 20. My emphasis. Elsewhere, I have shown that Arnold's representation of classical Greek culture is not Greek at all, but Roman and that its ideological purpose finally, like that of the Romans' representation of Greece, is to legitimize the imperial vision of

Victorian Britain. See "The Apollonian Investment of Modern Humanist Educational Theory: The Examples of Matthew Arnold, Irving Babbitt, and I. A. Richards," in Spanos, *The End of Education: Toward Posthumanism* (Minneapolis: University of Minnesota Press, 1993), pp. 65–117.

8. Martin Heidegger, *Being and Time*, trans. John Macquarrie and Edward Robinson (New York: Harper & Row, 1962), p. 359. Heidegger's emphasis.

9. Walter Benjamin, "Theses on the Philosophy of History," in *Illuminations*, ed. Hannah Arendt and trans. Harry Zohn (New York: Schocken Books, 1969), p. 257.

10. Samuel Beckett, *Watt* (New York: Grove Press, 1954), pp. 43–44.

11. James Joyce, *A Portrait of the Artist as a Young Man*, ed. Chester G. Anderson (New York: Viking, 1968), p. 205.

12. I. A. Richards, *Principles of Literary Criticism*, 2d ed. (London: Routledge & Kegan Paul, 1926), pp. 245–46.

13. Ibid., p. 247. Richards goes on to warn against the "temptation to analyse" the cause of this balanced poise "into sets of opposed characters in the object. . . . The balance is not in the structure of the stimulating object, it is in the response" (p. 248). But no sooner does he offer this admonition than he betrays it by making the famous culminating distinction between the structures of "exclusive" and "inclusive" poems, in which the former are judged to be "unstable" because their exclusion of opposing impulses makes them vulnerable to "ironic contemplation" and the latter "stable" because their inclusive "balance and reconciliation" of opposed impulses makes them invulnerable to irony: "Irony in this sense consists in the bringing in of the opposite, the complementary impulses; that is why poetry which is exposed to it is not of the highest order, and why irony itself is so constantly a characteristic of poetry which is" (p. 250).

14. Jacques Derrida, "Structure, Sign, and Play in the Discourse of the Human Sciences," *Writing and Difference*, trans. Alan Bass (Chicago: University of Chicago Press, 1978), p. 279.

15. Richards, *Principles*, p. 47.

16. Cleanth Brooks invokes the authority of the passage I am referring to from Richards' poetry of synthesis; the 'alliance of levity and seriousness' with Richards' tough reasonableness of Eliot's poetry of wit with the invulnerability to irony of Richards's poetry of synthesis; the 'alliance of levity and seriousness' with Richards' unification of opposed impulses; Eliot's 'sensibility which could devour any experience' with Richards' statement that 'tragedy (he holds tragedy to be the poetry of synthesis at its highest level) is perhaps the most general, all-accepting, all-ordering experience known. It can take anything into its organization.' One may suggest one more definition of metaphysical poetry, a definition based on Richards' terms: it is a poetry in which the opposition of the impulses which are united is extreme. . . .

"Such a definition of poetry places the emphasis directly on the poet as *maker*. . . . The metaphysical poet has confidence in the power of the imagination. He is constantly remaking his world by relating into an organic whole the amorphous and heterogeneous and contradictory" (*Modern Poetry and the Tradition* [New York: Oxford University Press, 1965], pp. 42–43).

17. Martin Heidegger, *Being and Time*, pp. 230–35, 391–96. See also Heidegger, "What is Metaphysics?" in *Basic Writings*, ed. David Farrell Krell (New York: Harper & Row, 1977), p. 103.

18. Claude Lévi-Strauss, *The Savage Mind*, (Chicago: University of Chicago Press, 1966), p. 23. My emphasis.

19. Jacques Derrida, "Force and Signification," in *Writing and Difference*: "In literary criticism, the structural 'perspective' is, according to Jean-Pierre Richard's expression 'interrogative and totalitarian.' The force of our weakness is that impotence separates, disengages, and emancipates. Henceforth, the totality is more clearly perceived, the panorama and the panoramagram are possible. The panoramagram, the very image of the structuralist instrument, was invented in 1824, as Littré states, in order 'to obtain immediately, on a flat surface, the development of depth vision of objects on the horizon.' Thanks to a more or less openly acknowledged schematization and spatialization, one can glance over the field divested of its forces more freely or diagramatically. Or one can glance over the totality divested of its forces, even if it is the totality of form and meaning, for what is in question, in this case, is meaning rethought as form; and structure in the *formal* unity of form and meaning. . . . Thus, the relief and design of structures appears more clearly when content, which is the living energy of meaning, is neutralized" (p. 5).

20. Henry Alonzo Myers, "The Tragic Meaning of *Moby-Dick*," in *Tragedy: A View of Life* (Ithaca, N.Y.: Cornell University Press, 1956), pp. 73–74.

21. Richard Sewall, "*Moby-Dick*," *The Vision of Tragedy*, new ed. (New Haven: Yale University Press, 1980), pp. 102–3.

22. Ibid., p. 103.

23. Ibid., p. 105. My emphasis.

24. R. P. Blackmur, "The Craft of Herman Melville: A Putative Statement," in *The Lion and the Honeycomb: Essays in Solicitude and Critique* (New York: Harcourt, Brace & World, 1955), p. 124.

25. Henry James, preface to *The Tragic Muse* (New York: Charles Scribner's Sons, 1922): "A picture without composition slights its most precious chance for beauty, and is moreover not composed at all unless the painter knows *how* that principle of health and safety, working as an absolutely premeditated art, has prevailed. These may, in its absence, be life incontestably . . . as Tolstoi's 'Peace and War' [has] it; but what do such large loose, baggy monsters, with their queer elements of the accidental and the arbitrary, artistically mean? We have heard it maintained . . . that things are 'superior to art'; but we understand least of all what *that* may mean. . . . There is life and life, and as waste is only life sacrificed and thereby prevented from 'counting,' I delight in a deep-breathing economy and an organic form" (p. x). See also Percy Lubbock, *The Craft of Fiction* (New York: Charles Scribner's Sons, 1929): "Here, then, is the reason . . . why the *general shape of "War and Peace" fails to satisfy the eye*—as I suppose it admittedly to fail.

It is a confusion of two designs, a confusion more or less masked by Tolstoy's imperturbable ease of manner, but revealed by the *look of his novel when it is seen as a whole. It has no centre*, and Tolstoy is so clearly unconcerned by the lack that one must conclude he never perceived it. If he had he *would surely* have betrayed that he had; he would have been found, at some point or other, trying to gather his two stories into one, *devising a scheme that would include them both, establishing a centre somewhere*" (p. 39). My emphasis. For a critique of this inscribed prejudice against decenteredness that demonizes its dissemination as "uneconomical" or as "waste," see the chapter entitled "Percy Lubbock and the Craft of Supervision," in Spanos, *Repetitions: The Postmodern Occasion in Literature and Culture* (Baton Rouge: Louisiana State University Press, 1987), pp. 149–88.

26. Blackmur, "The Craft of Herman Melville," p. 132. My emphasis. The echoes of Henry James and Percy Lubbock reverberate throughout Blackmur's essay: "Melville had no talent for making his dramatic scenes [in *Pierre*] objective except by aid of external and unrelated force . . . which is to say that the book had no compositional center at all. Something of the same sort may also be true of *Moby-Dick*. Is it possible to say that Ishmael, the narrator, provides only a false center? Is it not true that a great part of the story's theme escapes him, is not recorded through his sensibility, either alone or in connection with others? Then the real center would lie where?" (p. 135).

27. Roland Barthes, quoted in Alain Robbe-Grillet, "Nature, Humanism, Tragedy," in *For a New Novel: Essays on Fiction*, trans. Richard Howard (New York: Grove Press, 1965), p. 49. For Brecht's version, see Bertolt Brecht, "On the Use of Music in an Epic Theatre," in *Brecht on Theatre: The Development of an Aesthetic*, ed. and trans. John Wilett (New York: Hill and Wang, 1964), p. 87.

28. Herman Melville, *Pierre; or, The Ambiguities*, ed. Harrison Hayford, Hershel Parker, and G. Thomas Tanselle (Evanston, Ill.: Northwestern University Press and the Newberry Library, 1971), p. 208.

29. Martin Heidegger, "The Question Concerning Technology," in *The Question Concerning Technology and Other Essays*, trans. William Lovitt (New York: Harper and Row, 1977), pp. 14–23.

30. Michel Foucault, *Discipline and Punish: The Birth of the Prison*, trans. Alan Sheridan (New York: Pantheon Books, 1977), pp. 135–169.

31. Alexander Pope, *Selected Poetry and Prose*, ed. William K. Wimsatt, Jr. (New York: Rinehart, 1951), p. 137.

32. Herman Melville, *The Confidence-Man: His Masquerade*, ed. Harrison Hayford, Hershel Parker, and G. Thomas Tanselle (Evanston, Ill.: Northwestern University Press and the Newberry Library, 1984), pp. 208–220. The most overt manifestation in *The Confidence-Man* of Melville's project to demystify the American philosophical version of the doctrine of preestablished harmony—and the (pan)optics that puts seeing and seeming, Being and (mere) appearance, in a hierarchical binary opposition—occurs in the chapter ironically entitled "A Soldier of Fortune," in which the confidence man, in the guise of a herb doctor, cons a destitute and crippled veteran of America's imperial war with Mexico into abandoning his bitterness against "free Ameriky" and accepting

his disinherited and alienated lot—one might, looking both backward to the Puritans and forward to Thomas Pynchon, call it his "preterition"—on the grounds that the immediate "eye of reason" provides an "imperfect view" of the whole picture: "'You, my worthy friend, to my concern, have reflected upon the government under which you live and suffer. Where is your patriotism? Where your gratitude? . . . Grant, for the moment, that your experiences are as you give them; in which case I would admit that government might be thought to have more or less to do with what seems undesirable in them. But it is never to be forgotten that human government, being subordinate to the divine, must needs, therefore, in its degree, partake of the characteristics of the divine. That is, while in general efficacious to happiness, the world's law may yet, in some cases, have, to the eye of reason, an unequal operation, just as, in the same imperfect view, some inequalities may appear in the operations of heaven's law; nevertheless, to one who has a right confidence, final benignity is, in every instance, as sure with the one law as the other. I expound the point at some length, because these are the considerations, my poor fellow, which, weighed as they merit, will enable you to sustain with unimpaired trust the apparent calamities which are yours'" (pp. 98). This ironic disclosure of the complicity between "free Ameriky" and providential history in the ideological task of annulling by accommodating (colonizing) the dissent of those who have been socially and politically exploited and marginalized—of the preterited, as it were—will find its fullest and most radical expression, as the resonantly grim oxymoron of the title name and its occasion (the American Revolution) suggest, in Melville's *Israel Potter: His Fifty Years of Exile*, ed. Harrison Hayford, Hershel Parker, and G. Thomas Tanselle (Evanston, Ill.: Northwestern University Press and the Newberry Library, 1982).

33. Herman Melville, *Moby-Dick*, ed. Harrison Hayford, Hershel Parker, and G. Thomas Tanselle (Evanston, Ill.: Northwestern University Press and the Newberry Library, 1988), p. 68.

34. Wai-chee Dimock, *Empire for Liberty: Melville and the Poetics of Individualism* (Princeton: Princeton University Press, 1989): "Ahab, as it turns out, is not only named Ahab but also called 'immutable.' In an uncanny parallel, he seems to have been fashioned out of just those attributes antebellum Americans bestowed on the Indian. In Ahab, Melville tells us, 'There was an infinity of firmest fortitude, a determinate, unsurrenderable wilfulness, in the fixed and fearless, forward dedication of that glance.' 'The path to my fixed purpose is laid with iron rails,' Ahab himself says at one point" (p. 136). In attributing Ahab's unerring pursuit of his "fixed purpose" to Melville's Jeffersonian imperial libertarianism, Dimock's problematic blinds her, as we shall discover, to Melville's resonantly antimetaphysical irony: not simply to the diminishing overdetermination and inflation of the consonants in this passage, but, more tellingly, to the double meaning of the word "naught" in the sentence "'Naught is an obstacle . . . to the iron way!'" which clearly gives positive ontological status to what Ahab's metaphysical logic can only understand and reject as nullity. It is not Melville's "imperial folio," but the contradictory "naught" that *is* an obstacle to Ahab's iron way. See Martin Heideg-

ger, "What is Metaphysics?" *Basic Writings*, ed. David Farrell Krell (New York: Harper & Row, 1977), pp. 97–98. The word "unerring" recurs frequently in Melville's texts, and it is invariably intended to castigate by exposing the contradictions—the violence—in the single-minded pursuit of the logic of truth, the logic enabled by the Jacksonian version of the metaphysical principle of presence. See, for example, Melville's parodic account of the hegemonic custodians of American literature in the chapter of *Pierre* entitled "Young America in Literature": "A renowned cleric and philological conductor of a weekly publication of this kind, whose surprising proficiency in Greek, Hebrew and Chaldaic, to which he had devoted by far the greater part of his life, peculiarly fitted him to pronounce unerring judgment upon works of taste in the English, had unhesitatingly delivered himself thus: . . ." (p. 246). Implicitly, then, the word is also intended to endow "errancy" with positive meaning.

35. Melville, *The Confidence-Man*, p. 70.

36. For further commentary on the enchanter as principle of last resort, see my reading of Ishmael's reading of Father Mapple's sermon on the biblical Jonah text in chapter 3 below.

37. Job 1:7: "And the Lord said unto Satan, Whence comest thou? Then Satan answered the Lord, and said, From going to and fro in the earth, and from walking up and down in it." Melville's implicit interpretation of the function of Satan in the Book of Job is strikingly parallel to the modern existentialist reading, which, following Kierkegaard, represents Satan's encounter with God in the prelude as the original "author's" interrogation of the totalizing and dedifferentiating gaze of the Law. There is, however, an important distinction to be made. This "existentialist" tradition that rehabilitates the "satanic figure" tends to recuperate a *logos* by incorporating him into an accommodational theology—as in the discourse of Christian existentialists such as Rudolph Bultmann and Paul Tillich or in the literature of Christian existentialists such as T. S. Eliot (*Sweeney Agonistes, The Family Reunion*), Charles Williams (*Thomas Cranmer of Canterbury*), Graham Greene (*The Power and the Glory*), W. H. Auden ("New Year Letter") and François Mauriac (*Thérèse Desqueyroux*)—or into an accommodational existential humanism—as in work of Archibald MacLeish (*J.B.*), or Albert Camus (*The Fall*) or even Sartre (*The Flies*). Melville, on the other hand, finally resists that temptation.

38. Like Foucault, I use the word "Archive" to mean not simply the books privileged by Western culture, but more fundamentally, the rules of "discursive formation" and "practice" that, unknown even to the writer, make these privileged books possible. See *The Archaeology of Knowledge*, trans. A. H. Sheridan Smith (London: Tavistock, 1972), pp. 126–31. Unlike Foucault, who thinks of the Archive as historically discontinuous, I (with Heidegger) understand the rules of discursive formation to be a monolithic structure, however differentiated and asymmetrical its manifestations in history: a derivative measure—established by the Romans in translating the Greek *aletheia* to *veritas*, unconcealment to *adequaetio intellectus et rei*—which contains the mechanisms that allow the rules to be "re-formed" according to the exigencies of the historically specific moment.

39. Michael Foucault, "What is an Author?," *Language, Counter-Memory, Practice*, pp. 127–29.

40. Melville's overdetermination of his powerfully bitter critique of patriarchy in *Pierre* precludes or at least tempers the kind of simplistic criticism of his male chauvinism (most recently expressed simply by the relegation of his novels to irrelevant "history") that prevails in feminist accounts of American literary history. It should also retrospectively signal the antipatriarchal implication of *Moby-Dick*, where women are ostensibly located at the very distanced and vague margins of the world of the novel. I am referring to the phallic imagery pervading the deadly pursuit of the white whale.

41. Jean-Paul Sartre, *Nausea*, trans. Lloyd Alexander (New York: New Directions, 1959): "Things happen one way and we tell about them in the opposite sense. You *seem to start at the beginning:* 'It was a fine autumn evening in 1922. I was a notary's clerk in Marommes.' *And in reality you have started at the end. It was there, invisible and present, it is the one which gives to words the pomp and value of a beginning.* 'I was out walking, I had left the town without realizing it, I was thinking about my money troubles.' This sentence, taken simply for what it is, means that the man was absorbed, morose, a hundred leagues from an adventure, exactly in the mood to let things happen without noticing them. *But the end is there, transforming everything.* For us, the man is already the hero of the story. His moroseness, his money troubles are much more precious than ours, they are all gilded by the light of future passions. And the story goes on in the reverse: instants have stopped piling themselves in a lighthearted way one on top of the other, they are snapped up by the end of the story which draws them and each one of them in turn, draws out the preceding instant: 'It was night, the street was deserted.' *The phrase is cast out negligently, it seems superfluous; but we do not let ourselves be caught and we put it aside: this is a piece of information whose value we will subsequently appreciate. And we feel that the hero has lived all the details of this night like annunciations, promises, or even that he lived only those that were promises, blind and deaf to all that did not herald adventure.* We forget that the future was not yet there; the man was walking in a night without forethought, a night which offered him a choice of dull rich prizes, and he did not make his choice" (p. 57; my emphasis).

42. Edgar Dryden, "The Entangled Text: Melville's *Pierre* and the Problem of Reading," *boundary* 2, vol. 7 (Spring 1979), 145–73. See also Dryden, "Writer as Reader: An American Story," *boundary* 2, vol. 8 (Fall 1979), pp. 189–95.

3 THE ERRANT ART OF *MOBY-DICK*

1. Herman Melville, *Moby-Dick*, ed. Harrison Hayford, Hershel Parker, and G. Thomas Tanselle (Evanston, Ill.: Northwestern University Press and the Newberry Library, 1988) , p. 3. Page numbers cited in the text are to this edition.

2. Percy Lubbock, *The Craft of Fiction* (New York: Charles Scribner's Sons, 1929). The cunning absence of the omniscient proper author and his gaze is at the heart of Lubbock's (and R. P. Blackmur's) Jamesian representation of the "rendered" novel:

Maupassant, for example, "relates his story ["La Maison Tellier"] as though he had caught it in the act and were mentioning the details as they passed. There seems to be no particular process at work in his mind, so little that the figure of Maupassant, the *showman*, is overlooked and forgotten as we follow the direction of his eyes. . . . Certainly he is 'telling' us things, but they are things so immediate, so perceptible, that the machinery of his telling, by which they reach us, is unnoticed; the story appears to tell itself. Critically, of course, we know how far that is from being the case; we know with what judicious thought the showman is selecting the points of the scene upon which he touches. But the effect is that he is not there at all, because he is doing nothing that ostensibly requires any judgement, nothing that reminds us of his presence. He is behind us, out of sight, out of mind" (p. 113; my emphasis).

3. Ralph Waldo Emerson, "The American Scholar," in *The Collected Works*, ed. Robert C. Spiller and Alfred R. Ferguson (Cambridge, Mass.: Harvard University Press, 1971), p. 53.

4. Heidegger, *Being and Time*, trans. John Macquarrie and Edward Robinson (New York: Harper & Row, 1962), pp. 437–38. See also Søren Kierkegaard, *Repetition: An Essay in Experimental Psychology*, trans. Walter Lowrie (New York: Harper & Row, 1964): "Repetition and recollection are the same movement, only in opposite directions; for what is recollected has been, is repeated backwards, whereas repetition properly so called is recollected forwards" (p. 33). Later, Kierkegaard explains this distinction in terms of the role that interest (Heidegger's *Sorge* [Care]) plays in it: "The dialectic of repetition is easy; for what is repeated has been, otherwise it could not be repeated, but precisely the fact that it has been *gives to repetition the character of novelty*. When the Greeks said that *knowledge* is recollection [the reference is clearly to Plato's *anamnesis* (unforgetting) and his concept of the preexistent soul] they affirmed *that all that is has been*; when one says that life is a repetition one affirms *that existence which has been now becomes*. When one does not possess the categories of recollection or of repetition the whole of life is resolved into a void and empty noise. Recollection is the pagan life-view, repetition is the modern life-view; repetition is the *interest* of metaphysics, and at the same time the *interest* upon which metaphysics founders; repetition is the solution contained in every ethical view, repetition is a *conditio sine qua non* of every dogmatic problem" (pp. 52–53; my emphasis, except for Kierkegaard's telling italicization of both uses of the word "interest"). For a full analysis of Kierkegaard's distinction, its influence on Heidegger's understanding of repetition (*Wiederholung*), and its applicability to literary interpretation, see the chapter entitled "Heidegger, Kierkegaard, and the Hermeneutic Circle" in William V. Spanos, *Heidegger and Criticism: Retrieving the Cultural Politics of Destruction* (Minneapolis: University of Minnesota Press, 1993), pp. 53–80.

5. Both Paul Brodtkorb Jr., in *Ishmael's White World: A Phenomenological Reading of "Moby-Dick"* (New Haven: Yale University Press, 1965), and Edgar Dryden, in *Melville's Thematics of Form: The Great Art of Telling the Truth* (Baltimore: Johns Hopkins University Press, 1968), also call attention centrally to the initial ambiguity of Ishmael's name. But

both Brodtkorb's phenomenological and Dryden's broadly New Critical analysis of its function is radically different from mine. For both, without invoking Percy Lubbock, read Ishmael as a "central consciousness," not finally (though Brodtkorb is more ambiguous on this point) to be confused with Melville. Assuming an essentially New Critical approach to the text—and overlooking R. P. Blackmur's strictures about Melville's art (to which I will return in my text), Dryden, for example, interprets the narrator's use of a pseudonym as Melville's intention to focus on Ishmael as "storyteller" as opposed to "actor": "Ishmael's name . . . is a self-assumed one, a mask which at the most serves to define a role he had once chosen to play. Since he is at the time of writing a teller rather than an actor, his name is no more than a verbal convention: it designates a self which no longer exists. At the time of writing the narrator is called Ishmael precisely because he no longer plays the role identified by the name [the exiled "wild man" of Genesis 16:12, I take it]. No longer actor but teller, he names himself in order to reveal that all names are pseudonyms. By calling himself Ishmael, the narrator establishes his identity as a purely verbal one, and then goes on to explore the implications of his art by defining his past in obviously literary terms" (p. 82). More specifically, "Ishmael's achievement in *Moby-Dick* is the result of a victory of art over life. Finding the natural world a place which at first enchants, then confuses and terrifies, and recognizing that human constructs fail to explain it [thus the name Ishmael] he removes himself from both nature and society by retreating to a fanciful world of his own creation" (p. 112). (The fact that such a "fanciful world of his own creation" is itself a construct seems to escape Dryden.) Failing, that is, to perceive that writing can be a *praxis*, "Ishmael," for Dryden, becomes a "central consciousness"—a disengaged poet, as it were. Melville becomes the hidden "renderer" of a rendered text in the manner of Henry James and Percy Lubbock. And *Moby-Dick* becomes an "almost completely [a telling qualification] self-contained and self-referring [autonomous] text, always moving away from the objective and factual world and persistently calling attention to itself as fiction" (p. 87). Without being explicitly named as such, Melville's novel, in short, becomes a "Modernist" text that in T. S. Eliot's words, is capable of "controlling, of ordering, of giving a shape and a significance to the immense pan-orama of futility and anarchy which is contemporary history." "*Ulysses*, Order, and Myth," in *Selected Prose of T. S. Eliot*, ed. Frank Kermode (New York: Harcourt Brace Jovanovich, 1975), p. 177.

6. Everywhere in his text Ishmael/Melville makes it clear that he is addressing "landsmen"—the ultimate heirs, however re-affiliated, of a providentially inscribed American Puritanism—who, if they know anything about the "sea," know it only second-hand. See, for example, the chapter "The Affidavit": "So ignorant are most landsmen of some of the plainest and most palpable wonders of the world, that without some hints touching the plain facts, historical or otherwise, of the fishery, they might scout at Moby Dick as a monstrous fable, or still worse and more detestable, a hideous and intolerable allegory" (p. 205).

7. Genesis 16:12.

8. See 1 Chronicles, 8:38, 9:44; 2 Chronicles, 19:11; 23:1; Ezra, 10:22; 2 Kings, 25:23–25; and Jeremiah, 40–41 (the same as in 2 Kings).

9. Martin Heidegger, *Being and Time*, p. 195.

10. The first quotation from T. S. Eliot occurs in *Murder in the Cathedral* in *The Complete Poems and Plays, 1909–1950* (New York: Harcourt, Brace & World, 1952): Thomas, to the women of Canterbury, p. 182, and the fourth tempter to Thomas, p. 193. The second occurs in "Little Gidding," *Four Quartets* in *The Complete Poems and Plays:* "We shall not cease from exploration / And the end of all our exploring / Will be to arrive where we started / And know the place for the first time" (p. 145). These pivotal passages, needless to say, have been invariably invoked by sympathetic and adversary critics of Eliot's poetry and drama to focalize his commitment to a theocentric Origin. For a different reading, which calls this interpretation into question, see William V. Spanos, "Hermeneutics and Memory: Destroying T. S. Eliot's *Four Quartets*," *Genre*, vol. 10 (Winter 1978), pp. 523–73.

11. Walter E. Bezanson, "*Moby-Dick*: Work of Art," in "*Moby-Dick*": *Centennial Essays* ed. Tyrus Hillway and Luther S. Mansfield (Dallas: Southern Methodist University Press, 1953), pp. 36–37. According to Pease, Bezanson's essay represents "the clearest formulation of the opposition between Ahab's total constraints and Ishmael's freedom" (*Visionary Compacts: American Renaissance Writings in Cultural Context* [Madison: University of Wisconsin Press, 1987], p. 293. See p. 295, no. 10).

12. For a remarkable parallel between Melville's and Kierkegaard's understanding of the de-differentiating and reductive "virtues" of the recollective memory, see the appropriately entitled chapter "Retrospective" in *Pierre*: "Blessed and glorified in his tomb beyond Prince Mausolus is that mortal sire, who, after an honorable, pure course of life, dies, and is buried, as in a choice fountain, in the filial breast of a tender-hearted and intellectually appreciative child. For at that period, the Solomonic insights have not poured their turbid tributaries into the pure-flowing well of the childish life. Rare preservative virtue, too, have those heavenly waters. Thrown into that fountain, all sweet recollections become marbleized; so that things which in themselves were evanescent, thus became unchangeable, and eternal. So, some rare waters in Derbyshire will petrify birds'-nests. But if fate preserves the father to a later time, too often the filial obsequies are less profound; the canonization less ethereal. The eye-expanded boy perceives, or vaguely thinks he perceives, light specks and flaws in the character he once so wholly reverenced" (*Pierre; or, The Ambiguities*, ed. Harrison Hayford, Hershel Parker, and G. Thomas Tanselle [Evanston, Ill.: Northwestern University Press and the Newberry Library, 1971], p. 68). As my epigraph for chapter 2 is intended to suggest, Melville's most sustained interrogation of the monumentalizing memory at the site of sociopolitics is, of course, *Israel Potter*.

13. R. P. Blackmur, "The Craft of Herman Melville: A Putative Statement" in *The Lion and the Honeycomb: Essays in Solicitude and Critique* (New York: Harcourt, Brace & World, 1955), p. 132. In a characteristic gesture that distinguishes him from the New Critics,

with whom he is too easily associated, Blackmur allows Melville's "assured position—whatever that is—in American literature—whatever *that* is" (p. 124). But this tolerance—and this provocative uncertainty—is utterly belied by his criticism of *Moby-Dick* and *Pierre*.

14. Blackmur, "The Craft of Herman Melville," pp. 132–33.

15. Martin Heidegger, ". . . Poetically Man Dwells . . . ," in *Poetry, Language, Thought*, trans. Albert Hofstadter (New York: Harper & Row, 1971), pp. 221–23.

16. See Hans-Georg Gadamer, *Truth and Method* (New York: Seabury Press, 1975): "Every finite present has its limitations. We define the concept of situation by saying that it represents a standpoint that limits the possibility of vision. Hence an essential part of the concept of situation is the concept of 'horizon.' The horizon is the range of vision that includes everything that can be seen from a particular vantage point. Applying this to the thinking mind, we speak of narrowness of horizon, of the possible expansion of horizon, of opening up of new horizons, etc." (p. 274).

17. Ezra Pound, "Canto 59," *The Cantos* (New York: New Directions, 1970), p. 324. This is the point William C. Spengemann implies, if he does not explicitly make, in using the following quotation from Thoreau as the epigraph of his chapter on Herman Melville in *The Adventurous Muse: The Poetics of American Fiction, 1789–1900* (New Haven: Yale University Press, 1977): "A book should contain pure discoveries, glimpses of terra firma, though by shipwrecked mariners, and not the art of navigation by those who have never been out of sight of land" (p. 178). Spengemann, however, denies Ishmael this status in reading his negative capability as a manifestation of the domestic impulse: "Ishmael, the deposed protagonist of the early chapters, strongly resembles Tommo [in *Typee*]. He, too, is an innocent adventurer with a taste for perilous excitements, a desire to know the truth, and no past. But, like Tommo [and unlike Ahab], he betrays an instinctive reluctance to pay the price of that truth. As innocent adventurers, both Tommo and Ishmael derive ultimately from the pure heroine of the Domestic Romance. The domestic heroine represented an uneasy synthesis of two contrary middle-class ideals—a conservative obedience to parental authority and family tradition, and a progressive ambition to escape into a better life, to improve her situation" (p. 192).

18. Charles Olson, "Letter 5," *The Maximus Poems*, ed. George F. Butterick (Berkeley: University of California Press, 1983), pp. 26–27. For an amplification of Olson's affiliative relationship to Melville on this point, see William V. Spanos, "Charles Olson and Negative Capability," in *Repetitions: The Postmodern Occasion in Literature and Culture* (Baton Rouge: Louisiana State University Press, 1987), pp. 107–47; and "The Destruction of Form in Postmodern American Poetry: The Examples of Charles Olson and Robert Creeley," *Amerikastudien*, vol. 25, no. 4 (1981), pp. 375–404.

19. *Pierre*, p. 284. Ironically, the "book" Pierre is writing, which he invariably calls a failure because he is too immature for such an inclusive and grand cosmic project, will be "truer" to the "truth" of being than his life. For it is a constantly transforming process, replete with contradictions, and unending, like the "novel" implied in Mel-

ville's critique of novels that have teleological resolutions. Pierre, in other words, wants obsessively to write an "inclusive metaphysical Book." What he is *in fact* writing is a book that destroys the *Book*, that articulates, not the demonic/Titanic Word, but the *words* of their occasion. As author, Pierre, the founding and eternal rock of idealism, becomes the Heraclitean river of ambiguity, of temporal flux. Whether intentionally or not, this passage (like that comparing Pierre's pursuit of self-identity to the geologist's and the archeologist's futile pursuit of the origin) constitutes a tellingly detailed critique of Alexander Pope's specular aesthetics in "The Essay on Criticism":

A *little learning* is a dangerous thing;
Drink deep, or taste not the Pierian spring:
There shallow draughts intoxicate the brain,
And drinking largely sobers us again.
Fired at first sight with what the Muse imparts,
In fearless youth we tempt the heights of Arts,
While from the bounded level of our mind,
Short views we take, nor see the lengths behind;
But more advanced, behold with strange surprise
New distant scenes of endless science rise!
So pleased at first the towering Alps we try,
Mount o'er the vales, and seem to tread the sky,
Th' eternal snows appear already past,
And the first clouds and mountains seem the last;
But, those attained, we tremble to survey
the growing labours of the lengthened way,
Th' increasing prospect tires our wandering eyes,
Hills peep o'er hills, and Alps on Alps arise!

. . . .

In Wit, as Nature, what affects our hearts
Is not th' exactness of peculiar parts;
'Tis not a lip, or eye, we beauty call,
But the joint force and full result of all.
Thus when we view some well-proportioned dome,
(the world's just wonder, and even thine, O Rome!)
No single parts unequally surprise,
All comes united to th' admiring eyes;
No monstrous height, or breadth, or length appear;
The Whole at once is bold, and regular. (*Selected Poetry and Prose*, pp. 69–70)

In focalizing the deferral of presence (the whole picture) demanded by the imperial panoptic eye, Melville's critique is far more decisive than any English Romantic critique of Pope's neoclassic (Roman) measure.

20. Laurence Sterne, *The Life and Opinions of Tristram Shandy, Gentleman*, ed. Howard

Anderson (1767; reprint, New York: W. W. Norton, 1980), pp. 147. My pointing to the affiliation between Ishmael's "carnivalesque" discourse and Sterne's implication of John Locke with Enlightenment gravity is not gratuitous. It is intended to evoke and call into question Julian Markel's identification of Ishmael's epistemology and politics with John Locke's. "In perceiving Moby Dick as a symbol of universal warfare, in attributing the whale a Manichean provenance and to himself a messianic function, Ahab enacts a dramatic tragedy that passes into the open form of Ishmael's narrative comedy. Ishmael all along has been resisting Ahab's Hobbesian model through friendship with Quee-queg and his elaborate cetology that together comprise the bulk of the book and that model in surprising detail the politics and epistemology of Locke." *Melville and the Politics of Identity: From "King Lear" to "Moby-Dick"* (Urbana: University of Illinois Press, 1993), p. 88. On Melville's anti-Enlightenment cetology, see "Cetology and Discipline" in this chapter.

21. Michel Foucault, "Nietzsche, Genealogy, History," in *Language, Counter-Memory, Practice: Selected Essays and Interviews*, ed. Donald F. Bouchard, trans. Donald F. Bouchard and Sherry Simon (Ithaca: Cornell University Press, 1977), pp. 160–61.

22. Charles Olson, "Projective Verse," in *Selected Writings*, ed. Robert Creeley (New York: New Directions, 1966), p. 17. The word "forwarding" occurs in "I Maximus of Gloucester, to You," *The Maximus Poems*: "(o my lady of good voyage / in whose arm, whose left arm rests / no boy but a carefully carved wood, a painted face, a schooner! / a delicate mast, as bow-sprit for / forwarding" (p. 6). Olson dedicated *The Maximus Poems* to "Robert Creeley—the Figure of Outward." The coincidental relation between Olson's "forwarding" and Kierkegaard's (and Heidegger's) "repetition" should not be overlooked.

23. Martin Heidegger, "On the Essence of Truth," in *Basic Writings*, ed. David Farrell Krell (New York: Harper & Row, 1977), p. 135.

24. By "destructive phenomenology," perhaps needless to say, I do not mean that mode of thinking associated with Husserl and appropriated by George Poulet and the so-called Geneva Critics of Consciousness and (for Melville studies) by Paul Brodt-korb Jr. (*Ishmael's White World*). This "Husserlian" phenomenology assumes a "transcen-dental Ego" and a sympathetic interpretive process in which the exegete, by way of a spatialized reading of his/her *oeuvre*, tracks down or penetrates to the stable *cogito* of the author with whom he identifies in something like a mystical epiphany. The "phenome-nology" I am referring to is Heideggerian in origins. It rejects the notion of the transcendental Ego in favor of a decentered self, a self "grounded" in the absence of self-presence. This "self" is neither an "ontic" self—a self entirely inscribed by a dominant discourse—nor an "ontological" self—a self entirely free of inscription and thus positively capable of penetrating the surface of phenomena to their essence. As Heidegger says: "Is there not . . . a definite ontical way of taking authentic existence, a factical ideal of Dasein, underlying our ontological Interpretation of Dasein's exis-tence? That is so indeed. But not only is this Fact one which must not be denied and which we are forced to grant; it must also be conceived in its *positive necessity*, in terms of

the object which we have taken as the theme of our investigation. Philosophy will never seek to deny its 'presuppositions,' but neither may it simply admit them. It conceives them, and it unfolds with more and more penetration both the presuppositions themselves and that for which they are presuppositions" (*Being and Time*, p. 358). This "that for which they are presuppositions" I take to be the always already absent real.

25. Martin Heidegger, "On the Essence of Truth," pp. 136–37. My emphasis.

26. Martin Heidegger, *Introduction to Metaphysics*, trans. Ralph Manheim (New Haven: Yale University Press, 1959), p. 131. See also "The Origins of the Work of Art," in *Basic Writings*, ed. David Farrell Krell (New York: Harper & Row, 1977), p. 172–78.

27. Wai-chee Dimock, *Empire for Liberty: Melville and the Poetics of Individualism* (Princeton: Princeton University Press, 1989), pp. 109–39.

28. See Melville's letter of March 3, 1849 on Emerson to Evert A. Duyckinck: "I love all men who *dive*. And fish can swim near the surface, but it takes a great whale to go down five miles or more; & if he don't attain bottom, why all the Galena can't fashion the plumet that will. I'm not talking of Mr. Emerson now—but of the whole corps of thought-divers, that have been diving and coming up again with blood-shot eyes since the world began" (*The Letters of Herman Melville*, ed. Merrill R. Davis and William Gilman [New Haven: Yale University Press, 1960], p. 79). See especially "The Castaway," in which Ishmael recalls Pip's "dive" into the "wondrous depths," which culminated in the unspeakable knowledge of being that defies—and terrifies—rational understanding (*Moby-Dick*, p. 414). Richard H. Brodhead, in *Hawthorne, Melville, and the Novel* (Chicago: University of Chicago Press, 1976), invokes Melville's letter to Duyckinck as the basis of his suggestive chapter on the "Art of the Diver" to offer an interpretation of Melville's art that implicitly recognizes its immersed and explorative "phenomenological" perspective—and the limitations of traditional, especially New Critical, approaches to the question of Melville's "craft": "In devising techniques for his fiction he combines the conscious care of a dedicated craftsman with a remarkable tentativeness, a remarkable lack of commitment to his own achievements; he discards as readily as he invents. . . . Because each formulation seems to him to open up further vistas that require new formulations, he is always sailing on. His fictional technique, like the hypothesis in his letters, are both brilliantly adequate and instantly obsolete" (p. 124).

29. Henry Fielding, *Tom Jones*, ed. Sheridan Baker (New York: W. W. Norton, 1973): "Now lest this latter should be the Case [that the reader may "be no wiser than some of Shakespeare's editors"], we think proper, before we go any farther together, to give thee a few wholesome Admonitions; that thou may'st not as grossly misunderstand and misrepresent us, as some of the said Editors have misunderstood and misrepresented their Author.

"First, then, we warn thee not too hastily to condemn any of the Incidents in this our History, as impertinent and foreign to our main Design, because thou dost not immediately conceive in what Manner such Incident may conduce to that Design. This Work may, indeed, be considered a great Creation of our own; and for a little

Reptile of a Critic to presume to find Fault with any of its Parts, without knowing the Manner in which the Whole is connected, and before he comes to the final Catastrophe, is a most presumptuous Absurdity" (p. 398).

30. Thomas Pynchon, *The Crying of Lot 49* (1966; New York: Harper & Row, 1990): "Though she saw Mike Fallopian again, and did trace the text of *The Courier's Tragedy* a certain distance, these follow-ups were no more disquieting than other revelations which now seemed to come crowding in exponentially, as if the more she collected the more would come to her, until everything she saw, smelled, dreamed, remembered, would somehow come to be woven into The Tristero.

"For one thing, she read over the will more closely. If it was really Pierce's attempt to leave an organized something behind after his own annihilation, then it was part of her duty, wasn't it, to bestow life on what had persisted, to try to be what Driblette was, the dark machine in the centre of the planetarium, to bring the estate into pulsing stelliferous Meaning, all in a soaring dome around her? . . . Under the symbol she'd copied off the latrine of The Scope into her memo book [the ubiquitous posthorn], she wrote *Shall I project a world?* If not project then at least flash some arrow on the dome to skitter among constellations and trace out your Dragon, Whale, Southern Cross. Any thing might help" (p. 82).

31. 1 Kings 21:16–22.

32. The phrase derives from Heidegger's appropriation of Husserl's "Zu dem Sachen Selbst." But it is intended to recall Melville's definition of "visible truth" in his "No! in thunder" letter to Hawthorne: "By visible truth, we mean the apprehension of the absolute condition of present things as they strike the eyes of the man who fears them not, though they do their worst to him." Finally, as I will suggest later, to "return to the things themselves" does not mean to "penetrate the veil of language that obscures the referent." It means, rather, as in Heidegger, the always absent real that resists language understood as inscription or naming.

33. Heidegger, *Introduction to Metaphysics*: "Solely in the *enduring struggle between being and appearance* did [*the pre-Socratic Greeks*] wrest being from the essent, did they carry the essent to permanence and unconcealment: the god and the state, the temples and the tragedy, the games and philosophy; all this in the midst of appearance, beset by appearance, but also taking it seriously, knowing of its power. It was in the Sophists and in Plato that appearance was declared to be *mere appearance* and thus degraded. At the same time being, as *idea*, was exalted to a suprasensory realm. A chasm, *chorismos*, was created between the merely apparent essent here below and real being somewhere on high" (pp. 105–6).

34. This visual/siege metaphor, in which the distanced, panoptic, disciplinary perspective sanctioned by the "Truth" is also intended to guarantee immunity from criticism—in which, to appropriate Derrida's phrase, "a center elsewhere [is] . . . beyond the reach of freeplay"—recurs insistently in various guises in *Moby-Dick*. See, for example the chapter "Cetology," where Melville mocks the authority of the natural scientist, Linnaeus, who, from the secure distance of his study and by means of his

archival classification tables, pronounces the "edict" that "will fain banish the whale from the waters" (*Moby-Dick*, p. 136); and "The Mast-Head," where Melville deconstructs the panoptic perspective of Platonic/Emersonian metaphysics by disclosing the pantheistic "All" that it posits to be the domain of the Nothing (the zero zone): "Over Descartian vortices you hover" (*Moby-Dick*, p. 159). The metaphor also recurs with exactness and unmistakable ironic force in *The Confidence-Man*: "In short, with all sorts of cavilers it was best, both for them and everybody, that whoever had the true light should stick behind the secure Malakoff of confidence, nor be tempted forth to hazardous skirmishes on the open ground of reason. Therefore, he [the confidence man] deemed it inadvisable in the good man, even in the privacy of his own mind, or in communion with a congenial one, to indulge in too much latitude of philosophizing or, indeed, of compassionating, since this might beget an indirect habit of thinking and feeling which might unexpectedly betray him upon unsuitable occasions" (p. 66). Hershel Parker's note in the Norton edition of *The Confidence-Man* (New York: W. W. Norton, 1971) makes it quite clear that Melville is also thinking here of the fortresses he identifies with Father Mapple's pulpit: "A fort defended by the Russians in the Crimean War. The reference helps to date the composition of this passage, since Malakoff fell to the French on September 8, 1855. The *Berkshire Country Eagle* carried news of the siege of 'impregnable Malakoff' throughout the summer of 1855, and did not announce its fall until October 5, 1855" (p. 56).

35. Erich Auerbach, "Figura," in *Scenes from the Drama of European Literature: Six Essays*, trans. Ralph Manheim (New York: Meridian Books, 1959), pp. 53–54. See also, *Mimesis: The Representation of Reality in Western Literature*, trans. Willard Trask (Garden City, N.J.: Anchor Books, 1957), and William V. Spanos, "The Incarnation: The Sacramental Aesthetic," in *The Christian Tradition in Modern British Verse Drama: The Poetics of Sacramental Time* (New Brunswick, N.J.: Rutgers University Press, 1967), pp. 15–51. The list of Patristic exegetes in my text, does not, of course, discriminate between the two essentially different broad modes of interpretation of the Christian hermeneutic tradition. Nevertheless, what all these exegetes, allegorical and figural alike, have in common is the goal of accommodating the events recorded in the Old Testament to the event recorded in the New Testament on the basis of the Incarnation. What is of crucial importance for the American context is that it is essentially the figural rather than the allegorical hermeneutic tradition that determines the American Puritans'— and, it would seem, Father Mapple's—exegetical practice.

36. Despite Bercovitch's criticism of American "exceptionalism," his discourse remains curiously exceptionalist, thus obscuring the degree to which "America"—above all, its (self)representation of power relations—is *continuous* with "Europe"—and minimizing the viability of continental theory for American cultural critique. What now— in the wake of the emergence of the discourses of "the New World Order"—needs emphasis in any discussion of the Puritan heritage in America is precisely this continuity. The Puritans did, indeed, abandon the "Old World." But not because "Europe" was fundamentally grounded in the untruth. They rejected the "Old World Order"

because the latter had, in its practice, "corrupted" the abiding Word of God and its providential design. They did not represent themselves as radical revolutionaries as such, but as a "saving remnant" and/or as "relic- or seed-bearers": as the preordained present type of those Israelites, according to Isaiah (10–12), who would lead the people out of captivity, and/or of those Trojans (the exiled band of Aeneas), whose founding of Rome, according to medieval Christian exegetes, prefigured the rebuilding of the *civitas terrena* (the Holy Roman Empire). It is not an accident that, in focusing on the metanarrative of the saving remnant, the Puritans (as well as the post-Revolutionary founding fathers) represented their errand in the wilderness in precisely the figural terms that the medieval exegetes represented the "ultramontanism" of the Church: not simply on the prefigurative model of Aeneas's "planting" of the Roman empire, but also of the establishment of the *Pax Romana*. Bercovitch is aware of this relay, but it plays only a marginal role in *The American Jeremiad*. This, I suggest, is ultimately because to emphasize it would be to jeopardize the exceptionalist ideology of which he remains vestigially a captive. This marginalization of a crucially important motif in the discourse of the origins of American self-representation that would thematize the continuity between "America" and "Europe" against the thesis of American exceptionalism is manifested symptomatically by Bercovitch's relegation of the following resonant reference to Cotton Mather's appropriation of the above figural constellation in *Magnalia Christi Americana* to a footnote (quoted in a different context in chapter 1) devoted to challenging the prevailing thesis that the *Magnalia* represents "a cry of despair": "The significance of those deliverances [from Afflictive Disturbances . . . Suffered From Various Adversaries . . . (II, 487)] [is] indicated by the title of the last section of this last Book, 'Arma Virosque Cano,' a title that recalls the Virgilian invocation with which Mather opens the History (as well as the numerous echoes from the *Aeneid* thereafter), and so suggests the epic proportions of his narrative. For Mather . . . New England's story not only parallels but supersedes that of the founding of Rome, as his literary 'assistance' from Christ excels the inspiration of Virgil's muse, as the 'exemplary heroes' he celebrates resemble but outshine the men of Aeneas' band—not only as Christians but as seafarers and conquerors of hostile pagan tribes—and, most spectacularly, as the millennium towards which the Reformation is moving provides the far more glorious antitype of the Augustan *Pax Romana*. Undoubtedly, the proper title for Mather's work is the exultant one he gave it" (Sacvan Bercovitch, *American Jeremiad* [Madison: University of Wisconsin Press, 1978], p. 87).

37. Bercovitch, *The American Jeremiad*, pp. 12–13.

38. Herman Melville, *Redburn: His First Voyage*, ed. Harrison Hayford, Hershel Parker, and G. Thomas Tanselle (Evanston, Ill.: Northwestern University Press and the Newberry Library, 1969), pp. 139–40. Compare Michel Foucault, *Madness and Civilization: A History of Insanity in the Age of Reason*, trans. Richard Howard (New York: Vintage Books, 1988): "This basic poverty was in a sense inalienable: birth or accident, it formed a part of life that could not be avoided. For a long time, it was inconceivable to have a state in which there were no paupers, so deeply did need appear to be inscribed in man's fate

and in the structure of society: property, labor, and poverty are terms which remain linked in the thought of philosophers until the nineteenth century.

"Necessary because it could not be suppressed, this role of poverty was necessary too because it made wealth possible. Because they labor and consume little, those who are in need permit a nation to enrich itself, to set a high value on its fields, its colonies, its mines, to manufacture products which will be sold the world over; in short, a people would be poor which had no paupers. Indigence becomes an indispensable element in the State. In it is concealed the secret but also the real life of society. The poor constitute the basis and the glory of nations. And their poverty, which cannot be suppressed, must be exalted and revered: 'My purpose is merely to attract a share of that vigilant attention [that of the government] to the suffering portion of the People . . . ; the succor it is owed derives essentially from the honor and the prosperity of an Empire, of which the Poor are everywhere the firmest support, for a sovereign cannot preserve and extend his realm without favoring the population, the cultivation of the Land, the Arts, and commerce; and the Poor are the necessary agents of these great powers which establish the true strength of a People'" (pp. 229–30). (The closing quote is from the Abbé de Recalde, *Traité sur les abus qui subsistent dans les hôpitaux du royaume* [Paris, 1786], pp. ii, iii.) Foucault is speaking here of the birth of the idea of the state understood as "the people" in late monarchist France. But this new representation of the poor as the necessary and indispensable wheels of the sumptuous coach in which the privileged ride is not ultimately superseded by the rise of capitalist democracy.

It is no accident that after carefully reading several chapters of Adam Smith's *Wealth of Nations*, in hopes of finding "something like the philosopher's stone, a secret talisman, which would transmute even pitch and tar to silver and gold," Redburn, the impoverished gentleman turned seaman, finally decides that its best use is as a pillow "for which it answered very well" (p. 86–87). In this gesture indicating recognition not simply of the incommensurability of a totalizing Book and the historically specific actuality of power relations but of the comforting ideological agenda of such talismanic books, Redburn prefigures Pierre's itinerary vis à vis Plato, Spinoza, and Goethe and the "preposterous rabble of Muggletonian Scots and Yankees, whose vile brogue still the more bestreaks the stripedness of their Greek or German Neoplatonical originals" (p. 128). Not incidentally, his specific gesture is also proleptic of one of the essential demystifying gestures of the postmodern writer Samuel Beckett: "Not that for a moment Watt supposed that he had penetrated the forces at play [in the house of Knott (Not)], in this particular instance, or even perceived the forms that they upheaved, or obtained the least useful information concerning himself, or Mr Knott, for he did not. But he had turned, little by little, a disturbance into words, he had made a pillow of old words, for a head" *Watt* (New York: Grove Press, 1953), p. 117.

39. Edward W. Said, "Travelling Theory," *The World, the Text, and the Critic* (Cambridge, Mass.: Harvard University Press, 1983), pp. 226–47.

40. Geoffrey Whitney, *A Choice of Emblems* (Leiden, 1556), p. 229. The Great Seal of the United States, which also appears as an emblem on the American one-dollar bill, is a telling eighteenth-century American version of this ubiquitous Protestant emblem: an encircled pyramid, at the apex of which is an all-seeing eye, and at the base of which, the Roman numerals "MDCCLXXVI" (the entire temporal history of the Christian world over which its commanding gaze presides) and bearing the Virgilian mottoes: "Annuit coeptis" ("God has favored our beginnings") at the top, and "Novus Ordo Seclorum" ("New World Order") at the bottom. This conflation of the Puritan providential design and the imperial Roman project in an emblem intended to symbolize the cultural identity of America symptomatically captures its ideological itinerary in the secularized post-Revolutionary period. It also reflects the historical relationship between Puritanism and capitalism as developed by Max Weber. See also Dennis M. Arnold's stylized adaptation of this emblem for the cover design of the collection of "New Americanist" essays *Ideology and Classic American Literature*, ed. Sacvan Bercovitch and Myra Jehlen (Cambridge: Cambridge University Press, 1986). This synecdochical history should make forcefully clear the genealogy of the discourse of the "New World Order" enabled by the "end" of the Cold War.

41. Max Weber, *The Protestant Ethic and the Spirit of Capitalism*, trans. Talcott Parsons (New York: Charles Scribner's Sons, 1958), pp. 48–50, 159 ff., 180–83. See Melville's satirical representation of Franklin in *Israel Potter*, the novel which was intended to retrieve the "record of [its anonymous "hero's"] fortunes . . . long ago faded from print—himself out of being—his name out of memory" (p. 169). Like Weber, if more playfully, Melville, in this portrait, thematizes the calculative Protestant/bourgeois ethos that, in the name of the calling to rationalize the earth, reduces everything and everyone he encounters—especially the unelected (preterite)—to useful, expendable, and discardable objects.

42. Michel Foucault, *Discipline and Punish: The Birth of the Prison*, trans. Alan Sheridan (New York: Pantheon Books, 1977), p. 205. The English translation, it is worth observing, obscures Foucault's emphasis in the original French title—*Surveiller et punir*—the metaphorics of vision that marks the formation of the disciplinary society.

43. That Melville was aware of "the great debates of the 1830s" is evident in his recurrent references to John Howard (b. 1726, d. 1790), the English prison reformer, who, along with Blackstone, according to Foucault, established the general principles for the transformation of penal institutions in England and the United States into "reformatories" at the beginning of the nineteenth century. See, for example, *Redburn*, pp. 181, 293. Melville's references to Howard in *Redburn* are essentially favorable, but this, as his severe criticism of U.S. naval discipline in *White Jacket* makes clear, does not preclude his intuition into the general relationship between reformation and power. For a somewhat similar, if considerably less critical, account of post-Enlightenment penal reform in America, one that distinguishes the American from the continental initiative in terms of the former's effort to align its mechanism with the secular liberalism of postcolonial Jacksonian democracy, see David Rothman, *The Discovery of*

the Asylum: Social Order and Disorder in the New Republic (1971; rev. ed., Boston: Little, Brown, 1990).

44. See especially Cole's *Voyage of Life: Old Age* (1842). For an important discussion of the relation between Cole's banal painting and the domesticated and nationalized ("American") sublime, see Rob Wilson, *American Sublime: The Genealogy of a Poetic Genre* (Madison: University of Wisconsin Press, 1991), pp. 117–33.

45. This chapter begins: "Returning to the Spouter-Inn from the Chapel, I found Queequeg there alone, he having left the Chapel before the benediction sometime" (*Moby-Dick*, p. 49).

46. Henry Nash Smith, "The Image of Society in *Moby-Dick*," in *"Moby-Dick": Centennial Essays*, ed. Tyrus Hillway and Luther S. Mansfield (Dallas: Southern Methodist University Press, 1953), p. 64. My emphasis. This sanguine representation of Father Mapple's ferocious exhortation, in which a true Melvillean would take delight, is consistent with Smith's idealized representation of America, particularly the West, as the "Virgin Land," the romance, according to New Americanists—Richard Slotkin and Donald Pease, for example—that brutally annuls the history of the "divinely ordained" violence against the native Americans. As Pease puts it, "In *Virgin Land*, Smith idealized the American West as that permanent place in nature where Americans could separate from their pasts and recover the forever inviolable status of a new beginning. . . . As a romance-fulfillment of a wished-for America of endlessly renewable possibilities, . . . a *Virgin Land* eliminated ideological considerations about this place as un-American. But writing in the post-Vietnam era, Slotkin rereads *Virgin Land* in terms that recall American imperialism—its generalized domination of nature and native cultures. As an anti-romance of America's origins, Slotkin's *Fatal Environment* finds in Smith's *Virgin Land* a paradigmatic context for the naturalization of racist and sexist stereotypes. As the primal scene of America's endlessly recoverable origin, *Virgin Land*, Slotkin argues, is predicated upon the denial of the difference between 'virgin land' and every other place in the culture. After underscoring the violence in this denial, Slotkin associates the originary violence he finds in the denial of difference of America's primal self-image with the violence of America's western settlers directed against native peoples." "New Americanists: Revisionist Interventions into the Canon," *boundary* 2, vol. 17 (Spring 1990), p. 14. Implicit in this retrieved history are, of course, the American Puritan sermons, the prefigurative perspective of which justified the killing, burning, and destroying of native Americans by representing them as the diabolic agents of Satan, who threatened God's providential design in America. See also, Paul Brodtkorb Jr., *Ishmael's White World*, in which Father Mapple's text, if not Father Mapple himself, is represented as "Ishmael's" celebration of a Kierkegaardian-like "religious hero," who must act in a world where God has teleologically suspended the ethical (p. 75). For further commentary on this passage from Father Mapple's sermon, see "The American Adam and the Naming of the White Whale" later in this chapter.

47. Cotton Mather, *Magnalia Christi Americana; or, The Ecclesiastical History of New England*, Bks. 1 and 2, ed. Kenneth B. Murdoch with Elizabeth W. Miller (Cambridge, Mass.:

Harvard University Press, 1977), p. 129. Though Mather's representation of the natives of Massachusetts is by now well known, it is worth quoting from the *Magnalia* to suggest the remarkable similarity between the tonal resonance of its providential rhetoric and that of Father Mapple's sermon, that is, to suggest the force of Melville's parody: "And yet behold the watchful Providence of God over them that seek him! This *False-dealing* [of those neighbors in Holland who had contracted with the ship's captain] proved a *Safe-dealing* for the good People against whom it was used. Had they been carried according to their desire unto *Hudson's River*, the *Indians* in those parts were at this time so Many, and so Mighty, and so Sturdy, that in probability all this little feeble Number of Christians had been Massacred by these bloody Salvages, as not long after some others were: Whereas the good Hand of God now brought them to a Country wonderfully prepared for their Entertainment, by a sweeping *Mortality* that had lately been among the Natives. *We have heard with our Ears, O God, our Fathers have told us, what work thou didst in their Days, in the times of Old; how thou dravest out the Heathen with thy Hand, and plantedst them; how thou dids't afflict the People, and cast them out!* The *Indians* in these Parts had newly, even about a Year or Two before, been visited with such a prodigious Pestilence; as carried away not a *Tenth*, but *Nine Parts* of Ten, (yea, 'tis said, *Nineteen* of *Twenty*) among them: So that the *Woods* were almost cleared of those pernicious Creatures, to make Room for a *Better Growth*" p. 129.

48. In making this claim, I am in disagreement with Donald Pease's interpretation of the rhetorical uses to which Ishmael puts his language: "In speaking with the force of Ahab's demand for a world indistinguishable from his human will, but free of the consequences of that will, Ishmael can discover pleasure not quite in another world but in a prior world, in which the endless proliferation of possible deeds displaces the need for any definitive action. The pleasure in this prior world results from the endless delay of a conclusion to the pleasure-inducing activity. The capacity to experience this delay as pleasure (rather than frustration) also derives from Ahab. The fate befalling Ahab's decisive conversion of words into deed determines Ishmael's need for a realm in which the indeterminate play of endless possible actions overdetermines his indecision" (*Visionary Compacts: American Renaissance Writings in Cultural Context* [Madison, University of Wisconsin Press, 1987], pp. 272–73). Pease's interpretation of Ishmael's discourse is, at this point, intended to suggest the complicity of deconstruction (its textualization of the world in terms of *différance*) with the Old Americanists' Cold War "field-Imaginary"—in this case the apotheosis of Ishmael as the epitome of the self-reliant American Renaissance man—which internalizes historically specific conflicts. This interrogation is the necessary consequence of reading Ishmael's discourse as if it were co-present with the past events he is recalling. As I will make clearer later, what I am suggesting, rather, is that the present act of writing *Moby-Dick* is an emancipatory *praxis*, not in the sense of privileging a self-present (American) subject (as in the case of the Cold War critics), nor of privileging a textual or grammatological "self" (as in the case of deconstructive critics), but in the sense of proferring a de-centered subject who resists the coercive teleologically structured novel and the relay of imperial worldly

practices with which it is implicated and, in so doing, discloses the possibilities of a relay of collective emancipatory practices—a multisituated politics—which is "grounded, not on a principle of presence, but in its historically specific occasion."

49. I am referring to that peculiarly Cervantic form of parody that pursues the rigorous logic of the don's interpretive practice—his reading of worldly phenomena as particular signatures of a plenary Sacred Book—to its self-destructive or carnivalesque end. When the differential force of the recalcitrant real world manifests itself so powerfully that it can no longer be accommodated to and contained by the don's visionary problematic, he is compelled to appeal to the "enchanter." This is the ultimate outside principle of presence—the transcendental signified, as it were—that is the final guarantee of the legitimacy—but also the illegitimacy—of all logocentric and totalizing ontologies, the principle which is normally held in invisible reserve, but which is brought into play in crisis situations. The most telling example of this self-destructive movement occurs when the don, through the mediations of Sancho, finally "meets" his beloved Dulcinea in El Toboso and, unlike Sancho, who is Cervantes's destructive agent, finds her to be a rather plain-faced village girl riding an ass astride and stinking of raw garlic: "Do you see now what a spite the enchanters have against me, Sancho? See to what extremes the malice and hatred they bear me extend, for they have sought to deprive me of the happiness I should have enjoyed in seeing my mistress in her true person. In truth I was born a very pattern of the unfortunate, and to be the target and mark of the arrows of adversity. You must observe also, Sancho, that these traitors were not satisfied with changing and transforming my Dulcinea, but transformed and changed her into a figure as low and ugly as that peasant girl's. And they have deprived her too of something most proper to great ladies, which is the sweet smell they have from always moving among ambergris and flowers. For I must tell you, Sancho, that when I went to help my Dulcinaea on to her hackney—as you say it was, though it seemed a she-ass to me—I got such a whiff of raw garlic as stank me out and poisoned me to the heart" (*Don Quixote*, trans. J. M. Cohen [Hammondsworth, England: Penguin Books, 1950], Bk. 2, chap. 10, pp. 524–32.

50. Michel Foucault, "Nietzsche, Genealogy, History," in *Language, Counter-Memory, Practice*, pp. 160–61. See also Mikhail Bakhtin, *The Dialogic Imagination: Four Essays*, ed. Michael Holquist, trans. Caryl Emerson and Michael Holquist (Austin: University of Texas Press, 1981). As I have suggested, it is precisely this critical genealogy—this parodic logic that allows the reality constructed by the monumental historian to "unrealize" itself through its excesses—that is at work in Melville's *The Confidence-Man: His Masquerade*. In demonstrating the remarkable parallel between Melville's decentered parody and Foucault's "poststructuralist" or postmodern understanding of parody, I am implicitly disagreeing with Fredric Jameson's influential blanket identification of "postmodern parody" with *pastiche*: a "blank parody," which, in "the cannibalization of all styles of the past," has gone far to annul historical depth and affect. See *Postmodernism, or, The Cultural Logic of Late Capitalism* (Durham, N.C.: Duke University Press, 1991), pp. 16ff.

51. Foucault, "Nietzsche, Genealogy, History," p. 162.

52. Herman Melville to Nathaniel Hawthorne, April 16, 1851 (*The Letters of Herman Melville*, pp. 124–25). My emphasis.

53. In "The Craft of Herman Melville," Blackmur observed that "Melville never influenced the direction of the art of fiction. . . . He added nothing to the novel as a form. . . . It is not that he is inimitable but that there was nothing formally organized enough in his work to imitate or modify or perfect" (p. 125). Written in 1938, these remarks of a New Critic were intended to counter the indiscriminate enthusiasm of the revivalist critics, who paid little attention to the craft of Melville's fiction. Yet Blackmur is at one with the latter in his assumption that unity is the essential criterion of fictional value. A postmodern generation of American novelists has rendered Blackmur's conclusion anachronistic. If there is any earlier American novelist whose *art* this new generation has found "imitable," "modifiable," or "perfectable," it is precisely the Melville of *Moby-Dick* and after, as the testimony of Pynchon's *V.*, *The Crying of Lot 49*, and *Gravity's Rainbow*, of Robert Coover's *Public Burning*, of Joseph Heller's *Catch 22*, of John Barth's *Letters*, of E. L. Doctorow's *Book of Daniel*, bears witness.

54. Bercovitch, *The American Jeremiad*, p. 191.

55. Ibid., p 193.

56. I am, of course, putting all the terms of this quotation that reinscribe the principle of presence under erasure.

57. Richard Sewall, "*Moby-Dick*," in *The Vision of Tragedy* (New Haven: Yale University Press, 1980), p. 93.

58. On the surface, Ishmael/Melville characteristically attributes the source of the "Spirit of Equality" to God. But it is clear from the passage, especially where he invokes Him as "the great God absolute!" to define democratic equality, that he is, characteristically, putting the traditional idea of God under erasure.

59. This ironic metaphor, which Melville uses to suggest the act of imposing a symbolic, ritualistic meaning on the things themselves, is pervasive in *Moby-Dick*. It is more than likely that Melville is thinking of Shakespeare's insistent use of this trope to distinguish the human being's secondary, symbolized state from its primordial, initial condition: the inscribed and domesticated world of "culture" from the uncanny not-at-homeness (what Heidegger calls *Unheimlichkeit*) of a world "grounded" in nothing. See, for example, *King Lear*, in which Lear's journey into the chaos of the heath divests him—as he unknowingly prophesies it will in his magisterial opening ceremony of division, where he announces "we will divest us both of rule / Interest of territory, cares of state, while we / Unburdened crawl towards death" (1.1.103–4)—not only of his protective societal garments—his "lendings," he now realizes—but also of the analogous protective verbal trappings of ceremony, his earlier "tremendously centralized" and monolithic teleological rhetoric. In the midst of the raging storm that has torn to shreds the grand—and seemingly abiding—courtly image of King Lear, he cries (in unceremonial prose) to the naked "Madman" Edgar: "'Why, thou wert better in thy grave than to answer with thy uncover'd body this extremity of the skies.—Is man

more than this? Consider him well. Thou owest the worm no silk, the beast no hide, the sheep no wool, the cat no perfume.—Ha! here's three on's are sophisticate! Thou art the thing itself; unaccommodated man is no more but such a poor, bare, forkt animal as thou art. Off, off, you lendings!—Come, unbutton here.' (*Tear his clothes*)" (William Shakespeare, *Works* [New York: Oxford University Press, 1938], 3.4.103–12).

60. I am, of course, referring to Nietzsche's retrieval of the Dionysian dimension of Attic tragedy from the oblivion to which nineteenth-century European Apollonianism (spatial perception) had relegated it. But I am also thinking of Jacques Derrida's appropriation of Nietzsche's insight in his critique of "structuralism": his disclosure that the pursuit of "comprehension," of decidable meaning, is a will to power that annuls or pacifies the (Dionysiac) "force" of (temporal) writing: "*To comprehend* the structure of a becoming, the form of a force, is to lose meaning by finding it. The meaning of becoming and of force, by virtue of their pure, intrinsic characteristics, is the repose of the beginning and end, the peacefulness of a spectacle, horizon or face. Within this peace and repose the character of becoming and of force is disturbed by meaning itself. The meaning of meaning is Apollonian by virtue of everything within it that can be seen." "Force and Signification," in *Writing and Difference*, trans. Alan Bass (Chicago: University of Chicago Press, 1978), p. 26.

61. In his brilliant reading of this passage (which he calls a "scene of persuasion," prefiguring that of the Cold War discourse), Donald Pease claims that, by pointing to the superficiality of Starbuck's self-reliant argument, Ahab not only annuls his first mate's impulse to rebel, but in so doing transforms himself as totalitarian object of Starbuck's rebellion into the principle of rebellion itself: "Once transmuted onto his scene of persuasion, Ahab ceases to be a target for Starbuck's dissent; instead he elevates Starbuck's dissent into an apocalyptic plane where dissent and Ahab's wish for a final reckoning with the powers of the universe become indistinguishable from one another. In this elevation, however, Ahab also utterly separates the ideological motives for action—the struggle between an utterly self-reliant man and oppressive cosmic forces—from the set of actions possible for Starbuck. Once he has voiced his own rationale for hunting the whale, Ahab expects Starbuck not to hunt for the same reasons but to return to a scene more in keeping with Starbuck's career. . . .

"Having resituated the world of motives in a scene where he alone will have control over their resolution, Ahab places the crew in a second realm, one ideologically determined by the first. . . . His scene of persuasion collapses the space of argument, where dissent would otherwise be acknowledged, into an opposition—that between him and cosmic forces—whose terms carry their conclusion within the form of the organization" (pp. 239–40). (See also, pp. 242, 244.) Pease's reading is quite persuasive, but in order to achieve its larger purposes (the identification of Ishmael's narrative of resistance as no less a scene of persuasion than Ahab's and thus the exposure of the postwar criticism that privileged Ishmael over Ahab as determined by the Cold War scenario) it overlooks the fact that Ahab's projection of a profounder self-reliance than Starbuck's—what pits his person against "cosmic forces"—is intended by Melville to invoke the difference/identity of the material/capitalist representation of the "antagonism" between man and nature and the ontological, i.e., the tragic struggle, in order to deconstruct it. More important, it also overlooks, like virtually all the criticism that points to the superficiality of Starbuck's dissent, his resonant appeal, however discredited by the ideology preceding it, to "the things themselves," that is, as I shall show, to the most reiterated and important motif in *Moby-Dick*: that which posits being there—in the midst, in the destructive element, as it were—against seeing things as they are from a distance, i.e., meta-physically, or, what is the same thing, re-presentationally. This, as what precedes and will follow should make clear, is not to suggest that Melville is positing a self-identical "reality," a primordial reality free from inscription, which, in establishing Ishmael as a self-present subject, would justify Pease's poststructuralist argument against the Cold War criticism, the criticism that invokes Ishmael's American democratic spirit against Ahab's calculated totalitarianism. When Ishmael, echoing what Pease rightly calls Starbuck's "commonsense argument" (*Visionary Compacts*, p. 244), later insists that to know the whale one must go a-whaling, he is not positing an incommensurable distinction between naming and reality, interpretation and the thing itself; he is, I submit, referring to the "real" as "absent cause." The difference makes naming possible—and always already self-destructive.

62. Coming when it does in his text, this "expiation" on "the business of standing mast-head" suggests that it is precisely the young Ishmael's theoretical/meditative perspective that renders him oblivious to Ahab's ritual *use* of the figure to bend the world to his monomaniacal purpose.

63. See, especially, Ralph Waldo Emerson, "Nature," in *The Complete Works*, vol. 1, Centenary Edition, ed. Edward Waldo Emerson (Boston: Houghton Mifflin, 1903): "Standing on the bare ground,—my head bathed by the blithe air, and uplifted into infinite space,—all mean egotism vanishes. I become a transparent eyeball; I am nothing; I see all: the currents of the Universal Being circulate through me; I am part or parcel of God" (p. 16). F. O. Matthiessen has commented on this relationship between Emerson's "Neoplatonic" tendency to hover in a rarefied "cosmic" space and Melville's warning to "ye Pantheists": "Out of the depths of his consent to his lot welled up the opposite mood, his dilation in response to the flux. [T. E. Hulme, one of Matthiessen's theoretical authorities, called this "romantic" movement a rising into "the circumambient gas."] His enunciation of this mood is very like some of Melville's passages about standing the mast-head. Particularly in a letter that Emerson wrote from Nantasket in the summer of 1841 do his rhythms seem affected by the soothing monotonous movement of the waves as well as by his having just been rereading Plato: 'But is it the picture of the unbounded sea, or is it the lassitude of the Syrian summer, that more and more draws the cords of Will out of my thought and leaves me nothing but perpetual observation, perpetual acquiescence and perpetual thankfulness. . . .'" (*American Renaissance: Art and Expression in the Age of Emerson and Whitman* [London: Oxford University Press, 1941], p. 62). But Matthiessen exculpates Emerson by pointing to the latter's awareness of this tendency (though this particular passage does not clearly justify

Matthiessen's claim). He further does not interpret the passage from *Moby-Dick* as a critique of Emerson or Emersonianism (no doubt because his ideological project is to identify Melville's project with Emerson's), and, most tellingly, omits reference to the dire earthly consequences likely, according to Ishmael, to ensue from this kind of transcendental philosophical dreaming. For a strong deconstructive reading of the "transparent eyeball"—one that challenges mine or, rather, Melville's, in interpreting it as a *catachresis*, see Donald Pease, "Emerson, *Nature*, and the Sovereignty of Influence," *boundary* 2, vol. 8 (Spring 1980), 58–62.

64. The fact that Melville puts quotation marks around the word "interest" strongly suggests that, like Kierkegaard, he is aware of its etymological connotations: *interesse*, in the midst and thus in the realm where differential things make a difference: the existential structure that Heidegger calls "Care" (*Sorge*) in *Being and Time*.

65. Friedrich Nietzsche, "Of Redemption," in *Thus Spoke Zarathustra*, trans. R. J. Hollingdale (Hammondsworth, England: Penguin Books, 1969), p. 162. See also Martin Heidegger, "Who is Nietzsche's Zarathustra?" reprinted in *The New Nietzsche: Contemporary Styles of Interpretation*, ed. David B. Allison (New York: Dell, 1977), pp. 73ff.

66. Jacques Derrida, "Structure, Sign, and Play in the Discourse of the Human Sciences," *Writing and Difference*, p. 279.

67. Martin Heidegger, *Early Greek Thinking*, trans. David Farrell Krell and Frank A. Capuzzi (New York: Harper & Row, 1975), p. 57. My suggestion that Melville's interrogation of Ahab's American Adamic metaphysics anticipated Heidegger's interrogation of the Westernization of the planet is not as arbitrary as it may seem. In the last chapter I will try to show that Melville's interpretation of Ahab's American metaphysics as a totalizing paranoia speaks proleptically not simply to the occasion of the American intervention in Vietnam, but to America's unilateral assumption of leadership of the "New World Order" in the post–Cold War era.

68. Martin Heidegger, "The End of Philosophy and the Task of Thinking," in *Basic Writings*, ed. David Farrell Krell (New York: Harper & Row, 1977), p. 377. This, of course, is another way of putting Donald Pease's interpretation of Ahab's "argument" with Starbuck on the quarterdeck as discourse at "the scene of persuasion."

69. See especially, Thomas Pynchon, *The Crying of Lot 49*, p. 170.

70. Jean-François Lyotard, *The Postmodern Condition: A Report on Knowledge*, trans. Geoff Bennington and Brian Massumi (Minneapolis: University of Minnesota Press, 1984), p. 81. Melville's comportment toward the sublime is not to be confused with that "American Sublime" which, according to Rob Wilson, all too many American Renaissance writers, from the Puritan Ann Bradstreet through William Livingston to William Cullen Bryant and Walt Whitman, domesticated or accommodated, each in their own historically specific way, to the achievement of an expansionist national consensus. See Wilson, *The American Sublime*. On the contrary, Melville's discourse on the dreadful whiteness of the white whale is intended to subvert this kind of "Americanization" of the sublime. In this, too, he anticipates the postmodern rethinking of the sublime.

71. See especially, Lionel Trilling, "The Princess Casamassima," in *The Liberal Imagina-*

tion: Essays on Literature and Society, pp. 56–88. Following up on his recuperation of the "cold realism" of Hawthorne's romances from the oblivion to which the "progressive liberal" Parringtonian tradition would relegate them and speculating on Henry James's response to William James's liberal/progressive suspicion that his brother's "preoccupation with art was very close to immorality" (p. 74), Trilling argues: "[Henry] James even goes so far as to imply that the man of art may be close to the secret center of things when the man of action is quite apart from it. Yet Hyacinth [the "Jamesian" imagination] cannot carry out the orders of the people who trust him. Nor of course can he betray them—the pistol which, in the book's last dry words, 'would certainly have served much better for the Duke,' Hyacinth turns upon himself. A vulgar and facile progressivism can find this to be a proof of James's 'impotence in matters sociological'—'the problem remains unsolved.' Yet it would seem that a true knowledge of society comprehends the reality of the social forces it presumes to study and is aware of contradictions and consequences; it knows that sometimes society offers an opposition of motives in which the antagonists are in such a balance of authority and appeal that a man who so wholly perceives them as to embody them in his very being cannot choose between them and is therefore destroyed. This is known as tragedy" (pp. 76–77). This "defense" of Henry James can only take place in the nowhere of the universal—the internalized world of art presided over by a "secret cause"—where all things, not least, the balance of real sociopolitical power is equal, which is not *this world:* the late-nineteenth-century world which is the *mise-en-scène* of James's novel. The echoes of I. A. Richards's celebration of the balanced poise of opposites in tragedy in this spokesman for the American romance should not be overlooked.

72. See T. S. Eliot, "Hamlet and His Problems," in *Selected Essays* (New York: Harcourt, Brace, 1950): "The only way of expressing emotion in the form of art is by finding an 'objective correlative'; in other words, a set of objects, a situation, a chain of events which shall be the formula of that *particular* emotion; such that when the external facts, which must terminate in sensory experience, are given, the emotion is immediately evoked. If you examine any of Shakespeare's more successful tragedies, you will find this exact equivalence. . . . The artistic 'inevitability' lies in this complete adequacy of the external to the emotion; and this is precisely what is deficient in *Hamlet.* Hamlet (the man) is dominated by an emotion which is inexpressible, because it is in *excess* of the facts as they appear. And the supposed identity of Hamlet with his author is genuine to this point: that Hamlet's bafflement at the absence of objective equivalent to his feelings is a prolongation of the bafflement of his creator in the face of his artistic problem" (pp. 124–25).

73. See the chapters "The Albatross" (p. 237); "The Jeroboam's Story" (p. 216); "The Pequod Meets the Virgin" (p. 35); "The Pequod Meets the Rose-bud" (p. 404); "Leg and Arm: The Pequod, of Nantucket, Meets the Samuel Enderby, of London" (p. 436); "The Pequod Meets the Bachelor" (p. 494); "The Pequod Meets the Rachel" (p. 530); "The Pequod Meets the Delight" (p. 540).

74. Lionel Trilling, "The Princess Casamassima": "'But I have the imagination of

disaster—and see life as ferocious and sinister': James wrote this to A. C. Benson in 1896 and what so bland a young man as Benson made of the statement, what anyone then was likely to make of it, is hard to guess. But nowadays we know that such an imagination is one of the keys to truth.

"It was, then, 'the imagination of disaster' that cut James off from his contemporaries and it is what recommends him to us now. . . . [*The Princess Casamassima*] is a novel which has at its very center the assumption that Europe has reached the full of its ripeness and is passing over into rottenness, that the peculiarly beautiful light it gives forth is in part the reflection of a glorious past and in part the phosphorescence of a present decay, that it may meet its end by violence and that this is not wholly unjust, although, never before has the old sinful continent made so proud and pathetic an assault upon our affections" (p. 58). An analysis of this resonant passage, which epitomizes the essence of Trilling's critical discourse would tell us much about the ideological subtext of his Americanist "cultural criticism." Suffice it here to say that it is the last sentence that brings the meaning of James's oxymoron into focus.

75. Lionel Trilling, "The Princess Casamassima," pp. 58, 78, 79, 80.

76. Trilling's identification of the American romance and tragedy or, rather, his unstated assumption that tragedy constitutes the fullest artistic expression of the American romance is evident in the following remarks in "The Princess Casamassima": "If this [thickening of "the number of interesting events beyond our ordinary expectation"], in James or any other storyteller, leads to a straining of our sense of verisimilitude, there is always the defense to be made that the special job of literature is, as Marianne Moore puts it, the creation of 'imaginary gardens with real toads in them.' The reader who detects that the garden is imaginary should not be led by his discovery to a wrong view of the reality of the toads. In settling questions of reality and truth in fiction, it must be remembered that, although the novel in certain of its forms [not least the realist and the naturalist novel] resembles the accumulative and classifactory sciences . . . in certain other of its forms the novel approximates the sciences of experiment. And an experiment is very like an imaginary garden which is laid out for the express purpose of supporting a real toad of fact. . . . This seems to have been James's own view of the part that is played in his novels by what he calls 'romance.' He seems to have had an analogy with experiment very clearly in mind when he tells us that romance is 'experience liberated, so to speak; experience disengaged, disembroiled, disencumbered, exempt from the conditions that usually attach to it.' Again and again he speaks of the contrivance of a novel in ways which will make it seem like illegitimate flummery to the reader who is committed only to the premises of the naturalistic novel, but which the intelligent scientist will understand perfectly" (ibid., pp. 62–63).

77. Ibid., pp. 81–82. My emphasis.

78. R. W. B. Lewis, *The American Adam: Innocence, Tragedy, and Tradition in the Nineteenth Century* (Chicago: University of Chicago Press, 1955). For a powerful critique of Lewis's representation of American literature (and literary history) in terms of the

tragic/dialectical imagination, see Russel Reising, *The Unusable Past: Theory and the Study of American Literature* (New York: Methuen, 1986), pp. 107–23.

79. The rhetorical context of these penultimate moments of Ishmael's narrative is, of course, as those, like Matthiessen, who interpret Ahab's story as tragedy always point out, Shakespearean. But Melville's Shakespeare, I submit, is not the Shakespeare envisaged by the New Critics and the Americanist cultural critics who appropriated their poetics of "irony." It is not the Shakespeare of Robert Heilman, for example, in *This Great Stage: Image and Structure in "King Lear"* (Baton Rouge: Louisiana University Press, 1948), who resolves the differences disseminated by the Shakespearean "tragic" plot in a dialectically reconciled cosmic and formal end which has been present from the beginning. Melville's Shakespeare is, rather, the Shakespeare capable of parodying his audience's expectation of a comforting or consoling resolution by flagrant resort to the *deus ex machina* to set irreconcilable things right, as, say, in *Measure for Measure* or *All's Well That Ends Well*. As Melville's insistent refusal to name the mystery of being suggests, it is the Shakespeare implicit in the following speech of Lafeu in the latter, ironically entitled "problem play": "They say miracles are past; and we have our philosophical persons, to make modern and familiar, things supernatural and causeless. Hence is it that we make trifles of terrors; ensconcing ourselves into seeming knowledge, when we should submit ourselves to an unknown fear" (*Works* 2.3.1–6).

80. Paul Brodtkorb Jr., *Ishmael's White World*, p. 75. For Brodtkorb's extended analysis of this Kierkegaardian existentialist movement, see pp. 71–80. What Brodtkorb fails to notice, in attributing a transcendent and inexplicable religious "purpose" to Ahab's "insanity" is that Ishmael does not call it *insanity* as such, but "monomania," a name that has its source in his emergent recognition of Ahab's leveling or Same-making ontology of the One.

81. Michel Foucault, *Discipline and Punish*, p. 138.

82. Although Melville overdetermines his destruction of Captain Ahab's metaphysics (and Ishmael's antimetaphysics), a case can be made for his "feminism" on the basis of the insistent phallic resonance emanating from the rhetoric of instrumentality that Ishmael uses to characterize Ahab's will to power over the being of being.

83. G. W. F. Hegel, *Phenomenology of Spirit*, trans. A. V. Miller (Oxford: Oxford University Press, 1977): "The *goal*, Absolute Knowing, or Spirit that knows itself as Spirit, has for its path recollection [*Er-innerung*] of the Spirits [*Geister*], as they are in themselves and as they accomplish the organization of their realm. Their preservation, regarded from the side of their free existence appearing in the form of contingency is History; but regarded from the side of their philosophically comprehended organization, it is the science of knowing in the sphere of appearance: the two together, comprehended History, form alike the inwarding and the Calvary of absolute Spirit, the actuality, truth, and certainty of his throne, without which he would be lifeless and alone" (p. 493).

84. Charles Olson, *The Special View of History* (Berkeley: Oyez, 1970), pp. 29ff. Olson is, in fact, quoting a fragment from Heraclitus: "Man is estranged from that with which

he is most familiar," which he juxtaposes against Keats's definition of "negative capability" (to which I will return in my text). It is this Heraclitean fragment, not incidentally, that more than any other philosophical "source," constitutes the resonant point of departure ("step back") of Heidegger's destructive hermeneutics and his interrogation of Western metaphysics as a will to power over (temporal) being.

85. William V. Spanos, "The Un-Naming of the Beasts: The Postmodernity of Sartre's *La Nausée*," *Criticism*, vol. 20, no. 3 (Summer 1978), 223–80; reprinted in Spanos, *Repetitions*.

86. Charles Olson, "Human Universe," in *Human Universe and Other Essays*, ed. Donald Allen (New York: Grove Press, 1967), p. 11. It is too easily overlooked and forgotten by humanists who always invoke the masterful canniness and courage of Odysseus as the archetypal model qualities of the humanist hero that Homer, as Olson suggests, is equally appalled by Odysseus's careless exaltation of his will to power over being at the expense of the lives of the men who sail with him: "Then I would have shouted to the Cyclops, but my companions around me / from all sides tried to restrain me with soothing speeches. . . . / But in my angry spirit I answered him back: / Cyclops, if someone among mortal man should inquire / Of you about the unseemly blindness in your eye, / Say that Odysseus, sacker of cities, blinded it, / The son of Laertes, whose home is in Ithaca." It is precisely the excessive self-glorification, the egotistically sublime pride of this "man small and worthless and feeble" (as Homer has Polyphemus put it, to focus the paradox), who achieves mastery and domination over this giant "monstrosity" of being, that alienates Polyphemus's father Poseidon, the god of the sea of being, indeed, transforms him into an unrelenting enemy of Odysseus: "and then [Polyphemus] prayed to Lord Poseidon / . . . 'Hear me, earthholding Poseidon of the dark-blue locks, / If truly I am yours, and you declare you are my father, / Grant that the city-sacker Odysseus not go homeward, / The son of Laertes whose home is in Ithaca. / But if it is his fate to see his dear ones and arrive / At his well-established home and his fatherland, / May he come late and ill, having lost all his companions, / On someone else's ship and find troubles at home.' / So he said in prayer. The God with the dark-blue Locks heard him" (Homer, *The Odyssey*, trans. and ed. Albert Cook, Norton Critical Edition [New York: W. W. Norton, 1974], Bk. 9, ll. 492–505, 526–32). The continuous parallel between Ahab—his silencing of Starbuck to vent his anger against Moby Dick, his pitting of his puny manliness against a giant monstrosity at the expense of his crew's lives, and the retaliation of the "defeated" "object" of his wily wrath—should not be overlooked.

87. The teleological—and extraordinarily rigid—control Lewis holds over his materials is not simply a matter of history, but also of the literary production of the writer he is interpreting and of the particular text he is addressing. Thus, for example, Melville's career reenacts Lewis's dialectical narrative of American literary history, *Typee* representing the fictional manifestation of "the party of Hope," *Moby-Dick* (vestigially but crucially), of the "party of Memory," and *Billy Budd*, of the mediating "party of Irony."

Thus also, despite his high praise, he interprets *Moby-Dick*, not as representing the *essence* of Melville's imagination but as a novel on the way towards its perfect expression in the utterly balanced and transfiguring hopeful/tragic tensions of *Billy Budd*. As Lewis astonishingly puts it: "*Moby-Dick* is an elaborate pattern of countercommentaries, the supreme instance of the dialectical novel—a novel of tension without resolution. Ishmael's meditation, which transfigures the anger and sees beyond the sickness and the evil, is only one major voice in the dramatic conversation; and not until *Billy Budd* does this voice become transcendent and victorious. In *Moby-Dick*, Melville adopted a unique and off-beat traditionalism—a steadily ambiguous re-rendering of the old forms and fables once unequivocally rejected by the hopeful—in order to recount the total blasting of the vision of innocence. He went beyond a spurious artistic originality to give narrative birth to the conflict with evil: that evil against which a spurious and illusory innocence must shatter itself. In doing so, he not only achieved a sounder originality but *moved a great step toward perceiving a more durable innocence*. In *Pierre*, the following year, Melville faltered and went back once more over the old dreary ground of disillusion; but in *Billy Budd, he was to come home*" (p. 146, my emphasis). This geometric dialectical/teleological history exemplifies the reductive "preformationism" that Derrida attributes to all structuralisms with a vengeance. See "Force and Significa-tion," *Writing and Difference*, p. 23ff.

88. R. W. B. Lewis, *The American Adam*, p. 193.

89. See Louis Althusser, "'On the Young Marx': Theoretical Questions," in *For Marx* (London: New Left Books, 1977), pp. 55–70. Reading in the "future anterior" mode involves a retrospective orientation that privileges "tendency" over what would contra-dict it, which is to say, begins the futural process from a preconceived end. The Hegelianism that Althusser attributes to a certain "Marxist" reading of Marx, applies as well to R. W. B. Lewis's (as well as other Old Americanists') "dialectical" reading of Melville's literary career and of American literary history: "But this [tendentious reading] is the way Marx's early texts are only too often treated, as if they belonged to a reserved domain, sheltered from the *'basic question'* solely because they *must* develop into Marxism. . . . As if their meaning had been held in abeyance until the end, as if it was necessary to wait on the final synthesis before their elements could be at last resorbed *into a whole*, as if, before this final synthesis, the question of the whole could not be raised, just because all totalities earlier than the final synthesis have been destroyed. But this brings us to the height of the paradox from behind which this analytico-teleological method breaks out: this method which is constantly *judging* cannot *make the slightest judgement of any totality unlike itself*. . . . And to anyone whose response to the ultimate logic that I have drawn from this method is to say '*that is precisely what makes it dialectical'*—my answer is '*Dialectical, yes, but Hegelian!*" (p. 60).

90. That Ishmael is playing on "The Rime of the Ancient Mariner," especially the mariner's *repeated* efforts to "understand" the always already deferring meaning of experience, is clearly suggested in the chapter on the whiteness of the whale (which

includes Melville's resonant footnote on his memory of his first sighting of an albatross "during a prolonged gale, in waters hard upon the Antarctic seas"), where he alludes to Coleridge's poem (p. 190).

91. Jeremiah 31:15. In Matthew 2:16–18, Jeremiah's reference to "Rachel weeping for her children . . . because they were no more" becomes a *figura* of Herod's massacre of the male children of Israel.

92. Cotton Mather, *Magnalia Christi Americana*, Bk. I, p. 133. The Occidental myth of the saving remnant is derived, of course, from the Old Testament, but is mediated by Rome, especially by Virgil's *Aeneid*. This connection, as I have indicated earlier, is significant, since what is ultimately at stake in the Western, especially American, development of this myth about Adamic Man, naming, and the preservation of the word is empire.

93. Explicit recent appeals to the myth of the saving remnant can be found, for example, in Walter Jackson Bate, "The Crisis in English Studies," *Harvard Magazine*, vol. 85 (September–October 1987); William Bennett, "To Reclaim a Legacy: Report on Humanities in Education," *Chronicle of Higher Education* (November 28, 1984); and Allan Bloom, *The Closing of the American Mind: How Higher Education Has Failed Democracy and Impoverished the Souls of Today's Students* (New York: Simon and Schuster, 1987). For an amplified analysis and critique of the uses to which recent politically conservative intellectuals have put this perennial American myth, see William V. Spanos, "The Uses and Abuses of Certainty: Introduction," introduction to the special issue of *boundary 2*, "On Humanism and the University," vols. 12/13 (Spring/Fall 1984), pp. 1–17.

94. In that chapter, Ishmael writes, "The land seemed scorching to his feet. Wonderfullest things are ever the unmentionable; deep memories yield no epitaphs; this six-inch chapter is the stoneless grave of Bulkington. . . .

"Know ye, now Bulkington? Glimpses do ye seem to see of that morally intolerable truth; that all deep, earnest thinking is but the intrepid effort of the soul to keep the open independence of her sea; while the wildest winds of heaven and earth conspire to cast her on the treacherous, slavish shore?

"But as in landlessness alone resides the highest truth, shoreless, indefinite as God— so, better is it to perish in that howling infinite, than ingloriously dashed upon the lee, even if that were safety! For worm-like, then, oh! who would craven crawl to land! Terrors of the terrible! is all this agony in vain? Take heart, O Bulkington! Bear thee grimly, demigod! Up from the spray of thy ocean-perishing—straight up, leaps thy apotheosis!" (p. 107). In distinguishing chronicle from well-wrought urn, I am of course, reversing Cleanth Brook's privileging of the Metaphysical/Modernist autotelic (spatialized) poem over opened-ended, temporal/historical forms in his famous reading of Donne's "Canonization," in "The Language of Paradox," in *The Well Wrought Urn: Studies in the Structure of Poetry* (New York: Harcourt, Brace, 1947), pp. 3–21.

95. Richard Chase, *Herman Melville: A Critical Study* (New York: Macmillan 1949), p. 59.

96. Michel Foucault, "Nietzsche, Genealogy, History," p. 161.

97. That Melville consciously juxtaposes the "devious-cruising Rachel" against Cap-

tain Ahab's *unerring* course in order to thematize Ishmael's discovery of the belongingness together of erring and caring is suggested in "The Pequod Meets the Rachel,"
shortly before the *Pequod*'s encounter with Moby Dick. "Soon the two ships diverged
their wakes; and long as the strange vessel was in view, she was seen to yaw hither and
thither at every dark spot, however small, on the sea. This way and that her yards were
swung round; starboard and larboard, she continued to tack; now she beat against a
head sea; and again it pushed her before it; while all the while, her masts and yards
were thickly clustered with men, as three tall cherry trees, when the boys are cherrying
among the bows.

"But by her still halting course and winding, woful way, you plainly saw that this ship
that so wept with spray, still remained without comfort. She was Rachel, weeping for
her children, because they were not" (p. 533).

98. Herman Melville, *Pierre*, p. 89. This phrase, which suggests Melville's conscious
awareness of the etymological resonance I am foregrounding, occurs in a narrative
context that is precisely analogous to Ishmael's; namely, his de-centering following the
receipt of Isabel's letter, which estranges him from his mother and her secure but
repressive hegemonic world: "She was a noble creature, but formed chiefly for the
gilded prosperities of life, and hitherto mostly used to its unruffled securities; bred and
expanded, in all developments, under the sole influence of hereditary forms and world-
usages. Not his refined, courtly, loving, equable mother, Pierre felt, could unreservedly,
and like a heaven's heroine, meet the shock of his extraordinary emergence, and
applaud, to his heart's echo, a sublime resolve, whose execution should call down the
astonishment and the jeers of the world." The difference is that, in *Moby-Dick*, Melville
points to the positive revolutionary possibilities of Ishmael's decentering, whereas, in
Pierre, Pierre's liberation from the "hereditary forms and world-usages" that have
reduced him to "a noble boy, and docile" (pp. 18–19) precipitates a ferociously reactive
ressentiment in the hegemonic world, one that will destroy him in the end.

99. Letter from John Keats to George and Thomas Keats, December 21, 1817, in *The
Letters of John Keats*, vol. 1, ed. Hyder Edward Rollins (Cambridge, Mass.: Harvard
University Press, 1958), p. 193–94.

100. Lionel Trilling, "The Meaning of a Literary Idea," *The Liberal Imagination*, pp. 280–
81.

101. In thus questioning Trilling's version of negative capability, I am also expressing
my reservations about Daniel O'Hara's identification of Trilling's criticism with the
virtue of "magnanimity." See O'Hara, *Lionel Trilling: The Work of Liberation* (Madison:
University of Wisconsin Press, 1988), pp. 109ff.

102. Samuel Taylor Coleridge, *The Complete Works*, vol. 3, *Biographia Literaria*, ed.
W. T. G. Shedd (New York: Harper, 1860), pp. 363–64. As Coleridge notes (*Biographia*,
ch. 10, p. 272), his definition of the imagination as an "esemplastic power" is a coinage
derived ultimately "from the Greek words εἰς ·εὖ πλάττειν, to shape into one" and
immediately from Friedrich Schelling's *In-Eins-Bildung*, which, as noted by W. K.
Wimsatt and Cleanth Brooks in *Literary Criticism: A Short History* (New York: Vintage

Books, 1967), he mistakenly believes "is authorized by the German word *Einbildungs-kraft*" (p. 390). This is a revealing appropriation that goes far to confirm my point. For the etymology makes explicit the willful spatializing function of the Coleridgean imagination. It is, for Coleridge, as for his Modernist heirs, Trilling as well as the New Critics, a faculty, the "power" of which is positively capable of coercing the fragmentary and discontinuous into a "unified" or "whole" and flattened-out "picture."

103 For an amplification of this distinction, see the chapter entitled "The Indifference of *Differance*: Retrieving Heidegger's Destruction," in William V. Spanos, *Heidegger and Criticism*, pp. 81–131.

104. Michel Foucault, "Nietzsche, History, Genealogy," *Language, Counter-Memory, Practice*, p. 143.

105. Wallace Stevens, "An Ordinary Evening in New Haven," *The Collected Poems* (New York: Alfred A. Knopf, 1964), p. 469.

106. Charles Olson, "Human Universe," *Human Universe and Other Essays*, ed. Donald Allen (New York: Grove Press, 1967), pp. 3–16.

107. Charles Olson, "Equal, That Is, to the Real Itself," *Human Universe*, p. 117.

108. Thomas Pynchon, *Gravity's Rainbow* (New York: Viking Press, 1973), pp. 554–56.

109. T. S. Eliot, "*Ulysses*, Order, and Myth," *Selected Prose of T. S. Eliot*, ed. Frank Kermode (New York: Harcourt Brace Jovanovich, 1975), p. 178.

110. The degree to which *Pierre* is a "social text"—one that anticipates contemporary analyses of the discourse of hegemony—has not been adequately recognized in Melville criticism. The truth of "Revolutionary" American society, represented by Mrs. Glendinning and Saddle Meadows, makes it impossible to read Pierre's "emergency" (his "refusal of spontaneous consent" to its tenets, to use Gramsci's language) as anything other than madness, since to acknowledge Pierre's claims would be to acknowledge the interested fictiveness of its truth: to tear its fabric apart, as it were. This is most clearly suggested by Melville's conscious attempt to recall Mrs. Glendinning's early repeated references to Pierre as "sweet and docile" (pp. 16–20) at the precise moment when Pierre's estrangement from her person estranges his understanding of her truth and renders him another exiled Ishmael (pp. 88–91). The point is summarized by Pierre with great force later in a conversation with Isabel prior to their departure: "Isabel, though thou art all fearfulness to injure any living thing, least of all, thy brother; still thy true heart foreknoweth not the myriad alliances and criss-crossings among mankind, the infinite entanglements of all social things, which forbid that one thread should fly the general fabric, on some new line of duty, without tearing itself and tearing others" (p. 191).

111. Martin Heidegger, *Being and Time*, pp. 104–7.

112. W. B. Macomber, *The Anatomy of Disillusion: Martin Heidegger's Notion of Truth* (Evanston, Ill.: Northwestern University Press, 1967), pp. 154–64. See also pp. 43 ff.

113. Jacques Derrida, "The Ends of Man," in *Margins of Philosophy*, trans. Alan Bass (Chicago: University of Chicago Press, 1982), p. 126.

114. Martin Heidegger, *Being and Time*, p. 358. See also pp. 112, 457. For an amplified version of my interrogation of Derrida's critique of Heidegger's "phenomenological" hermeneutics, see the chapter entitled "The Indifference of 'Differance': Retrieving Heidegger's Destruction," in Spanos, *Heidegger and Criticism*, pp. 103–17.

115. It is important, at this critical juncture, to recall that the phrase "the spatialization of time," applied since Joseph Frank's seminal essays "Spatial Form in Modern Literature" (*Sewanee Review* 53 [Spring, Summer, Autumn, 1945], pp. 221–40, 433–45, 643–65; reprinted in Joseph Frank, *The Widening Gyre; Crisis and Mastery in Modern Literature* [New Brunswick, N.J.: Rutgers University Press, 1963], pp. 3–62) to characterize Modernist texts, was first used by Henri Bergson to define the operation of the empirical/scientific intelligence. In solidifying "our conscious states [duration]," this "realistic" intelligence, according to Bergson, "enables us to objectify them, to throw them out into the current of social life" (Bergson, *Time and Free Will: An Essay on the Immediate Data of Consciousness*, trans. F. L. Pogson [New York: Macmillan, 1910], pp. 230–31). In thus representing Modernist (as opposed to "Realist") texts such as Flaubert's *Madame Bovary*, Proust's *A la recherche de temps perdu*, Eliot's "The Waste Land," Djuna Barnes's *Nightwood*, and James Joyce's *Ulysses* as texts that "spatialize time," Frank was apparently unaware of Bergson's similar, yet potentially undermining, use of the phrase to refer to a mode of representation that Frank assumes to be antithetical to the Modernist. Nor does he indicate any awareness in "Spatial Form: An Answer to Critics," *Critical Inquiry*, vol. 4, no. 2 (Winter 1977), pp. 231–52, which rehearses the argument of the early essays and underscores its validity by invoking the intervening emergence of structuralist criticism. Indeed, despite the embarrassment that the bringing into play of Bergson's usage would cause, the term has achieved something like archival status as the continued use of the phrase by contemporary critics of fiction to define Modernist and even postmodernist novels testifies. See, for example, the essays honoring Frank in Jeffrey R. Smitten and Ann Daghistany, ed., *Spatial Form in Narrative* (Ithaca, N.Y.: Cornell University Press, 1981). Frank's and his filial heirs' implicit, if inadvertent, equation of objectivity and subjectivity, science and idealism, naturalism and symbolism, thus goes far to corroborate my argument that, despite surface variations, the romance, which the Old Americanists posited against the realistic novel in their effort to make an American canon, constitutes the substitution of one metaphysical center for another and thus is no less ideological than the fiction it would displace.

116. Claude Lévi-Strauss, *The Savage Mind* (Chicago: University of Chicago Press, 1966), pp. 23–24. The remarkable parallel between Lévi-Strauss's structuralist rhetoric *vis à vis* the relationship between the doll and a "living creature of real dimensions" and Ahab's metaphysics—his "miniaturization" of "all that most maddens and torments" man to Moby Dick—should not be overlooked.

117. See Martin Heidegger, *Discourse on Thinking*, trans. John M. Anderson and E. Hans Freund (New York: Harper & Row, 1966): "For all of us, the arrangements, devices, and machinery of technology are to a greater or lesser extent indispensable. It would be foolish to attack technology blindly. . . . But suddenly and unaware we find

ourselves so firmly shackled to these technical devices that we fall into bondage to them. . . . We can affirm the unavoidable use of technical devices, and also deny them the right to dominate us, and so to warp, confuse, and lay waste our nature. . . . We let technical devices enter our daily life, and at the same time leave them outside, that is, let them alone, as things which are nothing absolute but remain dependent upon something higher. I would call this comportment toward technology which expresses 'yes' and at the same time 'no,' by an old word, *releasement toward things* [*Die Gelassenheit zu den Dingen*]" (p. 54).

118. See especially, Jacques Derrida, "Structure, Sign, and Play," in *Writing and Difference*: "One cannot determine the center and exhaust totalization because the sign which replaces the center, which supplements it, taking the center's place in its absence—this sign, occurs as a surplus, as a *supplément*" (p. 286).

119. Herman Melville, *Billy Budd, Sailor (An Inside Narrative)*, ed. Harrison Hayford and Merton M. Sealts Jr. (Chicago: University of Chicago Press, 1962), pp. 130–31.

120. Martin Heidegger, *Being and Time*, p. 438.

121. Martin Heidegger, "The Question Concerning Technology," in *The Question Concerning Technology and Other Essays*, trans. William Lovitt (New York: Harper & Row 1977), pp. 55–61 ff.

122. R. P. Blackmur, "The Craft of Herman Melville," p. 125.

123. For Blackmur's critique of Babbitt's "Puritanism," see "Humanism and Symbolic Imagination: Notes on Re-reading Irving Babbitt," in *The Lion and the Honeycomb*, pp. 145–61. For an extended discussion of the continuing influence of the Puritan economy and its binary logic on Modernist Anglo-American fiction and literary criticism, see the chapter entitled "Percy Lubbock and the Craft of Supervision," in William V. Spanos, *Repetitions*, pp. 149–88. My reference to Henry James can be found in his preface to *The Tragic Muse* (1922). My critique of Blackmur's critique of Babbitt will be found in the chapter entitled "The Apollonian Investment of Modern Humanist Educational Theory: The Examples of Matthew Arnold, Irving Babbitt, and I. A. Richards," in *The End of Education: Toward Posthumanism* (Minneapolis: University of Minnesota Press, 1993), 87–93.

124. Charles Olson. "Letter 5," *The Maximus Poems*, p. 26.

125. Frank Lentricchia, *Ariel and the Police: Michel Foucault, William James, Wallace Stevens* (Madison: University of Wisconsin Press, 1988), pp. 20–21. The passage from Michael Herr is quoted from *Dispatches* (New York: Avon Books, 1978), p. 114.

126. Michael Herr, *Dispatches*, p. 74. It is not simply the problem of genre that allows our identification of Herr's *Dispatches* with *Moby-Dick*. Melville's novel is a subtextual "presence" in his book as a whole. Thus, for example, he describes (not without a self-irony that finally implicates his own American romance "irregularity" with the "regulars" who were devastating Vietnam in the name of America's Adamic mission) the fluid motley "community" of "irregulars" he associated with in Saigon and Danaang— "Lurps, seals, recondos, Green-Beret bushmasters, redundant mutilators, heavy rapists"—as "classic American types; point men, *isolatos* and outriders. . . ." (Herr's italics);

and his anxiety in the face of the dreaded Vietnamese jungles precisely in the Zero Zone terms Ishmael is compelled to use about the whiteness of the whale: "Cover the war, what a gig to frame for yourself, going out after one kind of information and getting another, totally other, to lock your eyes open, drop your blood temperature down under the 0, dry your mouth so a full swig of water disappeared in there before you could swallow, turn your breath fouler than corpse gas. There were times when you had to stop and watch the spin. Forget the Cong, the *trees* would kill you, the elephant grass grow up homicidal, the ground you were walking over possessed *malignant intelligence*, your whole environment was a bath" (p. 69; my emphasis, except for "trees").

127. Donald Pease, *Visionary Compacts*, pp. 272–73.

128. For my intervention in the debate over the politics of Heidegger's philosophical thought, see Spanos, "Heidegger, Nazism, and the 'Repressive Hypothesis': The American Appropriation of the Question," in *Heidegger and Criticism: Retrieving the Cultural Politics of Destruction* (Minneapolis: University of Minnesota Press, 1993), pp. 181–251.

129. See the chapter entitled "Heidegger, Foucault, and the Politics of the Commanding Gaze," in Spanos, *Heidegger and Criticism*, pp. 32–80.

130. Raymond Williams, *Marxism and Literature* (Oxford: Oxford University Press, 1977), pp. 109–10. The term as used in the critical practice of contemporary cultural criticism derives, of course, from Antonio Gramsci. See especially, *Selections from the Prison Notebooks*, ed. and trans. Quintin Hoare and Geoffrey Nowell Smith (New York: International Publishers, 1971), pp. 12, 56. Another version of this form of truth/power relations can be found in Michel Foucault's genealogy of "the repressive hypothesis," in which the post-Enlightenment understanding of truth as external to and the adversary of power is shown to be complicitous with, indeed, the agency of power. See *The History of Sexuality,* vol. 1, *An Introduction,* trans. Robert Hurley (New York: Pantheon Books, 1978), pp. 17ff. See also Edward Said's discussion of "affiliation" in "Reflections on American Literary 'Left' Criticism," *boundary* 2, vol. 13 (Fall 1979), pp. 26–27; rpr. in *The World, the Text and the Critic* (Cambridge, Mass.: Harvard University Press, 1983).

131. Max Weber, *The Protestant Ethic and the Spirit of Capitalism*, p. 117. See also pp. 108–9.

132. In *Empire for Liberty,* Wai-chee Dimock directly invokes the cetology chapters—specifically Melville's ironic declaration that "would you, you could not compress" the "mighty bulk" of the whale; that "he should only be treated of in imperial folio" (p. 455), to support her New Americanist representation of Ahab as the victim doomed by Melville's "American" ideology and *Moby-Dick* as a manifestation of the imperial imperatives of the American antebellum discourse on liberty: "Spatialized time is also what *Moby-Dick* invokes to make Ahab's fate legible. Reading that fate, Melville's prophets turn Ahab too into a doomed figure, spatializing his temporal endeavor into a timeless script. Melville's 'imperial folio,' then, logically shares the same temporal economy with its imperial environment, for a structure of dominion is inseparable

from a structure of time. . . . Fate in *Moby-Dick* and Manifest Destiny in antebellum America are kindred constructs. Ahab and America, bearers both of a timeless destiny, mirror each other in familial likeness" (p. 134). Dimock's representation of Melville's text as an "imperial folio" elides the narrative as a whole with Ishmael's comprehensive Book on cetology (see also pp. 109, 113). I can find no reference in the text in which Melville identifies *Moby-Dick* as such an "imperial folio." My point is that Dimock's own spatializing problematic precludes a kind of close reading that attends to the radical "digressions" of Melville's text—Father Mapple's sermon or, more immediately to the point, the cetology chapters—which quite pointedly disrupt by travestying the very spatializing gaze Dimock attributes to Melville. Despite her acute awareness of the operations of mastery associated with the spatializing eye, her reading of *Moby-Dick* is, as this telling slide shows, characterized precisely by such oversight. It blinds her to the possibility that Melville is marking the radical difference between Ishmael's narrative and the Book on cetology: that the latter might constitute a parodic geneal-ogy of the Linnaean system of classification then emerging in a rapidly industrializing America to claim dominion over and to exploit the differential or unnameable forces of nature, precisely the imperial project at the site of natural science. This elision is also manifest in Dimock's deliberate exclusion of Ishmael from the text: "My deepest disagreement with [virtually all "political" readings of *Moby-Dick*] has to do with my sense of Ahab not as villain but as victim. A new and important reading . . . from this perspective is Donald Pease, 'Moby-Dick and the Cold War,' in *The American Renaissance Reconsidered: Selected Papers from the English Institute, 1982–1983*. Pease, however, sees Ahab only as Ishmael's victim. I see Melville himself as being implicated in the process of victimization" (p. 233 n. 7).

133. Michel Foucault, *Discipline and Punish*, p. 148. That Foucault, like Melville, has Linnaeus particularly in mind is suggested earlier in his text, where the eighteenth-century project to codify crimes is shown to find its primary model in Linnaeus's taxonomic system: "The code-individualization link was sought in the scientific mod-els of the period. Natural history no doubt offered the most adequate schema: the taxonomy of species according to an uninterrupted gradation. One sought to con-stitute a Linnaeus of crimes and punishments, so that each particular offence and each punishable individual might come, without the slightest risk of any arbitrary action, within the provisions of a general law. 'A table must be drawn up of all the genera of crimes to be observed in different countries. According to the enumeration of crimes, a division into species must be carried out. The best rule of this division is, it seems to me, to separate the crimes according to their objects. This division must be such that each species is quite distinct from another, and that each particular crime, considered in all its relations may be placed between that which must precede it and that which must follow it, in the strictest gradation; lastly, this table must be such that it may be compared with another table that will be drawn up for penalties, in such a way that they may correspond exactly to one another' ([P. L. de] Lacretelle, 351–352)." See also Foucault, *The Birth of the Clinic*, trans. A. M. Sheridan Smith (New York: Vintage Books,

1975): "The clinic was probably the first attempt to order a science on the exercise and decisions of the gaze. From the second half of the seventeenth century, natural history had set out to analyse and classify natural beings according to their visible characters. All this 'treasure' of knowledge that antiquity and the Middle Ages had accumulated—and which concerned the virtues of plants, the powers of animals, secret correspondences and sympathies—since Ray, all this had become marginal knowledge for naturalists. What remained to be discovered, however, were 'structures,' that is, forms, spatial arrangements, the number and size of elements: natural history took upon itself the task of mapping them, of transcribing them in discourse, of preserving, confronting, and combining them, in order to make it possible, on the one hand, to determine the vicinities and kinships of living beings (and therefore the unity of creation) and, on the other, to recognize rapidly any individual (and therefore his unique place in creation).

"The clinic demands as much of the gaze as natural history. As much, and to a certain extent, the same thing: to see, to isolate features, to recognize those that are identical and those that are different, to regroups them, to classify them by species or families. The naturalist model, to which medicine had partly been subjected in the eighteenth century, remained active. The old dream of Boissier de Sauvages of being the Linnaeus of diseases was not entirely forgotten in the nineteenth century" (p. 89). For a productive application of Foucault's analysis of the disciplinary imperatives of Linnaeus's system of classification to the imperial project, see Mary Louise Pratt, *Imperial Eyes: Travel Writing and Transculturation* (London: Routledge, 1992). In demonstrating the absolute complicity of Linnaeus's natural science with the colonization—the domestication and exploitation—of the indigenous peoples of South Africa and America and their earth, Pratt's book constitutes a significant contribution to the contemporary critique of the discourse and practice of imperialism. Like virtually all historicist critiques of imperialism, however, Pratt's critique is limited by her failure to thematize the ontological "base" on which not only the relay between Linnaeus's system of classification and colonization rests, but also the relay of metaphorics—the eye/other senses, light/dark, maturity/immaturity, cultivation/barbarism, and so on—that this base enables and naturalizes, the hegemonized metaphorics, that is, that circulate as truth in the discourses of the travel writing Pratt analyzes. A similar criticism can be made against David Spurr, *The Rhetoric of Empire: Colonial Discourse in Journalism, Travel Writing, and Imperial Administration* (Durham, N.C.: Duke University Press, 1993). For a recent theorization of the imperial project that goes some way to overcome this limitation by thinking what I call the ontological imperialism of metaphysics, see Robert Young, *White Mythologies: Writing History and the West* (London: Routledge, 1990).
134. Michel Foucault, *The Order of Things: An Archaeology of the Human Sciences* (New York: Vintage Books, 1973), p. xv.
135. My rhetoric derives from Heidegger's *Being and Time*, but it is, in fact, the American poet and Melville scholar Charles Olson who provides the appropriate gloss on the paradoxical estrangement that, according to Ishmael's destructive cetology,

accompanies the logical economy of classification. We will recall that Melville, according to Olson, anticipated the anti-Euclidean geometries of Bolyai and Lobatschewsky and the new mathematics of Riemann, who distinguished between "[t]wo kinds of manifold, the discrete (which would be the old system, and it includes discourse, language as it had been since Socrates) and, what [Melville] took to be more true, the continuous" ("Equal, That Is, To the Real Itself," p. 117). In "Human Universe," Olson explains, "We stay unaware how two means of discourse the Greeks appear to have invented hugely intermit our participation in our experience, and so prevent discovery. They are what followed from Socrates' readiness to generalize, his willingness (from his own bias) to make a 'universe' out of discourse instead of letting it rest in its most serviceable place. (It is not sufficiently observed that logos, and the reason necessary to it, are only a stage which a man must master and not what they are taken to be, final discipline. Beyond them is direct perception and the contraries which dispose of argument. The harmony of the universe, and I include man, is not logical, or better, is post-logical, as is the order of any created thing.) With Aristotle the two great means appear: logic and classification. And it is they that have so fastened themselves on habits of thought that action is interfered with, absolutely interfered with, I would say" (p. 4).

136. In response to the possible objection that Pierre falls victim to the disclosure of the abyss of nothing, I would suggest that it is not the impasse that destroys him, it is the discourse and practice of hegemony: the "truth" of Saddle Meadows, that is, "Revolutionary America."

137. The "landsman" natural scientist is, in this respect, much like the cartographer Martin Behaim, the figure of the archival poet, in Charles Olson's "On first Looking out through Juan de la Cosa's eyes," *The Maximus Poems*, pp. 77–81. Unlike Juan de la Cosa, Columbus's cartographer, who *was there* and thus whose map is virtually a *periplus* that first disclosed the existence of the "new world," Behaim, the German map maker who produced the first map of the world that represents it as a globe, was *not there*. Basing his representation on hearsay (i.e., received authority), he thus presents a blank space between the Old World and Japan (Cipangu): "Behaim—nothing / insular Azores to / Cipangu. . . ." In contrast to the landsman, Behaim, the metaphysical cartographer who relies on the authority of the archive, the seaman La Cosa, for Olson, represents the postmodern projective poet (and thinker), who risks his prejudices in the face of the things themselves: "before La Cosa, nobody / could have / a mappemunde." See William V. Spanos, "The De-struction of Form in Postmodern American Poetry," pp. 385–90. Admittedly Olson here, as often in Melville, is representing the "New World" from the colonial perspective that reduces its native inhabitants to nonexistence. Seen in the larger context of his poetry and criticism at large, not least "The Kingfisher" and *The Mayan Letters*, which recall the genocidal European assault on the native civilization of the Mayans, however, this apparent blindness to the native other is radically modified. Indeed, as in Melville, the filling in of the blank space constitutes

a postcolonial discursive gesture that finally operates to retrieve the other world annulled by the Occidental discourse of the "New World."

138. Charles Olson, *The Special View of History*, p. 21. See also "Letter 23," *The Maximus Poems*:

The odish-man sd: "Poesy
steals away men's judgment
by her *muthoi* (taking this crack
at Homer's sweet-versing

"and a blind heart
is most men's portions." Plato
allowed this divisive
thought to stand, agreeing

that *muthos*
is false. *Logos*
isn't—was facts. Thus
Thucydides.

I would be a historian as Herodotus was, looking
for oneself for the evidence of what is said . . . (p. 104)

139. Olson, *The Special View of History*, p. 29. The first and last emphases are mine. This is also what I take Olson to mean when, in *Call Me Ishmael: A Study of Melville* (San Francisco: City Light Books, 1947), he writes: "Logic and classification had led civilization towards man, away from space [presumably, the indissoluble regions of being]. Melville went to space to probe and find man. Early man did the same: poetry, language and care of myth, as Fenellosa says, grew up together. . . . He [Melville] has a pull to the origins of things, the first day, the first man, the unknown sea. . . . He sought prime" (pp. 14–15).

140. This is Richard Brodhead's essential thesis in *Hawthorne, Melville, and the Novel*. Taking his lead from Ishmael's account of the whale's eyes, Brodhead concludes that Melville's purpose in *Moby-Dick* is to posit undecidability concerning the "two visions of reality"—the mysterious (symbolic) and the domestic (realistic) that the novel proffers: "Melville's fiction bounces us back and forth between two visions of reality that are radically incommensurate and arranged in such a way that from within one of them we simply cannot see the other. . . . Ishmael tells us that since the whale's eyes are on different sides of its head he 'must see one distinct picture on this side, and another distinct picture on that side.' The alternation of portentous romance and comic realism in his narration makes us see in a similar way. It makes us enter into both of its visions and see each, by turns, as yielding a true image of reality, but we cannot, if we would, put the two of them together" (p. 145). What Brodhead leave unsaid, however, is that

Melville is positing undecidability not for its own sake but (1) to call into question the Ahabian ontological monomania (and the institutions of knowledge production which have legitimized it), i.e., to focus the destructive will to power over being that informs the Adamic impulse to name; and (2) to give undecidability a positive (negatively capable) value. This failure to perceive the otherwise disparate intent of Melville's destructive projective project is also evident in Paul Brodtkorb's reading of *Moby-Dick*.

141. By "bearing witness," I mean, with Søren Kierkegaard and Charles Olson, who insist on the distinction, an interested "looking for myself for the evidence of what is said" ("Letter 23," *The Maximus Poems*, p. 104), rather than relying on the archival authority that lies behind the humanistic ideal of objectivity: or, better, a seeing care-fully from *interesse* (in the midst), rather than from the care-less panoptic distance of a center elsewhere. To bear witness means to be morally responsible to the occasion of bearing witness.

142. Charles Olson, *Call Me Ishmael*, p. 23. Elsewhere, Olson writes: "Whaling was production, as old as the colonies and, in capital and function, forerunner to a later America, with more relation to Socony than to clippers and the China Trade" (p. 18). Olson admits that he's "putting a stress Melville didn't on whaling as *industry*. Cutting out the Glory: as book *Moby-Dick* turns out to be its glory. We still are soft about industries, wonder-eyed. What's important [in Melville's text, I take it] is the energy they are a clue to, the drive in the people" (pp. 20–21). Nevertheless—and despite his focus on the "tragedy" of Ahab—Olson makes it explicit that it is this capitalist spirit that constitutes the political unconscious of Melville's commentary on the American whaling industry. "It's what lies under," as Olson puts it in the title of the chapter in which he writes about the economics of whaling.

143. If the masculine virtues of the idealized American frontiersman, as for example in James Fenimore Cooper's Natty Bumppo stories or in Robert Montgomery Bird's *Nick of the Woods*, are recalled in the context of the phallic resonances emanating from Melville's identification of the *Pequod* as murderous instrument/weapon and the ambiguous nature of Ishmael's and Queequeg's friendship, it would not, as I have been suggesting throughout, be an imposition to add gender relations to this list of ideological sites of struggle, despite the necessary restriction of the *mise-en-scène* to a male space.

144. Max Weber, *The Protestant Ethic and the Spirit of Capitalism*, p. 162. The page numbers cited in these two paragraphs refer to this book, unless otherwise noted.

145. If one attends to the insistent overdetermination of the Puritan origins of Israel Potter, it will be seen that Melville's retrieval of this discarded and forgotten American life constitutes a synecdochical history of America that reverses the narrative promised by the figural hermeneutics of the Puritans and their secularized progeny (represented in the novel—and in Weber's text—by Benjamin Franklin). The elected Israel which, according to the providential logic of Puritan history, was to be brought home out of exile to the rich spiritual and material promised land, is buried in the oblivion of a "Potter's Field" (*Israel Potter: His Fifty Years of Exile*, ed. Harrison Hayford, Hershel Parker,

and G. Thomas Tanselle [Evanston, Ill.: Northwestern University Press and Newberry Library, 1982], p. 168).

146. According to Weber, "[T]he Quaker ethic also holds that man's life in his calling is an exercise in ascetic virtue, a proof of his state of grace through his conscientiousness, which is expressed in the care and method with which he pursues his calling. What God demands is not labour, but rational labour in a calling" (*The Protestant Ethic and the Spirit of Capitalism*, pp. 161–62).

147. Michel Foucault, *Discipline and Punish*, p. 144–45. One thinks here, especially where Foucault invokes the factory supervisor, of Melville's reiteration of the dreaded figure of the master-at-arms in *White-Jacket* and more centrally in *Billy Budd*: the "sort of high constable and schoolmaster, wearing citizen's clothes, and known by his official ratan. He it is whom all sailors hate. His is the universal duty of a universal informer and hunter-up of delinquents. On the birth-deck he reigns supreme; spying out all grease-spots made by the various cooks of the seamen's messes, and driving the laggards up the hatches, when all hands are called. It is indispensable that he should be a very Vidocq in viligance" (*White-Jacket; or, The World in a Man-of-War*, Harrison Hayford, Hershel Parker, and G. Thomas Tanselle [Evanston, Ill.: Northwestern University Press and the Newberry Library, 1970], p. 26). Melville's allusion to Vidocq is to the master criminal turned master policeman in Balzac's *Lost Illusions* (1837–43) and *Splendor and Misery of Courtesans* (1838–47), and it is not incidental. Vidocq is the exemplary instance of the Janus-like figure who emerges with the emergence of the realistic novel, which, according to Foucault, in stripping away the "fourth wall" of the hitherto unobserved private lives of marginalized social constituencies, "forms part of the great [panoptic] system of constraint by which the [post-Enlightenment, bourgeois/capitalist] West compelled the everyday to bring itself into discourse" [in order to be known]" ("The Life of Infamous Men," in *Power, Truth, Strategy*, ed. Meaghan Morris and Paul Patton, trans. Paul Foss and Meaghan Morris [Sydney, Australia: Feral Publications, 1979], p. 91). See also Mark Seltzer, "*The Princess Casamassima*: Realism and the Fantasy of Surveillance," in *American Realism: New Essays*, ed. Eric Sundquist (Baltimore: Johns Hopkins University Press, 1982), pp. 110–11; reprinted in Seltzer, *Henry James: The Art of Power* (Ithaca, N.Y.: Cornell University Press, 1984).

148. We may infer Melville's awareness of the disciplinary function of the division of labor on board the whaling vessel by invoking *White-Jacket*, his devastating critical analysis of the disciplinary economy on board the ships of the United States Navy. (See especially, chapter 3, "A Glance at the Principal Divisions into which a Man-of-War's Crew Is Divided.") This is not, as it might superficially appear, an arbitrary juxtaposition, if we recall Foucault's genealogy of the mass production system of the capitalist factory: its origins in the supervision of detail in the training of soldiers, the organization of space and time of the military camp, and the strategies of tactics that emerged during the Enlightenment. (See "Docile Bodies," *Discipline and Punish*, pp. 135–69.) What Melville is intuiting in this insistent comparative concern is that the division

of labor on the whaling ship constitutes a mimesis of that on the naval vessel, but in a way that "liberalizes"—that is, conceals by internalizing—the more overtly oppressive and exploitative power relations that, as Melville insistently notes in *White-Jacket*, obtain aboard the man-of-war.

149. Michel Foucault, *Discipline and Punish*, pp. 137–38.

150. Charles Olson, *Call Me Ishmael*, p. 23.

151. R. W. B. Lewis, *The American Adam*, pp. 132–33.

152. See Bercovitch, *The American Jeremiad*, p. 176. Wai-chee Dimock invokes this passage in her reading of *White-Jacket*, where she identifies Melville's "rhetoric of reform" in that novel with American imperial expansionism. See *Empire for Liberty*, pp. 101–2. But this passage clearly determines her reading of *Moby-Dick* as an "imperial folio" in the next chapter of her book.

153. Walter Benjamin, "Theses on the Philosophy of History," in *Illuminations*, ed. Hannah Arendt, trans. Harry Zohn (New York: Schocken Books, 1969), p. 256.

154. Donald Pease, *Visionary Compacts*, p. 271–72.

155. Gramsci's concept of the "historical bloc" was intended to call into question the essentialism of the orthodox Marxist base/superstructure model, in which the Communist Party, as the determining center, reduced the differential identities of the historically specific occasion to the totalized and dedifferentiated (idealized) concept of the working class. In opposition to this essentialist—and tremendously concentering—view of struggle, Gramsci's appeals to the "historical bloc": the alliances of differential, historical, social constituencies or subject positions. My own understanding of the historical bloc derives in part from Ernesto Laclau and Chantal Mouffe's radicalization of Gramsci's decentering impulse. See *Hegemony and Socialist Strategy: Towards a Radical Democratic Politics* (London: Verso, 1985).

156. Drawing from Gramsci's substitution of the "organic intellectual" for the class of universal intellectuals, who "are the dominant group's 'deputies' exercising the subaltern functions of social hegemony and political government" (*Selections from the Prison Notebooks*, (p. 12), Foucault proffers the "specific" against the "universal" or "general" intellectual as the appropriate agency of thoughtful practice in a world in which power relations are determined by the discourse of truth rather than by force: "In the most recent upheaval [the 'events of May 1968'], the intellectual discovered that the masses no longer need him to gain knowledge: . . . they know far better than he and they are certainly capable of expressing themselves. But there exists a system of power which blocks, prohibits, and invalidates this discourse and this knowledge, a power not only found in the manifest authority of censorship, but one that profoundly and subtly penetrates an entire societal network. Intellectuals are themselves agents of this system of power—the idea of their responsibility for 'consciousness' and discourse forms part of the system. The intellectual's role is no longer to place himself 'somewhat ahead and to the side' in order to express the stifled truth of the collectivity; rather it is to struggle against the forms of power that transforms him into its object and instrument in the sphere of 'knowledge,' 'truth,' 'consciousness,' and 'discourse'" ("Intellectuals and

Power: A Conversation between Michel Foucault and Gilles Deleuze," in *Language, Counter-Memory, Practice*, p. 207). See also, Paul Bové, *Intellectuals in Power: A Genealogy of Critical Humanism* (New York: Columbia University Press, 1986).

157. Foucault introduces the concept of the "repressive hypothesis" in *The History of Sexuality*, vol. 1, pp. 155 ff. But it is based on the inaugural distinction Foucault makes in *Discipline and Punish*, between power relations in the period of monarchy and in the post-Enlightenment, between the overt use of power in the *"ancien régime"* and the harnessing of knowledge production to power in the "regime of truth."

158. For amplification of this oxymoron and of the need to think it in the context of the contemporary occasion, in which the pervasive retrieval of difference from total-itarian (Stalinist) or hegemonic (Western democratic) identities is taking the form of reinscribing virulent forms of identity (racial, sexual, ethnic, and so on) that manifest themselves in violent acts of differential "cleansing," see Spanos, *The End of Education: Toward Posthumanism*, especially the chapter entitled "The Intellectual and the Posthu-manist Occasion: Toward a Decentered *Paideia*," pp. 187–221.

159. This American exceptionalist, "Thoreauvian" tradition is brought into the pres-ent revisionary context by Leo Marx, "Pastoralism in America," in *Ideology and Classic American Literature*, ed. Sacvan Bercovitch and Myra Jehlen (Cambridge: Cambridge University Press, 1986), pp. 36–69. In this extremely nostalgic essay, Marx identifies the communal impulse of the "New Left" of the 1960s—the "move away from the complex world of organized power in the direction of nature" (p. 64)—with the antitechnological pastoral impulse of mid-nineteenth-century America.

160. Martin Heidegger, ". . . Poetically Man Dwells . . . ," pp. 217–18.

161. The sense of Melville's unelaborated improvisational (as opposed to providen-tial) "visionary compact" *vis à vis* the American *polis* I am trying to convey is suggested by the decentered neo- or poststructuralist Gramscian model of social democracy articulated by Ernesto Laclau and Chantal Mouffe in *Hegemony and Socialist Strategy*. See especially, pp. 149–93.

162. Martin Heidegger, ". . . Poetically Man Dwells . . . ," p. 221.

163. Martin Heidegger, "Building Dwelling Thinking," in *Poetry, Language, Thought*: "A boundary is not that at which something stops but, as the Greeks recognized, the boundary is that from which something *begins its presencing*. That is why the concept is that of *horismos*, that is, horizon, the boundary" (p. 154).

164. See Paul Royster, "Melville's Economy of Language," in *Ideology and Classic American Literature*, ed. Sacvan Bercovitch and Myra Jehlen: "*Moby-Dick* is an exuberant paean to labor, an elaborate celebration of human energy and industry of nineteenth-century America. Yet what it converts to metaphor is a particular set of economic relations: Whaling is a capitalist enterprise, an industry that produces commodities for a market and employs labor to return a profit on investment. Ishmael's advocacy of 'the honor and glory of whaling' does not separate labor from capital, as being distinct parts of the industry. He is as proud of the number, size, and efficiency of the American whaling fleet as of the skill, productivity, and dedication of its seamen. Both the labor

and the physical means of production emerge from Ishmael's account in favorable colors. Meanwhile, he invests the process of producing whale oil with additional symbolic meanings, which make it an extended metaphor for various social and metaphysical referents. Ishmael is never so happy as when he is finding in some dull, arduous, or onerous task an allegory of universal truth. Work takes on extra value when Ishmael can interpret it symbolically, when it assumes the pattern of some large structure or condition of human life" (pp. 313–14).

165. Wai-chee Dimock, *Empire for Liberty*, p. 134.

166. Sacvan Bercovitch, *The American Jeremiad*, p. 191.

167. Ibid., p. 193. This is also the conclusion Bercovitch draws about Henry Adams's *Education*: "The distinctive quality of the *Education* is that it reverses all the effects of the jeremiad while retaining intact the jeremiad's figural-symbolic outlook. . . . The symbol he projects in himself [the manikin which stands "for the great 'inheritance with which (Adams) took his name'"] deprives us of alternatives" (p. 196). There is, perhaps, greater justification for this conclusion in Adams than in Melville. But as in the case of his reading of *Moby-Dick*, Bercovitch reduces the admittedly tentative emancipatory parodic/genealogical impulse of the *Education* to "the ['sick'] humor of the anti-jeremiad" (p. 196). It could as easily be demonstrated, especially if one attended to the antiexceptionalist global context of his thought, that the continuity Adams posits between his great New England name and the manikin he has become in "the fullness of (American) time" is intended to release us from the paranoid logic of American patriarchal/dynastic models. One very significant instance of this genealogical impulse, which Bercovitch ignores, is Adams's identification of American cultural identity with the patriarchal male; i.e., his protofeminism. For a path-breaking refocusing of Adams's discourse, which rejects the "Americanist" perspective in favor of Adams's "rigorously global perspective on the U.S. which specifically cannot be assimilated to the statist project of American Studies or its recent reformist incarnations," see Paul Bové, "Anarchy and Perfection: Henry Adams's Anti-American Discourse," in *Essay in Honor of Joseph Riddel*, ed. Joseph Kronick and Kathryne Lindberg (Baton Rouge: Louisiana State University Press, 1995), 168.

168. I am, of course, putting all the terms of this quotation that reinscribe the principle of presence under erasure.

169. In opposition to Bercovitch, it is one of Donald Pease's central theses about Melville that he offers the possibility of a counterhegemonic discourse grounded in his "visionary compact" with Hawthorne. I will address Pease's version of this counterhegemonic possibility below. Suffice it to say here that, in the absence of an argument to the contrary, it could be objected that the visionary compact he discovers in Melville's relationship with Hawthorne recuperates a logocentrism.

170. Herman Melville to Nathaniel Hawthorne, June 29, 1851. *The Letters of Herman Melville*, p. 133.

171. Henry A. Murray, "In Nomine Diaboli," in *Moby-Dick: Centennial Essays*, ed. Tyrus Hillway and Luther S. Mansfield, p. 20.

172. The double meaning of "différence," as Jacques Derrida has suggested in working

out the grammatological implications of his coinage *différance*, is still present in the French *différer*. See Jacques Derrida, "Différance," in *Speech and Phenomena and Other Essays on Husserl's Theory of Signs*, trans. David B. Allison (Evanston, Ill.: Northwestern University Press, 1973).

173. This anxiety-provoking ontological insight, perhaps needless to say, lies behind the accommodational impulse of post-Reformation Christian theology that renders the fall of man into time a *"felix culpa"* (fortunate fall). John Milton, for example, especially in the "Areopagitica," recognized that in "paradise," where difference does not exist, nothing makes a difference and that to act in this differential world according to this transcendental representation would be disastrous for the *logos*: "I cannot praise a fugitive and cloistered virtue unexercised and unbreached that never sallies out and seeks her adversary, but slinks out of the race, where the immortal garland is to be run for, not without dust and heat. Assuredly we bring not innocence into the world, we bring impurity much rather. That which purifies us is trial, *and trial is by what is contrary.* That virtue therefore which is but a youngling in the contemplation of evil, and knows not the utmost that vice promises to her followers and rejects it, is but a blank virtue, not pure; her whiteness is but an excremental whiteness" (*Areopagitica*, ed. with commentary by Sir Richard C. Jebb [Cambridge: Cambridge University Press, 1918], p. 20; my emphasis). In its existentialist phase, on the other hand—in the thinking of Søren Kierkegaard, Rudolph Bultmann, Paul Tillich, and Dietrich Bonhoeffer, for example—this impulse might properly be called destructive.

174. Herman Melville, *Billy Budd*, p. 53. Barbara Johnson invokes this passage in "Melville's Fist: The Execution of *Billy Budd*," in *The Critical Difference: Essays in the Contemporary Rhetoric of Reading* (Baltimore: Johns Hopkins University Press, 1980), pp. 79–109. While I find a certain critical gesture in this brilliant deconstructive reading of Melville's text—namely, her disclosure that "the stutter 'mars' the [traditional allegorical] plot in that it triggers the reversal of roles between Billy and Claggart" (innocence becomes guilt; guilt becomes innocent)—productive in its estranging of powerful, sedimented, metaphysical categories (the self-evident binary polarity of good and evil), Johnson's reading, which is undertaken in the name of a more just justice, finally constitutes an injustice to Melville's text. This is because her reading, like that of so many American followers of Derrida, who have appropriated deconstruction for reading literary texts, reduces Melville's critical judgment of the historically specific questions of moral comportment and politics he is addressing in his novella—specifically, his awareness of *the imbalances of power* that actually obtain in the world of the novel and the world to which it refers—to a free-floating, undecidable textuality, that is, to a no-place where all things are equal.

This is suggested in what follows immediately after the passage quoted above: "Yet in another sense this reversal does not mar the plot, it constitutes it. Here, as in the story of Eden, what the envious 'marplot' mars is not the plot, but the state of plotlessness that exists 'in the beginning.' What both the Book of Genesis and *Billy Budd* narrate is thus not the story of a fall but a fall into story" (p. 87). By "fall into story,"

I take it, Johnson means what Derrida calls "writing" and Paul de Man, "rhetoric": that mode of language that the Occident has historically subordinated to speech because it has "fallen away"—has "become separated from"—the self-identical voice and is thus contaminated by *aporias* (gaps) and undecidability (*différance*). Understood in these terms, one cannot but agree with Johnson, but at the same time conclude that this way of putting it is inadequate in that it reduces the historically specific reference (if not source) of Melville's destruction of the traditional allegorical plot—the official political narrative of the *Somers* mutiny (which is reflected in parodic form in the official "account of the affair" published in an "authorized" "navy chronicle of the time" [p. 130]) to the functioning of plots (understood from a deconstructive perspective) in general: "If all plots somehow tell the story of their own marring, then perhaps it could be said that all plots are plots against authority, that authority creates the scene of its own destruction, that all stories necessarily recount by their very existence the subversion of the father, of the gods, of the consciousness, of order, of expectations, or of meaning" (p. 88). Thus when Johnson brings history into play in the form of Captain Vere's judgment of Billy Budd—the (decidable) story into which his historical situation compels him to put Billy and Claggart—it is to show that Captain Vere's externalization of internal ambiguities into bipolar opposites (into a decidable plot) constitutes a violence against *différance* similar to the violence of *all* plots. In other words, it is to show that historical judgment (praxis), like deciding about the meaning of a text, is impossible: "It would seem . . . that the function of judgment is to convert an ambiguous situation into a decidable one. But it does so by converting a difference *within* . . . into a difference *between*. . . . A difference *between* opposing forces presupposes that the entities in conflict be knowable. A difference *within* one of the entities in question is precisely what problematizes the very *idea* of an entity in the first place, rendering the 'legal point of view' inapplicable. In studying the plays of both ambiguity and binarity, Melville's story situates *its* critical difference neither within nor between, but in the *relation between the two* as the fundamental question of all human politics" (p. 106). From the infinitely negative perspective, Johnson cannot see that the "difference *between* opposing forces" in the *historical world* can also invoke the recognition and thus the *will* to redress the balance of power. Her anti-universal universal deconstructive problematic reduces the imbalance of power that obtains between Billy Budd and the sociopolitical constituency composed of Claggart, Captain Vere, and the British navy—to the same, thus canceling each out. Johnson's frame of reference positively makes invisible the very visible fact that Billy, as his impressment itself suggests, doesn't stand a chance in the political "plot" he's trapped in. In other words, it renders her necessarily blind to the possibility that Melville can both challenge the principle of presence—take his lead from the *dia-bolos*—and still make moral and political judgments about historically specific injustices.

175. Samuel Taylor Coleridge, *Biographia Literaria*, pp. 363–64. As Coleridge notes (*Biographia Literaria*, chap. 10, p. 272), his definition of the imagination as an "esemplastic power" is a coinage that derives ultimately "from the Greek words εἰς ἕν πλάτ-

τειν, to shape into one," and immediately from Friedrich Schelling's "In-Eins-Bildung, which, as noted by W. K. Wimsatt and Cleanth Brooks in *Literary Criticism*, he mistakenly believes "is authorized by the German word *Einbildungskraft*" (p. 390). This is a revealing relay of appropriations that goes far to confirm my point about the Symbolic imagination. As the etymology makes explicit, it is informed by the will to power over difference and serves not simply to internalize and sublimate external conflict, but also to spatialize temporality. It is, for Coleridge, Emerson, and the American Renaissance writers in general, as for their Modernist heirs, not simply the New Critics, but those Americanists like the Matthiessen of *American Renaissance*, the Trilling of *The Liberal Imagination*, and the Feidelson of *Symbolism and American Literature*, a faculty the "power" of which is capable of coercing the recalcitrantly differential being of being-in-the-world into a "unified" or "whole" and flattened out mental "picture."

176. Lionel Trilling, "Reality in America," *The Liberal Imagination*, pp. 9–10. By "dialectic," it should be recalled, Trilling is invoking that "inclusive" mode of *poiesis*, sponsored by I. A. Richards and the New Critics against an "exclusive" (didactic) *poiesis*, that, in its internalizing and resolving of external contradictions, is "impervious to irony." It suggests something like the Hegelian *Aufhebung*. See my discussion of this relay of names in chapter 1.

177. Milton R. Stern, *The Fine Hammered Steel of Herman Melville* (Urbana: University of Illinois Press, 1957), p. 9.

178. Ibid., p. 16.

179. Herman Melville, *Billy Budd*, pp. 130–31. For all its emphasis on the question of representation in *Billy Budd*, recent poststructuralist criticism of this novella, Barbara Johnson's, for example, has failed to perceive the degree to which it constitutes Melville's committed attempt to reclaim a history for those whom History—specifically the monumental American History that claims its origins in the Puritan errand in the wilderness—has denied a history. Lest my invocation of Foucault's genealogical discourse be taken as an example of "travelling theory," it is worth recalling that what I have said above about Melville's historical sense could as well be put in Thomas Pynchon's terms: Criticism has been blind to the degree to which *Billy Budd* constitutes an effort to retrieve a history for those "preterites"—the "disinherited"—that American History has "passed over." It is also worth recalling that this project of retrieving the forgotten "other" from the amnesiac American Cultural Memory is, as his sardonic prefatorial address to "His Highness the Bunker-Hill Monument," suggests, the fundamental project of Melville's *Israel Potter: His Fifty Years of Exile*. Melville's retrieval from oblivion of forgotten texts of this sort is remarkably proleptic of Foucault's retrieval of the histories of those whom official history has forgotten. One thinks, for example, of *I, Pierre Rivière, Having Slaughtered My Mother, My Sister, and My Brother: A Case of Parricide in the 19th Century*, ed. Michel Foucault, trans. Frank Jellinek (New York: Random House, 1975); and *Herculine Barbin: Being the Recently Discovered Memoirs of a Nineteenth-Century Hermaphrodite*, trans. Richard McDougall (New York: Pantheon, 1980).

180. Joseph N. Riddel, "Decentering the Image: The 'Project' of 'American' Poetics?"

in *The Problems of Reading in Contemporary American Criticism*, a special issue of *boundary 2*, vol. 8 (Fall 1979), pp. 165–66; reprinted in *The Question of Textuality: Strategies of Reading in Contemporary American Criticism* (Bloomington: University of Indiana Press, 1982). See also Edgar Dryden, "The Entangled Text: Melville's *Pierre* and the Problem of Reading," *boundary 2*, vol. 7 (Spring 1979), pp. 145–73, and Rodolphe Gasché, "The Scene of Writing: A Deferred Outset," *Glyph* 1 (Baltimore: Johns Hopkins University Press, 1977), pp. 150–71. This last essay is a brilliant deconstructive reading of the "Cetology" chapter, which, however, finally *uses* Melville's text as a pretext, not for reading *Moby-Dick*, but for articulating a, by now, all-too-familiar theory of writing as *différance*.

181. Joseph Riddel, "Decentering the Image," p. 185.

182. For an extended critique of deconstruction as it has been practiced by American literary critics, see "The Indifference of Differance," in Spanos, *Heidegger and Criticism: Retrieving the Cultural Politics of Destruction* (Minneapolis: University of Minnesota Press, 1993), pp. 81–131. See also Fredric Jameson, *Postmodernism, or, The Cultural Logic of Late Capitalism*, in which he identifies deconstruction with the postmodern cultural production that is complicitous with the formation of the simulacral world of late capitalism: "The new spatial logic of the simulacrum can now be expected to have a momentous effect on what used to be historical time. The past is thereby itself modified: what was once, in the historical novel as Lukàcs defines it, the organic genealogy of the bourgeois collective project—what is still . . . for the resurrection of the dead of anonymous and silenced generations, the retrospective dimension indispensable to any vital reorientation of our collective future—has meanwhile itself become a vast collection of images, a multitudinous photographic simulacrum. . . . In faithful conformity to poststructuralist linguistic theory, the past as 'referent' finds itself gradually bracketed, and then effaced altogether, leaving us with nothing but texts" (p. 18). See also the section on Paul de Man in the chapter entitled "Theory," pp. 217–59.

183. See the chapter entitled "Heidegger, Kierkegaard, and the Hermeneutic Circle," in Spanos, *Heidegger and Criticism*, especially the discussion of Kierkegaard's existentialist critique of Friedrich Schlegel's novel *Lucinde*, pp. 65–70.

184. See the chapter entitled "The Indifference of Differance," in Spanos, *Heidegger and the End of Criticism*, pp. 99 ff.

185. See Jacques Derrida, "Force and Signification," *Writing and Difference*, pp. 3–30.

186. Charles Olson, *Call Me Ishmael*, p. 14. See also "I, Maximus of Gloucester, to You," *The Maximus Poems*: "O my lady of good voyage / in whose arms, whose left arm rests / no boy but a carefully carved wood, a painted face, a schooner! / a delicate mast, as bow-sprit for / forwarding" (p. 6).

4 *MOBY-DICK* AND THE CONTEMPORARY AMERICAN OCCASION

1. The firepower of the atomic bombs exploded by the United States in World War II was, of course, technically greater (though quantitatively less devastating) than that of

the weaponry used in Vietnam. Unlike the ideological circumstances surrounding the unleashing of American technological violence in Vietnam, however, the ideological circumstances in which this atomic firepower was unleashed obscured—and continues to obscure—the essential continuity between the atomic bomb used against Japan and the "conventional" weaponry used in Vietnam: the recognition, in other words, that the use of nuclear weapons constitutes the (unfulfilled) apocalyptic fulfillment of the ontological, cultural, and sociopolitical logic of America's justification of its wars. This complicity, not incidentally, is precisely what Francis Ford Coppola's great "Melvillean" movie about "America's" intervention, *Apocalypse Now,* ironically thematizes. (We should not be misled by the film's overdetermined indebtedness to Joseph Conrad's *Heart of Darkness.*) In pitting Captain Willard's assignment by MACV (Military Assistance Command, Vietnam) to "terminate" Colonel Kurtz's command "with extreme prejudice" against Kurtz's "unsound methods," this film points with bitterly ferocious irony to the insanity of the "sound," "rational," or "civilized" methods of the United States' command in Vietnam: to the complicity, that is, between the "conventional" technology of extermination and Kurtz's "unconventional"—"Ahabian"—desire, written in blood across a page of his journal, to "Drop the bomb. Exterminate them all!" One should recall at this juncture the famous "unconventional" declaration of General Curtis LeMay, chief of staff of the U.S. air force during the Eisenhower administration: "We're going to bomb them back into the Stone Age." For an extended discussion of the difficult question of the commensurability of forms of modern violence (which includes the Nazi's "Final Solution"), see the chapter entitled "Heidegger, Nazism, and the 'Repressive Hypothesis,'" in William V. Spanos, *Heidegger and Criticism: Retrieving the Cultural Politics of Destruction* (Minneapolis: University of Minnesota Press, 1993), pp. 181–251.

2. Fredric Jameson, *Postmodernism, or, The Cultural Logic of Late Capitalism* (Durham, N.C.: Duke University Press, 1991) p. 44.

3. Ibid., p. 45.

4. Ibid., p. 16.

5. Gerald Graff, *Professing Literature: An Institutional History* (Chicago: University of Chicago Press, 1987), pp. 12–13.

6. Jacques Derrida, "Structure, Sign and Play in the Discourse of the Human Sciences," in *Writing and Difference,* trans. Alan Bass (Chicago: Chicago University Press, 1978), p. 279.

7. Michael Herr, *Dispatches* (New York: Avon, 1978), pp. 113–14.

8. Frank Lentricchia, *Ariel and the Police: Michel Foucault, William James, Wallace Stevens* (Madison: University of Wisconsin Press, 1988), pp. 20–21. See also pp. 112–14. Because Lentricchia's brilliant reading of Stevens's poem estranges the sedimented New Critical reading, I quote the poem in full: "I placed a jar in Tennessee, / And round it was, upon a hill. / It made the slovenly wilderness / Surround that hill. // The wilderness rose up to it, / And sprawled around, no longer wild. / The jar was round upon the ground / and tall and of a port in air. // It took dominion everywhere. // The

jar was gray and bare. / It did not give of bird or bush, / Like nothing else in Tennessee." Since, further, Lentricchia attributes such great importance to Herr's "perversely perfect mixed metaphor of the 'planted jar,'" it is worth recalling what should be a commonplace: that "colony" (from the Latin *colonus*: tiller, planter, cultivator, settler, and *colere*: to cultivate, to plant) and "plantation" are interchangeable in the early history of the settlers of the "New World"—their domestication of the "slovenly wilderness" by encirclement and cultivation—and that these genetic metaphors always constitute the major terms in a series of empowering binary oppositions that has been fundamental to the legitimation and extension of the hegemony of the Colonizer/planter: Culture/barbarism, Capital/provinces, for example; that, in other words, their genealogical origins contradictorily betray the complicity of their benign organic or "sym-bolic" logic—the process of the fructification of the planted seed—with the polyvalent imperial will to dominate and master the "other."

9. Michael Herr, *Dispatches*, p. 50–51. For further reference to the Puritan identification of the natives with Satan, see *Dispatches*, p. 100. For an important but neglected genealogy of the American national identity that, like Herr, is cognizant of this "secret history"—how deeply "backgrounded" the U.S. involvement in Vietnam was—see Richard Drinnon, *Facing West: The Metaphysics of Indian-Hating and Empire-Building* (Minneapolis: University of Minnesota Press, 1980). See also John Hellman, *The American Myth and the Legacy of Vietnam* (New York: Columbia University Press, 1986). Alden Pyle is the central character in Graham Greene's *The Quiet American* (1956), in his novel about the last days of French colonial rule in Indochina and the assumption of the *"mission civilatrice"* by the United States. Pyle, modeled on the legendary intelligence officer Edward G. Landsdale, is represented by Greene as a contemporary American frontiersman—what Herr calls a "spook" in *Dispatches*—fortified by the Cold War writings of one York Harding, the author of *The Advance of Red China*. What Greene is satirizing by way of his portrait of Alden Pyle in this prophetic novel is epitomized by Landsdale himself in the preface of his autobiography: "You should know one thing at the beginning: I took my American beliefs with me into these Asian struggles, as Tom Paine would have done. Ben Franklin once said, 'Where liberty dwells, there is my country.' Paine's words form a cherished part of my credo. My American beliefs include the conviction of the truth of the precept that 'men are created equal, that they are endowed by their Creator with certain unalienable Rights' and in the provision of our Bill of Rights to make the great precept a reality among men. Along with other Americans, I feel a kinship with Thomas Jefferson when he declared, 'I have sworn upon the altar of God eternal hostility against every form of tyranny over the mind of man.' These are principles for an American to try to live by wherever he goes, even two centuries after. Thus, I endeavored to practice my beliefs among embattled people abroad" (*In the Midst of Wars: An American's Mission to Southeast Asia* [New York: Harper & Row, 1972], pp. ix–x). Landsdale's raison d'être as an American bears witness to the abiding power of what Wai-chee Dimock, by way, not incidentally, of quoting a letter of Thomas Jefferson to James Madison (27 April 1809), identifies as the essence of the

founding American cultural identity: its self-representation as an "empire for liberty." It is an irony of massive proportions that Dimock invokes Jefferson's phrase as the title of a book that would implicate Melville centrally in this Jeffersonian ideology. See especially, the introductory chapter, "Nation, Self, and Personification," in *Empire for Liberty: Melville and the Poetics of Individualism* (Princeton: Princeton University Press, 1989), pp. 3–41.

10. In fairness to Lentricchia, it should be noted that he does, indeed, invoke both the Jacksonian occasion and the Puritan "errand in the wilderness" in his commentary on the historical resonances evoked by the jar Stevens places in Tennessee: "What are the limits of the historical horizon within which we would situate 'Tennessee'? How far back does it go? To the Cherokee Indians? How far forward? Maybe all the way to Vietnam" (p. 16); "The journey from 'a lot of pathological Germans and Poles' [i.e., the early William James], to James's critique of philosophy's shining marble temple on a hill, to Stevens' critique of the jar on a hill in Tennessee, to Herr's meditation on Vietnam, Khe Sanh upon a hill, perhaps began with John Winthrop's unwittingly ugly interpretation of that city when, years after he had coined the phrase, he banished Anne Hutchinson for antinomian heresy" (p. 114). As the separation of the two passages suggest, however, these are, despite their heuristic force, unfocused insights, which fail to adequately thematize not simply the indissoluble continuity between the ontological site and the cultural and sociopolitical, but the weight given by the discourse of America—and this triad of critics—to the ontological site in this relay. This, I suggest, is one significant reason why Melville's *Moby-Dick* plays no part in Lentricchia's otherwise ground-breaking revisionist reading of several synecdochical moments in American cultural and political history.

11. There are at least two overt allusions to *Moby-Dick* in *Dispatches*: (1): Herr's identification of the community of "irregulars"—Sean Flynn, Tim Page, Dana Stone—with whom he identifies (but not without awareness and self-criticism of its frontier origins) in Saigon as "classic essential American types; point men, *isolatoes* and out-riders" (p. 35) and (2) his characterization of the dreadfully threatening silence of the terrain he was supposed to cover as possessing a "malignant intelligence" (p. 69).

12. See, for example, Simon During, "Postmodernism or Postcolonialism Today," *Textual Practice*, vol. 1 (1987), pp. 32–47; and Rey Chow, "Rereading Mandarin Ducks and Butterflies: A Response to the 'Postmodern Condition'," *Cultural Critique*, vol. 5 (1986), pp. 69–93, both of which criticize Fredric Jameson's "postmodern" reading of Third-World texts as imperial precisely because of his commitment to the idea of the postmodern as a cultural dominant that, however sympathetically, determines—speaks for, as it were—the "other."

13. See Andrew F. Krepinevich Jr., *The Army and Vietnam* (Baltimore: Johns Hopkins University Press, 1988): "To paraphrase General of the Army Omar Bradley, the United States can look back on Vietnam as the wrong war—at the wrong place, at the wrong time, with the wrong army. Simply stated, the United States Army was neither trained nor organized to fight effectively in an insurgency conflict environment. To

understand why, it is necessary to examine the evolution the Army has undergone over its history, particularly in this century—an evolution that has provided the United States with a superb instrument for combating the field armies of its adversaries in conventional (or 'mid-intensity') wars but an inefficient and ineffective force for defeating insurgent guerrilla forces in a 'low-intensity' conflict.

"The key to understanding this condition is a recognition that the Army's approach to war, referred to here as the Army Concept, is the product of an organizational character that has evolved over time and that, because of its high regard for tradition, has become deeply embedded in the service's psyche.

". . . The characteristics of the Army Concept are two: a focus on mid-intensity, or conventional, war and a reliance on high volumes of firepower to minimize casualties—in effect, the substitution of material costs at every available opportunity to avoid payment in blood" (pp. 4–5). What Krepinevich says but necessarily leaves unsaid in this in-house (disciplinary) critique of the U.S. army's conduct of the war in Vietnam (he is assigned to the Executive Secretariat in the office of the Secretary of Defense) is that the evolution of "the organizational character" of the "Army Concept" into a traditional perspective that "has become deeply imbedded in the service's psyche" is continuous with the evolution of the American cultural identity.

14. I am, of course, invoking Louis Althusser's analysis of the affiliative relationship between the ostensibly distinct (repressive) state apparatuses and the ideological state apparatuses in "Ideology and Ideological State Apparatuses," in *Lenin and Philosophy and Other Essays* trans. Ben Brewster (New York: Monthly Review Press, 1971), specifically that moment in the relationship when, in the face of the refusal of consent to the latter, the distinction evaporates, when, that is, the state apparatuses are invoked as a last resort to fulfill the blocked agenda of the ideological apparatuses or the ideological apparatuses assume the power relations characteristic of the repressive state apparatuses. This transformative—and self-destructive—moment is powerfully suggested by Frances FitzGerald in her great book on the Vietnam War, above all, in her account of the radical revision of American foreign policy following the political crisis that precipitated the Guam Conference of 1967: "At the Guam conference President Johnson took the long-awaited step of putting all civilian operations under the command of General Westmoreland. His move signified that Washington no longer gave even symbolic importance to the notion of a 'political' war waged by the Vietnamese government. The reign of the U.S. military had begun and with it the strategy of quantity in civilian as well as military affairs.

"As an assistant to Westmoreland, Robert Komer [director of CORDS, Civilian Operations and Revolutionary Development Support; i.e., chief of the pacification program] had something of the general's notion of scale. After all the history of failed programs, he believed that the only hope for success lay in saturation. . . . The U.S. government had no choice but to force its supplies upon the Vietnamese people: thousands of tons of bulgar wheat, thousands of gallons of cooking oil, tons of pharmaceuticals, enough seed to plant New Jersey with miracle rice, enough fertilizer for the same, light bulbs, garage trucks, an atomic reactor, enough concrete to pave a province, enough corrugated tin to roof it, enough barbed wire to circle it seventeen times, dentist's drills, soybean seedlings, sewing kits, mortar, machine tools, toothbrushes, plumbing, and land mines" (*Fire in the Lake: The Vietnamese and the Americans in Vietnam* [1972; New York: Vintage Books, 1989], p. 433). This is the Ahabian "Robert 'Blowtorch' Komer" about whom Michael Herr says, in pointing to the complicitous relation between "military arms and civilian arms" (and evoking the Virgilian resonance) in the strategy of "pacification," "If William Blake had 'reported' to him that he'd seen angels in the trees, Komer would have tried to talk him out of it. Failing there, he'd ordered defoliation" (*Dispatches*, p. 45).

15. Tim O'Brien, *Going after Cacciato* (New York: Delta/Seymour Lawrence, 1989), pp. 224–25.

16. Michael Herr, *Dispatches*, p. 111.

17. Ibid., pp. 174–75. See also the film, *The Battle of Khe Sanh* produced by the Department of Defense (1968), which ends with a proclamation by General Westmoreland that Khe Sanh was a decisive American victory.

18. Philip Caputo, *A Rumor of War* (New York: Ballantine, 1977), p. 273.

19. Tim O'Brien, *Going after Cacciato*, p. 240.

20. Herr's parodic ventriloquizing of the Command's identification of the Vietnamese enemy in terms of the third person masculine pronoun should not be overlooked. This reduction of the Vietnamese insurgent force, which included women as well as men, is another aspect of the Occidental concept of war. This same insight into the "Ahabian" will of the American military command is at the heart of Stanley Kubrick's great film *Full Metal Jacket*.

21. Herman Rapaport, "Vietnam: The Thousand Plateaus," in *The 60s without Apology*, ed. Sohnya Sayres, Anders Stephanson, Stanley Aronowitz, and Fredric Jameson (Minneapolis: University of Minnesota Press in cooperation with *Social Text*, 1984), p. 139. The quotation is from Truong Son, "American Failure," *Vietnamese Studies*, vol. 20, ed. Nguyen Khac Vien (Hanoi: Government of North Vietnam, December 1968). As Rapaport notes, "*Vietnamese Studies* is a series of pamphlets written during the 1960s and 1970s which cover various aspects of Vietnam, from medicine, farming, history, to chemical warfare (Agent Orange). These pamphlets have been distributed through Foreign Languages Publishing House in Hanoi and are no longer permitted to be imported into the United States, by order of the United States Government" (p. 146).

22. This contradictory course of the logic of "America" is synecdochically embodied in the progress of Colonel Kurtz in Francis Ford Coppola's *Apocalypse Now* (1978), one of the two Hollywood films about the Vietnam War that have read the American Cultural Memory of the postwar period against the grain. The other is Stanley Kubrick's *Full Metal Jacket*. Oliver Stone, the noted "liberal" film director, employs Melville's *Moby-Dick* in a centrally intertextual way in his prize-winning *Platoon* (1987). Particularly prominent is the motif involving Ahab's scene of persuasion, in which Ishmael (Chris Taylor) takes the oath to commit himself to Ahab's (Sergeant Barnes's)

revenge against the elusive white whale (the Vietcong): as Chris says in the voice over "Sergeant Barnes was our Ahab." But Stone's structural strategy constitutes an internalization of the external political conflict in America (exacerbated by America's extension of military operations in Cambodia: the *mise-en-scène* of *Platoon*) as a psychomachia with Puritan origins. More specifically, he transforms the historical specificity of the external political context into a morality romance. It thus becomes clear that Stone's understanding of his Ishmael is determined precisely by the "liberal imagination": by the terms, that is, of the hegemonic discourse that shaped the representation of Melville's novel in the Cold War era. A similar criticism can be mounted against John M. Del Vecchio's novel, *The 13th Valley* (New York: Bantam Books, 1982), which, like Stone's *Platoon*, would extend its symbolic resonance to incorporate the American cultural identity by modeling its narrative structure on *Moby-Dick*.

23. Michel Foucault, "Nietzsche, Genealogy, History," in *Language, Counter-Memory, Practice: Selected Essays and Interviews*, ed. Donald F. Bouchard and trans. Donald F. Bouchard and Sherry Simon (Ithaca, N.Y.: Cornell University Press, 1977), p. 152. See also Antonio Gramsci on hegemony and the state or political society in *Selections from the Prison Notebooks*, ed. and trans. Quintin Hoare and Geoffrey Nowell Smith (New York: International Publishers, 1971), p. 12.

24. Michael Herr, *Dispatches*, p. 2.

25. Ibid., p. 74.

26. See the discussion of the relation between the centered circle and the metropolis of imperialism in the chapter entitled "The Apollonian Investment of Modern Humanist Educational Theory: The Examples of Matthew Arnold, Irving Babbitt, and I. A. Richards," in Spanos, *The End of Education: Toward Posthumanism* (Minneapolis: University of Minnesota Press, 1993), pp. 106–17. See also Spanos, "Culture and Colonization: The Imperial Imperatives of the Centered Circle," in *Nationalism(s), Culture and the Shape of the World*, ed. Henry Schwarz and Richard Dienst, Politics and Culture, vol. 4 (Boulder, Co.: Westview Press, 1995).

27. Henrique Dussel, *Philosophy of Liberation*, trans. Aquilina Martinez and Christine Morkovsky (Maryknoll, N.Y.: Orbis Books, 1985). See also Dussel, "Eurocentrism and Modernity: Introduction to the Frankfurt Lectures," in *The Postmodern Debate in Latin America*, a special issue of *boundary 2*, ed. John Beverley and José Oviedo, vol. 20 (Fall 1993), pp. 65–76.

28. Lentricchia verges on thematizing this strategy in, quite appropriately, invoking the passage from Michel Foucault's *Archaeology of Knowledge*, which constitutes one of my epigraphs: "Foucault's antidote [to discipline: the agency that 'takes us all through the gate of modernization, into safe port, where individuality is studied so much the better to be controlled'] is writing: not as a space for the preservation of identity and the assertion of voice, but as a labyrinth into which he can escape, to 'lose myself,' and, there, in the labyrinth, never have to be a self . . . —write yourself off, as it were, 'write in order to have no face.' Give no target to discipline: 'Do not ask who I am and do not ask me to remain the same: leave it to our bureaucrats and our police to see that our

papers are in order. At least spare us their morality when we write.' If for [William] James 'individuality' translates into a philosophical positive—a given of liberalism—a holdout in freedom and the site of the personal and of 'full ideality,' then for Foucault undisciplined individuality may be precisely the unintended effect of a system which would produce individuality as an object of its knowledge and power (the disciplinary appropriation of biography), but which instead, and ironically, inside its safe, normalized subject, *instigates the move to the underground where deviant selfhood may nurture sullen counterschemes of resistance and revolution" (Ariel and the Police*, p. 26; my emphasis). As in the case of his analysis of the historical backgrounding of America's Vietnam, this passage comes immediately after his reference to Michael Herr's and Don DeLillo's writing as "a counterdiscourse, working to undermine discourses of abstraction and domination" (p. 25). But like them it is invoked in behalf of the *individuality* that Marxism "dismisses by calling [it] a bourgeois illusion" (p. 23). That is, it is not clearly the postmodern insight instigated by the postmodernity of the "other's" fracturing strategy. Could it be that Foucault is, in fact, alluding specifically to this fracturing strategy of the National Liberation Front in the play on underground tunnelings, facelessness, and nomadic mobility in this passage? After all, *The Archaeology of Knowledge* was first published in 1969, when the problem of the facelessness of the Vietnamese "other" was becoming an American obsession. The parallel between this Foucauldian refusal to be answerable to the "police" of the disciplinary society with the strategy of migrant or nomadic resistance in the postcolonial period articulated by Edward Said in *Culture and Imperialism*, and to which I will return at the end of this book, should not be overlooked.

29. Herr, *Dispatches*, p. 280. I am, of course, extending the point Lentricchia is making in thematizing American "jar placing" as metonymic representation of a "repetitive action of domination hard to separate from the course of American history" (*Ariel and the Police*, p. 16), in which we *as* Americans have been and continue to be implicated.

30. The racism informing Ahab's self-reliant will to power over being—which parallels the racism Herr points to in the passage invoking Stevens's "Anecdote" ("a vision of as many as 40,000 of them out there in the open, fighting it out on our terms, fighting for once like men, fighting to no avail") is disclosed in the opening contrast between "turbaned Turk" and "hired Venetian or Malay." It renders the American character (the implicit "us" in the passage) more malicious than that of the Oriental (the overt "them" in the passage) whose demonic identity is the consequence of an Occidental naming intended to justify its privileged identity and its cultural and political domination over the Oriental worlds. In this, not incidentally, Melville anticipated Nietzsche's and Foucault's inversion of the classical European binary opposition that privileges the Greek/Roman over the Egyptian.

31. It is no accident, I think, that Edward Said invokes Melville's *Moby-Dick* in *Culture and Imperialism* at two crucial conjunctures to demonstrate the degree to which America's self-representation in the cultural terms of its errand in the wilderness has been complicitous not simply with its nineteenth-century but also its twentieth-century imperial project, especially in Vietnam and the Middle East: "Enough work has been

done by American cultural historians for us to understand the sources of the drive to domination on a world scale as well as the way that drive is represented and made acceptable. Richard Slotkin argues, in *Regeneration Through Violence*, that the shaping experience of American history was the extended wars with the native American Indians; this in turn produced an image of Americans not as plain killers . . . but as 'a new race of people, independent of the sin-darkened heritage of man, seeking a totally new and original relationship to pure nature as hunters, explorers, pioneers and seekers.' Such imagery keeps recurring in nineteenth-century literature, most memorably in Melville's *Moby-Dick*, where, as C. L. R. James and V. G. Kiernan have argued from a non-American perspective, Captain Ahab is an allegorical representation of the American world quest; he is obsessed, compelling, unstoppable, and completely wrapped up in his own rhetorical justification and his sense of cosmic symbolism" (*Culture and Imperialism* (New York: Alfred A. Knopf, 1993) p. 288). Later Said adds: "Anyone who has read *Moby-Dick* may have found it irresistible to extrapolate from that great novel to the real world, to see the American empire preparing again, like Ahab, to take after an imputed evil. First comes the unexamined moral mission, then, in the media, its military-geo-strategic extension. The most disheartening thing about the media—aside from their sheepishly following the government policy model, mobilizing for war right from the start—[and here Said seems to be relating the media's utterly reductive cultural representation of the "elusive and inscrutable" Middle East to Ahab's ontological monomania *vis à vis* the white whale]—was their trafficking in 'expert' Middle East lore, supposedly well-informed about Arabs. All roads lead to the bazaar; Arabs only understand force; brutality and violence are part of Arab civilization; Islam is an intolerant, segregationist, 'medieval,' fanatic, cruel, anti-woman religion. The context, framework, setting of any discussion was limited, indeed frozen, by these ideas. There seemed considerable but inexplicable enjoyment to be had in the prospect that at last 'the Arabs' as represented by Saddam were going to get their comeuppance. Many scores would be settled against various old enemies of the West: Palestinians, Arab nationalism, Islamic civilization." Said's citation of V. G. Kiernan is *America: The New Imperialism: From White Settlement to World Hegemony* (London: Zed, 1978), p. 206.

32. Herman Melville, "Bartleby, the Scrivener" in *The Piazza Tales, and Other Prose Pieces, 1839–1860*, ed. Harrison Hayford, Alma A. MacDougall, G. Thomas Tanselle, and others (Evanston, Ill.: Northwestern University Press and the Newberry Library, 1987), 13– 46.

33. Said, *Culture and Imperialism*, pp. 332–33.

34. Donald Pease, *Visionary Compacts*, p. 275.

35. For Pease's powerful critique of Bercovitch's politics of dissensus, see his introduction to *New Americanists: Revisionist Interventions into the Canon*, a special issue of *boundary 2*, vol. 17 (Spring 1990): "Because he cannot envision any political culture in the United States other than one organized according to the supernumerary binarity of the cold war consensus, Bercovitch . . . proposes a dissensus politics. But, as his placement

within the cultural conversation makes clear, Bercovitch's politics of dissensus only elevates *The American Jeremiad* into the consensus principle of the cold war liberals. And when, in the Cambridge project, it becomes the anthology's principle for the reorganization of American literary history, it continues the cold war consensus by taking opposition to a point of powerless dissensus. Without any arena for articulating different, dissenting voices into an empowering reconstruction of the field of American Studies, these individual, dissenting voices become simulacra of the structuring oppositions that articulated the cold war" (p. 29).

36. By "horizonal comportment," I mean with Hans-Georg Gadamer, the comportment toward knowledge that, against the idea of the knower as "seer," acknowledges the radical finiteness of its interpretive "situation" or occasion: "Every finite present has its limitations. We define the concept of situation by saying that it represents a standpoint that limits the possibility of vision. Hence an essential part of the concept of situation is the concept of 'horizon.' The horizon is the range of vision that includes everything that can be seen from a particular vantage point. Applying this to the thinking mind, we speak of narrowness of horizon, of the possible expansion of horizon, of the opening up of new horizons, etc." (*Truth and Method* [New York: Seabury Press, 1975], p. 267). What needs to be emphasized, by way of qualifying a recuperative tendency in Gadamer, is that a "horizonal comportment" is, in its finiteness, *always* horizonal.

37. Donald Pease, *Visionary Compacts*, p. 274.

38. Francis Fukuyama, *The End of History and the Last Man* (New York: Free Press, 1992). This book is a greatly expanded version of the "Hegelian" thesis presented in Fukuyama's much-discussed essay "The End of History?" *The National Interest*, vol. 16 (Summer 1989), pp. 2–18. Though the Cold War literary critics did not specify their commitment to dialectical narrative and historical processes by calling it "Hegelian," as Fukuyama, in a bold reversal of Marx's representation of universal history, does, the prefigurative continuity between the two is remarkable. It is as if his politically conservative discourse represents the fulfillment of the logical economy of the "liberal imagination." It is worth observing, *à propos* of the question of countering this representation of contemporary history, that prominent Marxist reviewers of Fukuyama's book in the prestigious *New Left Review* no. 193 (May–June 1992) have, despite significant qualifications, found his Hegelian analysis in many ways persuasive and useful. Such a nostalgic gesture in the face of the alternative of a world politics "grounded" in a decentered ontology is symptomatic at the site of political science of the inadequacy I am trying to thematize at the site of American literary history.

39. Pease, *Visionary Compacts*, p. 243.

40. Noam Chomsky, *Deterring Democracy* (New York: Hill and Wang, 1992).

BIBLIOGRAPHY

Abrams, M. H. "Belief and the Suspension of Disbelief." In *Literature and Belief*. English Institute Essays. New York: English Institute, 1957.

Althusser, Louis. "From *Capital* to Marx's Philosophy." In *Reading Capital*. London: Verso, 1979.

———. "Ideology and Ideological State Apparatuses." In *Lenin and Philosophy and Other Essays*. Trans. Ben Brewster. New York: Monthly Review Press, 1972.

———. "'On the Young Marx': Theoretical Questions." In *For Marx*. London: New Left Books, 1977.

Arac, Jonathan. "F. O. Matthiesson: Authorizing an American Renaissance." In *The American Renaissance Reconsidered: Selected Papers from the English Institute, 1982–1983*. Ed. Walter Benn Michaels and Donald E. Pease. Baltimore: Johns Hopkins University Press, 1985.

Arnold, Matthew. "On the Modern Element in Modern Literature." *The Complete Prose Works*, vol. 1. Ed. R. H. Super. Ann Arbor: University of Michigan Press, 1974.

Auerbach, Erich. "Figura." In *Scenes from the Drama of European Literature: Six Essays*. Trans. Ralph Manheim. New York: Meridian Books, 1959.

———. *Mimesis: The Representation of Reality in Western Literature*. Garden City, N.J.: Anchor Books, 1957.

Bakhtin, Mikhail. *The Dialogic Imagination: Four Essays*. Ed. Michael Holquist, trans. Caryl Emerson and Michael Holquist. Austin: University of Texas Press, 1981.

Bate, Walter Jackson. "The Crisis of English Studies." *Harvard Magazine*, vol. 85 (September–October 1987), pp. 46–53.

Beckett, Samuel. *Watt*. New York: Grove Press, 1953.

Benjamin, Walter. "Theses on the Philosophy of History." In *Illuminations*. Ed. Hannah Arendt, trans. Harry Zohn. New York: Schocken Books, 1969.

Bennett, William. "To Reclaim a Legacy: Report on Humanities in Education." *Chronicle of Higher Education* (November 28, 1984), pp. 19–21.

Bercovitch, Sacvan. *The American Jeremiad*. Madison: University of Wisconsin Press, 1978.

Bercovitch, Sacvan, and Myra Jehlen, eds. *Ideology and Classic American Literature.* Cambridge: Cambridge University Press, 1986.

Bergson, Henri. *Time and Free Will: An Essay on the Immediate Data of Consciousness.* Trans. F. L. Pogson. New York: Macmillan, 1910.

Bezanson, Walter. "*Moby-Dick*: Work of Art." In *Moby-Dick: Centennial Essays.* Ed. Tyrus Hillway and Luther S. Mansfield. Dallas: Southern Methodist University Press, 1953.

Bickman, Martin, ed. *Approaches to Teaching Melville's "Moby-Dick."* New York: Modern Language Association of America, 1985.

Blackmur, R. P. "The Craft of Herman Melville: A Putative Statement." In *The Lion and the Honeycomb: Essays in Solicitude and Critique.* New York: Harcourt, Brace and World, 1955.

———. "Humanism and Symbolic Imagination: Notes on Re-reading Irving Babbitt." In *The Lion and the Honeycomb: Essays in Solicitude and Critique.* New York: Harcourt, Brace and World, 1955.

Bloom, Allan. *The Closing of the American Mind: How Higher Education Has Failed Democracy and Impoverished the Souls of Today's Students.* New York: Simon and Schuster, 1987.

Booth, Wayne. *The Company We Keep: An Ethics of Fiction.* Berkeley: University of California Press, 1988.

Bové, Paul. "Anarchy and Perfection: Henry Adams's Anti-American Discourse." In *Essays in Honor of Joseph Riddel.* Ed. Joseph Kronick and Kathryne Lindberg. Baton Rouge: Louisiana State University Press, 1995.

———. *Intellectuals in Power: A Genealogy of Critical Humanism.* New York: Columbia University Press, 1986.

———. "Introduction: In the Wake of Theory." In *In The Wake of Theory.* Hanover, N.H.: Wesleyan University Press, 1992.

———. "Notes toward a Politics of 'American' Criticism." In *In the Wake of Theory.* Hanover, N.H.: Wesleyan University Press, 1992.

Brecht, Bertolt. "On the Use of Music in an Epic Theatre." In *Brecht on Theatre: The Development of an Aesthetic.* Ed. and trans. John Wilett. New York: Hill and Wang, 1964.

Brodhead, Richard H. *Hawthorne, Melville, and the Novel.* Chicago: University of Chicago Press, 1976.

———, ed. *New Essays on "Moby-Dick; or, The Whale."* Cambridge: Cambridge University Press, 1986.

Brodtkorb, Paul, Jr. *Ishmael's White World: A Phenomenological Reading of "Moby-Dick."* New Haven: Yale University Press, 1965.

Brooks, Cleanth. "The Language of Paradox." In *The Well Wrought Urn: Studies in the Structure of Poetry.* New York: Harcourt, Brace, 1947.

———. *Modern Poetry and the Tradition.* New York: Oxford University Press, 1964.

Caputo, Philip. *A Rumor of War.* New York: Ballantine, 1977.

Carafiol, Peter C. "In Dubious Battle: American Literary Scholarship and Poststructuralist Theory." Intro. to *The American Renaissance: New Dimensions.* Ed. Harry R. Garvin and Peter C. Carafiol. Lewisburg, Pa.: Bucknell University Press, 1983.

Cervantes. *Don Quixote*. Trans. J. M. Cohen. Hammondsworth, England: Penguin Books, 1950.

Cesarano, James, Jr. "The Emergence of *Moby-Dick*: An Archaeology of Its Critical Value." Ph.D. dissertation. State University of New York at Binghamton, 1984.

Chase, Richard. *The American Novel and Its Tradition*. Garden City, N.Y.: Doubleday, 1957.

————. *Herman Melville: A Critical Study*. New York: Macmillan, 1949.

Chomsky, Noam. *Deterring Democracy*. New York: Hill and Wang, 1992.

Chow, Rey. "Rereading Mandarin Ducks and Butterflies: A Response to the 'Postmodern Condition.'" *Cultural Critique*, vol. 5 (1986), pp. 69–93.

Coleridge, Samuel Taylor. *The Complete Works*, vol. 3: *Biographia Literaria*. Ed. W. T. G. Shedd. New York: Harper, 1860.

Crews, Frederick. *The Critics Bear It Away: American Fiction and the Academy*. New York: Random House, 1992.

————. Foreword. In *After Poststructuralism: Interdisciplinarity and Literary Theory*. Ed. Nancy Easterlin and Barbara Riebling. Evanston, Ill.: Northwestern University Press, 1993.

————. "Whose American Renaissance?" In *The Critics Bear It Away*. Originally published in *New York Review of Books*, vol. 35, no. 16 (October 27, 1988).

Derrida, Jacques. "The Ends of Man." In *Margins of Philosophy*. Trans. Alan Bass. Chicago: University of Chicago Press, 1982.

————. "Force and Signification." In *Writing and Difference*. Trans. Alan Bass. Chicago: University of Chicago Press, 1978.

————. "Structure, Sign, and Play in the Discourse of the Human Sciences." In *Writing and Difference*. Trans. Alan Bass. Chicago: University of Chicago Press, 1978.

Dimock, Wai-chee. "Blaming the Victim." In *Empire for Liberty: Melville and the Poetics of Individualism*. Princeton: Princeton University Press, 1989.

————. "Nation, Self, and Personification." In *Empire for Liberty: Melville and the Poetics of Individualism*. Princeton: Princeton University Press, 1989.

Drinnon, Richard. *Facing West: The Metaphysics of Indian-Hating and Empire-Building*. Minneapolis: University of Minnesota Press, 1980.

Dryden, Edgar. "The Entangled Text: Melville's *Pierre* and the Problem of Reading." *boundary 2*, vol. 7, no. 1 (Spring 1979), pp. 145–73.

————. *Melville's Thematics of Form: The Great Art of Telling the Truth*. Baltimore: Johns Hopkins University Press, 1968.

————. "Writer as Reader: An American Story." *boundary 2*, vol. 8 (Fall 1979), pp. 189–95.

D'Souza, Dinesh. *Illiberal Education: The Politics of Race and Sex on Campus*. New York: Free Press, 1991.

During, Simon. "Postmodernism or Postcolonialism Today." *Textual Practice*, vol. 1 (1987), pp. 32–47.

Dussel, Henrique. "Eurocentrism and Modernity: Introduction to the Frankfurt Lectures." In *The Postmodern Debate in Latin America,* special issue of *boundary 2.* Ed. John Beverley and José Oviedo, vol. 20 (Fall 1993), pp. 65–76.

——. *Philosophy of Liberation.* Trans. Aquilina Martinez and Christine Morkovsky. Maryknoll, N.Y.: Orbis Books, 1985.

Duyckinck, Evert A. "Melville's *Moby-Dick; or, The Whale.*" *Literary World,* November 22, 1851. Reprinted in Herman Melville, *Moby-Dick,* ed. Harrison Hayford and Herschel Parker. New York: W. W. Norton, 1967.

Eagleton, Terry. "The Rise of English." In *Literary Theory: An Introduction.* Minneapolis: University of Minnesota Press, 1983.

Eliot, T. S. *Four Quartets.* In *Complete Poems and Plays, 1909–1950.* New York: Harcourt, Brace and World, 1952.

——. "Hamlet and His Problems." In *Selected Essays.* New York: Harcourt, Brace, 1950.

——. *Murder in the Cathedral.* In *Complete Poems and Plays, 1909–1950.* New York: Harcourt, Brace and World, 1952.

——. "*Ulysses,* Order, and Myth." In *Selected Prose.* Ed. Frank Kermode. New York: Harcourt, Brace, Jovanovich, 1975.

Emerson, Ralph Waldo. "The American Scholar." In *The Collected Works.* Ed. Robert C. Spiller and Alfred R. Ferguson. Cambridge, Mass.: Harvard University Press, 1971.

——. "Nature." In *The Complete Works.* Ed. Edward Waldo Emerson. Centenary edition, 12 vols. Boston: Houghton Mifflin, 1903–4.

Escoubas, Éliane. "Heidegger, la question romaine, la question impériale. Autour du 'Tournant.'" In *Heidegger: Questions ouvertes.* Ed. Éliane Escoubas. Paris: Éditions Osiris, 1988.

Fielding, Henry. *Tom Jones.* Ed. Sheridan Baker. New York: W. W. Norton, 1973.

FitzGerald, Frances. *Fire in the Lake: The Vietnamese and the Americans in Vietnam.* New York: Vintage Books, 1989.

Foucault, Michel. *The Archaeology of Knowledge.* Trans. A. H. Sheridan Smith. London: Tavistock, 1972.

——. *The Birth of the Clinic.* Trans. A. Sheridan Smith. New York: Vintage Books, 1975.

——. *Discipline and Punish: The Birth of the Prison.* Trans. Alan Sheridan. New York: Pantheon Books, 1977.

——. *The History of Sexuality.* Vol. 1: *An Introduction.* Trans. Robert Hurley. New York: Pantheon, 1978.

——. "Intellectuals and Power: A Conversation between Michel Foucault and Gilles Deleuze." In *Language, Counter-Memory, Practice: Selected Essays and Interviews.* Ed. Donald Bouchard, trans. Donald Bouchard and Sherry Simon. Ithaca, N.Y.: Cornell University Press, 1977.

——. "The Life of Infamous Men." In *Power, Truth, Strategy.* Ed. Meaghan Morris and Paul Patton, trans. Paul Foss and Meaghan Morris. Sydney, Australia: Feral Publications, 1979.

————. *Madness and Civilization: A History of Insanity in the Age of Reason*. Trans. Richard Howard. New York: Vintage Books, 1988.

————. "Nietzsche, Genealogy, History." In *Language, Counter-Memory, Practice: Selected Essays and Interviews*. Ed. Donald F. Bouchard, trans. Donald F. Bouchard and Sherry Simon. Ithaca, N.Y.: Cornell University Press, 1977.

————. *The Order of Things: An Archaeology of the Human Sciences*. New York: Vintage Books, 1973.

————. "Revolutionary Action: 'Until Now.'" In *Language, Counter-Memory, Practice: Selected Essays and Interviews*. Ed. Donald Bouchard, trans. Donald Bouchard and Sherry Simon. Ithaca, N.Y.: Cornell University Press, 1977.

————. "What Is an Author?" In *Language, Counter-Memory, Practice: Selected Essays and Interviews*. Ed. Donald F. Bouchard, trans. Donald F. Bouchard and Sherry Simon. Ithaca, N.Y.: Cornell University Press, 1977.

————, ed. *Herculine Barbin: Being the Recently Discovered Memoirs of a Nineteenth-Century Hermaphrodite*. Trans. Richard McDougall. New York: Pantheon, 1980.

————, ed. *I, Pierre Rivière, Having Slaughtered My Mother, My Sister, and My Brother: A Case of Parricide in the 19th Century*. Trans. Frank Jellinek. New York: Random House, 1975.

Frank, Joseph. "Spatial Form in Modern Literature." In *Sewanee Review* 53 (Spring, Summer, Autumn, 1945). Reprinted in *The Widening Gyre; Crisis and Mastery in Modern Literature*. New Brunswick, N.J.: Rutgers University Press, 1963.

————. "Spatial Form: An Answer to the Critics." *Critical Inquiry*, vol. 4, no. 2 (Winter 1977), pp. 231–52.

Fukuyama, Francis. "The End of History." *The National Interest*, vol. 16 (Summer 1989), pp. 2–18.

————. *The End of History and the Last Man*. New York: Free Press, 1992.

Gadamer, Hans-Georg. *Truth and Method*. New York: Seabury Press, 1975.

Gasché, Rodolphe. "The Scene of Writing: A Deferred Outset." *Glyph* 1. Baltimore: Johns Hopkins University Press, 1977.

Graff, Gerald. *Professing Literature: An Institutional History*. Chicago: University of Chicago Press, 1987.

Gramsci, Antonio. *Selections from the Prison Notebooks*. Ed. and trans. Quintin Hoare and Geoffrey Nowell Smith. New York: International Publishers, 1971.

Hegel, G. W. F. *Phenomenology of Spirit*. Oxford: Oxford University Press, 1977.

Heidegger, Martin. *An Introduction to Metaphysics*. Trans. Ralph Manheim. New Haven: Yale University Press, 1959.

————. *Being and Time*. Trans. John Macquarrie and Edward Robinson. New York: Harper and Row, 1962.

————. *Discourse on Thinking*. Trans. John M. Anderson and E. Hans Freund. New York: Harper and Row, 1966.

————. "Poetically Man Dwells." In *Poetry, Language, Thought*. Trans. Alfred Hofstadter. New York: Harper and Row, 1971.

———. "Building Dwelling Thinking." In *Poetry, Language, Thought*. Trans. Alfred Hofstadter. New York: Harper and Row, 1971.

———. *Early Greek Thinking*. Trans. David Farrell Krell and Frank A. Capuzzi. New York: Harper and Row, 1975.

———. "On the Essence of Truth." In *Basic Writings*. Ed. David Farrell Krell. New York: Harper and Row, 1977.

———. "The End of Philosophy and the Task of Thinking." In *Basic Writings*. Ed. David Farrell Krell. New York: Harper and Row, 1977.

———. "Who is Nietzsche's Zarathustra?" In *The New Nietzsche: Contemporary Styles of Interpretation*. Ed. David B. Allison. New York: Dell, 1977.

———. "The Origins of the Work of Art." *Basic Writings*. Ed. David Farrell Krell. New York: Harper and Row, 1977.

———. *Basic Writings*. Ed. David Farrell Krell. New York: Harper and Row, 1977.

———. "The Question Concerning Technology." In *The Question Concerning Technology and Other Essays*. Trans. William Lovitt. New York: Harper and Row, 1977.

———. *Parmenides*. Translated by André Schuwer and Richard Rojcewicz. Bloomington: University of Indiana Press, 1992.

Heilman, Robert. *This Great Stage: Image and Structure in "King Lear."* Baton Rouge: Louisiana University Press, 1948.

Hellman, John. *American Myth and the Legacy of Vietnam*. New York: Columbia University Press, 1986.

Herr, Michael. *Dispatches*. New York: Avon Books, 1978.

Hirsch, E. D. *Cultural Literacy: What Every American Needs to Know*. Boston: Houghton Mifflin, 1982.

Homer. *The Odyssey*. Trans. and ed. Albert Cook. Norton Critical edition. New York: W. W. Norton, 1974.

Howe, Susan. *The Birth-Mark: Unsettling the Wilderness in American Literary History*. Hanover, N.H.: Wesleyan University Press, 1993.

James, C. L. R. *Mariners, Renegades and Castaways: The Story of Herman Melville and the World We Live In*. Detroit: Bewick Editions, 1978.

James, Henry. *Preface to "The Tragic Muse."* New York: Charles Scribner's Sons, 1922.

Jameson, Fredric. *Postmodernism, or, The Cultural Logic of Late Capitalism*. Durham, N.C.: Duke University Press, 1991.

Johnson, Barbara. "Melville's Fist: The Execution of *Billy Budd*." In *The Critical Difference: Essays in the Contemporary Rhetoric of Reading*. Baltimore: Johns Hopkins University Press, 1980.

Joyce, James. *A Portrait of the Artist as a Young Man*. Ed. Chester G. Anderson. New York: Viking, 1968.

Keats, John. *The Letters of John Keats*. Ed. Hyder Edward Rollins. Cambridge, Mass.: Harvard University Press, 1958.

Kierkegaard, Søren. *Repetition: An Essay in Experimental Psychology*. Trans. Walter Lowrie. New York: Harper and Row, 1864.

Kimball, Roger. *Tenured Radicals: How Politics Has Corrupted Our Higher Education*. New York: Harper and Row, 1990.

Knapp, Steven, and Walter Benn Michaels. "Against Theory." In *Against Theory: Literary Studies and the New Pragmatism*. Ed. W. J. T. Mitchell. Chicago: University of Chicago Press, 1985.

Krepinevich, Andrew F., Jr. *The Army and Vietnam*. Baltimore: Johns Hopkins University Press, 1988.

Laclau, Ernesto, and Chantal Mouffe. *Hegemony and Socialist Strategy: Towards a Radical Democratic Politics*. London: Verso, 1985.

Lansdale, Edward G. *In the Midst of Wars: An American's Mission to Southeast Asia*. New York: Harper and Row, 1972.

Lentricchia, Frank. *Ariel and the Police: Michel Foucault, William James, Wallace Stevens*. Madison: University of Wisconsin Press, 1988.

Lewis, R. W. B. *The American Adam: Innocence, Tragedy, and Tradition in the Nineteenth Century*. Chicago: University of Chicago Press, 1955.

Lévi-Strauss, Claude. *The Savage Mind*. Chicago: University of Chicago Press, 1966.

Lubbock, Percy. *The Craft of Fiction*. New York: Charles Scribner's Sons, 1929.

Lyotard, Jean-François. *The Postmodern Condition: A Report on Knowledge*. Trans. Geoff Bennington and Brian Massumi. Minneapolis: University of Minnesota Press, 1984.

Macomber, W. B. *The Anatomy of Disillusion: Martin Heidegger's Notion of Truth*. Evanston, Ill.: Northwestern University Press, 1967.

Markel, Julian. *Melville and the Politics of Identity: From "King Lear" to "Moby-Dick."* Urbana: University of Illinois Press, 1993.

Marx, Leo. "Pastoralism in America." In *Ideology and Classical American Literature*. Ed. Sacvan Bercovitch and Myra Jehlen. Cambridge: Cambridge University Press, 1986.

Mather, Cotton. *Magnalia Christi Americana*. Ed. Kenneth B. Murdoch with Elizabeth W. Miller. Cambridge, Mass.: Harvard University Press, 1977.

Matthiessen, F. O. *American Renaissance: Art and Expression in the Age of Emerson and Whitman*. London: Oxford University Press, 1941.

Melville, Herman. "Bartleby, the Scrivener." In *The Piazza Tales and Other Prose Pieces, 1839–1860*. Ed. Harrison Hayford, Alma A. MacDougall, G. Thomas Tanselle, and others. Evanston, Ill.: Northwestern University Press and the Newberry Library, 1987.

———. *The Confidence-Man: His Masquerade*. Ed. Harrison Hayford, Hershel Parker, and G. Thomas Tanselle. Evanston, Ill.: Northwestern University Press and the Newberry Library, 1984.

———. *Israel Potter: His Fifty Years of Exile*. Ed. Harrison Hayford, Hershel Parker, and G. Thomas Tanselle. Evanston, Ill.: Northwestern University Press and the Newberry Library, 1982.

———. *The Letters of Herman Melville*. Ed. Merrill R. Davis and William Gilman. New Haven: Yale University Press, 1960.

————. *Moby-Dick.* Ed. Harrison Hayford and Hershel Parker. Norton Critical Edition. New York: W. W. Norton, 1967.

————. *Moby-Dick.* Ed. Harrison Hayford, Hershel Parker, and G. Thomas Tanselle. Evanston, Ill.: Northwestern University Press and the Newberry Library, 1988.

————. *Pierre; or, The Ambiguities.* Ed. Harrison Hayford, Hershel Parker, and G. Thomas Tanselle. Evanston, Ill.: Northwestern University Press and Newberry Library, 1971.

————. *Redburn: His First Voyage.* Ed. Harrison Hayford, Hershel Parker, and G. Thomas Tanselle. Evanston, Ill.: Northwestern University Press and Newberry Library, 1969.

————. *White-Jacket; or, The World in a Man-of-War.* Ed. Harrison Hayford, Hershel Parker, and G. Thomas Tanselle. Evanston, Ill.: Northwestern University Press and Newberry Library, 1970.

Michaels, Walter Benn. *The Gold Standard and the Logic of Naturalism.* Berkeley: University of California Press, 1987.

Michaels, Walter Benn, and Donald E. Pease, eds. *The American Renaissance Reconsidered: Selected Papers from the English Institute, 1982–1983.* Baltimore: Johns Hopkins University Press, 1985.

Milton, John. *Areopagitica.* Ed. with commentary by Sir Richard C. Jebb. Cambridge: Cambridge University Press, 1918.

Mumford, Lewis. *The Golden Day: A Study of American Experience and Culture.* New York: Boni and Liveright, 1926.

————. In *Herman Melville.* New York: Harcourt, Brace, 1929.

Murdoch, Kenneth B. "The *Magnalia.*" In Cotton Mather, *Magnalia Christi Americana,* ed. Kenneth B. Murdoch with Elizabeth W. Miller. Cambridge, Mass.: Harvard University Press, 1977.

Murray, Henry. "In Nomine Diaboli." In *Moby-Dick: Centennial Essays.* Ed. Tyrus Hillway and Luther S. Mansfield. Dallas: Southern Methodist University, 1953.

Myers, Henry Alonzo. "The Tragic Meaning of *Moby-Dick.*" In *Tragedy: A View of Life.* Ithaca: Cornell University Press, 1956.

Nietzsche, Friedrich. *"On the Genealogy of Morals" and "Ecce Homo."* Trans. Walter Kaufmann. New York: Vintage Books, 1969.

————. *Thus Spoke Zarathustra.* Trans. R. J. Hollingdale. Hammondsworth, England: Penguin Books, 1969.

O'Brien, Tim. *Going after Cacciato.* New York: Delta/Seymour Lawrence, 1989.

O'Hara, Daniel T. *Lionel Trilling: The Work of Liberation.* Madison: University of Wisconsin Press, 1988.

Olson, Charles. *Call Me Ishmael: A Study of Melville.* San Francisco: City Lights Books, 1947.

————. "Human Universe." In *Human Universe and Other Essays.* Ed. Donald Allen. New York: Grove Press, 1967.

————. "Equal, That Is, to the Real Itself." In *Human Universe and Other Essays.* Ed. Donald Allen. New York: Grove Press, 1967.

―――. "Projective Verse." *Selected Writings.* Ed. Robert Creeley. New York: New Directions, 1966.

―――. *The Maximus Poems.* Ed. George F. Butterick. Berkeley: University of California Press, 1983.

―――. *The Special View of History.* Ed. Ann Charters. Berkeley: Oyez, 1970.

Pease, Donald. "Emerson, *Nature,* and the Sovereignty of Influence." *boundary 2,* vol. 8 (Spring 1980), 43–74.

―――. "*Moby-Dick* and the Cold War." In *The American Renaissance Reconsidered: Selected Papers from the English Institute, 1982–1983.* Ed. Walter Benn Michaels and Donald E. Pease. Baltimore: Johns Hopkins University Press, 1985.

―――. "New Americanists: Revisionist Interventions into the Canon." In *New Americanists: Revisionist Interventions into the Canon* 1. Special issue of *boundary 2,* vol. 17, no. 1 (Spring 1990), pp. 1–37.

―――. "Visionary Compacts and the Cold War Consensus." [and other chapters, named and unnamed] In *Visionary Compacts: American Renaissance Writings in Cultural Context.* Madison: University of Wisconsin Press, 1987.

Pope, Alexander. *Selected Poetry and Prose.* Ed. William Wimsatt, Jr. New York: Rinehart, 1951.

Pound, Ezra. *The Cantos.* New York: New Directions, 1970.

Pratt, Mary Louise. *Imperial Eyes: Travel Writing and Transculturation.* London: Routledge, 1992.

Pynchon, Thomas. *The Crying of Lot 49.* 1966; New York: Harper and Row, 1990.

―――. *Gravity's Rainbow.* New York: Viking Press, 1973.

Rapaport, Herman. "Vietnam: The Thousand Plateaus." In *The 60s without Apology.* Ed. Sohnya Sayres, Anders Stephanson, Stanley Aronowitz, and Fredric Jameson. Minneapolis: University of Minnesota Press, in cooperation with *Social Text,* 1984.

Reising, Russell. *The Unusable Past: Theory and the Study of American Literature.* New York: Methuen, 1986.

Reynolds, David S. *Beneath the American Renaissance: The Subversive Imagination in the Age of Emerson and Melville.* Cambridge, Mass.: Harvard University Press, 1988.

Richards, I. A. *Principles of Literary Criticism.* 2d ed. London: Routledge and Kegan Paul, 1926.

Riddel, Joseph N. "Decentering the Image: The 'Project' of 'American' Poetics?" In *The Problems of Reading in Contemporary American Criticism.* Special issue of *boundary 2,* vol. 8 (Fall 1979), pp. 165–66. Reprinted in *The Question of Textuality: Strategies of Reading in Contemporary American Criticism.* Bloomington: University of Indiana Press, 1982.

Robbe-Grillet, Alain. "Nature, Humanism, Tragedy." In *For a New Novel: Essays on Fiction.* Trans. Richard Howard. New York: Grove Press, 1965.

Rogin, Michael Paul. *Subversive Genealogy: The Politics and Art of Herman Melville.* Berkeley: University of California Press, 1985.

Rosovsky, Henry. "Report on the Core Curriculum." Cambridge, Mass.: Faculty of Arts and Sciences of Harvard University, February 15, 1978.

Rothman, David. *The Discovery of the Asylum: Social Order and Disorder in the New Republic.* 1971; rev. ed. Boston: Little, Brown, 1990.

Royster, Paul. "Melville's Economy of Language." In *Ideology and Classic American Literature.* Ed. Sacvan Bercovitch and Myra Jehlen. Cambridge: Cambridge University Press, 1986.

Said, Edward W. *Culture and Imperialism.* New York: Alfred A. Knopf, 1993.

————. "Reflections on American Literary 'Left' Criticism." *boundary* 2, vol. 13 (Fall 1979), pp. 26–27.

————. "Travelling Theory." In *The World, the Text, and the Critic.* Cambridge, Mass.: Harvard University Press, 1983.

Sartre, Jean-Paul. *Nausea.* Trans. Lloyd Alexander. New York: New Directions, 1959.

Seltzer, Mark. "*The Princess Casamassima*: Realism and the Fantasy of Surveillance." In *American Realism: New Essays.* Ed. Eric Sundquist. Baltimore: Johns Hopkins University Press, 1982. Reprinted in Seltzer, *Henry James: The Art of Power.* Ithaca, N.Y.: Cornell University Press, 1984.

Sewall, Richard. "*Moby-Dick.*" In *The Vision of Tragedy.* New ed. New Haven: Yale University Press, 1980.

Shakespeare, William. *King Lear.* In *Works.* New York: Oxford University Press, 1938.

Slotkin, Richard. *Regeneration through Violence: The Mythology of the American Frontier, 1600–1860.* Middleton, Conn.: Wesleyan University Press, 1973.

————. *The Fatal Environment: The Myth of the Frontier in the Age of Industrialization, 1800–1890.* New York: Atheneum, 1985.

Smith, Henry Nash. "The Image of Society in *Moby-Dick.*" In *Moby-Dick: Centennial Essays.* Ed. Tyrus Hillway and Luther S. Mansfield. Dallas: Southern Methodist University Press, 1953.

————. *Virgin Land: The American West as Symbol and Myth.* New York: Random House, 1961.

Smitten, Jeffrey R. and Ann Daghistany, eds. *Spatial Form in Narrative.* Ithaca, N.Y.: Cornell University Press, 1981.

Son, Truong. "American Failure." *Vietnamese Studies*, vol. 20. Ed. Nguyen Khav Vien. Hanoi: Government of North Vietnam, December 1968.

Spanos, William V. "Culture and Colonization: The Imperial Imperatives of the Centered Circle." In *Nationalism(s), Culture and the Shape of the World.* Eds. Henry Schwarz and Richard Dienst, Politics and Culture, vol. 4. Boulder, Co.: Westview Press, 1995.

————. "The De-struction of Form in Postmodern American Poetry: The Examples of Charles Olson and Robert Creeley." *Amerikastudien*, vol. 25, no. 4 (1981), pp. 375–404.

————. "The Detective and the Boundary: Some Notes on the Postmodern Literary Imagination." *boundary* 2, vol. 1, no. 3 (Fall 1972), pp. 1163–65. Reprinted in *Repetitions.*

————. *The End of Education: Toward Posthumanism.* Minneapolis: University of Minnesota Press, 1993.

———. *Heidegger and Criticism: Retrieving the Cultural Politics of Destruction*. Minneapolis: University of Minnesota Press, 1993.

———. "Hermeneutics and Memory: Destroying T. S. Eliot's *Four Quartets*." *Genre*, vol. 10 (Winter 1978), pp. 523–73.

———. *Repetitions: The Postmodern Occasion in Literature and Culture*. Baton Rouge: Louisiana State University Press, 1987.

———. "The Un-naming of the Beasts: The Postmodernity of Sartre's *La Nausée*." *Criticism*, vol. 20, no. 3 (Summer 1978), pp. 223–80. Reprinted in *Repetitions*.

———. "The Uses and Abuses of Certainty: Introduction." In *On Humanism and the University*. Special issue of *boundary 2*, vols. 12/13 (Spring/Fall 1984), pp. 1–17.

———. *The Christian Tradition in Modern British Verse Drama: The Poetics of Sacramental Time*. New Brunswick, N.J.: Rutgers University Press, 1967.

Spengemann, William C. *The Adventurous Muse: The Poetics of American Fiction, 1789–1900*. New Haven: Yale University Press, 1977.

Spurr, David. *The Rhetoric of Empire: Colonial Discourse in Journalism, Travel Writing, and Imperial Administration*. Durham, N.C.: Duke University Press, 1993.

Stearns, Harold, ed. *Civilization in the United States: An Inquiry by Thirty Americans*. New York: Harcourt, Brace, 1922.

Stern, Milton. *The Fine Hammered Steel of Herman Melville*. Urbana: University of Illinois Press, 1957.

Sterne, Laurence. *The Life and Opinions of Tristram Shandy, Gentleman*. Ed. Howard Anderson 1767; New York: W. W. Norton, 1980.

Sussman, Henry. "The Deconstructor as Politician: Melville's *Confidence-Man*." *Glyph* 4. Baltimore: Johns Hopkins University Press, 1980.

Trilling, Lionel. In *The Liberal Imagination: Essays on Literature and Society*. New York: Harcourt Brace Jovanovich, 1949.

———. *Matthew Arnold*. New York: Meridian, 1969.

Weber, Max. *The Protestant Ethic and the Spirit of Capitalism*. Trans. Talcott Parsons. New York: Charles Scribner's Sons, 1958.

Whitney, Geoffrey. *A Choice of Emblems*. Leiden, 1556.

Williams, Raymond. *Marxism and Literature*. New York: Oxford University Press, 1977.

Wilson, Rob. *American Sublime: The Genealogy of a Poetic Genre*. Madison: University of Wisconsin Press, 1991.

Wimsatt, W. K., and Cleanth Brooks. *Literary Criticism: A Short History*. New York: Vintage Books, 1967.

INDEX

Abrams, M. H.: on canon formation, 283n

Acker, Kathy, 182, 246; *Blood and Guts in High School*, 162

Adams, Henry, 70, 286; Sacvan Bercovitch on, 338

Adorno, Theodor, 273

Althusser, Louis, 3, 21, 252; anti-Hegelianism of, 323n; on ideological state apparatuses, 346n; on the problematic, 279–280n

American Adam, 70, 71, 77–78, 110, 112, 121, 144–147, 161, 173, 179–180, 183, 197–198, 221–222, 246, 271, 276–277; Ahab as, 122–123, 137–138, 184, 246, 267–269; circular journey of, 145–146; and discipline, 185; and naming, 125–127, 137, 140, 187–188; and the saving remnant, 152–153, 221, 287n. See also *Moby-Dick*

American canon, 3, 161, 172, 174, 267; and monumental history, 247–249, 251–252; and the promise/fulfillment structure, 79–80, 88–92, 223–224

American Cultural Memory, 28–29, 248–249

American exceptionalism, 231–233, 249, 265–266, 268, 277–278, 308–309n, 337n

American Jeremiad, 19, 28, 33, 38, 89, 91, 96–106, 231–232, 245; and imperialism, 99, 222, 265. *See also* American Puritans; Sacvan Bercovitch; Figural interpretation

American Puritans, 14–16, 19–21; and capitalism, 185–224, 205–225, 311n; and discipline, 204; and imperialism, 98, 309n, 311n; and the "errand in the wilderness," 2, 91, 97–98, 107, 125, 154, 198, 204, 221, 256, 265, 271, 281n; and figural interpretation, 88–89, 91, 93, 96–99, 110, 125, 132, 191, 223, 226, 284n; and the Old World, 308–309; as "saving remnant," 152–153, 223, 226, 309n; narrative imperatives of, 79; and panoptic gaze, 101–104, 125–127, 173; and preterition, 155, 164–166, 208–209, 227; and providential history, 88–89, 112, 155, 225, 231. *See also* American Adam; American Jeremiad; Figural interpretation

American Renaissance, 31, 32, 37–38, 45, 113, 127, 159, 223, 231, 235, 236. *See also* F. O. Matthiessen

Anaximander, 282–283n

Anderson, Quentin: *The Imperial Self*, 23

Arac, Jonathan, 31

Aristotle, 168, 282n; on tragedy, 51, 147

Arnold, Dennis A., 311n

Arnold, Matthew: *Culture and Anarchy*, 18; humanism and, 17–18; on deliverance, 48, 51, 58; Melville revival and, 21, 23, 44, 48–49, 56, 57; "On the Modern Element in Modern Literature," 293n

Auden, W. H.: "New Year Letter," 298n
Auerbach, Erich: on figural interpretation, 96–97
Auster, Paul, 182

Babbitt, Irving, 181, 328n
Bakhtin, Mikhail, 60, 85, 192, 314n
Balzac, Honore de, 335n
Baraka, Amiri, 181
Barnes, Djuna: *Nightwood*, 327n
Barth, John, 246, 315n
Barthelme, Donald, 182, 246
Barthes, Roland: on tragedy, 60
Bate, Walter Jackson, 3, 28; and saving remnant, 324n
Baxter, Richard: and Puritan work ethic, 101, 208–209
Beckett, Samuel: *Watt*, 49, 63, 310n
Being: as indissoluble continuum, 25–26, 45, 73, 113, 187–190, 225, 226–232, 244–245, 269–270, 291–282n. *See also* Martin Heidegger
Benjamin, Walter: "Theses on the Philosophy of History," 1, 223
Bennett, William, 28
Bentham, Jeremy: and the Panopticon, 102–104, 213
Bercovitch, Sacvan, 23, 24, 28, 37, 222, 229, 275, 280n, 288n; and American exceptionalism, 308–309n; on "dissensus," 41, 274, 351n; and figural interpretation, 97–98; on *Moby-Dick* as anti-jeremiad, 113–114, 230–231, 338n. *See also* American Puritans; Figural interpretation
Bergson, Henri: and spatial form, 327n
Bewley, Marcus: *The Eccentric Design*, 23
Bezanson, Walter, 73; on Ishmael as self-present self, 79, 80, 115, 148, 302n. *See also* Old Americanists
Bird, Robert Montgomery, 2
Blackmur, R. P., 74, 90, 233, 299n, 301n, 328n; as Jamesian critic, 296n; on Melville's influence, 314n; and New Critical reading of *Moby-Dick*, 58–60, 80–82, 112, 167, 180–181. *See also* New Critics
Blake, William, 232

Bloom, Allan, 3, 28
Bonhoeffer, Dietrich, 339n
Boone, Daniel, 2
Booth, Wayne, 3
Borges, Jorge Luis, 195, 196
Bové, Paul: on the New Americanists, 24–25, 281n, 288n, 337n, 338n
Brecht, Bertolt, 40, 42, 60; "On the Use of Music in an Epic Theatre," 296n
Brodhead, Richard H., 306n, 333–334n
Brodtkorb, Paul, Jr.: on Ahab as Kierkegaardian hero, 137; on Father Mapple's sermon, 312n; on Ishmael's name, 300–301n
Bronson, Orestes, 145
Brooks, Cleanth, 341n; on metaphysical poetry, 294n; and Modernist poetics, 325n; on I. A. Richards, 294–295n. *See also* New Critics
Brooks, Van Wyck, 16
Bultmann, Rudolph, 298n, 339n
Bushnell, Horace, 145, 146
Byron, Lord Gordon, 232

Cameron, Sharon, 23
Camus, Albert: *The Fall*, 298n
Canon formation, 2–12
Caputo, Philip: *A Rumor of War*, 260–261
Carafoil, Peter, 287n
Carlyle, Thomas, 14, 64
Carson, Kit, 2
Cervantes, Miguel de, 246; *Don Quixote*, 11; and the enchanter as principle of last resort, 108, 234, 314n
Cesarano, James, 284n, 285n
Chase, Richard, 31, 111, 167, 179, 180, 224, 235; *The American Novel and Its Tradition*, 23; and American romance, 131, 239; on Bulkington, 154–155. *See also* Old Americanists; Romance
Cheney, Lynne, 28, 289n
Chow, Rey, 346n
Circle, centered: and American literary history, 146; and de-centering, 142–144, 151–156, 160, 167, 178–179, 191, 232, 248–249, 261–263, 265–266, 271–272, 276–278; and em-

pire, 174, 221–222, 246; and fictional form, 121, 167–174; as figure of domination, 120; and logocentrism, 5; and periphery, 9–10, 258; and tragic vision, 53–54; and the Vietnam War, 262; as will to power, 60, 114–121, 147, 262–266. *See also* Metaphysics; Panopticism; Spatialization; Vision

Cold War: end of, 3, 27–28, 271–272, 275–278, 311n; and New Americanists, 31–36, 131, 251, 275; and New World Order, 30, 35, 251–252, 275–278; as ontological scenario, 37; and saving remnant, 152–153; and Vietnam, 26–27, 256, 267. *See also* New World Order

Cole, Thomas, 104–105, 312n

Coleridge, Samuel Taylor, 51, 89; and the esemplastic imagination, 44–45, 130, 160, 235–236, 341n; influence on American Renaissance, 293n; Keats on, 159; "The Rime of the Ancient Mariner," 93, 324n. *See also* Negative capability

Conrad, Joseph: *The Heart of Darkness*, 343n

Cooper, James Fenimore, 2, 146, 151, 334n; *The Deerslayer*, 79; *The Pioneers*, 153

Coover, Robert, 246: *The Public Burning*, 162, 184

Coppola, Francis Ford: *Apocalypse Now*, 343n, 348n

Cosa, Juan de la, 332–333n

Creeley, Robert, 142, 181, 246

Crews, Frederick, 4, 28, 36

Crockett, Davy, 2

Dana, Richard Henry, Jr.: *Two Years before the Mast*, 12

Danforth, Samuel: *Brief Recognition of New England's Errand into the Wilderness*, 97–98. *See also* American Puritans; Sacvan Bercovitch; Figural interpretation

Dante: *The Divine Comedy*, 79

Davies, Sir John, 291

Deconstruction: political limitations of, 28, 313–314n, 339–341n. *See also* Jacques Derrida; Martin Heidegger

Deleuze, Gilles, 261–262, 273

DeLillo, Don, 182, 246, 349n

Del Vecchio, John M.: *The Thirteenth Valley*, 348n

De Man, Paul, 279n

Derrida, Jacques: on canon formation, 283–284; and the "center elsewhere," 19, 51, 52, 55, 124, 132, 188, 198, 255, 307–308n; and deconstruction, xi, 11, 110, 242–243; and destruction, 38, 46; and *differance*, 78, 234, 240, 269, 339n; on Dionysian "force," 53, 245, 295n, 316n; and errancy, 104; on Heidegger, 170; and ontological decentering, 45, 151; on supplementarity, 129, 176, 195; *See also* Deconstruction; Martin Heidegger

Diderot, 246

Dimock, Wai-chee, 23, 38, 73, 275; on Melville's imperialism, 64, 73, 88, 101, 111, 114, 222, 229–230, 232, 290–291n, 292–293n, 330n, 336n, 345n. *See also* New Americanists

Doctorow, E. L., 182, 315n

Donne, John, 228

Dorn, Edward, 181, 246

Dreiser, Theodore, 163, 236, 237

Drinnon, Richard: *Facing West*, 344n

Dryden, Edgar, 28, 72, 239, 300–301n

D'Souza, Dinesh, 4, 28

During, Simon, 346n

Dussel, Henrique, 264

Duyckink, Evert, 13–14, 73, 306n

Eagleton, Terry, 18

Edwards, Jonathan, 68

Eliot, T. S., 44, 168, 301n; *The Family Reunion*, 298n; *Four Quartets*, 143; *Murder in the Cathedral*, 78; and the objective correlative, 131, 319–320n; *Sweeney Agonistes*, 298n; "The Waste Land," 327n

Elkin, Stanley, 182, 246

Emerson, Ralph Waldo, 2, 14, 31, 75, 146, 151, 159, 161, 186, 235, 341n; and the "Emersonian" perspective, 120–121, 125–127, 130, 145, 160, 186, 235, 242, 317–318n; and optimism, 60, 64, 110, 198; and representation, 172, 191; and self-reliance, 17, 35, 148, 204, 226

Enlightenment: and disciplinary practice, 25

Errancy, 85–87, 112–113, 132, 174, 183, 228; words and, 156, 176–177. *See also* Martin Heidegger; Herman Melville; *Moby-Dick*

Euripides, 246

Faulkner, William, 157; *The Bear*, 161

Feidelson, Charles, 31, 131, 239, 341n; *Symbolism and American Literature*, 32

Fiedler, Leslie, 167, 180; *Love and Death in the American Love*, 23

Fielding, Henry, on narrative structure, 99, 306–307n; *Tom Jones*, 153

Figural interpretation, 96–99; and the American Jeremiad, 96–106; and difference, 107; and metaphysical vision, 66–67; Puritan version of, 68. *See also* American Jeremiad; Sacvan Bercovitch; Metaphysics

Fitzgerald, F. Scott: *The Great Gatsby*, 161–162

FitzGerald, Frances: *Fire in the Lake*, 346–347n. *See also* Vietnam War

Flaubert, Gustave: *Madame Bovary*, 11, 327n

Foucault, Michel, 47, 107, 151, 195, 250, 254, 288n, 349n; and Antonio Gramsci, 336–337n; *Archaeology of Knowledge*, 298n, 349n; disciplinary technology, 139, 187, 192–193, 204, 211–212, 214–215, 283n, 335–336n; *Discipline and Punish*, 10–11, 41, 54; "Egyptianism, 262–263, 284n; on figural exegesis, 68–69, 284n; and genealogy, 19, 28, 60, 63; 86, 100, 108–110, 155, 161–162, 192, 227, 239, 314n, 315n; on history, vii, 278, 284n, 341–342n; *History of Sexuality*, 8; and on the humanist subject, 20; "The Life of Infamous Men," 283n, 335n; on Linneaus, 330–332n; "Nietzsche, Genealogy, History," 41; and the "other," 227; on panopticism, 54, 102–104, 133, 213; on pauperism and the state, 309–310n; and "the repressive hypothesis," 8–10, 226, 249, 329n, 337n; "What is an Author?" 68–69, 284n. *See also* Genealogy; Panopticism

Frank, Joseph: and spatial form, 327–328n

Franklin, Benjamin, 101, 208; in *Israel Potter*, 208–209, 311n, 335n

Freeman, John, 15, 16

Fukuyama Francis, and the "end of history," 30, 351–352n. *See also* G. W. F. Hegel; New World Order

Gadamer, Hans-Georg, 303n, 351n

Gaddis, William, 246

Gasché, Rodolphe, 239, 342n

Genealogy, 28, 46, 68, 104; posthumanism of, 41

Graff, Gerald, 254

Gramsci, Antonio: on hegemony, 7–8, 24, 29, 254, 288n, 329n, 348n; on the historical bloc, 225–226, 271, 336n. *See also* Hegemony

Greene, Graham: *The Power and the Glory*, 298n; *The Quiet American*, 344n

Guattari, Félix, 261–262, 273

Harvard University: and the Cold War, 32; *General Education in a Free Society* ("The Harvard Redbook"), 32, 288n; and Vietnam, 28

Hawthorne, Nathaniel, 31, 144, 146, 151, 161, 232, 245, 307n; and the American romance, 131; Donald Pease on, 274, 338–339n; *House of the Seven Gables*, 110–112; Lionel Trilling on, 319n

Hegel, G. W. F.: and the dialectic, 40, 57, 76, 80, 136, 163–164, 199, 206, 341n; on memory, 322n; and the New World Order, 351–352n. *See also* Old Americanists; Lionel Trilling

Hegemony, 7–8, 29–30, 45, 240–242, 265; Raymond Williams on, 189. *See also* Antonio Gramsci

Heidegger, Martin, 120, 151; and *a-letheia*, 78, 86, 113, 174, 203; and *Auseinandersetzung*, 38, 90, 178, 192, 203, 228, 245, 275, 292n; and being as continuum, 281–282n; and being there (*Dasein*), 217, 228; and being with, 150, 160; on care, 156, 168, 300n, 318n; and destruction, xi–xii, 38, 49, 89, 90, 110, 121, 149, 159–160, 168–169, 187–190, 224, 305–306n; dread (of nothing), 53, 128; and the end of philosophy, 110–111; on enframement, 63, 124, 179; on errancy, 85–87, 112; on *Gelassenheit*, 156, 175, 327n; on the hermeneutic circle, 78, 155, 245; on humanism, 10–11, 126; on imperialism, 5–7; *das Man*, 120, 155; on measure, 81–82, 229; and Nazism, xii; on the nothing, 269–270, 297–298n; and the ontic/ontological nexus, 170–172, 187–188, 192, 307n; on the ontological difference, xi, 62, 161, 244; "The Origins of the Work of Art," 203; and the question of being (*Seinsfrage*), 234; on Repetition, 76, 80, 176–178, 226; and *dies Unheimlichkeit*, 153; "What Is Metaphysics?" 269, 298n. *See also* Being

Heilman, Robert, 321n

Heller, Joseph, 182, 315n

Hellman, John: *American Myth and the Legacy of Vietnam*, 279n, 344n

Hemingway, Ernest, 157, 237; the "Nick Adams" stories, 161–162

Heraclitus, 202, 292n, 304n

Herodotus, 142, 202, 246, 333n

Herr, Michael, 182, 344n, 349n; and carnival, 263–264, 347n; *Dispatches*, 41, 162, 182, 184–185, 252–257, 259–260, 263–265, 266–268; and *Moby-Dick*, 329n, 345–346n. *See also* Frank Lentricchia; Vietnam War

Hirsch, E. D., Jr., 3, 28

Holderlin, Friedrich, 291n

Homer, *The Odyssey*, quoted, 322–323n

Howard, John, 311n

Hulme, T. E., 318n

Humanism, 10–11, 126, 143; and pluralism, 247. *See also* Posthumanism

Hussein, Saddam, 184

Husserl, Edmund, 305–306n, 307n

Imperialism, 5–7, 124; and metaphysics, 5, 37–38, 62–63, 71–72, 80, 82, 172–174, 235, 264. *See also* Metaphysics

Irigaray, Luce, 151

Jackson, Andrew: and democracy, 33, 110, 114, 198, 211, 222, 232, 242, 246, 311n; Frank Lentricchia on, 345n

James, C. L. R., 100, 115, 350n

James, Henry, 58, 75–76, 131, 161–162, 181, 319n; on narrative economy, 295–296n; *The Princess Casamassima*, 135, 153, 320–321n

James, Henry, Sr., 145, 146, 151, 219

James, Williams, 256, 319n

Jameson, Fredric, 342n, 346n; on parody, 314n; on postmodernity of the Vietnam War, 251, 252–257. *See also* Frank Lentricchia; Vietnam War

Jefferson, Thomas, 345n

Jerome, Saint: *De Viris Illustribus*, 69. *See also* Figural interpretation

Job, 65–66, 198, 234, 298n

Johnson, Barbara, 28, 239; on *Billy Budd*, 339–341n. *See also* Deconstruction

Johnson, Lyndon, 27, 36, 262

Joyce, James: *A Portrait of the Artist as a Young Man*, 50, 52, 53; *Ulysses*, 11, 327n

Keats, John, 142; and negative capability, 156–157, 159

Kennedy, John F., 262; and the "New Frontier," 2, 27, 36, 258

Kierkegaard, Søren, 57, 62, 120, 121, 137, 177, 243, 244, 298n, 334n, 339n; on the Hegelian recollection/

285n; as parodist, 108–109, 298n, 314n; *Pierre*, 12, 62–63, 70–73, 80, 84–86, 153, 156, 196, 238, 240–242, 286n, 293n, 298n, 299n, 302n, 303–304n, 325n, 326n; and the *polis*, 227–230; and political economy, 204–226, 336n; and posthumanism, 181–182, 269–278; as precursor of postmodern fiction, 40–41, 246, 315n; reception of, 12–23; *Redburn*, 44, 99–100, 310n, 311n; and representation, 169–174, 176–178, 191, 197–201, 317n; *Typee*, 12, 44, 285n, 303n, 323n; and vision, 84–85; on the whaling industry, 204–224; *White-Jacket*, 13, 44, 116, 222–224, 226, 311n, 335n, 336–337n. See also *Moby-Dick*

Melville revival, 25, 106–107, 183, 233; Mendeleev, 211; and *Moby-Dick*, 20–21, 38–40; and tragic vision, 60–61

Metaphysics: and figural exegesis, 65–70; as imperial mode of perception, 5, 37–38, 172–174, 235, 264; Melville's critique of, 62–74; and naming, 187–203; and spatial form, 50–54, 172–174. *See also* Circle; Panopticism; Spatialization; Tragedy; and Vision

Michaels, Walter Benn, 37, 280n

Milton, John: on *felix culpa*, 339n

Moby-Dick: and Ahab's monomania, 114–121; 123–127, 128, 130, 132, 174–175, 192, 205–207, 216–219, 231, 267–269; and the American Adam, 123–127, 173; as American classic, 4–5, 20, 58; as R. P. Blackmur's New Critical reading of, 59–60, 80–82, 167; Bulkington in, 154–155; and canon formation, 4–5; cetology in, 191–203, 307–308n, 330–331n; and the Cold War, 23–35; as counterhegemonic text, 45–46, 114, 231–232, 244–245, 267, 271–278; as diabolic book, 68, 226, 232–245; as destructive text, 60–61, 76–77, 80, 86–87, 110–111, 146–149, 167–172, 183, 196, 203, 227, 267–278; and e-mergence, 148, 149–155; and Father Mapple's sermon, 61, 87–114, 116, 126–127, 135, 139, 167, 174–175, 178, 184, 180, 198, 209, 212, 226, 231–232, 263; humanist reading of, 55–58, 247–249; and the imperial gaze, 114–121, 132, 173–174, 230; and Ishmael's errant narrative, 37–38, 45, 46–47, 54, 55, 77–87, 112–113, 132, 147, 167–180, 183, 186, 227, 239, 267, 270–275; and monumental history, 58, 70, 112, 155; and naming, 124–127, 137, 174, 176, 184–185, 247–249, 267–270; and negative capability, 111, 156–166, 201–202; New Americanist reading of, 36–40, 88, 122–123; Old Americanist reading of, 33–34, 36–37, 57, 79, 88, 131–138; and orphanage, 151–156, 161, 167; and patriarchy, 299n; political economy in, 204–225; polyglossia of, 14, 192; and polyvalency of, 113–114, 148, 190–192, 242–243, 270–272; and prophecy/fulfillment structure, 87–91; and representation of the whale, 170–172, 191, 197–201; as social text, 148, 186; as (American) tragedy, 38–42, 44–47, 55–57, 161; and unnaming, 127–131, 269–270; and the Vietnam War, 183–185, 266–272; and the white whale (as the "Naught"), 132–133, 140–145, 148, 149, 267–269, 315–316n. *See also* Melville

Mouffe, Chantal, 336n, 337n

Mumford, Lewis, 15, 16, 39, 58, 73, 285–286n

Murray, Henry A., 232–233

Myers, Henry Alonzo, 56–57, 58

New Americanists: field-Imaginary of, 23–25, 31; limits of, 36–42, 44–45, 229–232, 244–245, 248–249, 251, 265–266, 274–278; and New Historicism, 40, 41, 186, 271, 274–275, 280–281n. *See also* Old Americanists

New Critics, 21, 112, 131, 136, 161, 185, 321n, 341n; and canon formation, 283n; and the Old Americanists, 21–23, 31–36, 131, 148, 166–167, 180, 235, 243–244; and spatial form, 50–52, 144, 147

New Historicism, 4, 7, 28, 37, 41, 186, 265, 271, 280–281n. *See also* New Americanists

New World Order: and American capitalism, 311n; and "end of history," 30, 36, 41–42, 248–249, 251, 276–278, 289n, 308–309n. *See also* Cold War; G. F. W. Hegel

Nietzsche, Friedrich, 14, 47, 120, 151, 156, 206, 350n; on Dionysiac force, 53, 316n; and genealogy, 60, 108–109, 161–162, 315n; and "Egyptianism," 262–263; on tragedy, 38, 47, 117. *See also* Michel Foucault

Nixon, Richard, 27, 35, 36, 262, 276

Occasion, 38, 81, 86, 130, 132, 154, 167, 179; etymology of, 291–292n

O'Brien, Tim, 259, 260–261

O'Hara, Daniel: on Lionel Trilling, 326n

Old Americanists: apotheosis of Ishmael, 33–34, 36–37, 159, 243–244; as Cold War critics, 21–23, 33–35, 41–42, 224–226, 229, 235–236, 317n, 351–352n; and end of ideology, 31, 131, 180, 188, 229, 240, 251; field-Imaginary of, 21–23, 31–36, 131, 161, 282n; on *Moby-Dick* as tragedy, 33–36, 38–40; as Modernists 38–39, 131, 167, 235; and spatial form, 50–54, 55. *See also* New Americanists; New Critics

Olson, Charles, 86, 181, 182, 246, 305n, 334n; affiliation with Melville, 163–164; *Call Me Ishmael*, 216; and Heraclitus, 322n; and Herodotus, 333n; *The Maximus Poems*, 162, 333n (quoted); on the measure of care, 83, 181, 332–333n; and negative capability, 163–164, 201–202; and ontological invasion, 142, 322–323n;

and representation, 201–202; on Socratic classification, 332n, 333n; *The Special View of History,* 201–202; on the whaling industry, 206, 212, 216, 334n

Panopticism, 6, 80; and canon formation, 10; of the critics of the Melville revival, 48–49, 58; and the disciplinary gaze, 71–73, 98, 109, 114–121, 125, 133, 173, 175, 179, 198, 202, 213, 242, 259; in Father Mapple's sermon, 93–94, 102–104; as polyvalent figure, 103–104; of the symbolic imagination, 246. *See also* Circle; Foucault; Metaphysics; Spatialization; Vision

Parker, Hershel, 308

Parker, Theodore, 2

Parrington, V. L., 33, 236; and the Parringtonian tradition, 21, 54, 131, 135, 180, 163, 167, 236–238, 319n. *See also* Lionel Trilling

Pease, Donald, 23, 73; on Ahab, 122–123, 207, 316–317n, 319n; on counterhegemony, 41–42, 338–339n; on covenant, 274–275; on "dissensus," 351n; on Ishmael, 186, 224–225, 243–244, 274–275, 313–314n; on *Moby-Dick* as tragedy, 36–40; and the New Americanists, xiii, 31, 114; on the Old Americanist Cold War "field-Imaginary," 21–23, 31–36, 131, 148, 243–244, 302n, 312n. *See also* Cold War; New Americanists; *Moby-Dick*; Old Americanists

Petronius, 246

Plato, 282n, 291n, 307n, 310n

Poe, Edgar Allan, 31

Poirier, Richard: *A World Elsewhere,* 23

Pope, Alexander: "Essay on Man," 63–64, 179, 304n (quoted)

Posthumanism, 2–3, 148, 181, 187, 190, 246; and destruction, 37, 41

Poulet, George, 305n

Pound, Ezra: and periplus, 82–83

Pratt, May Louise, 331–332n

Problematic, 3; definition of, 279–280n